1|99

TIDEWATER TIME CAPSULE:
History Beneath the Patuxent

Other Books by the Author

TIDEWATER TIME CAPSULE:
History Beneath the Patuxent

Donald G. Shomette

TIDEWATER PUBLISHERS
Centreville, Maryland

Library of Congress Cataloging-in-Publication Data

Shomette, Donald.
    Tidewater time capsule : history beneath the Patuxent / Donald Shomette. — 1st ed.
        p.   cm.
    Includes bibliographical references (p.) and index.
    ISBN 0-87033-463-8 (casebound)
    1. Underwater archaeology—Maryland—Patuxent River. 2. Patuxent River (Md.)—Antiquities. 3. Excavations (Archaeology)—Maryland—Patuxent River. I. Title.
F187.P38S485 1995
975.2′401—dc20   94–39900

Manufactured in the United States of America
First edition

For Dale

In the sea there is everything to record.

— Honor Frost, *Under the Mediterranean*, 1963

Contents

Preface

The wardroom of the big oceangoing research ship *Mt. Mitchell*, moored at the dock in front of Phillips Restaurant in Baltimore's famed Inner Harbor, was crowded, stuffy, and hot on the morning of November 1, 1988. Outside, a dull, cold rain had begun, driving the normal bustling crowds of the harborplace indoors. But aboard the ship, pride of the National Oceanic and Atmospheric Administration's fleet, there was an air of anticipation, for important events in the somewhat arcane field of underwater archaeology were about to commence. In the wardroom, newspaper reporters and television crews, and more than a few politicians, jockeyed for a position close to an arrangement of tables at which a singular ceremony would soon occur. Some jostled for a strategic vantage point, while others, mostly state officials, pressed forward merely to be near and to be seen by the focal point of the proceedings, Governor William Donald Schaefer of Maryland. The few invited guests had early on relinquished their own positions to the more aggressive media and politicians, and were obliged to catch whatever snatches of the historic proceedings they could from the back of the room. I stood quietly among this small but privileged group.

On the table from which the governor was to speak sat several documents and a simple blue and gray stoneware inkwell of the early nineteenth century. The rather nondescript little container, noted the ornate press kit prepared for the media, was to be used in the ceremonial signing of a historic agreement between the state of Maryland and NOAA announcing the commencement of a major initiative in the field of underwater archaeology. I was all too familiar with both the initiative and the inkwell, the latter of which may have been used by one of both Maryland's and the nation's foremost naval heroes, Commodore Joshua Barney. The diminutive artifact had witnessed a great deal of history, indeed, and was about to add another chapter to its unique résumé. It had, in fact, been chosen because of its particularly symbolic nature as a historic prop for the events that were about to begin. Although from my limited vantage point at the back of the room I could not see it, I knew its vita well. The little inkwell was one of twenty-six such items purchased at Baltimore in the latter half of the War of 1812 for use on board a hurriedly built naval force commanded by Barney and charged with the defense of the Chesapeake Bay. The vessels of this tiny mosquito squadron were collectively and officially referred to as the U.S. Chesapeake Flotilla, but to those destined to shed their blood on them, they were affectionately known as Barney's Barges. The inkwell had sailed from Baltimore with Barney's squadron, bound for an attack on the main British base in the Bay, Tangier Island, in May 1814. The object had borne mute witness to the little flotilla's months of gallant but ultimately futile combat against overwhelmingly superior British naval forces in Maryland's Patuxent River. Indeed, many of Commodore Barney's brave dispatches from the scenes of battle may have been penned in ink carried in the tiny, battered jug. Finally, in late August, as enemy forces landed and marched up the Patuxent, hell-bent on the destruction of the nation's capital, the infant city of Washington, the flotilla was scuttled to prevent capture. And along with it went the inkwell. One hundred and sixty-six years later, I had enjoyed the privilege of superintending its safe recovery and restoration, along with that of scores of other artifacts, during the first major underwater archaeological excavation of a historic shipwreck in Maryland waters—one of Barney's own.

At 10:15 A.M. sharp, J. Rodney Little, director of the Maryland Historical Trust, under whose newly vested authority, ordained by a recent act of the state legislature, all underwater archaeology in Maryland was to be managed, presented a few opening remarks. Little then introduced assistant secretary of NOAA, B. Kent Burton, who disclosed his agency's role in the historic agreement about to be signed. Then came Dr. Michael Hooker, president of the University of Maryland/Baltimore County (UMBC). Finally, with a flourish, came the governor himself.

As I looked about the room filled with the powerful and the influential, the movers and shakers of state and national politics, policies, and programs, I saw few faces who were aware of, or who had actually participated in, the events of the previous fifteen years that had helped launch Maryland to the forefront in the field of underwater archaeology. Perhaps it was just as well, for we stood this day on the threshold of a new order and a new way of doing things that would escort underwater archaeology in the Tidewater region from the Dark Ages into the twenty-first century. In Maryland, we were finally leaving the era of the enterprising underwater antiquarian and armchair archaeocrat behind us. In its place we were now ceremonially and officially embracing that of the scientist, the historian, the professional resource manager, and the trained archaeologist, comfortable in the water, in the museum laboratory, or lobbying in the halls of the state legislature for the preservation and study of our submerged cultural resources. Under the leadership of Governor Schaefer, Maryland had finally established the first comprehensive state-supported underwater archaeology program in its history. The missions of this new operation, dubbed the Maryland Maritime Archaeology Program (MMAP), were both bold and multifaceted: to locate, investigate, and document submerged archaeological sites in state waters; to protect those resources and historic properties therein; to educate and certify the general and diving public regarding the state's submerged cultural resources; to issue and administer permits allowing for the excavation of submerged archaeological sites; and to establish a program of voluntary registration by the sport diving public of artifacts removed from significant underwater archaeological sites. In June, Maryland had reached around the world to Australia to hire its first marine archaeologist to administer MMAP, and publicly dedicated itself to establishing a major program for maritime preservation, designed to be a model for the nation.

Now Governor Schaefer was announcing several even more historic initiatives: the establishment of a National Center for Maritime Preservation Technology (a joint pilot research program with NOAA on the relationship between climatic change and the archaeological record); the establishment of a major graduate program in underwater archaeology at UMBC; and, finally, the nomination of the resting site of the U.S. Chesapeake Flotilla as a National Marine Sanctuary to be managed and studied under the auspices of NOAA's landmark Marine Sanctuary Program, an honor afforded only one other vessel in American history, the USS *Monitor*. The Chesapeake Tidewater, it seemed, would soon become a vast natural laboratory for the study and advancement of underwater archaeological research and technology in a scientific and social experiment that would benefit a nation.

As the politicians and officials droned on for the benefit of the media and their constituents, my thoughts drifted back to an earlier day when the pursuit of the past beneath the waters was considered little more than adventurous foolishness rather than scientific inquiry; when every underwater archaeological investigation, every survey, every excavation was an experiment in new concepts and methodologies, often as not carried out by amateurs and scoffed at or ignored by terrestrial-bound professionals; indeed, when underwater archaeology in the Chesapeake was in its infancy.

I was fortunate to have been one of the numerous participants in these formative, fledgling years. In April 1974, I had the privilege of being named director of a newly formed nonprofit corporation chartered in the state of Maryland and dedicated to the promulgation of underwater archaeological research. The company was called Nautical Archaeological Associates, Incorporated (NAA), and would serve, until its demise in December 1988, as the platform from which many, indeed most, underwater archaeological research projects in Maryland waters would be launched.

For me and my colleagues, archaeologists (professionals and amateurs alike), historians, engineers, museologists, cultural resource managers, oceanographers, marine biologists, and many others who had participated, it had been an exciting time, a stimulating period of personal and professional growth. It was a wonderful era when the watery shroud of history beneath the Tidewaters was first penetrated. It was a time when the Chesapeake witnessed the nascent discipline of underwater archaeology mature and ripen, providing a cultural, a historical, and an educational boon hitherto unknown and untapped. It was, simultaneously, a time when a new appreciation for our maritime heritage, long in decline, began to grow in the public consciousness. Museums began to exhibit the discoveries gleaned from the pursuit of history beneath the waves. And a new awareness and appreciation of the historical and cultural values of the resources resting on the bottoms of our waters began to emerge in the deliberative bodies of our governments.

As a participant in this wonderful period of discovery, the greatest satisfaction of all has been the privilege of being able to reach out and touch the history that has helped make us who and what we are today. I have certainly not been alone in my pursuits for there are many who have labored long and hard to roll back the waters of time for the sake of history, documenting the past from the physical record left behind. Nor could I hope to adequately chronicle the marvelous totality of underwater archaeological endeavors that have been conducted over the years throughout the Chesapeake Tidewater. Many superb efforts, such as the landmark Yorktown Shipwreck Project, would produce volumes of their own. I could never hope to describe them all. Thus, I have sought to present herein a chronicle of one of those projects that I have been intimately involved with—the search for the lost history of one of Maryland's most important waterways, the Patuxent River.

Many individuals have made this journey and this book possible. A special note of appreciation must first be addressed to my colleagues in NAA, Dr. Fred Hopkins, Jr., Dr. Ralph E. Eshelman, Eldon Volkmer, Kenneth Hollingshead, Nicholas Freda, Larry Pugh, and my brother Dale Shomette, without all of whom there would have been nothing.

I would be remiss if I did not offer thanks to those many individuals and institutions that have supported efforts in the field and archives, in the laboratory, and in the halls of government, to bring underwater archaeology in Maryland to maturity. First and foremost I would like to extend my gratitude to Former Maryland Governor William Donald Schaefer for demanding that we protect, preserve, and study the evidence of our past hidden beneath our waters and for playing an instrumental role in urging passage of the federal Abandoned Shipwreck Act of 1987. Indeed, archaeology in Maryland certainly never had a truer friend. A note of appreciation must also be extended to J. Rodney Little, Director of the Maryland Historical Trust, who graciously agreed to share with me his vision for the future of underwater archaeology in Maryland. I must also recognize the many institutions that have generously supported the work this publication has sought to document. These include the University of Baltimore, the Calvert Marine Museum, the U.S. Navy, the Maryland National Capital Park and Planning Commission, the University of Maryland, Yellow Cat Productions, the U.S. Department of the Interior, the Maryland Geological Survey, the Chesapeake Biological Laboratory, and the Bethlehem Steel Corporation. The most capable staffs of many more institutions, including the Library of Congress, the National Archives and Record Service, and the Smithsonian Institution in Washington, the Maryland Historical Society in Baltimore, and the Public Record Office in London must be cited for their unstinting guidance and aid during my research efforts.

Recognition for their valuable assistance must also be given to Paul Berry; David Bohaska; Leslie Bright; John Burton; Wayne E. Clark; Andrew Creed, USN; Laura Curran; Richard Dolesh; Evelyne Eshelman; Michael Ford; Emily Graves; Wesley Hall; Steven and Barbara Israel; Daniel Koski-Karell; Leroy "Pepper" Langley; Colin Drury Languedoc; James McEvoy; Lt. Commander Michael McMillan, USN; John Mitchell; Robert Neyland; Claude "Pete" Petrone; Sarah Ruhl; Galloway Selby; E.B. Shelly; Sharon Shomette; Peter Schwenk; Iva Volkmer; all of whom have contributed immeasureably to the making of this history.

For her tireless work at editing the manuscript, as she has done for so many of my other works, I am indebted to my longtime friend and colleague at the Library of Congress, Jennifer Rutland.

And finally, I would like to express my heartfelt appreciation to my wife, Carol, for her encouragement and patience during the writing of this work.

Introduction

As a youth I was a voracious reader, given to consuming every book I could lay my hands on. I was particularly fond of the pulp science fiction paperbacks that seemed to proliferate in geometric proportion to my minuscule allowance. One such book, the title of which has long since escaped me, was destined to have an enormous influence on the development of my interest in the field of underwater archaeology. Specifically, the book dealt with an epochal geological catastrophe that occurred sometime in the not-too-distant future. The cataclysm was, in fact, a terrible earthquake in the far Pacific at the base of the Marianas Trench, the deepest recess on the face of the globe. It was a disaster that portended, as this particular genre of science fiction frequently does, the ultimate demise of the human race, for the quake had caused a terrible tear in the earth's crust through which the waters of the oceans began to pour. Rapidly, the seas of the world receded until finally the only waters that remained were a few Alpine lakes and the ice caps of the polar regions.

What fascinated me, however, was not the ultimate fate of the world or the manner in which humankind struggled for its salvation, but what the rolling back of the seas revealed, the wonders of the past long hidden beneath the waves. There were the remnants of sunken cities and forgotten civilizations, Spanish galleons and Roman triremes, English carracks and ill-fated ocean liners scattered about on the now-dry ocean bed. There were the ghost fleets of mighty empires, the ships of a thousand different nations and ages, all but forgotten by even time itself. Yet each was an individual link with the past, with its own story to tell, forgotten by history and unscathed by the human hand from the very second it had slipped beneath the waves.

In the more than three decades since I read that story, fact has all but outstripped fiction. Through the relatively nascent science of underwater archaeology, many of these things and more have been revealed to the wonderment of mankind, but more importantly to the enhancement of human knowledge. Even as these words are written, underwater archaeological excavations of the oldest known shipwreck located to date, a late Bronze Age vessel sunk in the fourteenth century B.C. off the Ulu Burun promontory near the coast of Turkey, are under way. Ultrasonic surveys and excavations of the infamous buccaneer stronghold of Port Royal, Jamaica, swallowed by the sea during a cataclysmic earthquake in 1692, have been completed. Ancient Roman harbors, such as King Herod's noble Cesarea on the coast of Israel, and the foundations of seaside Greek temples such as the Sanctuary of Apollo at Halieis in southern Greece, long hidden beneath Mediterranean waters, have become daily grist for scientific and scholarly investigations. In the Far East, the magnificent thousand-ship fleet of the great Kublai Khan, destroyed by the Divine Winds, the Kamikazi, while attempting the invasion of Japan, has been located beneath the silts of the Straits of Tsushima by Japanese archaeologists. Henry VIII's mighty war carrack *Mary Rose*, the first true battleship, has been meticulously excavated by English archaeologists and raised from her silt-covered tomb in the Solent off Portsmouth, England. And the majestic *Titanic* herself has been located, and her ghostly image broadcast for the world to see.

The long list of wonderful discoveries made beneath the sea during the last quarter of a century is truly remarkable and is exceeded only by the enormity of those underwater archaeological resources still awaiting to be revealed and studied. Each site has its own résumé patiently waiting to be read. And each has a contribution to make toward a better understanding of just who we are, where we came from, and where we belong in the grand scheme of things.

The seas are richly endowed with the cultural remnants of past ages which the seas have claimed for their own. But are such resources universal? Indeed, what would we find if we were to roll back the waters of our own Chesapeake Bay, the thousands of miles of rivers, creeks, and streams that flow into it, or of the Atlantic coast of the Delmarva Peninsula? Are there the lost towns and shipwrecks of ages past awaiting discovery? Are there the remnants of forgotten cultures and ancient peoples still to be found? And if, indeed, those things do exist, of what importance are they to us? Can their discovery and study contribute to the wider dominion of social history and science, or to a better understanding of human behavior? Can they help fill in the lost chinks of histories unwritten or altogether forgotten?

Before we can attempt to address the answers to these questions, we must first define how we can accomplish these ends, namely, through the science of archaeology.

Derived from the terms *archaeos,* meaning ancient, and *logos,* meaning word, discussion, or region, we may say that archaeology is, quite specifically, the scientific study of human life, culture, and activities in ages past through the systematic evaluation of the material evidence left behind. While the historian delves into the written record to glean, synthesize, and reconstruct the proceedings and progress of humankind, the archaeologist must locate and analyze the very products of human handiwork,

Introduction

the artifacts they created, the implements they adopted for their use, the buildings they constructed, the vessels they sailed, the food they cooked, and even the spaces they altered for their use, to provide data where the written record is inadequate, suspect, biased, incorrect, or nonexistent. But most important, the archaeologist formulates and reconstructs from artifactual evidence social and behavioral patterns undocumented by the written word, or of preliterate times, which make up the cultural components of humankind.

By extension, underwater archaeology is merely archaeology carried out underwater, utilizing the same basic principles of systematic investigation and inquiry to achieve its objectives, albeit employing a far wider array of technologies to promulgate and sustain such efforts in an environment alien to humans.

Marine archaeology may be addressed as a discrete subcomponent of underwater archaeology in its specific concern with maritime affairs, such as maritime technology and other aspects of seafaring. A corollary to this is that marine archaeology also can involve sites that are not submerged but that relate to shipping, shipbuilding, or other marine endeavors, and that may be encountered in a terrestrial setting as well.

But what exactly constitutes underwater archaeological resources, and how do they compare with dry land resources?

Quite broadly, we may say that any vessel, building, structure, manmade object, material, or spatial arrangement of value in historic, architectural, or other cultural terms lying beneath a body of water may be considered a submerged cultural resource. To this we may also add all information sources that can be used to understand past activities specifically related to maritime endeavors or the intentional alterations of the marine environment itself. This particular resource base includes not only cultural remains such as artifacts, structures, features, activity areas, and so forth, but any part of the natural and cultural environments that were used or modified by people in the past and that can aid in expanding our understanding of the relationship of people to the marine environment they utilized.

The submerged cultural resource base—that is, those resources of an archaeological or a historical nature lying partially or entirely submerged beneath the waters—may be divided into four discrete categories: inundated terrestrial sites, insert sites, random deposition sites, and vessel remains.

Inundated terrestrial sites incorporate the entire spectrum of humankind's cultural remains, activity areas, and spatial alterations commonly found on dry land. From pre-Holocene time to the present, the coastlines of the world have been constantly evolving, more often than not retreating from an ever-encroaching sea. It has been estimated by some scientists that fourteen thousand years ago, sea levels were over 100 meters below those of today. Then, as the last Ice Age came to a close, the glaciers began to melt and receded, and the seas began a slow but steady rise. Other influences, such as the dynamics of plate tectonics (that is, the ever-shifting motions of the earth's crust) and terrestrial subsidence, also play key roles in the variations of sea level rise and fall through the ages. A growing corpus of work by geologists and archaeologists suggests that during the last two thousand years the hitherto even rate of sea level rise suddenly and unaccountably accelerated threefold. As a consequence of this surprising geological event, coastal areas of the Chesapeake Tidewater and the Atlantic frontier of the Eastern Shore, along which the first native American arrivals in the region camped, hunted, fished, foraged, fought, and manufactured their tools ten thousand to fifteen thousand years ago, are now drowned lands lying as deep as 60 to 360 feet or more below the surface. On the Atlantic frontier such sites now lie many miles seaward of the modern shoreline. Even colonial towns, forts, plantations, and other habitation or activity areas of the first European settlers, almost always situated along the water's edge, were destined to fall victim, in part or entirely, to the unrelenting march of the sea. It is, indeed, a continuation of these very same marine depredations that are experienced by modern society in the unending battle against tidal action, erosion, and inevitable coastal inundation.

Marine transgressions against the shorelines of the Middle Atlantic seaboard are typical of those experienced worldwide in the ongoing confrontation between land and sea. Natural sea level rise during the Holocene Epoch and the consequent erosion and inundation of land gave birth to and permitted the growth of the Chesapeake Bay from the modest ancestral riverine trunk of twelve thousand years ago to the magnificent estuary we know today. The effects of this continual assault on the shorelines, resulting in the drowning of untold numbers of prehistoric and historic dry-land archaeological sites, are staggering. A seven-year study of the Chesapeake by the U.S. Environmental Protection Agency illustrates the severity of those transgressions. Of 4,360 miles of Maryland shoreline (one of the longest in the nation), 1,340 are eroding, 376 of them at more than two feet per year. An estimated total of twenty-five thousand acres of land in the state has been lost to erosion and drowning in the last century alone. In Virginia an estimated twenty thousand acres has succumbed to the sea. Entire island systems in the Chesapeake, such as Sharps, Three Sisters, Watts, and Tangier Archipelago, have been totally lost or will soon disappear. Poplar Island, a thousand-acre landmass in Captain John Smith's time, is now little more than an islet of a few acres extent, patiently awaiting the denouement.

Ironically, as the Bay increases in size, resultant filling of its body with eroded soils proceeds unhindered at a rate of two to four million tons of sediment annually. Hence, the average depth of the Bay is decreasing at a steady 0.8 millimeter per year. As the waters continue their relentless creep, and coastal development by man proceeds with little concern for the environment, wetlands are also rapidly filling with sediments both

Introduction

naturally and artificially. A 1954 survey counted 614 thousand acres of wetlands in Maryland. By 1966, an average of 14 percent had been filled in the upper seven counties of that state alone, and in one county the figure was 35 percent.

On the Atlantic frontier of the Eastern Shore, as elsewhere along the seaboard, the sea is relentlessly on the march, claiming territory and forcing people to retreat ever westward. On Assateague, one of the barrier islands ensconced along the Maryland coast, the stumps of cedar forests once growing on the west, or sound, side at the beginning of the present century can now be seen on the Atlantic beach extending beyond the surf line hundreds of yards seaward, bearing mute testimony to nature's march. Certainly this is not very encouraging news for the condominium owners and real estate brokers in the resort towns that pepper the coast, yet it is substantial evidence of the natural forces at work. This inexorable march of the sea also helps to create a major component of the submerged cultural resource base.

The inundation or drowning of terrestrial archaeological sites, however, is not always due to natural causes. The building of dams and reservoirs, man-made lakes, and ponds also creates such sites artificially. In Maryland, which possesses no major naturally enclosed aquatic system, a number of artificial lakes and reservoirs such as Deep Creek, Tridelphia, and others have been created to provide power, community water supplies, and recreational areas. Thousands of farmers throughout the tri-state area of Maryland, Delaware, and Virginia have created small ponds and reservoirs for the benefit of their crops and livestock and have in the process occasionally inundated dry-land archaeological resources.

Clearly, the potential for submerged archaeological resources that were once terrestrial sites is, from a geological viewpoint, enormous. Indeed, anything that a terrestrial archaeologist might encounter on dry land, be it a prehistoric campsite, an ossuary, a colonial town site, or a Civil War fort, may also be found beneath the waters of the Chesapeake Tidewater and off the Atlantic frontier of the Eastern Shore.

Unlike inundated sites, *insert sites* may be defined as those components of human handiwork, artifacts, constructions, or structures, intentionally inserted into or erected within the subaqueous environment, with order and regularity, to perform a specific function or service. Such sites include piers; wharves; jetties; harbor facilities; aids to navigation; artificial islands; fishing installations such as weirs, rock traps, and net stands; hunting installations; stilted dwellings; privies; bridge foundations; causeways; piped sewer, water, drainage, or other flowing systems; and defense works such as gun mounts, mines, chains, harbor gates, and various kinds of military obstructions to navigation. Alterations of the environment itself, such as the dredging of artificial channels, canals, or anchorages, or the erection of harbor moles, breakwaters, or bulkheads may also be considered in this category. Such alterations represent either man-made structural and/or spatial relationships in a hitherto natural setting for the benefit of people, or are undertaken with the objective of achieving other specific functional goals.

The third category of submerged cultural resources consists of *sites of random deposition*. Such sites include any object or collection of objects deposited into the marine environment without singular order or regulation of placement. Such sites may be composed of both intentionally or unintentionally inserted objects or clusters of objects. Intentionally inserted components may consist of such diverse items as offerings to deities, burials at sea, goods abandoned during natural catastrophes and accidents, ballast dumping, military projectiles fired or dropped into the water during combat or training, and so forth. Unintentional deposition may occur when objects are simply lost or tossed aside. Sites of random deposition may be created by dropping objects into the water from boats, airplanes, bridges, adjacent shorelines, or platforms of any kind on or adjacent to the water. Such sites differ from insert sites in that they are not placed in the water to serve a function, although the placement process itself may indeed have some ascribed purpose.

The final category, that of *vessel remains,* is perhaps the most commonly known and controversial component of the submerged cultural resource base. This category may be divided into two broad subsections, which I shall simply call shipwrecks and abandonments. For the sake of definition, we can address a *shipwreck* as being any vessel lost at sea either from environmental causes such as storms, lightning, or ice, or other factors such as fire, collision, explosion, military encounters, stranding, poor seamanship, the physical condition of the vessel itself, or from the action of people through scuttling or other means. Such sites may be considered significant in that shipwrecks usually represent the deposition of a culturally discrete unit at a single moment in time. The normal consequence of such an event is the inadvertent creation of a veritable time capsule, a frozen moment, within which is contained a microcosm of a specific maritime society. The goods that the vessel carried and the mission it was addressing at the time of loss represent an integral component of a larger parent society.

Then, there is the vessel itself. Simply put, the ship is usually representative of the highest level of technology of the era during which it was constructed and of the society that built it, be it a Chesapeake Bay log canoe, a Venetian galley, a side-wheel steamer, or a nuclear-powered submarine. As the late marine archaeologist Keith Muckleroy once noted, from prehistoric times through the nineteenth century, the ship was the largest and most complex machine built by man. Indeed, as an archaeological entity, the ship itself must be considered as a single artifact, whose architecture and construction were usually determined by the specific

Introduction

mission in life addressed to it by the society that built it, be it fishing, military, communications, transportation, commerce, or exploration.

Anthropologically, the ship was one of the more important components of many societies on a large scale and the focal point of that considerable but discrete suborder we call maritime society. Indeed, the ship was a social container, within which was housed a distinct culture of its own, a closed society unto itself, with its own laws, economics, customs, and folkways. Only at the beginning and end of each voyage was that closed society opened to the influences and regulatory social order of the terrestrial world. Yet, the ship's myriad assortment of missions, its very reason for being, made it a major contributing factor to the worldwide diffusion of culture, technology, and society. Hence, a shipwreck may present to the archaeologist a fixed moment in time in which not only that particular society of the mariner—a social class that migrated from port to port leaving precious few records of their lives on tax lists or probate records—can be studied and evaluated, but also that of the larger society from which it sprang and which it invariably served.

Abandonments constitute a singularly important variation of the shipwreck category. This subcategory may be divided into two sections: abandonments at sea, usually as a result of an impending disaster such as a foundering, fire, battle, or other factors such as an outbreak of plague or a mutiny; and abandonments of old or useless vessels. Abandonments at sea may be accompanied by the removal of some or all of the various inventories of goods on board. These could include cargo, personal belongings of the crew and passengers, or ship's stores, as well as useful or valuable parts of the ship itself such as rigging, furniture, and ordnance. Abandonments of old or useless vessels, however, are far more common and, in fact, provide the largest category of historic (and probably prehistoric) vessel resources in the Chesapeake Tidewater. Such vessels were normally abandoned after having outlived their utility or when they became economically impossible to maintain or field. Some were simply outmoded by the advance of industry, improvements in technology, or the imposition, for one reason or another, of regulatory actions of society. Most were disposed of by simply being hauled into an isolated backwater and left moored to their fates or by being sunk in some convenient bywater. Some were deliberately broken up and their components recycled or disposed of in a variety of ways. On occasion, abandoned vessels were incorporated in the construction of wharves and breakwaters or were used as fill material for land reclamation projects. Because vessels in this subcategory were usually stripped of all usable, valuable, or marketable items, including parts of the craft itself, before or shortly after their abandonments, the cultural value of such sites lay almost solely in the record of their architecture and construction. Such sites may be encountered submerged, partially submerged, or even on or in dry land.

Tidewater Time Capsule

Not surprisingly, the greatest concentration of scholarly attention in underwater archaeology has tended to focus on the category of vessel remains as the most fertile field of study. The reasons for this bias are many, but the philosophic underpinnings are sound. The role of watercraft and the waterways they traverse in the evolution, cultural definition, and technological development of humankind, from prehistory to the present day, has been among the most significant features of the vast, untapped archaeological resource base of the Middle Atlantic seaboard of the United States. Ironically, until recent years, the maritime component of the archaeological resource base was also one of the most ignored, owing primarily to its inaccessibility, but also to a general ignorance of its importance in archaeological, anthropological, and historical terms. Yet, its value is pivotal to a comprehensive understanding of the sequence of human events and cultural evolution of the region, indeed, of who we were and how we came to be who we are. Dr. George Bass, one of the pioneers of underwater archaeology, rather succinctly noted that it would be as impossible to consider the history of civilization without taking into account the spread of ideas, goods, and humankind itself by water as it would be difficult to chart the history of nations without observing the influences of battles fought upon the waves. Thus, it would be equally absurd, indeed negligent, to undertake the evaluation of the cultural dynamics of a largely maritime-oriented culture, society, or geopolitical entity such as the state of Maryland without incorporating a representative analysis of the prehistoric and historic record deposited in and about its waters.

Whenever water is present, people have found that the easiest and most efficient methods of transportation, communication, and commerce have been by watercraft. A vessel rowed, sailed, or paddled was, as Dr. Bass notes, capable of greater speed, carried a greater load, and was generally more reliable than either man or beast of burden. Watercraft, until the advent of powered flight, often provided the only means of penetration, settlement, and development of extremely inaccessible or hostile areas. It was the boat that permitted primitive people access to the bounties of the Chesapeake Tidewater and allowed them to carry on trade, communication, war, and other social interactions with their neighbors. It was the boat which carried the first Europeans to America and permitted the extensive explorations of the Chesapeake Bay, its innumerable major tributaries, and the far recesses of its many minor feeders. Early settlement was restricted to the water's edge because of a total and slavish reliance on watercraft for rapid communication and transportation. In the Chesapeake Tidewater, it was watercraft upon which the economic well-being and security of Maryland and Virginia often relied. The strategy for urban development, uppermost in the minds of the colonial governments in the seventeenth and eighteenth centuries, focused on one all-important component—the proximity of urban centers to navigable waters. And finally, to defend, capture, or control the cumulative fruits of these important maritime-dependent societies (namely, the commerce, ports, harbors, shipyards, and the very watercraft that made it all possible), specialized vessels of war, along with the professional and paraprofessional establishments specifically developed to achieve such ends, were created time and again.

The accumulated physical remnants of humankind's prehistoric and historic heritage are still to be found throughout the waters of Maryland in as yet undetermined, but certainly great, quantities. These important resources, however, are both finite and nonrenewable. In recent years, without laws and specific regulations to manage and protect them, or to provide for scholarly investigation and evaluation of them for the public benefit, they have become endangered and frequently controversial commodities as have most archaeological resources in this modern, teeming world we live in. Fortunately, over the last three decades we have witnessed an archaeological renaissance made possible by the invention of the self-contained underwater breathing apparatus (SCUBA), by Emile Gagnan and Jacques Cousteau in 1943, which permitted the application of archaeological precepts to the undersea environment. In those pioneering days, archaeologists were limited to working at depths of less than one hundred feet, and by modern standards, with relatively primitive equipment. Worse, there was no body of comparative work upon which to proceed. Yet, every step forward provided the building blocks upon which those who followed might learn and progress with scientific thoroughness and deliberate methodology.

Today, although underwater archaeologists have added to their tool kits such modern and diverse trappings as submersibles, robotics, underwater video, electronic photography, lasers, computers, ultrasonics, and a mind-boggling array of ever-developing technologies, and they will soon be capable of working with scientific precision at any depth, the mission has remained the same: to carry out the systematic evaluation of the material evidence humans have left in their wake down through time.

The search for evidence of our heritage and history beneath the waters of Maryland and Virginia is not a recent phenomenon, or even a modern preoccupation. As early as 1824, efforts were carried out by dedicated antiquarians in southern Maryland to wrest from the waters of the St. Mary's River historically important artifacts relating to the first settlement and capital of Lord Baltimore's infant colony. During the mid-1930s, the same sort of interest on the part of the National Park Service and the Mariners' Museum of Newport News, Virginia, led to the salvage of artifacts belonging to British ships sunk in Virginia's York River during the Battle of Yorktown in 1781. Neither effort, however important in antiquarian terms, was carried out archaeologically. But it was a start.

Tidewater Time Capsule

Not until the 1970s were archaeologically sound precepts applied in earnest to the search for and documentation of historic and prehistoric sites lying beneath the waters of the Chesapeake Tidewater. Then, in heady succession, the Yorktown Shipwreck Project, the Londontown Survey, the Patuxent River Submerged Cultural Resources Survey, the Point Lookout Survey, the *New Jersey* Shipwreck Project, and the Claiborne Project were among many that were carried out. They were also to be among the more exhaustive archaeological efforts undertaken within the territorial waters of Maryland and Virginia—efforts built upon the foundations of a discipline begun a decade earlier in the far-off Mediterranean.

The first major underwater historical recovery project began at the site of the 1930s effort on the York River. Decades later, nine ships of the fleet of Lord Cornwallis, sunk or scuttled during the Siege of Yorktown, were located and, beginning in the 1970s, one of the most significant archaeological excavations in American history was undertaken within the confines of a cofferdam of revolutionary design. At the site of the former seventeenth century port of Londontown, Maryland, historic foundations, port facilities, and artifacts spanning a three-hundred year period were documented in the first underwater archaeological survey in Maryland history. During the course of the Patuxent River Survey (the first holistic archaeological and historical survey of an entire navigable river system in the United States), a fleet of warships from the War of 1812 was located and one of its intact members excavated within the confines of a small cofferdam. The fleet, of course, was that of Commodore Joshua Barney. The project boasted many firsts, including the earliest known use of underwater video in the Tidewater for archaeological documentation. During the survey, the fragmentary remains of possibly the oldest small-craft vessel (circa 1680–1720) of Euro-American manufacture discovered to that time in American waters were located and surveyed. By the project's end, a total of 142 historic shipwreck and abandoned vessel sites, scores of landings, wharves, and extinct town sites were documented, along with the first inundated prehistoric site to be examined in the state. At Point Lookout, Maryland (the site of the largest Union prisoner-of-war camp of the Civil War era, one-third of which is now drowned land), an intensive survey of underwater archaeological remains was carried out. Shipwrecks, building foundations, and an intact section of an inundated fort were discovered and archaeologically documented. In 1975 the largely intact remains of a Chesapeake Bay steamer, the Old Bay Line freighter *New Jersey*, built in 1862 and sunk in 1870 with hundreds of tons of cargo, were located in the Bay in forty to seventy feet of water. As a consequence of this discovery and subsequent damage to the site by relic hunters, archaeologists undertook the first effort at an entirely robotic underwater archaeological survey of a shipwreck and the first open-water deployment of a revolutionary mapping technology for an archaeological purpose. And finally, in 1989-90, an effort was launched to locate the inundated remnants of the first European settlement in Maryland, in the waters off Kent Island. None of these efforts, it should be observed, were without their flaws or difficulties, and most were filled with human errors and misjudgments (many of which were my own) that usually go hand-in-hand with the process of investigation and discovery where there are few models to follow.

The importance of these and many other projects undertaken during the 1970s and early 1980s was significant, for Maryland was at a crossroads. During this period, the state was faced with a series of challenges that had long plagued other states regarding jurisdiction over, and management of, historic and archaeological properties lying beneath state waters. Treasure salvors, relying upon the ancient code of admiralty law and the rights of salvage, proliferated and began to seek alleged treasure ships lost in many states' waters. In Maryland, efforts were initiated by several groups to locate and recover the legendary treasure of the Spanish galleon *La Galga,* lost off Assateague Island in 1750, as well as that of several other purported treasure wrecks, most notably the *San Lorenzo de Escoral, Santa Clara, Santa Rosalea,* and *Royal George.* Lawsuits and admiralty court proceedings abounded. In nearby Delaware, the long-sought remains of HMS *De Braak,* a purported treasure ship that never had any treasure, were discovered and raised, promulgating one of the worst maritime archaeological disasters in American history. Spurred by such events, in Maryland and throughout the United States, and directly influenced, in great measure, by the support of Maryland's governor and Congressional delegation resulting from the impact of the *New Jersey* Project, a long-simmering national controversy was brought to a boil, ending in the passage of landmark federal antiquities legislation, the Abandoned Shipwreck Act of 1987. For the first time, historic shipwrecks and other submerged cultural resources were removed from the realm of admiralty law and placed in the hands of those states willing to address them as the priceless resources they are. No longer would they be considered as mere commodities to be mined for treasure and artifacts by anyone with enough panache and money to do so. In this act, the seeds for Maryland's own mandate to assess and manage her vast submerged cultural resource base for the benefit of her citizens and the nation were finally planted.

The fields are fertile, and with a liberal dose of attention, intelligent management, and a great deal of hard work by those charged with their care, they should do well. But to ignore them is to forever lose the past. The choice is simple, for, as the late Peter Throckmorton, the famed pioneer of underwater archaeology, once wrote, "Everyone who gets involved in marine archaeology today soon discovers that he is struggling to learn more things than he ever imagined existed. None of us knows enough."

THE PATUXENT

*It is little known. It has neither cult nor a lore.
It is the most sparsely inhabited and least known,
probably, of all the rivers of Tidewater Maryland.*

Paul Wilstach, *Tidewater Maryland*

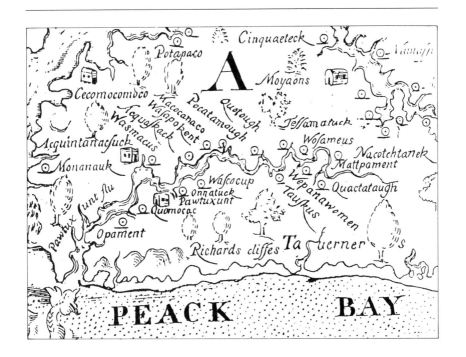

Of a Lesse Proportion

As I drew near the 140-foot-high apex of the Thomas Johnson Bridge on a bright, cold day in late December 1977, the panorama before me seemed without parallel on the Chesapeake. The magnificent bridge, which crossed Maryland's Patuxent River and some of the deepest waters in the Tidewater, had been dedicated and opened to the public only a few days earlier, and I had intentionally come the long way down from my home in Upper Marlboro to cross it for the first time. The new bridge had, after all, made obsolete one of the last ferryboat services in southern Maryland and joined two of the state's most isolated and rural counties, St. Mary's and Calvert, an event bound to have significant impact on the entire region.

My approach was from the St. Mary's side, over a placid little waterway called Town Creek, which had once been selected to be the site of one of Maryland's earliest towns but, as with the best-laid schemes, had never gotten beyond the planning stage. Ahead and to the east, set firmly in the glittering sunlit waters, was the dogleg form of Solomons Island, with its bent knee at Sandy Point cutting sharply into the Patuxent. Close behind the island, I could see the silhouette of Molly's Leg, a small islet once used for drying fishing nets and grazing horses, and as a sailor's burial ground. The islet was strategically ensconced by nature at the confluence of several waterways and the main river, and daily oversaw a bustle of waterborne traffic erupting from the rabbit warren of marinas nestled within the harbor area. Further to the east I spied Drum Point, billed by the Calvert County tourist board as the gateway to the Patuxent and a well-known natural landmark for mariners plying the Bay and river. To the north of the bridge lay the slim, sandy finger of Point Patience, jutting out from the shore into the 130-foot-deep paleochannel of the river. If Drum Point was the gateway to the Patuxent, I thought, then Point Patience was most certainly the door to its heart—and nearly 10 percent of the landmass of Maryland that drained into it. Further upstream, I could barely make out the entrance to St. Leonard's Creek, once touted as the most beautiful and historic waterway in the Tidewater, but soon to be blighted by housing developments.

I slowed on the downhill side of the bridge, trying to pick out the local landmarks and buildings immediately in front of me. To my left I could see the sprawling Naval Surface Weapons Center, which had played an important role in the development of American military technology during World War II. Ahead, I discerned, was the anchorage site where the once famed but now forgotten "Ghost Fleet" of the German Lloyd Line had been interned and moored from 1927 to 1940. Beyond, on the neck of land adjoining Solomons Island with the main, I could see a little red county schoolhouse to which children had once been regularly transported via school boat—the only such service vessel east of the Mississippi. I could also see less renowned but no less important local landmarks. There was the famous Chesapeake Biological Laboratory; and the old J. C. Lore Oysterhouse, first opened in 1922; the Our Lady Star of the Sea Catholic Church; the onetime sites of the M. M. Davis Shipyard; Swift's Ferry Terminal; the Isaac Solomon Oyster Canning Company; the Maryland, Delaware & Virginia steamboat wharf; and the J. T. Marsh Shipyard.

Yet here, lying beneath the ancient river banks and in its waters, beneath these filters of modern civilization, were still layered the history and artifacts of early Maryland, compacted and hidden, awaiting resurrection. Here, Native Americans had settled, communed, fought, farmed, and worshipped their gods for thousands of years before the coming of the Europeans. Here, too, Christian men of the cloth prayed for souls and lived lives of ascetic devotion among the native inhabitants. Here, simple settlers bent on improving their lots in the world pushed back the Chcsapcakc frontier, cleared the lands, plowed the fields, raised their families and crops, gathered oysters and finfish in their log canoes, and built their farms, plantations, and towns. They constructed their ferries and flats for local communication and commerce. They built ships that sailed the Bay and the seas beyond, spreading the bounty of the Chesapeake Tidewater to the four corners of the earth. Here, Marylanders had fought one another over religion, land, power, God, and king, fended off cruel invaders time and again, and prospered despite it all.

As I glanced over the miles of open fetch upriver, I pondered the considerable history that awaited discovery beneath its muddy waters. I thought of the meeting I was to have in a few minutes with the energetic young director of the Calvert Marine Museum, Dr. Ralph E. Eshelman, and of the content of my company's presentation to him. It would, I hoped, prove to be an auspicious meeting, because my firm, Nautical Archaeological Associates, Incorporated, was seeking to join forces with his new museum to conduct the first comprehensive underwater archaeological survey of an entire river system in the United States. The Patuxent was a river that was still little known and less understood, yet one with an enormously rich history and archaeological potential. Just how rich it was remained to be known. And it was our objective to find out before our urban civilization injured or destroyed it.

16

Of a Lesse Proportion

In the year 1588, near the end of the month of May, a small Spanish reconnaissance expedition, under the leadership of Captain Vincente Gonzáles, and consisting of approximately thirty soldiers and sailors under the command of Sergeant Major Juan Menéndez Marqués, set sail in a tiny bark from the presidio of Saint Augustine, Florida. The objective of this daring foray was the exploration of the American coast north of Florida, indeed as far as the recently discovered Bahia de Madre de Dios, in the mysterious region known to the Spanish as Ajacán, in order to reconnoitre newly reported English settlements and fortifications. [1]

In June the Spanish arrived in the Chesapeake Bay, lingered briefly in the vicinity of a fine, deep harbor, situated within the mouth of a grand tributary, and then continued their journey northward to explore the far reaches of the great estuary itself. Between 1617 and 1620, in his very descriptive *Relacion* of the Spanish exploration efforts in the region, the Spanish missionary Fra Luis Gerónimo de Oré wrote of Gonzáles's discoveries:

> As they continued to sail north, the land from the east jutted into the bay. It became narrower in such a manner that at its narrowest place, from the western shore whence it stretched toward the eastern part, it was 2 leagues. After that they discovered inlets and coves as well as rivers along the western shore. Then they came upon a large fresh-water river, which, where it entered the bay, was more than 6 fathoms deep. To the north there was a very high land, with ravines, but without trees, delightful and free, which had the aspect of a green field and was pleasant to behold. On the south shore of this river the beach is very calm and is lined with small pebbles. Farther up on the south bank of the same river there appeared a delightful valley, wooded, and pleasant land which seemed to be fertile and adaptable to stock raising and farming. This river was located in latitude 38. They named it San Pedro. They continued to sail north along the western shore and passed the night in a small inlet under the protection of high and well-shaded land. The next day many Indians came to the beach, and one among them who appeared to have the greater dignity, wore a necklace, which seemed to be of fine gold. [2]

After securing an American Indian hostage for presentation to the court, the Spanish pressed cautiously onward up the great estuary in which "they discovered many other ports and important rivers which entered the bay from the western shore" until they reached latitude thirty-nine degrees. There they entered and proceeded to explore the banks of yet another great river afoot for many miles before returning homeward.[3]

That the Spanish expedition under Captain Gonzáles conducted the first comprehensive European exploration of the two-hundred-mile length of Bahia de Madre de Dios was of significance, for the enormous estuary they had so carefully probed would soon host the first permanent English settlement in America. The bay, of course, was the Chesapeake, the Rio San Pedro was the Potomac River, and the great headwaters were the peaceful Susquehanna River. The Spanish were probably the first Europeans to lay eyes upon, and possibly penetrate, the strategically situated Patuxent River, one of the Bay's most important tributaries. It also seems likely that they may have secured their notable shelter in some inlet near the Patuxent, probably under Drum Point. The Spanish, however, were not obliged, nor did they see the need to tarry. Closer examination by European explorers of this great and gentle river that had entered the Bay at its midpoint was not to come for another two decades. But come it would.

With the establishment of a permanent English settlement at Jamestown, Virginia, in 1607 it was inevitable that further exploration of the Chesapeake would soon be undertaken. In June 1608 that inveterate soldier of fortune, Captain John Smith, set out with a tiny party specifically to conduct the first English exploration of the far reaches of the Bay and its tributaries. Smith, however, was infinitely more thorough and descriptive when writing of the waterway to the immediate south of the "high and well shaded cliffs" described by Oré, and of its native inhabitants, than were his predecessors.

> The fifth river is called Pawtuxunt, of a lesse proportion then the rest; but the channell is 16 fadome deepe in some places. Here are infinit skuls of divers kindes of fish more then elsewhere. Upon this river dwell the people called Acquintanackuak, Pawtuxunt, and Mattapanient. Two hundred men was the greatest strength that could be perceived. But they inhabit together, and not so dispersed as the rest. These of all we found most civill to give entertainment.[4]

Smith, unlike his predecessor, did not tarry to take hostages, but pressed on with his explorations and eventually produced a remarkably accurate map of the Patuxent as part of a delightful, grand chart of the Chesapeake Bay region. Included on the chart were the numerous native towns located along the banks of the river. Fortunately for Smith and his party, the tribes they encountered were (at least along the Patuxent), quite peaceful and friendly. These natives proved to be members of the Piscataway tribe, of Algonquin linguistic stock, and derived their living from farming corn and reaping the bounty of the Bay and river. The richness of these waters, including its oysters (reported to be as large as horses' hooves, almost four times the size of English oysters, and so large they had to be cut to be swallowed), startled the colonists.

Indeed, the very name *Chesapeake,* said to have been derived from the Indian word meaning "Great Shellfish Bay," reflected their incredulity.[5]

Captain Smith noted on his chart a total of seventeen Native American villages or major settlements situated on the Patuxent.[6] A number of these sites were quite extensive, such as the village established on the mouth of what would one day be called Battle Creek where, over the years, the natives had developed extensive cornfields upon the rich land.

After Smith's departure the Patuxent remained untainted by European contact until 1621 when an expedition from Virginia, led by John Pory and Etinien Moll, came to explore.[7] Six years later, the enterprising secretary of state of Virginia, William Claiborne began to barter with the natives, preparatory to establishing a major fur trading station on Kent Island.[8] Not long after Claiborne came the Virginia trader Henry Fleet. Fleet, like the secretary, always had an open eye for the fur and corn trade. The captain examined the river to its far corners, became intimately acquainted with the natives along its banks, learned their traditions and language, and proceeded to carry on a commerce with them.[9]

In 1634 the first permanent Catholic settlement in Maryland was established on the shores of the nearby St. Mary's River with the arrival of a band of colonists aboard the ships *Ark* and *Dove.* Five years later, Governor Leonard Calvert gave a small party of Jesuit missionaries permission to erect a permanent mission amidst the Indians on the river, among whom the kindly Father White, and later the superior of the mission, Father Ferdinand Poulten, had been warmly received. The chief of the Patuxents, Macquacomen, welcomed the missionaries with a gift of land called Mattapany, not far from St. Mary's City. Mattapany was situated on the southern lip of the mouth of the Patuxent, at the terminus of an Indian trail leading from St. Mary's to the river, on grounds now occupied by the Patuxent Naval Air Test Center. The priests proceeded to fence in a segment of land; construct a permanent residence, warehouse, and farm buildings; cultivate the soil; and convert the natives, all with considerable success. Moreover, the waters off the site provided superb fishing grounds and an excellent anchorage for sailing vessels, which the priests frequently employed on their missionary forays upriver. Mattapany thus became the first permanent European settlement on the Patuxent, a center dedicated not to commerce, trade, or agriculture, but to the saving of souls.

The colonists soon spread out from their original close-knit community at St. Mary's City, and by 1641, despite occasionally ugly incidents with the local natives, there were thirty to forty inhabitants dwelling on Mattapanian Hundred. By 1642 one Henry Bishop had established a residence on a beautiful little waterway dubbed St. Leonard's Creek, becoming the first English settler on the north shore of the river. The European's spread along the banks of the Patuxent had thus begun, unfortunately at the expense of the native population. But there would be occasional setbacks for the colonists. In 1644 a major Susquehannock attack was made upon the Indians of southern Maryland, in the course of which the Jesuit mission at Mattapany was captured and sacked. Governor Calvert, for reasons both political and military, was soon obliged to take control of the little settlement. The mission was disbanded, and a strong stockaded fort was erected near the river mouth, which soon became one of the chief military centers in Maryland, serving in that capacity for the next forty-five years.

By 1646 the spread of English settlements up the Patuxent had become epidemic, and the establishment of a communications system became a necessity. Ferry operations were opened between Millstone Point and the north shore. Soon afterward, another service was begun at Point Patience. The river was rapidly becoming the central avenue of civilization from the frontier to the interior. Settlers on the Patuxent and, indeed, throughout the Chesapeake Tidewater were obliged to remain close to the water. For most it was a source—their only source—of rapid communication, and commerce, while also providing for a great bulk of their sustenance.

But of equal importance, it provided the most convenient and expeditious manner of transportation possible. In fact, travel during this early period was practically impossible except by water. The land was densely forested, opened only here and there by age-old animal and Indian trails, while streams and creeks penetrated the hinterland in every direction and afforded a ready means of travel. "Early travelers," as historian Charles Francis Stein once pointed out, "described these creeks and streams as being crystal clear, with but few shoals and sand bars to impede navigation." The larger waterways feeding into the river were navigable for even the larger vessels of the day. Not surprisingly, each plantation erected along the Patuxent had access to its own or a neighbor's wharf; this insured early and continued employment of the river and its tributaries as a means of communication and transportation.

Early local travel along the myriad waterways of the Patuxent region was facilitated by the ready adoption of Native American watercraft and watercraft construction. The principal vessel type in question was the dugout canoe, a cheaply produced boat employed widely in the Tidewater that could be manufactured from readily available resources. "The manner of making their boates in Virginia," wrote Thomas Harriot, one of the first Englishmen to record and publish a description on the construction of the dugout,

is verye wonderfull. For wheras they [the Indians] want Instruments of yron [iron], or other like unto ours, yet they know howe to make them as handsomelye, to saile with whear they liste in their Rivers, and to fishe with all, as ours. First they choose some longe, and thicke tree, accordinge to the bignes of the boate which they would frame, and make a fyre on the grownd about the Roote thereof, kindlinge the same by little, and little with drie mosse of trees, and chipps of woode that the flames should not mounte opp to highe, and burne to muche of the lengthe of the tree. When yt is almost burnt through, and readye to fall they make a new fyre, which they suffer to burne untill the tree fall of yt owne accord. Then burninge of the topps, and boughs of the tree in such wyse that the bodie of the same may Retayne his just lengthe, they raise yt uppon potes laid over cross wise uppon forked posts, as such as reasonable heighte as they may handsomelye work uppon yt. Then take they of the barke with certayne shells: they reserve the, innermost parte of the lonnke, for the nethermost parte of the boate. On the other side they make a fyre according to the lengthe of the bodye of the tree, sawinge at both the endes. That which they thinke is sufficientlye burned they quenche and scrape away with shells, and makinge a new fyre they burne yt agayne, and soe they continue somtymes burninge and sometymes scrapinge, until the boate have sufficient hollownes. Thus god indueth these savage people with sufficient reason to make thinges necessarie to serve their turnes.[10]

"The manner of makinge their boates in virginia" by Theodor de Bry. This famous engraving included in Thomas Harriot's *A Brief and True Report of the New Found Land of Virginia* is the earliest illustration depicting native American boatbuilding methods on the Middle Atlantic seaboard during the Contact Period. Courtesy of the Library of Congress

Although the white man's tools alleviated much of the labor and certain improvements were made in the design, the dugout canoe—forerunner of the noted Chesapeake Bay bugeye—remained basically intact as an individual craft type, surviving in some areas well into the nineteenth century.

The white settlers of the Patuxent region, however, did not rely on indigenous vessel types entirely, and employed watercraft of European construction or design whenever possible. In 1642 the Jesuits described a missionary voyage in one such craft:

> We are carried in a pinnace, or galley, to wit: the father, the interpreter, and a servant—for we use an interpreter, as will be stated hereafter—two of them propel the boat with oars, when the wind fails or is adverse; the third steers with the helm. We take with us a little chest of bread, butter, cheese, corn, cut and dried before it is ripe, beans and a little flour —another chest, also, for carrying bottles, one of which contains wine for religious purposes, six other holy waters for the purpose of baptism; a casket with the sacred utensils, and a table as an altar for performing sacrifice; and another casket full of trifles, which we give the Indians to conciliate their affection—such as little bells, combs, fishing-hooks, needles, thread and other things of this kind. . . . In our excursions we endeavour, as much as we can, to reach by evening some English house, or Indian village, but if not, we land, and to the father falls the care of mooring the boat fast to the shore. . . .[11]

In 1648 the northern movement of white settlement in Maryland took an important step forward with the migration of 118 Puritan settlers, led by one Richard Bennett, to what was later to become Anne Arundel County. The Puritans, prohibited from practicing their religious beliefs in Anglican Virginia, had sailed north and settled at Greenbury Point. By 1649 they had erected the community of Providence, on the Severn River. The following year, after the new immigrants had sworn an oath of allegiance to the lord proprietor Governor William Stone and the General Assembly, then convened at St. Mary's City, caused "An Act for the erecting of Providence into a County by name of Annarundell County." [12]

In 1650 the arrival of Robert Brooke, a favorite of King Charles I, was welcomed by the governor of Maryland with pomp and circumstance. Lord Baltimore saw fit to erect another new county along the Patuxent with Brooke as its "Commander."[13] The county was initially dubbed Charles County, but was reestablished on July 3, 1654, as Calvert County.[14] Brooke was to personally receive a grant of two thousand acres in Resurrection Hundred, on the west side of the river, from which to conduct his administrations. This grant he promptly dubbed De la Brooke Manor. The senior Brooke received an additional tract of two thousand acres directly across the Patuxent and adjoining a large creek, a delightful waterway he named Battle Creek in honor of his wife Mary Baker, whose family had lived at Battle, Sussex, England, site of the Battle of Hastings.[15]

Soon, settlers were spreading westward from the South and Severn Rivers toward the upper reaches of the Patuxent as well as northward from the initial settlement base near the river's mouth. All along its banks land grants were parceled out and settlement was encouraged.

The admission of Bennett's Puritans into Maryland was to have a profound effect upon the tranquil settlements along the Patuxent River. In 1642 civil war between the Puritan-led forces of Parliament and those of King Charles I had burst forth like a firestorm upon the English countryside. On January 30, 1649, the king was beheaded, and in 1651 Oliver Cromwell assumed the dictatorial mantle of government control by becoming the lord protector. These events had severe repercussions in the Chesapeake region, particularly along the Patuxent drainage, which soon became a political battleground between loyal Catholic Royalists and the largely Puritan supporters of Cromwell, with the political authority and properties of Lord Baltimore serving as the focal point of struggle.

In 1652 Cromwell, irritated with Virginia for its refusal to come to heel and with Maryland for its noncommitment to any cause, even though the civil war in England was over, dispatched a force of 750 soldiers to reduce resistance to his authority in both colonies. Governor William Berkeley of Virginia capitulated without a fight in early March.[16] A commission was then sent to Maryland where negotiations were opened with Governor William Stone. On March 29, Cromwell's Virginia Commission issued an edict vesting the powers of the Maryland government in a new commission.[17] Eventually, authority was delegated to a six-man council, the president of which was none other than Commander Robert Brooke of Calvert County. On July 3, 1654, Lord Baltimore, obviously upset with this turn of events, ordered Stone not to cooperate with the Puritan government of Maryland and to maintain his own office as governor.[18] Stone, in a hollow effort to assert his authority, attempted to divest Brooke of his position by simply issuing a proclamation.[19]

The Puritan Assembly, despite Stone's proclamations, proceeded to assert its own authority and quickly moved to erase even nominal linkage to the regime of the Calverts. On October 20, 1654, the Puritans changed the name of Calvert County to Patuxent County, and St. Mary's County became Potomac County.[20] Richard Preston's plantation, grandly situated on the scenic east shore of the Patuxent, was selected as the meeting place for the new government. Preston, one of the early Puritan settlers in Calvert County, was himself an ardent member of the new Maryland commission. Learning of this move, Lord Baltimore dispatched a special messenger, William Eltonhead, to Maryland with orders for Stone to recover his authority. Stone received his instructions in January 1655, organized an armed party in St. Mary's County, and sent a force to capture Preston and the commissioners at Preston Plantation. Though Preston escaped, the seat of government, all of its records, and the Great Seal of Maryland were quickly seized by the Catholics.[21] Stone was encouraged and set sail with a force of 130 armed men to subdue the major Puritan stronghold of Providence. This time he was not as fortunate as he had been at Preston Plantation: his tiny army was defeated at the Battle of the Severn on March 25-26, 1655.[22]

Despite the outcome of the fight, it was soon obvious that the dispute between the Puritans and Lord Baltimore would be settled in London rather than on the battlefields of Maryland. Baltimore was more of a politician and diplomat than a soldier, and on November 30, 1658, he was able to successfully negotiate the return of his lands and authority through appeals to the commissioners of trade in England.[23]

□   □   □

With the end of Puritan rule in Maryland, the inhabitants along the Patuxent, both Protestant and Catholic, returned to a longed-for peace, and their plantation systems began to develop in earnest. Great manors, some already established and others yet to flourish, began to dominate the social system. Forests were felled, lands were cleared, wharves constructed, shallops and flats built, and crops of tobacco planted. Estates of noble size began to emerge. Manors became the commercial, economic, and social centers of the day, and most were situated close to the water, if not directly on the river or one of its tributaries. The Patuxent River, it seemed, was rapidly becoming the most important waterway in the colony. Even the proprietor of Maryland was not impervious to its allure. In 1667 Charles Calvert himself removed to Mattapany where he erected "a fair House of Brick and Lumber."[24]

Ferry connections were soon serving several sections of the Patuxent well above earlier crossings, such as Hallowing Point, at a narrows in the river where the natives had maintained a ferry long before the Europeans' arrival.[25] By 1673 a private ferry crossed the Patuxent into Anne Arundel County, with its main terminus point situated somewhere near the mouth of Lyons Creek on the eastern bank. Another site, which may have been in use during this early period but which certainly had been employed by the beginning of the eighteenth century, was at a crossing now known as Queen Anne's, at the head of deep-water navigation.[26]

And still the settlers came.

During the final third of the seventeenth century the proprietor of Maryland began to experiment with the development of an urban basis upon which to expand and exploit the commercial and maritime resources of the colony and to facilitate the collection of revenues and taxes.

Of a Lesse Proportion

On June 5, 1668, Charles Calvert, Lord Baltimore, issued a proclamation designating eleven sites in the colony as "Sea Ports Harbours creekes & places for the discharging and unlading for goods and merchandizes out of shippes & boates and other vessells." [27] Despite the proclamation, development of towns or ports along the Patuxent River seemed to have been as retarded as any along the entire range of colonial Maryland waterfrontage. Yet a semblance of several rudimentary towns did exist. In 1671 John Ogilby published, in his famous account of America, an indication of the first town development on the river.

> These are Foundations laid of Towns, more or less in each County, according to his Lordships Proclamation, to that effect issu'd forth in the year 1668. In Calvert County, about the River of Patuxent, and the Adjacent Cliffs, are the Bounds of three Towns laid out, one over against [*opposite*] Point Patience, called Harvington, another in Battel-Creek, cau'd Calverton, and a third upon the Cliffs, cau'd Herrington, and Houses already built in them, in uniform, and pleasant with Streets, and Keys on the Water side. [28]

None, however, were towns in any modern sense of the word. Harvington, also referred to as Harvey Town, was situated on the west bank of the Patuxent at Town Creek, in Harvey Hundred, a part of Mattapany; Calverton, of course, lay upon Battle Creek; and Herrington lay ensconced on the Cliffs of Calvert overlooking the Chesapeake; but none had moved to anything resembling a township by this date, except on paper.

In 1669 Lord Baltimore tried again. By "an Ordinance of the . . . Lord Proprietary" he specifically ordered all exports and imports to be routed through twelve designated ports of entry. Though in many parts of the colony this ordinance was met with stout opposition by the planters who would be obliged to divert transportation of their tobacco stocks from their own or their neighbors' private wharves and shipping, at least one effort was made to follow the edict on the Patuxent. Under the 1669 ordinance William Berry, a Puritan residing on the opposite shore of Battle Creek, across from a plantation known as Brooke Place Manor, moved to have twenty acres laid out as a town. His request was carried out under a warrant issued by the proprietor and the nucleus of the town of Calverton was formed. Commander Brooke proceeded to build a courthouse, jail, customs house, and appropriate harbor installations necessary to encourage trade. [29]

Though not specifically designated in the 1669 ordinance, it has been suggested by some urban historians that the port of St. Leonard's, either at the head or mouth of St. Leonard's Creek, was laid out about this time but was never fully recorded until 1707. Yet the first two town acts had met with opposition by the planters of Maryland, and Governor Calvert was obliged to again repeat the provisions, enlarging the number of overall sites in the colony to fifteen, in 1671. It has also been suggested that the origin of St. Leonard's Town was to stem from this particular act and that settlement was soon afterwards begun at the head of St. Leonard's Creek.[30]

Despite the hoped-for development, Lord Baltimore continued to be frustrated in the new town attempts, especially throughout the important Patuxent River region. In 1676 Governor Calvert informed the lords of trade, despite his efforts, that excepting the rude settlement at St. Mary's City, town development in Maryland was at a veritable standstill. "Other places wee have none That are called or cann be called Townes. The people are not affecting to build nere each other but soe as to have their houses nere the Watters for conveniencye of trade."[31] Thus, in 1682, new town measures were again taken up for consideration, and on November 6, 1683, the lord proprietor signed a bill creating a total of thirty-one ports of entry in the province. Supplemental measures and additional sites were added in 1684, 1686, and 1688, along with the mention of specific sites designated for port development. The port of St. Leonard's was officially recognized in the 1683 bill. Another site called Bowlington was situated slightly above present-day Nottingham and was mentioned in both the 1683 bill and the 1688 measure. Calverton, the only site along the Patuxent that could by any stretch of the imagination be considered a town, was also mentioned in the same two measures.[32]

Coxtown, later to become the port of Lower Marlborough (Lower Marlboro), was established by the 1683-84 bills. This townsite, well situated on the banks of the east shore of the Patuxent in Calvert County, was to serve for a considerable period as the principal port of the upper-middle river reach and as the principal outlet for the commerce of Lyons Creek Hundred. The town ultimately grew to a level of importance that rivaled the county seat of Calvert County, Calverton, which was less accessible to the planters of the upper Patuxent region.[33]

Each of these new towns was to be designated by selected commissioners appointed by the governor and was to be one hundred acres in extent, "marked staked out and divided into Convenient streets, Laines & allies, with Open Space places to be left on which may be Erected Church or Chappell, & Marckett house, or other publick buildings, & the remaining part of the said One hundred acres of Land as near as may be into One hundred equall Lotts."[34]

Still, development of the new-town systems was impossibly slow. Many, if not most, of the planters, particularly along the Patuxent, were opposed to alterations in the established system, and they were concerned with the expense and inconvenience of transporting goods to and from the ports. As the prescribed date of property sales approached, the government and the lord proprietor became increasingly concerned over the commissioners' failure to move forward. Many of the commissioners, being planters themselves, were obviously reluctant to take actions that they felt might be economically unfavorable to them should the law be carried out. By the end of February 1684, a proclamation had to be issued directing that

> all and singular the Commissioners of the respective Counties . . . putt in Execution the said Act . . . by causeing the several Port Townes and places of Trade . . . to be forthwith layd out; . . . and that noe failure be thereof made as they will answer the Contrary at their Perill, by not only incurring our displeasure for their contempt of the said Act . . . but also running the hazard of being excluded and exempt from any future benefitt or advantage to be obtained of us. . . . [35]

Like it or not, the new towns of the Patuxent region were finally off to a start.

□   □   □

The period following the restoration of the Baltimores was one marked by material progress and rapid advances in civilization along the Patuxent. The wilderness was daily being pushed back, and the soil turned to the production of "the stinking weed," tobacco, the focal point of Maryland agriculture, the chief export commodity, source of revenue, and main barter medium. "In Virginia and Maryland," bemoaned Benedict Calvert, "Tobacco, is our Staple, is our all, and indeed leaves no room for anything Else."[36] And it begat a problem of epic proportions.

As early as 1671 in an effort to balance its budget, which was in a perennial state of deficit, the government enacted legislation providing for a new tax on every hogshead of tobacco exported, and increased duties levied on articles imported from England. To facilitate the maintenance of order in the collection process, the province had to be divided into three naval districts, of which the Patuxent was one.[37]

The Patuxent had much to offer early maritime endeavours. "Vessels of up to three hundred tons burden," wrote the traveler Andrew Burnaby later in the eighteenth century, "travelled fifty miles upstream. . . ."[38] Thus, access to major water commerce could be given to planters as far north as the region later dominated by the town of Queen Anne's. Navigation of Chesapeake estuaries such as the Patuxent in the seventeenth and eighteenth centuries presented few obstacles for experienced mariners. Native pilots employed in bringing vessels up the Bay were discharged where the rivers met the Bay, the chief obstructions to navigation of the rivers being only branches and trees felled by local inhabitants for fishing. The Patuxent, at least at this early stage, had yet to silt up.

The lifeblood of the Patuxent region was its fine tobacco, and the arrival of the annual tobacco fleet from Europe spurred the only real business activity of the year. It was normal procedure for the ship captains to invite planters along the river to board their ships to discuss the crops, tobacco markets, prices, and freight. The planters then struck bargains for their tobacco by barter, consignment, or direct sale. While the planters and captains negotiated, the seamen flocked ashore to spend their hard-earned wages in the local taverns or ordinaries.

Then commenced the backbreaking work of rolling the great hogsheads of tobacco from the plantations to the local wharves, loading them aboard small vessels, droughers, or flats, and transporting them to the seagoing ships in the river. Tobacco flats employed in this service were described as "large, flat-bottom'd boats, capable of carrying some Tons of Goods, and used in the Tobacco countries to unlade vessels with. They have also a kind of Sloops, clumsily built, which may be called Tobacco druggers, of 70 or 80 Tons Burden. . . ."[39]

A typical flat was capable of carrying nine to twelve hogsheads, or the equivalent of two or three tons of shipping space. Thus, tobacco hauled by 20 or 30 flats, or the equivalent in trips of fewer vessels, filled a typical drugger. Ships occupied the pinnacle of the tobacco hauling hierarchy and their carriage capacity ranged from 50 to 500 tons, with the average being about 170 tons. A ton was considered the measure of space allotted rather than weight. One ton was approximately the equivalent of sixty-four hogsheads. Thus filling a 500-ton vessel required six sloops and 120-180 flats or the equivalent in trips.[40]

There were small craft aplenty. In the 1680s, in All Hallows Parish, Anne Arundel County, the western border of which lay on the Patuxent River and whose eastern border lay on the South River, 22.6 percent of all estates possessed either boats, canoes, flats, shallops, or sloops.[41] By the last quarter of the seventeenth century there were innumerable estates situated along the entire stretch of the river, many of which would undoubtedly have regularly employed the services of such craft and, during the peak selling season, larger flats and druggers. In his famous chart of Maryland, Augustine Hermann indicated that at least one hundred plantations were situated on the river or its tributaries, all subject to the need for waterborne communications.[42]

□   □   □

With the termination of the Cromwell era, Charles II assumed the throne of England. In 1685 his death brought to the crown James II, a despotic and religious zealot bent on the full restoration of the powers of the Catholic Church in England, who, within three years, had roused zealous opposition in both the Whig and Tory parties of the nation. These rarely united political factions, seeking the replacement of the king, invited William of Orange of the United Provinces of the Netherlands to come to London and seize the crown. Without support, James was obliged to flee, and William and his wife, Mary, became rulers of Great Britain on February 13, 1689. As during the days of Cromwell, these far-off events were felt with considerable force on the Patuxent.

In Maryland the Catholic population was now outnumbered by Protestants by twenty-five to one. With the accession of William and Mary, Lord Baltimore was ordered to inform the colony of the new order. Hoping to await the outcome of several rebellions that might influence the tenure of the new monarchs, Baltimore delayed. By June 1689 the Protestants of Maryland, still not officially informed of the change of government but entirely aware of the situation, were becoming restive. Baltimore defended himself by claiming he had sent the proclamation but that his messenger had died.[43] His stalling tactics, however, were to no avail.

Many citizens of Maryland, under the leadership of Captain John Coode of St. Mary's County and Colonel Henry Jowles and Major Ninian Beall of Calvert County, decided to take matters into their own hands. Secretly they formed an "Association of Protestant Gentlemen in Arms for the Defense of the Protestant Religion and for asserting the right of King William and Queen Mary to the Province of Maryland and all the English Dominions." The association rapidly began to assemble arms and men[44] and was soon marching on the capital. St. Mary's City fell without bloodshed. But combat seemed inevitable.[45]

The council of state, which was panicked by the fall of St. Mary's, instructed Colonel William Digges to muster a defensive force, but Digges was unable to gather more than a hundred men loyal to Lord Baltimore. With the capture of the capital, the council had little alternative but to withdraw to the defense works at Mattapany, the strongest fortified position in the province. The Protestant forces, now swollen to 700 men, were soon marching on the old fort and the colony arsenal, then defended by 160 Catholics recruited by Nicholas Sewall and Henry Darnall. Coode's men promptly surrounded the works and ordered the council to surrender. The demand was refused, whereupon Major Beall brought up two cannon taken from an English ship lying in the Patuxent and prepared to pound the Catholics into submission. Coode, however, was now faced with a serious bout of hesitancy among his troops, many of whom were reluctant to conduct a direct assault on their erstwhile governor and council. Captain Coode thus resorted to a ruse to urge them on. A horseman, appearing almost exhausted from a long journey, was instructed to dash through the Protestant camp shouting that the Indians were slaughtering the settlers in the northern sections of the county. The false message rallied the troops to finish the work at hand, and turn their attentions to the menace in the north. The governor and council, being badly outnumbered and possessing no cannon, surrendered on August 1, 1689.[46] The Revolution of 1689 had been completed, practically without bloodshed, yielding a total Protestant victory.

Once again peace prevailed over the settlements of the Patuxent region, and local attention returned to more domestic concerns. Lands along the river's edge and along her creeks and streams were increasingly denuded of virgin forests and ground cover and turned over to the untender mercies of the plow. For the first time, a small but noticeable loss of land through erosion and an incumbent silting up of small feeder creeks and even some shoaling of the river itself began to draw governmental attention. The first and foremost river highway of the colony was beginning to feel the fledgling symptoms of its ultimate fate. Government placed the onus of guilt not on the farmer, who stripped the land and depleted the soil, but upon the itinerant mariner, whose age-old habits of dumping ballast when new cargo was taken aboard was thought to be the cause of river blockage. In 1692 and again in 1704, acts were passed making it illegal for ships to dump ballast into the water and further requiring that if the ballast were to be left behind, it must be carried ashore and deposited on dry land. To reinforce the act, a penalty of two thousand pounds of tobacco was to be levied against violators.[47]

In 1692 Sir Lionel Copley became the first royal governor of Maryland but upon his death was replaced by his lieutenant governor, Francis Nicholson. The new governor's first act was to remove the seat of government from St. Mary's to what would soon become the city of Annapolis. The colony's population center had for several years been creeping inexorably northward, focusing on the fulcrum of the "Ridge," which formed the Patuxent–Chesapeake drainage divide. Though opposition to the move was loud, Nicholson noted that the new seat of government would afford a more convenient and accessible location from which to administer the province. On October 11, 1694, the Assembly convened in Annapolis and formally enacted the transfer. The following year an act was passed partitioning Calvert County, part of which was incorporated into the establishment of a new political subdivision along the Patuxent, which was to be called Prince George's County.[48]

Now that peace had been fully established and the political process of stabilization seemed quite in hand, English colonial officials were once again hopeful that Maryland might prosper and that a town-based culture might develop in lieu of the plantation system that still prevailed. Many, if not most, of the new towns established by Lord Baltimore's earlier attempts had fallen by the wayside, and some existed only on paper. Coxtown, Calverton, and St. Leonard's survived on the Patuxent, but others such as Bowlington, Harvington, St. Joseph's, and St. John's never got off the drawing boards. Thus, the Maryland executive was soon the recipient of a directive "to move the assembly to pass an act for the building of towns, warehouses, wharves, and keys . . . upon the rivers of Potomac, Pattuxent, and on the opposite shore in our Province of Maryland."[49]

In 1706, 1707, and 1708, at the urging of Governor Seymour, the Maryland General Assembly again undertook the passage of new-town legislation. Despite specific instructions that only eight towns be created, a total of forty-two sites were designated by the Act of 1706, and forty-eight by the Act of 1707. Finally, by the Act of 1708, a grand total of fifty-two sites were designated. All trade was to be funneled through these ports, and at these places "all Ships and Vessels trading into this Province shall unlode and put on shoare all Negroes, wares, goods, merchandizes and Commodities whatsoever. . . ."[50]

Only two of the 1683 towns on the Patuxent, St. Leonard's and Coxtown (Lower Marlborough), were redesignated by the 1706 legislation, although several new sites were added. The new sites were Benedict-Leonard Town, situated opposite Hallowing Point; Huntingtown, at the head of Hunting Creek; Nottingham, on the western shore of the Patuxent and abreast of the earlier paper-town of Bowlington; Charles Town, at the conflux of the Western Branch and the Patuxent; Upper Marlborough (later shortened to Upper Marlboro), at the head of navigation on the Western Branch, and Queen Anne's Town, at the head of seaborne navigation on the Patuxent itself.[51]

Directions were issued to the various county commissioners to superintend the business of town and port development. By 1707 county surveyors had been directed to deliver to the commissioners plats of each town. They were also empowered to acquire half-acre sites for public landings at convenient locations on the rivers and creeks to which hogsheads of tobacco and other commodities could be brought and stored to await shipment to convenient designated towns.[52]

Primitive industry in Maryland was at last permitted to take root. In Anne Arundel County valuable deposits of clay and carbonite ore were explored. Much of the clay contained iron and could be made into good common brick. Moreover, the iron ore deposits found along the upper Patuxent were close enough to the water's edge for easy transport and were in ready proximity to large stands of timber suitable for providing charcoal for the smelting process. Not surprisingly, several well-to-do families, such as the Snowdens and Dorseys, found a ready incentive to construct furnaces and forges to produce iron for export and local use. The Snowdens, in fact, became so important to the local economy and well-being of the region that the Patuxent itself was frequently referred to as "Snowden's River."[53]

By the 1720s, the new towns were finally beginning to mature, and overland travel again played an important part in Patuxent development. In 1719 the governor entreated the Assembly to provide for a bridge over the river at Queen Anne's Town, and another on the Eastern Shore: "These two places being the great road, through the Heart of this Country and also the usuall and Shortest passage for all travellers to, and from his Majestys plantations on this continent."[54] The bridge construction effort, however, the first ever on the Patuxent, was turned over to Anne Arundel and Prince George's Counties and the project soon bogged down, stifled by political differences and infighting.[55]

In 1721 and 1722 the Anne Arundel County Court ordered a ferry to cross the Patuxent between Queen Anne's Town and a sister village directly across the river known as Kilkenny Town.[56] In 1722 another crossing was established downriver at Mount Pleasant, which "by the computation of Severall Gentlemen is much the nearest way for all comers & goers from St. Marys and Charles County to & from Annapolis."[57] The Mount Pleasant crossing was extolled as superior to the Queen Anne's Ferry due to the "Difficulty of Passing & Repassing over at Queen Anne Town, Occasioned by the freshes of the River at Some Seasons, wch is quite contrary at Mount Pleasant. . . ."[58]

Although easy river access to the growing port of Queen Anne's Town at the head of Patuxent navigation was more or less assured, development of commercial and agricultural interests north of the town were making demands on the government to dredge the river. In 1733 the government finally passed "An Act to empower the Inhabitants of Anne-Arundel and Prince George Counties, to make the main Branch of the River Patuxent navigable above Queen Anne's Town, in Prince George County. . . ."[59] In 1736 a supplementary series of acts were passed specifically prohibiting the obstructing of the branch by hedges, weirs, or fences, or by the felling of trees "either for the conveniency of fishing or any other reason. . . ." Soon, flat-bottomed barges began to haul ore, produce, and tobacco from points nearly twenty miles above Queen Anne's down to the town for transfer to seagoing vessels bound for Europe.[60]

The Queen Anne's Ferry, despite competition at Mount Pleasant Landing, remained in operation at least until 1743 when the government again moved to have a bridge constructed there.[61] In August of 1744 the court drew up an agreement with John Fowler for the building of an arched bridge over the Patuxent at Queen Anne's Town. The cost was to be one hundred pounds and was to be equally shared by Prince George's and Anne Arundel Counties.[62] Unlike before, bicounty cooperation was so successful in this endeavor that between 1744 and 1773, agreements were made for the construction of more than sixteen bridges over the river above the town. Development and commerce, however, were not the main reasons for such a large number of spans being agreed upon. The primary justification for so many bridges was, in fact, due to the ravages of nature. A new bridge was needed at Queen Anne's only ten years after the first had been constructed, because the older bridge had succumbed to wear and the forces of the river. Between 1754 and 1777, two more bridges had to be constructed at the town as a result of these same natural forces.[63]

Maritime commerce on the river was as hearty as ever during this period, as evidenced by the newsworthiness of the comings and goings of shipping and the day-to-day events along the banks that made the weekly "headlines" in the colony press, the *Maryland Gazette.*

Yet the newspaper reported not only the major events of the day relating to the river, such as who was being appointed naval officer of the district or what vessels were entering, unloading, and departing but the seemingly mundane matters of everyday life as well. Typical of this genre was an advertisement that appeared in the newspaper on Tuesday, June 10, 1729:

> RUN away from the Ship *Sea-Horse,* a Sailer, named John Brand, a thin Man, a Dutch Man, speaks broken English. He had a Pair of Screws and Rowlers with him. Whoever secures him and brings him to me the Subscriber, on Board the said Ship, shall have 2-Shillings Reward. [64]

The notice was signed by Thomas Davidson, master of the *Sea Horse.* Another type of notice was that which reported the escape or loss of black slaves.

> Stray'd or stolen, the 2d Inst. from the Plantation of Mr. Richard Hall, near Hall's Creek, in Calvert County, a Negroe Boy between 3 and 4 Years old, of a very Black Complexion. Whoever secures the said Negroe to me, at the Plantation aforesaid, shall have Two Pistoles Reward. Richard Hall.[65]

The escape or death of a black slave, be it accidental or otherwise, was as significant as any other loss incurred by a Patuxent planter, for a slave represented a long-term investment that was expected to pay for itself in terms of lifelong labor. The replenishment and enlargement of this labor pool represented a significant commercial undertaking in Maryland, with considerable profits promised for those bold enough to invest in the slaving trade. It was often a physically hazardous and economically debilitating venture for its managers and the personnel but was indeed nothing compared to the unendurable and degradingly painful experience suffered by the human chattel it dealt in.

The first black slave in Lord Baltimore's Maryland was probably purchased at the island of Barbados, in the West Indies, by Richard Thompson and arrived along with the settlers aboard the *Ark* and the *Dove* in 1634. Four years later, the first active attempt to import slaves into the province was initiated by Lord Baltimore. Richard Kemp, the proprietor's agent, was ordered to purchase for the use of Lord Baltimore's personal household "Fortye neate Cattle, ten Sowes, Forty Henns and Ten Negroes to be Transported to St. Maryes."[66]

The trade was initially centered at St. Mary's City and was apparently quite small, with individual planters procuring slaves from Barbados and the West Indies whenever possible. By the end of the seventeenth century the importation of slaves had increased moderately, for in the period between midsummer of 1698 and Christmas of 1707 (the first period for which solid statistics on importation of blacks exist), a total of 2,290 slaves had been brought into the province, averaging approximately 250 individuals per year. After this period, however, slave importation jumped between two- and fourfold; a substantial portion of the slaves were carried into the Patuxent. In 1708, nearly 20 percent of all slaves imported into Maryland were brought into the Patuxent Naval District. In fact, one of the better anchorages for slaving vessels entering the river seems to have been in the sheltering waters of the mouth of St. Leonard's Creek.[67]

One typical slave-trading venture ending in the Patuxent in this particular year was initiated by a consortium of investors led by Sir Thomas Webster. Webster had secured the services of, or possibly owned, a London galley called the *Alexander*, which he intended to employ in a slaving voyage to the Guinea Coast of Africa. The *Alexander* was a vessel of 160 tons burden and carried twelve guns and a complement of twenty-six men. She was commanded by Captain Giles Loame who, upon Webster's orders, fitted her out with the myriad accoutrements necessary for a slaving voyage. After Webster secured approval of a "Petition to clear [the] Alexander for Guinea, then with Slaves to Patuxant R. Md.," the expedition got under way. Loame successfully acquired a cargo of slaves on the African coast and, on October 25, 1708, arrived in the Patuxent with 119 African blacks. Traders and sponsors of the expedition such as William Loame, Godfrey Webster, John Dene, and Thomas Stringer now stood to make a large fortune upon the sale of this human cargo.[68]

By 1726, between five hundred and one thousand blacks were being imported annually and the flow of slaves into Maryland via the Patuxent and other rivers continued unabated. The Royal African Company, established by royal charter specifically to exploit the African slave trade, figured prominently in many of the Maryland enterprises. One such undertaking was recorded on April 6, 1720, when the company agents wrote: "Capt. Lambert joyned with Mr. Wm. Younge on a Trading Voyage to Windward. . . . Will consign the Negros to Mr. James Bowles at Puttuxent River in Maryland." Three months later the agents reported the successful acquisition of a large cargo of black men, women, and children: "Shipd on board 260 Slaves vizt. 124 Men 111 Women and 26 boys and 8 girls. Consign'd to Mr. Ja. Bowles at Puttuxent River in Maryland."[69]

By the 1770s it had become common practice among some local investors in the slave trade, such as James Dick of London Town, Anthony Stewart of Annapolis, and others, to enter into partnership agreements with sea captains and ship owners not normally involved in the trade to import slaves on a large scale. One such shipowner, a former sea captain named Judson Coolidge, was a typical example. In 1771 the *Maryland Gazette* reported that the ship *Mary* (Captain Samuel Haycroft commanding) had arrived from Africa with "A Small Parcel of about One Hundred Slaves, consisting of Men, Women, Boys and Girls, which will be sold, on Monday next, the Tenth Instant [of July], at Selby's Landing, on Patuxent River, for Bills of Exchange, or Current Money, by the Subscribers. James Dick and [Anthony] Stewart [and] Judson Coolidge."[70] Coolidge's partner, James Dick, was one of the more enterprising of Maryland's merchants to operate in the trade and made the Patuxent his major district of entry, favoring either Selby's Landing or Nottingham as the center of his slave sales. Frequently, Dick even formulated favorable partnerships with his competition to carry out operations. Men such as Stephen West, Jr., of Upper Marlborough, and Richard Snowden of Annapolis were but a few. Vessels such as the *Mary* or others with more exotic names such as *Kouli Kan* were employed regularly by Dick and his associates and figured prominently in the records of middle and late eighteenth century shipping on the Patuxent.[71]

Merchants and entrepreneurs were not oblivious to the other merits of the Patuxent either. The river flowed directly through the heart of the colony's primary tobacco-growing region, and thus made available a veritable gold mine for the industrious and enterprising trader. English and Scottish concerns were quick to see the advantages offered by such ready access to tobacco stocks, and were equally sharp to observe the profits available by providing the necessities of civilized life to the planters of the Patuxent region. In 1713, with the signing of the Treaty of Utrecht, the War of the Spanish Succession, a twelve-year conflict that had sapped the lifeblood of all the European powers, came to a close. Many English and Scottish merchant houses, as well as local Maryland speculators, reasoned that a lasting European peace had finally been achieved, and thus began to explore avenues of commercial expansion in the English-speaking colonies of America. One of the most lucrative fields of investment, of course, was the Chesapeake tobacco trade. Many firms, through agents and factors, began to look for ports in the colony offering advantageous geographic locations and potentials for future growth. The Patuxent region and its many young towns fit the bill. It was precisely from this moment in time that the new towns along the river actually blossomed.

Villages such as Queen Anne's, Upper Marlborough, Nottingham, and St. Leonard's began to attract the attentions of local merchants and English and Scottish concerns alike. The European houses opened up lines of commerce and trade by sending company representatives to operate stores in the colony, providing a share of the profits in return for healthy credit extensions, ready outlets for tobacco, and imports suitable for merchandising on the local markets. Many of these factors, however, saw advantages in independent trade or became enamoured with the colony itself and entered other occupations as well. In 1716, for instance, Isaac Hyde came to Maryland as factor of Gilbert Higgenson of London. Not unlike a number of European merchant representatives, Hyde preferred being his own man, moved to Queen Anne's Town, rented a tavern, and operated the ferry.[72] Many more, however, carried out their original assignments profitably. Some, such as William Mollenson, at St. Leonard's Town, began to dominate the trade of entire sectors of the river. [73] Others, of a more local character, such as Stephen West, Jr., son of a wealthy merchant at London Town on the South River, found the Patuxent more desirable than other locations. West, in fact, ultimately maintained a chain of at least eleven different stores throughout the colony, including several on the Patuxent, and employed Upper Marlborough, where he also operated a ropewalk, as his base of operations.[74]

In 1735 an Act of Assembly authorized a new and even larger St. Leonard's Town to be established adjacent to the old town site.[75] Tobacco grown along the lower cliffs of Calvert, on the Chesapeake, and along the shores of St. Leonard's Creek was being shipped from the town directly to England, and American wharf facilities had become inadequate to meet the expanding needs of the planters and merchants alike. Such was the case at many of the new towns. Imperceptibly, however, alterations in the mosaic of commerce and transportation were beginning to influence the growth of the region. By the late 1740s a shift in the colony's traffic patterns began to reflect the out-migrations pushing north into the upper Patuxent and Potomac valleys. German pioneers began developing settlements in the Monocacy Valley, and urban centers such as Baltimore and Bladensburg began to siphon off commercial expansion in the central county areas and along the Patuxent drainage. Yet even on the eve of the American Revolution the "Great Road" of the colony still passed through Queen Anne's where ferry service had been resumed.

Although a demographic shift in colony population patterns was becoming a notable villain in slowing development of the Patuxent valley, sedimentation and obstruction to river navigation were becoming even more of a concern with every passing year. A crude survey of soil taken from one riverfront plantation, Anne Arundel Manor, in 1767 classified 218.5 acres of eroded land out of a 10,894.5-acre total. Soil deposition, however, had already become a serious problem at the navigable head of the river as early as 1712. At that time the inhabitants of a settlement on the South River had petitioned for a road over to Kilkenny Town because boat traffic from South River, via the Chesapeake and up the Patuxent, was frequently being stymied by increased shoaling.[76]

In 1733 the river above Queen Anne's Town was cleared for nearly twenty-five miles upstream. Yet, there were numerous places where shoals and rapids were preventing flatboat and barge traffic, so that banks had to be cleared and roads built to permit men or beasts of burden to portage their vessels. In 1750, during an extremely bad period of weather, the river made a breach across the main street of Queen Anne's Town, which had to be filled in before town traffic could resume.[77] Twenty years later, the channel area above the town had become so narrow and clogged that dredging was imperative if river barge traffic was to reach the town wharves.[78]

Other towns on the upper Patuxent had their problems as well. In 1759 the Western Branch became so choked with rubbish, dead trees, and sediment that Upper Marlborough was practically cut off from its access to the main river. Its commerce suffered accordingly. In May of this same year several merchants of the town proposed a lottery scheme to raise money to construct a new wharf on the branch, and to clear a passage down to the river. A total of fifteen hundred tickets, at two pieces of eight each, were offered for sale, with 496 prizes guaranteed, totaling twenty-five hundred pieces of eight. The surplus five hundred pieces of eight raised by the lottery would be used to finance the construction of the wharf and to clear the Western Branch. The scheme was so successful that all of the tickets were sold almost immediately, and the lottery was held in the Prince George's County Courthouse in July, six months earlier than planned.[79]

The continued and frequent blockage of the Patuxent River was only one of the problems facing the ports and landings along her banks. With the alterations of the private traffic and commercial patterns and new road development to the north and west, local county governments situated along the river found themselves out of touch with population centers. The Patuxent was simply becoming less important in the colony communications system. In 1722 the Assembly passed an act directing the movement of the Calvert County Government from its seat at Calverton, to a more centralized position in the county. The site selected was on a tract of land below the head of Battle Creek, and above Parker's Creek, on the backbone of the Patuxent–Chesapeake drainage divide. The new

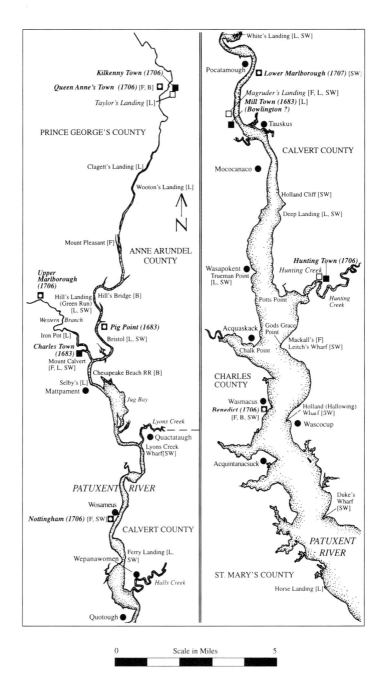

Colonial towns, landings, ferries, and tobacco inspection stations on the Patuxent River. (This and facing page. See key on page 39.)

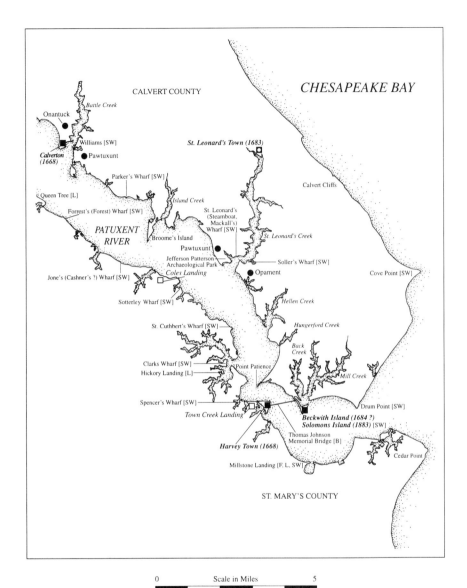

CALVERT COUNTY

Battle Creek

Onantuck

Williams [SW]

Calverton (1668)

Pawtuxunt

Parker's Wharf [SW]

Queen Tree [L]

Forrest's (Forest) Wharf [SW]

Island Creek

PATUXENT RIVER

Broome's Island

Pawtuxunt

Jefferson Patterson Archaeological Park

Coles Landing

Jone's (Cashner's ?) Wharf [SW]

Sotterley Wharf [SW]

St. Cuthbert's Wharf [SW]

Clarks Wharf [SW]

Hickory Landing [L]

Spencer's Wharf [SW]

Town Creek Landing

Point Patience

CHESAPEAKE BAY

St. Leonard's Town (1683)

Calvert Cliffs

St. Leonard's (Steamboat, Mackall's) Wharf [SW]

St. Leonard's Creek

Soller's Wharf [SW]

Opament

Cove Point [SW]

Hellen Creek

Hungerford Creek

Back Creek

Mill Creek

Drum Point [SW]

Beckwith Island (1684 ?) Solomons Island (1883) [SW]

Thomas Johnson Memorial Bridge [B]

Harvey Town (1668)

Millstone Landing [F, L, SW]

Cedar Point

ST. MARY'S COUNTY

0   Scale in Miles   5

● Conjectured location of Native Village Sites Based Upon John Smith Map

■ Riverport/Port of Entry

◘ Tobacco Inspection Station and Port of Entry

☐ Tobacco Inspection Station at Landings

[F]   Ferry Service

[B]   Bridge

[L]   Landing

[SW] Public and/or Steamboat Wharf

39

county seat was called Prince Frederick, in honor of the eldest son of King George I.[80] Upper Marlborough was selected at about the same time to become the county seat of Prince George's County despite opposition from the merchants of Charles Town, the original seat of government.[81]

By the mid-1740s, the threat of economic disaster loomed large on the horizon. The state of the tobacco trade, and the economy to which it was married, had been subjected to severe setbacks due to a variety of causes, not the least of which was an annual glut of the leaf on European markets. An alarmingly high percentage of this glut was made up of inferior quality "trash" tobacco which brought poor returns to the planters whose time, energy, and economic resources had gone into its production. As prices declined, the indebtedness of Maryland planters increased, with the fortunes of dependent tradesmen and the merchant community suffering accordingly as depression set in. By 1747 the Maryland tobacco was earning less than half a penny per pound, and total collapse of the colony's economic structure seemed imminent.[82]

The government was forced to take drastic measures. Legislation modeled after a successful Virginia law was enacted and was entitled "An Act for amending the Staple of Tobacco, for Preventing Frauds in His Majesty's Customs, and for the Limitation of Officers Fees." This law provided for the establishment of fixed stations throughout Maryland where tobacco inspectors would examine all produce destined for export. The inspectors were ordered to burn all trash tobacco on the spot and issue receipts for quality stock passing inspection.[83]

Obviously, sites chosen for the establishment of stations and warehouses employed in the process were likely to become, if they were not already, the focal points of local tobacco commerce. The post of inspector soon became a lucrative, much sought-after sinecure. Twelve public warehouses and inspection stations were selected for the Patuxent region, through which all tobacco being exported from each locale would be funneled.

The effect of the Tobacco Inspection Act on the Patuxent region was multifaceted. In the past, rising tobacco prices, a hoped-for result of the new law, had indeed heralded prosperity for all—merchants, planters, and the towns. Yet the 1747 Act resulted in lower production, offsetting gains made by the higher prices. Worse, with lowered production, fewer merchants were required to market the crops. In All Hallow's Parish, bordering on the upper Patuxent and serviced by Taylor's Landing, tobacco production was halved. Small planters and tenant farmers, unable to rotate planting because of their limited resources and land, often lost half of their crops at inspection stations.[84]

In 1771 the Tobacco Inspection Act expired, and exports from the colony increased substantially: 22.9 percent the first year and 41.2 percent the second. And with the restoration of trade volume on the river, a greater number of merchants once again began to employ the towns and landings of the Patuxent to their benefit. In 1775, for instance, the firm of Wallace, Davidson and Johnson opened up stores at Queen Anne's Town and Nottingham to promote their import sales and handle export tobacco. One of the principals of the firm was particularly anxious to receive consignments from Calvert County planters because the farmers usually took their profits in goods and rarely drew on their London balances in bills of exchange. For such firms as Wallace, Davidson and Johnson this was advantageous since the businessmen gained a commission from tobacco sales and profits from store goods priced far above cost. The return of prosperity, however, was to be terribly short-lived.[85]

▢   ▢   ▢

The numerous wars of empire into which the American colonies of England had been thrust time and again usually had little effect on the docile Patuxent region. Beginning with the Stamp Act in 1765, however, efforts to force the colonies to pay a portion of the debts incurred by the most recent of these contests, the Seven Years War, began to sow significant discontent in Maryland, not the least of which was with the disintegrating moral fabric of the proprietary government and the British aristocracy. The system was simply breaking down and Marylanders began to join the ranks of protest. Finally, in June 1769 a large body of merchants in Annapolis and Baltimore formed public assemblies and joined with counterparts in other colonies to set up a boycott of British importations to protest the costly corruption and heavy-handed tactics of Parliament. The protest was strongly supported on the Patuxent, especially in Prince George's County. On April 7, 1770, the first challenge to the issue of nonimportation and test of the boycott's strength was raised. "Several Ships from Great-Britain being daily expected to arrive in Patuxent River, with European Good," it was noted in the *Maryland Gazette*, "the Inhabitants of Prince George's County thought it necessary to meet, in order to appoint proper Committees to SUPPORT THE ASSOCIATION."[86] Accordingly, two dozen merchants—six from Queen Anne's Town, eight from Upper Marlborough, five from Nottingham, and five from Magruders Landing—were elected. It was thereafter resolved "That we will support the Association of the 22nd June 1769, and that the above Committee be directed to take care that the same be carried into Effect with the utmost strictness."[87]

The confrontation was not, however, destined to occur on the Patuxent, but at Annapolis. Here, the vessel *Good Intent*, belonging to James Dick and Anthony Stewart, was held up when it was learned she had broken the boycott. Maryland's unified merchant community, including those along the Patuxent, obliged the owners to send her back to England unloaded. Ultimately, the legislation that had aroused the latest protest, the Townsend Act, was revoked.[88]

Unfortunately for England, the seeds of discontent were allowed to grow. In May 1773, when the British government again attempted to enforce its will on the colonies by imposing a tax on tea, Maryland again embarked on another nonimportation scheme.

On March 1, 1774, James Dick's and Anthony Stewart's brigantine *Peggy Stewart* lay at anchor at Selby's Landing on the Patuxent "ready to take on board tobacco at seven pounds per ton, consigned to Wallace, Davidson and Johnson." Her master, Richard Jackson, busily superintending the loading, was anxious to be off, and it was advertised that "those...who incline to take advantage of an early market, are requested to have their tobacco ready with a view of dispatching her."[89]

Several months had already passed since the already-famous protest against the tea tax at Boston by the time the *Peggy Stewart* was being loaded. And it was only a few weeks after her sailing that Parliament set about to punish that port by ordering it closed. Few realized that the *Peggy Stewart*'s return would touch off an even more violent incident in Maryland. Again a boycott was called for. On October 19, 1774, soon after the arrival of the brigantine back from England, Stewart was forced by an angry mob to burn his vessel in Annapolis Harbor for attempting to ignore the boycott.[90]

Exactly six months later to the day "the shot heard 'round the world" was fired at Lexington Green. The American Revolution had begun, and the Patuxent was certain to bear its share of the suffering.

TWO

Up the Patuxent Plundering

With the onset of the American War of Independence, the Patuxent River region was to suffer from few major military actions, but was to become the target of repeated depredations by British and loyalist raiders. As early as March 1776, enemy naval forces had begun to conduct their first punitive operations near the river, and landings were feared to be in the making as close as Point Lookout in St. Mary's County. On March 5 a militia unit under the command of Captain John Allen Thomas had marched to the mouth of the Patuxent and then to Point Lookout on the Potomac, to defend the area against an expected enemy attack. The British, however, operating freely upon the waters, possessed superior mobility and simply sailed around the landbound Marylanders. Several days later three armed vessels moved into the mouth of the Patuxent and captured a merchant vessel laden with flour. Captain Thomas, unable to move his unit back across the river, or even fire upon the foe, was helpless. Reinforcements under Lieutenant John Steward responded as rapidly as possible, but to no avail. In frustration, Thomas requested permission from the Maryland Council of Safety to purchase a Virginia pilot boat to convoy his troops between St. Mary's and Calvert Counties as necessary. Permission, however, was denied when the threat of immediate incursions subsided.[1] But alarms were frequent. In July, southern Maryland was again thrown into a panic when a large naval force commanded by Virginia's royal governor, James Murray (the Earl, Lord Dunmore), hove to with nearly one hundred vessels off St. Mary's County and proceeded to make armed landings at St. George's Island and other places along the Potomac River. The Patuxent was spared.[2]

With Dunmore's departure the Patuxent region fell into a state of total military stagnation, always exposed, but never quite threatened enough to warrant a military buildup or fortifications. Defense of the river fell to local militia units. Two garrisons were maintained in the area: one, under Captain Thomas's command, was situated at Point Lookout, at the mouth of the Potomac; the other was stationed at the mouth of the Patuxent at Drum Point. Neither garrison exceeded fifty men. Duty was monotonous at best, and desertion was a constant problem.[3]

By the end of the summer of 1777, inactivity was taking its toll on regional defense preparedness. On September 15 Governor Thomas Johnson, a native of Calvert County and Maryland's first freely elected chief executive, was notified by an officer stationed at Leonardtown, in St. Mary's County, that southern Maryland had become the most poorly armed sector of the entire state (albeit still the most exposed) and was practically defenseless. Moreover, the danger from internal upheaval was as menacing as that offered by the British. The slave population of the region was, by many accounts, becoming "very insolent," and with local defenses and morale at such a low ebb, the possibility of an uprising had become more than a little worrisome. Although a company of militia was still being maintained on the Patuxent, the dissipated unit at Point Lookout had by that time been broken up and returned home. British attacks were one thing. After all, that was white against white. But a possible slave revolt! In light of the restive black population, another militia unit was readily formed and dispatched to Point Lookout.[4] Despite the unrest, all would remain quiet on the river for the next three years.

The year 1780 was to prove more disconcerting to the Patuxent region than any thus far, as enemy naval attention began to focus on the Chesapeake. In early July a large convoy of more than twenty American ships, brigs, and assorted smaller merchant vessels had set sail from the upper Bay intent on slipping through the British naval blockade at the Virginia capes and into the open sea. On July 11, it was reported, the convoy had proceeded as far south as Smith Point on the Virginia lip of the Potomac, but had encountered a strong enemy naval force and was obliged to retire into the Patuxent for safety. The convoy remained locked in the river for weeks, causing dismay in the highest circles of state government. The Maryland Council of Safety berated the state delegates to the Continental Congress and the Congress itself for its inability to cope with British naval depredations in the Bay. "Our Coast," the council wrote, "is much infested with the Privateers and Cruisers of the Enemy, our Trade & Navigation obstructed & many of our Vessels captured. . . ."[5]

Yet day-to-day life on the river varied little, despite the threat of enemy activity. On August 30, 1780, Captain John Smith was appointed inspector at St. Cutherbert's Creek even though tobacco exporting had ground to a virtual halt. Enemy landing parties occasionally raided private estates on the exposed shores of the western side of the Bay, above and below the mouth of the Patuxent, but life on the river itself seemed to plod along much as always. On August 23, during one such raid, however, British invaders had moved dangerously close, landing at nearby Point Lookout and destroying most of the plantation of one Robert Armstrong. On September 4, as a result of these attacks, a committee composed of Nicholas Sewall, Robert Watts, and Thomas Dillon informed the Council of Safety that the enemy was not only harassing the Chesapeake in general, but seemed to be specifically targeting the Patuxent and Potomac regions. The committee requested arms and ammunition, which were still in terribly short supply, for their defense. Again, it was a case of too little too late. Eight days later, on September 12, Point Lookout was again hit by enemy raiders. British and loyalist depredations were soon becoming a common expectation, and so upsetting to the local population that another, stronger request for defensive measures was forwarded on September 20 to Governor Thomas Sims Lee by Colonel Richard Barnes, commander of the St. Mary's County Militia. Again, the request was ignored, and the consequences were predictable.[6]

On November 5, 1780, the enemy struck directly at the Patuxent. Three armed schooners, one of which mounted eight- and six-pounders, and another mounting four three- and four-pounders, swivels and small arms, entered the river and proceeded directly toward Point Patience. This narrow, sandy peninsula of land jutting into the river from the Calvert County shore, belonged to John Parran. The British landed unopposed, burned Parran's house and furniture, "took several negroes & what stock they could collect & two Vessels loaded with 8 hhds of Tobacco," and retired downriver. When they hove to again, they were off Rousby Hall, the estate of Colonel William Fitzhugh. There, they immediately dispatched a flag ashore and informed the Marylander that if the flag were accepted and provisions provided, they would do no harm. The flag was, unfortunately for the Marylanders, "refused & . . . [the attackers] immediately Cannonaded & burnt the Colonel's house."[7]

The enemy continued to menace the Patuxent region for months on end effecting a virtual blockade. On January 3, 1781, Captain Joseph Ford, in charge of the St. Mary's County Commissary Department, reported that enemy barges were watching the river so closely that all transfer of supplies by water had become quite hazardous if not impossible.

Efforts, however, were continually made to test the blockade whenever feasible. Late in January one such trial was undertaken, with disastrous results. Three merchantmen (the privateer brig *Cato*, Captain Benjamin Wickes commanding; the schooner *Hawk*, Captain Bull commanding; and the schooner *Nautilus*, Captain James Kierstad commanding; laden with cargoes of flour) had departed Baltimore and were sailing under a secret charter from the Maryland Council of Safety and were intent on running the Chesapeake Bay blockade. On January 22, off the mouth of the Patuxent, the three ships encountered an enemy man-of-war, believed to be HMS *Isis*, of fifty guns and 350 men, and were driven ashore between Cedar Point and St. Jerome's Creek, near the estate of a certain Mr. Bellwood. The *Hawk*, being the furthest out and the most exposed to capture, was immediately set afire by her crew and abandoned. The *Nautilus*, an eighty-five-ton vessel of shallow draft, struck bottom relatively close in-shore. The *Cato*, unfortunately, struck further out and, with *Hawk* afire and no longer of interest to the enemy, became the first target of convenience for British boarding parties. The brig's commander, for want of ammunition, was unable to defend his vessel, which was quickly carried. The British immediately commenced plundering the prize.[8]

Whether Captain Wickes had prepared a trap for the enemy or the following events were entirely accidental is uncertain, but the end result was catastrophic for all concerned. Several of the British seamen, no doubt in pursuit of plunder, managed to break into the brig's magazine, which for unknown reasons suddenly "blew up carrying 10 of theirs & six of our [American] people." The explosion was awesome, and the vessel's stores were hurled as far forward as her pumps, and in some cases entirely away. More than a third of the ship had been blown to bits. A raging fire soon encompassed the remaining wreck as water ebbed and flowed through giant gaps in her shattered hull. The *Nautilus*, throughout the whole affair, remained unmolested and was later reported to be "high up & will be saved." [9]

Despite the terrible loss of the *Hawk* and *Cato*, two hundred barrels of flour from the smoking hulk of the latter were saved. It was hoped a good portion of the remaining cargo might also be recovered, as the water had not penetrated more than an inch into the powdered flour despite immersion in the Bay. Soon after the incident Colonel Samuel Smith of Baltimore arrived on the scene and by January 27 had managed to extract nearly two hundred additional barrels of flour from the wreck of the *Nautilus*. Both Bull and Smith encountered great difficulties in their ongoing salvage work. Unfortunately the "avarice, avidity & Lazyness of the [local] Inhabitants" prohibited the ready advancement of the work at hand. The crew of the *Cato* had embezzled much of that vessel's cargo before Smith's arrival, selling it to the nearby residents at a great profit, and the crew of the *Nautilus* refused "to preserve anything but their rigging and furniture" even though the wreck was in a salvageable condition. Smith promptly dismissed the now-sulking crew of the *Cato* and hired a work gang of whites and black slaves to proceed with the salvage. At the same time, pumping and bailing began on the *Nautilus*. The following day Smith suggested to Major Ignatius Taylor, in overall charge of the actual recovery operations, that Taylor offer the local militia a one-eighth share of the salvaged flour as payment to induce them to assist in the work. Thus by January 28 a total of seven hundred barrels had been removed and stored on the beach front of Mr. Bellwood's estate. Thanks to Smith's and Taylor's valiant efforts, *Nautilus* was saved. On February 7 the Maryland Council of Safety determined to have the flour, finally tallying over eight hundred barrels, transferred to Baltimore where it was to be baked and repacked for later usage.[10]

Up the Patuxent Plundering

Isis soon departed the area, but the enemy was not to leave the Patuxent region alone for long. On March 27, 1781, Joseph Wilkinson of Calvert County informed the governor of the foe's return:

> In consequence of five of the enemy's Vessels laying off the Clifts, I have ordered the Militia on Guard and directed them to secure all Craft in the Bay & River. The enemy has been several times in the mouth [of the] Patuxent, they landed last Wednesday night in St. Mary's and plundered several Gentlemen of the whole of their furniture, wearing apparel, corn, meat, &c.[11]

News of enemy raids in the Patuxent region was soon being reported in Annapolis with dismal regularity. One foggy day in April, for instance, enemy barges penetrated "all the way up the Patuxent." Worry was expressed as far upriver as Upper Marlborough, where merchant Stephen West wrote of distinct concern. "Every hours experience shows the necessity of having some armed vessels in . . . the Patuxent & Potomac."[12]

On April 7, a "picaroon" barge of loyalists commanded by Captain Jonathan Robinson, with a crew principally composed of runaway slaves, ascended to Lower Marlborough, plundered the town and local tobacco warehouses, and carried off the shipping tied up at the town wharf. The home of former Maryland State Navy Commander John David was burned to the ground.[13]

Details were often sketchy, but the enemy's vicious presence in or about the undefended river was often felt. On one typical occasion soon after the Robinson raid, two ships and a brig were discovered heaving to off the mouth of the Patuxent, and an enemy landing was expected. On April 10 Wilkinson again wrote Governor Lee from Lower Marlborough, informing him that on the evening of the ninth an enemy barge had landed at Cedar Point "and last night a House was seen on fire near the place supposed to be Mr. Nicholas Sewall's. . . ."[14]

Two weeks after the barge landing, enemy marauders again ascended the Potomac and, it was feared, might pose some immediate danger to the Patuxent as well. Three senior militia officers, Colonels Jordan, Fenwick, and Thomas, advised the government that, in the absence of a state naval defense, at least 120 men might be raised immediately, 30 of whom should be employed as mobile mounted troops to react to potential trouble spots more readily. These 120, they suggested, should be stationed on the Patuxent. In fact, enemy vessels were in a position to ascend the river at any time if they had so desired. At least one enemy warship, the New York loyalist privateer *Jack o' the Lanthorn*, of six guns and thirty-six men, was at that moment cruising off the river's mouth, with a recently captured prize sloop in company awaiting any unwary vessel that might happen her way.[15]

For once, however, luck was on the American side. On April 27 two Baltimore privateers, the *Antelope* and *Felicity*, returning from the West Indies, engaged and captured the loyalist and her prize a little below Cedar Point. "The Chaps had with them," it was reported after the affair, "a pretty deal of very good wearing apparel such as Shirts, Breeches, Waistcoats &c, Summer Ware. . . ." The cargo of clothing, it was learned, belonged to none other than the Marquis de Lafayette and had only recently fallen into the enemy's hands with the capture of "Middleton's Boat in which it had been shipped." "Middleton's Boat" was undoubtedly the aforementioned prize sloop taken by the loyalists sometime earlier.[16]

Unable to secure help from the state government, the merchants along the Patuxent drainage, under Colonel Fitzhugh's leadership, finally organized themselves into a self-defense force known as the Board of Patuxent Associators. With the blessings of the state government and by pooling their resources, they purchased the hard-luck *Nautilus*, then lying at Fells Point on the Patapsco River and armed her with eight cannon. Soon afterwards, the newly outfitted river-defense boat was sailed to the port of Nottingham to take on the mission of defending the Patuxent. By August, however, *Nautilus* was found to be far too costly for a handful of merchants to sponsor alone, and had proved less than effective for such work. She was offered up for sale.[17]

On July 1 British barges again returned to the mouth of the Patuxent, where they fell in with and captured a small bay schooner ostensibly laden with tobacco. The owner of the schooner, a young man by the name of James Thomas, was in fact running military supplies up the Chesapeake to the Head of Elk, and was wounded in the encounter.[18]

Alarm followed alarm. On August 4 it was reported that some forty enemy vessels were coming up the bay. A circular was carried up and down the western shore of the Chesapeake urgently requesting teams be recruited to remove public stores and papers. Little did the citizens of southern Maryland and the Patuxent region realize that the arrival of the large enemy flotilla in the lower Bay was but the opening round in a military campaign that would lead to the defeat of an entire British Army under Lord Cornwallis on the fields of Yorktown, Virginia, and, ultimately, to the end of the Revolutionary War. Despite the American victory at Yorktown, however, loyalist guerilla and naval activities in the Patuxent region would continue unabated for another two years.[19]

In March 1782, less than five months after the British defeat at Yorktown, enemy naval depredations had resumed on the Chesapeake, with raiders penetrating as high as Sharps Island. The Maryland Council of Safety, in desperation, appealed to the commander of the French naval forces in the Bay to help bring the raiders to a halt. The state's remaining barges, the Council explained, the last of the Maryland State Navy, were in no condition for use, and there were even fewer men to sail them. The French diplomatically declined.[20]

The following year the enemy struck again at the Bay, and once more zeroed in on the Patuxent. Though rumors of peace were afloat throughout Maryland, local loyalist forces, many of them freed slaves, were intent on wreaking as much havoc as possible in the little time left. In February enemy barges and privateers seemed to be everywhere. Richard Barnes reported from his headquarters in Leonardtown that three loyalist barges, manned by an "abandoned Set of Men" had been sighted on the Potomac and had recently landed on St. George's Island, taking up the black slaves as well as the usual plunder. In an enclosure to his report to Governor William Paca, Barnes included a bit of bad news from Nicholas Sewell at Mattapany: three privateers, two sloops, and a schooner from the British fleet had just captured a bay craft at Cedar Point and had moved into the Patuxent.[21]

Governor Paca appealed directly to the merchants of Baltimore for help against the enemy in the river. Loyalist naval strength was now reported at one sloop, two schooners, and thirteen armed barges, and there was "no Force belonging to Government able to oppose them. . . ." The enemy was at that moment "in Patuxent doing great Damage. . . ." Paca thus pitched upon the merchant community to provide three armed sloops or schooners of eight or ten guns apiece, and 150 men over and above the crew complements necessary to man them, in order that he might put the few dilapidated state naval barges into service.[22]

It was, unfortunately for the Patuxent, already too late. On February 21 Paca sadly informed General George Washington of the extent of the uncontested British attack:

> On Thursday last a Party under the Command of Joseph Whaland went up the Patuxent, plundering the town of Benedict [in Charles County] and burnt and destroyed the dwelling house and out Houses of Mr. Benjamin Mackall [in Calvert County] with his furniture, Tobacco and other moveable Property. Col. Plater [in St. Mary's County] was also plundered of some of his Negroes. . . .[23]

The bankrupt Maryland government, under Paca's prodding, lethargically responded to the enemy attack and began to enlist men to serve on the state barge force, but the governor was uncertain when they could be equipped for service. The French naval commander in the region was again requested to provide aid and eventually promised the governor the use of an armed vessel, but qualified his donation of services with the provision that "Repairs were wanting, that Circumstance may still detain her. . . ."[24]

And circumstances of sorts did detain her. By the time the French naval aid was available, the American War of Independence had come to an end.

□   □   □

The years following the war proved, for the most part, peaceful and prosperous in the Patuxent Valley. Declines in the tobacco market, and competition for maritime trade from the ports of Baltimore, Alexandria, and Norfolk began to siphon off the more commercial prosperity of the valley, but a shift from tobacco to grains reinforced stability. Ironically, with the erection of the national capital city of Washington on the banks of the Potomac only a few miles away and the adoption of a new federal Constitution, the towns, villages, and farms along the river began to slip into a mild slumber interrupted only now and then by events of occasionally disturbing nature.

With the onset of the nineteenth century, as affairs in Europe degenerated and France, under the command of a brilliant young general named Napoleon, began its ascendancy, America had sought desperately to remain neutral in the conflict that ensued. It was an uneasy role at best and the drift toward war was marked. In January 1806 a French seventy-four-gun man-of-war named *L'Eole* became trapped in Chesapeake Bay by a pursuing British squadron and was soon joined by two of her sisters, *Patriot* and *Cybelle*. Almost immediately, a British blockade was thrown up to prevent their escape. Despite American protest, the British remained. The French commander dispatched *L'Eole* to Annapolis, *Patriot* to the Patuxent, and *Cybelle* remained at Norfolk to better facilitate the provisioning of their respective companies during the long standoff. Upset by the blockade and in an effort to show the flag and demonstrate American sovereignty, the secretary of the navy ordered the U.S. frigate *Chesapeake* on a brief cruise out of the Bay and through the line of blockaders. Claiming that British deserters were aboard the frigate, the British man-of-war *Leopard* opened fire on the vessel and then boarded her. It was a humiliating moment for the young nation, and talk of a new war with England was again heavy in the air. [25]

But the British were not the only ones to suffer from desertions. On the Patuxent the big seventy-four-gun man-of-war *Patriot* (Commodore Hiacinthe Krohn commanding) had also experienced the flight of crew members. Many of *Patriot*'s deserters had made their way to Baltimore, and one party determined to purchase a pilot-boat schooner, which was dubbed *General Massena* after one of Napoleon's leading commanders, and go a-pirating. Their first and only victim proved to be the Boston merchantman *Othello* (Captain John Glover, as master), bound for Baltimore from Liverpool. Captured near Sharps Island on August 23, 1807, and then released after the pirates realized that they could not escape from the Chesapeake, *Othello*'s arrival at Baltimore induced a major controversy and a diplomatic incident. *Patriot*, whose deserters had formed the crew of the *General Massena*, was accused of promulgating the capture, and a diplomatic break with France was being considered, even as expeditions were fitting out in Baltimore, Annapolis, and Norfolk to capture the pirates. On August 27, a volunteer force out of Baltimore, commanded by Captain David Porter in the armed schooner *Volunteer*, encountered the *Massena* in the mouth of the Patuxent; *Massena* was attacked, boarded, and captured within minutes, bringing to an end the last episode of piracy in Chesapeake history. *Patriot* was cleared and the incident was concluded peacefully. But during the next five years the slow and steady drift toward war with England could not be restrained.[26]

On June 18, 1812, President James Madison finally issued a formal declaration of war. The second conflict with Great Britain had begun, and the Patuxent River Valley was destined to become one of the major seats of combat.[27]

THREE

I Am Anxious to Be at Them

On the morning of February 4, 1813, when the long-expected vanguard of a powerful British fleet arrived at the Chesapeake capes to institute a blockade of the Bay, the farmers and merchants of the Tidewater braced themselves for the worst. And not without reason.[1]

At the outset of hostilities, the U.S. Navy could boast of only seven frigates and a handful of lesser vessels to contend with the Royal Navy, nearly a thousand ships strong and the most powerful force afloat in the world. In a desperate effort to correct the imbalance, America was obliged to submit to a slavish reliance on the age-old practice of privateering, that is the commissioning of privately owned and operated ships of war to attack and capture enemy commerce for private profit. The initial effect was stunning. Within a month of President Madison's declaration of war (which had incorporated provisions for such action within the actual manifesto itself), no fewer than 65 privately owned and armed American ships had put to sea to actively decimate enemy commerce. By the war's end, from Maryland alone but primarily from the port of Baltimore, more than 117 privateers would be fielded and capture over 455 prizes, over a third of the 1,338 vessels taken by all American ships sailing under letters of marque and reprisal during the war. Many Maryland privateersmen, such as Joshua Barney and Thomas Boyle, would repeatedly humiliate both the British merchant marine and the Royal Navy on the high seas. On a single voyage in the twelve-gun Baltimore schooner *Rossie*, Captain Barney took four ships, eight brigs, three schooners, and three sloops— 3,698 tons of shipping in all, valued at $1.5 million, as well as 217 prisoners—and had fought no less than three spirited actions in the process. In one combat, Barney had taken on His Britannic Majesty's armed packet ship *Princess Amelia* and, after a severe battle of an hour's duration that was fought at pistol-shot range, captured her. Boyle, sailing in the swift fourteen-gun Baltimore schooner *Chasseur*, captured or destroyed more than 30 vessels valued at millions of dollars and also fought several engagements in the process.[2]

The British response to such depredations was to direct the Royal Navy on December 26, 1812, to blockade the Chesapeake and Delaware Bays, the two principal nests of privateers. Five weeks later, a strong Royal Navy

I Am Anxious to Be at Them

Commodore Joshua Barney. Courtesy of the Franklin D. Roosevelt Library, Hyde Park, New York

squadron under the command of Admiral Sir George Cockburn, which consisted of ten ships of the line and lesser warships and mounted 491 cannons, dropped anchor in Hampton Road. With brief exception, the Chesapeake Bay would henceforth become a British lake.[3]

Although lacking strong ground forces suitable to occupy a site for long, the British roved about the Tidewater as they saw fit, raiding, burning, and plundering. No place close to the water's edge was immune to assault and Cockburn ranged far and wide. On April 16 the port of Baltimore was menaced. A week later, Spesuite Island, near the mouth of the Susquehanna, was taken. Annapolis was blockaded. One by one, the undefended islands in the Bay were attacked, captured, and plundered. In quick succession, Sharps, Pooles, Tilghman, and Poplar Islands were taken and the inhabitants looted. The tiny port of Frenchtown was sacked and burned to the ground and its shipping carried off. Havre de Grace fell on May 3, with slight resistance. Georgetown and Fredericktown were destroyed soon afterwards. The arrival of Admiral Sir John Borlase Warren from Bermuda with additional warships and 2,650 marines, infantry,

Admiral Sir George Cockburn. Courtesy of the Public Archives, Ottawa, Canada

artillerymen, and a body of independent foreigners boded even worse for the Tidewater defenders. At the battle of Craney Island, at the mouth of Virginia's Elizabeth River, the invaders suffered their first defeat, a setback that resulted in their failure to capture the port of Norfolk. In a fit of revenge, they turned their rapacious attention upon the village of Hampton. The village was taken without much fight and was sacked. Its citizens were outraged by wanton rape, murder, and plunder, which Cockburn attributed to be the acts of a detachment of French Canadians, the Chasseurs Britanniques.[4]

In July the British entered the Potomac, conducting raids and landings at Mattox Creek, Blackistone, St. Catherine's and St. George's Islands, and at Point Lookout, inducing slaves to run away, plundering tobacco stocks, and burning crops as they proceeded. Again, the invaders moved up the Bay to menace Baltimore and Annapolis, while conducting brief forays ashore at such places as Sandy Point and Kent Island (which was forcefully occupied). On August 7, the invaders organized thrusts against

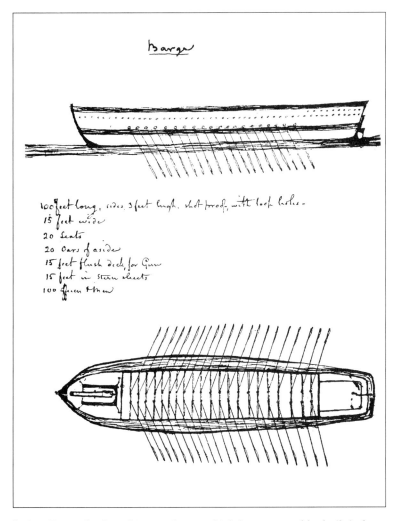

Joshua Barney's plans for a war barge which he suggested be built in large numbers to shadow British naval forces and interdict enemy landings. Barney's rough design was submitted with his "Defense of the Chesapeake" plan to Secretary of the Navy William Jones on July 4, 1813, but his barge design was altered radically. Courtesy of the National Archives and Record Service

Queenstown, on the Eastern Shore, and three days later against the port of St. Michaels, where they were repulsed.[5]

Aside from the infrequent and inept resistance by local militia, the USS *Constellation*, effectively blockaded within the Elizabeth River, and a handful of federal warships and gunboats being built or outfitted at Washington and Baltimore, the Chesapeake was devoid of naval defenses. Moreover, the major portion of the U.S. Army had been moved north to the

Canadian theater of operations, leaving the Tidewater to the untender mercies of the enemy.[6]

President James Madison and Secretary of the Navy William Jones were not unaware of the dangers of permitting the Chesapeake to remain a British lake for long. Should the enemy be able to throw a large body of troops into the region, their tactical and strategic advantage would be enormous. To counter the risk, the government needed money, men, and ships, all of which were in critically short supply. They needed a plan of action for the Chesapeake that stood a modest chance of success, and a capable man determined to implement it.

□　　□　　□

Captain Joshua Barney, a native Marylander and bona fide hero of the American Revolution, was fifty-three years old at the outbreak of the War of 1812. He had led a storybook life of adventure and travel. Going to sea as a child of thirteen, he had assumed command of his first ship at the age of fourteen, and during the Revolution served as a privateersman and as the youngest commander ever of a Continental Navy frigate. Several times captured by the British, he had been paroled or escaped after each. While in command of the privateer *Hyder Ally*, he had fought the last naval engagement of the war. The action, against the British warship *General Monk*, had been termed "one of the best fought actions on record," and Barney was dubbed "the prince of privateers." Afterwards, he had been entrusted to carry important dispatches regarding the peace negotiations to Benjamin Franklin in Paris, and was introduced at court, where he kissed the cheek of Marie Antoinette. He was a guest of General George Washington at Mount Vernon, to whom he delivered the ceremonial ship *Federalist*, on behalf of the citizens of Baltimore. In 1795, his fame and reputation as a daring naval commander brought him an offer from the French government, for whom he actively served for five years, bearing the rank of commodore before retiring to his native land and the life of a country gentleman at Elk Ridge in Anne Arundel County.[7]

At the outbreak of the War of 1812, Barney had been denied a command in the U.S. Navy because of his loss of seniority while in the service of France. He accepted the next best thing, the command of the *Rossie*. After his stunning cruise in that ship, he again retired to Elk Ridge. There, he watched in despair as the British conducted their forays against the Tidewater with increasing ferocity, and against little or no opposition. By midsummer 1813, he could no longer restrain himself.[8]

On July 4, 1813, private citizen Joshua Barney submitted to the secretary of the navy his own detailed plan, entitled "Defense of Chesapeake Bay," replete with sketches of the vessels he suggested be built to implement it. He began by noting that the enemy's strength on the American Station and in the Chesapeake was over 82 warships (11 ships of the line, 33

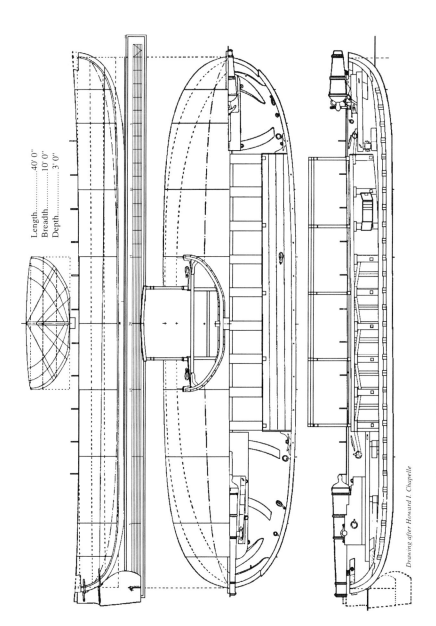

Length..............40' 0"
Breadth..............10' 0"
Depth..............3' 0"

Drawing after Howard I. Chapelle

Row galley designed by William Doughty, naval constructor.

frigates, 38 sloops of war, and numerous schooners and other craft) and an available manpower of 8,200 men suitable for landings. The primary objectives of the British were the destruction of the cities and navy yards at Washington, Norfolk, and Baltimore. Due to the shallowness of most of the Chesapeake, however, the attacks and landings would have to be launched from frigates, sloops, schooners, barges, and smaller craft.[9]

The only way to counter the overwhelming superiority of the enemy, with only two American frigates in the Bay (both blockaded in) and a handful of clumsy old gunboats, was with "a kind of barge or row galley, so constructed, as to draw a small draft of water, to carry oars, light sails, and one heavy gun." They could be built in three weeks each, and furnished easily—with men from Baltimore if necessary—without having to utilize regular Navy personnel or officers. Such a force could be formed into a flying squadron, which could hound the enemy, watching and annoying him whenever possible, by taking advantage of the shoals of the Bay, where the larger warships dare not venture. A force of twenty barges manned with a thousand seamen and marines and a thousand land troops could hover about the enemy and interdict any attacks on the Bay shore. During the summer, they could harass the enemy's big men-of-war at night, and fire with impunity. Being small, fast, and armed with twenty-four-pounder long-guns, the barges would make difficult and dangerous targets for enemy gunners. And as for their utility in the defense of major ports:

> Should the enemy land all their forces with a design on any of our large cities, they must be met in the field, but unless their heavy ships can cover the landing, and receive them on board again, the barge squadron might, and would cut off a retreat, by acting in concert with our troops ashore.[10]

Obstructions might be sunk in the Potomac, and defended by the frigate *Adams* and the force of old Jeffersonian Navy gunboats at Washington. Similar defenses might be produced for Baltimore. Norfolk was already adequately defended by gunboats and the frigate *Constellation*. A single barge would cost barely three thousand dollars, and after service was over, could be sold as a commercial coaster. Fifty barges would cost less than half the price of a conventional frigate. Such a flotilla force could be fielded as an entirely separate entity from the regular U.S. Navy flotilla force, with officers and men for this barge flotilla recruited for short terms, until the emergency was over, with but a single regiment of regular troops annexed to it. Marines would be under the command of a capable officer and a colonel "with powers to correspond, not only with the general government, but with the Governors of Virginia and Maryland, and act in concert whenever circumstances required...." It was imperative

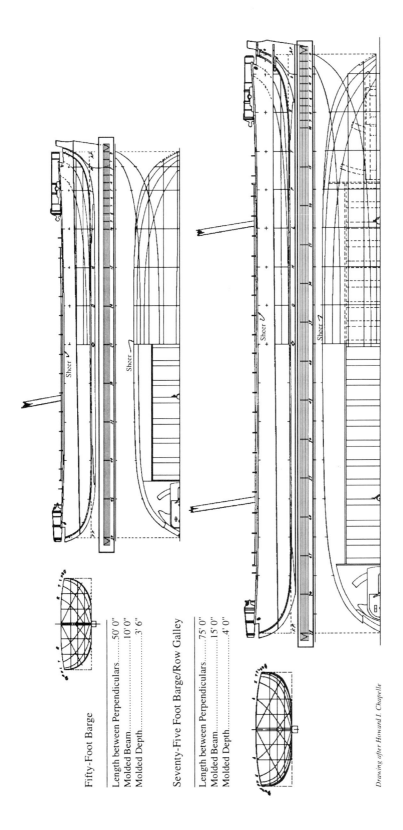

Fifty-Foot Barge

Length between Perpendiculars	50' 0"
Molded Beam	10' 0"
Molded Depth	3' 6"

Seventy-Five Foot Barge/Row Galley

Length between Perpendiculars	75' 0"
Molded Beam	15' 0"
Molded Depth	4' 0"

Drawing after Howard I. Chapelle

Barges designed by William Doughty, naval constructor.

to adopt the scheme, he told Jones. "In fact, we have no other mode of defense left us." [11]

Jones was desperate, and the old seadog's plans made sense. But more importantly, they seemed to offer an economically feasible answer to an insoluable problem. On August 20, 1813, Joshua Barney was appointed acting master commandant in the U.S. Navy for the "special purpose" of assuming the distinct and separate command of the United States Flotilla "in the upper part of the Chesapeake," composed of such vessels as designated by the Navy Department. He was to be answerable only to the secretary of the navy and the president, for Barney's command was to be completely unconnected with the regular Navy establishment. His concept on the defense of the Chesapeake had been accepted. Now all he had to do was build a flotilla force from scratch, man it, field it, fight with it, and emerge victorious![12]

Barney worked with protean zeal. He immediately set to buying and building the force needed and recruiting the manpower necessary to field it. On September 29, the Navy Department, at his behest, purchased the row galley *Vigilant* (Captain John Rutter commanding) for $1,800. Two armed barges that had originally been fielded by Baltimore for its own defense were purchased from the city. These were barges *No. 5*, costing $1,725, and *No. 8* (Captain William Flanagan commanding) costing $1,875. Secretary Jones dispatched the galley *Black Snake*, recently outfitted at the Washington Navy Yard; a three-gun fifty-seven-ton schooner called *Asp*, recently purchased at Alexandria, Virginia; and an old but battle-tested gunboat named *Scorpion*.[13]

Barney, however, did not intend to simply adopt every old tub the Navy sent him. Within a short time, contracts had been awarded to build a fleet and to supply it with the necessities of the flotilla. Spencer's Shipyard at St. Michaels was contracted to construct six to eight thirty-man barges, while the Fells Point, Baltimore, yard of Thomas Kemp, famed builder of both *Rossie* and *Chasseur*, would build at least three of the remainder for $2,350 each. Soon, eight vessels were under construction, mostly seventy-five-foot barges and galleys. Barney's barges were generally constructed along the lines of a new class of warcraft designed by chief naval constructor William Doughty. In appearance, the vessels were somewhat like double-ended whaleboats, mounting a single long gun aft and a carronade forward, but fuller, however, at both ends to better bear the weight of cannon. The long guns ranged from twelve- to forty-two-pounders, while the carronades varied from twenty-four- to forty-two-pounders.[14]

The first barge designs called for a 50-foot-long craft, with a 12-foot moulded beam, and a hold of 3 feet 6 inches in depth, and mounting a single lateen sail. After trial runs in September, however, Barney suggested heavier construction to better withstand the shock of artillery fire. Doughty quickly produced a plan for a 75-foot vessel, 15 feet abeam, and

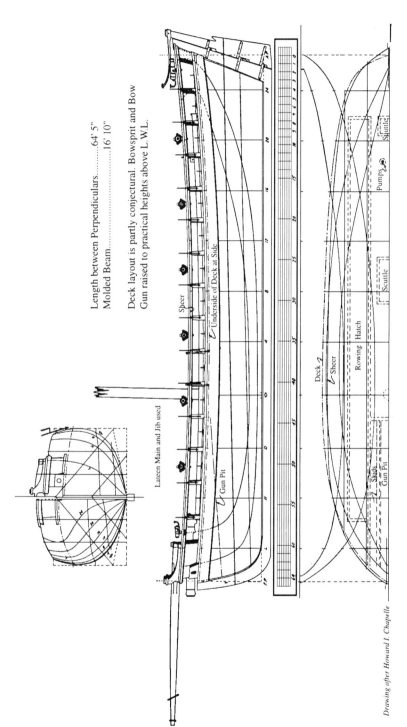

Length between Perpendiculars..........64' 5"
Molded Beam......................16' 10"

Deck layout is partly conjectural. Bowsprit and Bow
Gun raised to practical heights above L.W.L.

Underside of Deck at Side

Sheer

Lateen Main and Jib used

Gun Pit

Deck

Sheer

Rowing Hatch

Pumps

Scuttle

Scuttle

Skids
Gun Pit

Drawing after Howard I. Chapelle

Captain James Barron's first draft design for a gunboat (1806).

Tidewater Time Capsule

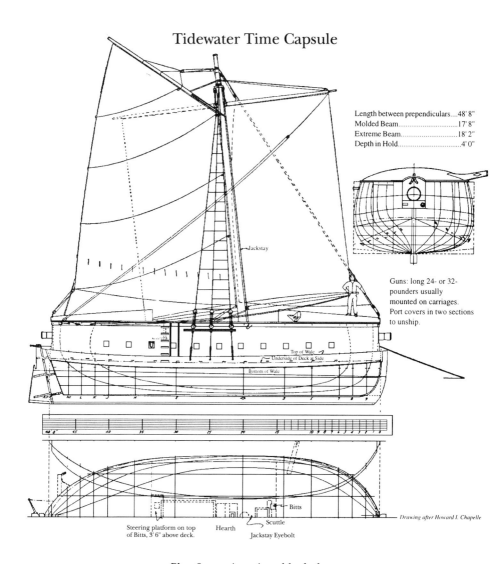

Length between prependiculars....48' 8"
Molded Beam............................17' 8"
Extreme Beam............................18' 2"
Depth in Hold.............................4' 0"

Guns: long 24- or 32-
pounders usually
mounted on carriages.
Port covers in two sections
to unship.

Jackstay

Top of Wale
Underside of Deck at Side
Bottom of Wale

Bitts
Scuttle
Jackstay Eyebolt

Steering platform on top
of Bitts, 3' 6" above deck.   Hearth

Drawing after Howard I. Chapelle

Plan for an American block sloop.

4 feet deep in hold, mounting two lateen sails, fore and aft. Later, a third
class of vessel, 40 feet in length, 10 feet abeam, and 3 feet in hold, fitted
for oars only, was also begun.[15]

Two sloop-rigged gunboats, built along lines laid out by Commodore
James Barron in 1806 and constructed by one William Price in the latter's
yard at the end of Thames Street, Fells Point, were also added to the
flotilla. Both vessels were capable of being propelled by 20 sweep of
20-foot-long oars. Each was 64 feet 5 inches long on deck, 16 feet 20 inches
abeam, and 6 feet 6 inches deep in hold. The two gunboats, *No. 137* and
No. 138, had both served as regular Navy vessels. *No. 137* had been
attached to the Potomac Flotilla in March of 1813 and had participated

in operations on the lower river later in the year. *No. 138* had been assigned to Captain Charles Gordon's five-boat Chesapeake defense squadron stationed at Baltimore.[16]

Barney's flagship was to be the USS *Scorpion*, a four-gun vessel variously described as a gunboat, a large sloop, a block sloop, a cutter, and a topsail sloop. Originally built as *No. 59* in a gunboat construction series begun in 1809, probably by naval architect George Hope at Hampton, Virginia, along lines of a prototype drawn up by Captain James Barron, she had cost eleven thousand dollars when fully outfitted. Rebuilt and renamed at the Washington Navy Yard in 1812, she had seen considerable action during her wartime career. Initially stationed at Norfolk, she had been ordered to join Commandant Arthur Sinclair's Potomac Flotilla in late March 1813. On July 14, while reconnoitering the mouth of the Potomac in company with the U.S. schooner *Asp*, she had briefly participated in a hard-fought action against HMS *Contest* and *Mohawk*. On September 2, less than two weeks after Barney had been offered the "special command" of the Chesapeake Flotilla, *Scorpion* was transferred to his control but continued to patrol the Potomac for some time thereafter.[17]

By December, Barney was ready to embark upon his recruiting campaign. He began by inducing Captain Solomon Frazier, a Revolutionary War veteran of some fame and the most popular mariner and state legislator on the Eastern Shore, to resign his Maryland Senate seat and take up arms as Lieutenant Frazier of the U.S. Flotilla Service. The move was designed to serve as an inducement for other Eastern Shore mariners to enlist, and Frazier was promptly dispatched to spearhead the recruitment drive. Bounties were offered for those willing to join up, with promises that they would be home by October 1, 1814. Still, manpower shortages, caused by the drain of able-bodied mariners to the more profitable pursuit of privateering, stymied recruiting efforts. To man the flotilla, seamen were soon being stripped from the complements of uncompleted U.S. warships abuilding at Baltimore. Yet the barge building program continued in fits and starts.[18]

The work at Baltimore and St. Michaels, regularly reported on in the press, did not go unnoticed by the British, who would soon begin construction on their own small barge flotilla at their fortified naval base on Tangier Island. An arms race, it seemed, had begun. Barney, however, remained unflappable. When informed of the British program, he replied simply: "I am anxious to be at them." [19]

On April 17, 1814, a completed and manned segment of the Chesapeake Flotilla, including ten barges, gunboat *No. 138*, and *Scorpion*, set out on a shakedown cruise, to investigate reported enemy incursions off the Potomac. Though Barney's force was short by an average of ten men per vessel, and though several flaws (mostly correctable) were discovered in the new barge designs, the shakedown proved a success even though the enemy had retired down bay before it could be engaged. But it would be back. And soon.[20]

In late April the large British seventy-four-gun man-of-war *Dragon* (Captain Robert Barrie commanding) and several armed tenders arrived at the mouth of the Potomac to reestablish a temporary blockade, secure fresh water, and conduct patrols as high up the river as Blackistone Island. Their presence on Maryland's southern border was not taken lightly, for now the invaders were conducting raids designed not only to plunder, but to free the black slaves of the Tidewater for the purpose of recruiting and training them as soldiers in a new unit called the Black Colonial Corps. Although barely three hundred slaves had escaped to join the invaders, and far fewer had actually accepted the British call to arms on Tangier Island, the planters of southern Maryland were terrified at the specter of a black insurrection. Fighting white men was one thing, but fighting one's escaped slaves was definitely something else! After all, who knew what savagery they might be capable of? Barney, however, was more concerned with the enemy's growing barge force said to be abuilding on the island.[21]

By the spring of 1814, the Chesapeake Flotilla was well along but, owing to material shortages, lack of funding, and the priority being given to the Canadian theater, was still far from complete. Only two-thirds of the vessels were ready for sea. Manpower to sail them was still less than adequate, several of the vessels were not yet entirely seaworthy, and naval stores were in short supply. But delay was no longer possible. On May 24, with barely a month's provisions for the entire flotilla stuffed aboard one of his two older gunboats, Barney sailed from Baltimore with a force of eighteen vessels to attack the main enemy stronghold in the Bay, Tangier Island. Perhaps, a surprise raid on the fortified island would not only succeed in destroying the enemy's infant barge fleet, but might also drive him from the secure haven to which the slave population of the Tidewater had begun to flock. A link-up with the barge flotilla in the Elizabeth River might even be capable of challenging the blockade at Norfolk. It was a bold venture, entirely out of keeping with Barney's plan of nearly a year earlier for the defense of the Chesapeake. But it was one of the first truly aggressive American offensives to be undertaken on the Bay since the war had begun.[22]

On or about May 31, accompanied by a small convoy of merchantmen intent on slipping through the British blockade, Joshua Barney brought his squadron to a temporary anchorage under Drum Point, at the mouth of the Patuxent, to await the next favorable tide for a fast, evasive sprint across the Bay to Hooper's Straits.

◻   ◻   ◻

As Barney was heaving to under Drum Point, Captain Barrie of HMS *Dragon* was personally embarking on a reconnaissance of St. Jerome's

Creek, less than twenty miles south of the American flotilla's position and immediately north of Point Lookout, with boat crews from the British schooner *St. Lawrence* and the tender *Catch-up*. By 5:00 A.M., June 1, the reconnaissance was well under way. The wind was from the north, light and inclined. Only four hours into their mission, the boat crews sighted the flotilla bearing down from the north. Barney's lookout boat and the row galley *Vigilant* had sighted the British nearly an hour earlier and had already signaled the commodore that two schooners were in the offing. Barney smelled blood, and immediately ordered "sail and oar." [23]

With his forces scattered and vulnerable, Barrie promptly fired guns to summon the reconnaissance parties back and to alert the *Dragon*, at anchor off Smith Point on the Potomac, to come up immediately. After picking up his men, the British commander began to retire toward Point Lookout and to make an impromptu rendezvous with *Dragon* even as the American flotilla pressed southward after him. By 1:00 P.M. Barney was off St. Jerome's, and finally spied the big seventy-four beating to cross the river against the wind. Desperately, the Americans charged for the shelter of the Potomac, before *Dragon*, under a full press of sail, could cut them off. [24]

Suddenly the wind shifted and began to blow out of the southwest. Barrie now had the weather gauge. Outgunned by more than two to one, Barney had little choice but to retreat northward. The stiff breezes brought not only the enemy, but a deadly rain squall that threatened to swamp many of the little barges on the open Chesapeake. Barrie was quick to take advantage and pressed on in full pursuit with his powerful warships.[25]

By 4:00 P.M. Barney was off Cedar Point, where another dramatic sea fight between the Americans and the British had occurred nearly thirty-three years earlier. Again the wind shifted, blowing from the west now, denying the flotilla easy entry into the sanctuary of the Patuxent. Barney ordered oars only and the distance between the two forces began to increase.[26]

Barrie sought to delay the American escape and ordered *Dragon*'s barge and cutter to cut off a schooner lagging behind in the American rear. The vessel proved to be gunboat *No. 137*, carrying the bulk of the flotilla's provisions. Unwilling to lose the important vessel, Barney turned to assist her up the river, and to face the oncoming foe. *Scorpion* and *No. 138* were brought to anchor, and extra men were dispatched to assist the struggling storeboat. Within minutes, *St. Lawrence*, seven enemy barges, and the cutter from *Dragon* were under heavy fire from the Americans and obliged to retreat. The flotilla pressed the attack by attempting to follow and opened a peppery fire on the enemy at long range. This time, however, the British responded with a secret weapon hitherto unused on the Chesapeake—the Congreve rocket. The weapon was the invention of a British artillery officer, Sir William Congreve, and though far from accurate or destructive, served to thoroughly terrorize the Americans. Its fame was soon to be widely castigated in the American press. But its fearsome long-range utility in battle was unquestionable.[27]

Having been aborted in his designs, Barney quickly ordered the flotilla to retire into the temporary sanctuary of the Patuxent and came to anchor three miles up the river. Barrie immediately established a blockade of the river mouth, and sent for reinforcements that were of shallow enough draft to venture in. In the interim, he contented himself with the usual British pastime of plundering local plantations of livestock and slaves. Meanwhile, Joshua Barney licked his wounds and contemplated his desperate situation.[28]

FOUR

Determined to Something Decisive

Captain Robert Barrie was a conservative tactician. He had cornered the only significant American naval force of any consequence on the upper Chesapeake and was not about to begin playing the game recklessly. That Commodore Joshua Barney would be attacked was certain, but only when overwhelming forces were at hand. And they were not slow in coming up. On June 6, 1814, Barrie's expected reinforcements began to arrive when *Dragon* and *St. Lawrence* were joined by the sloop-of-war brig *Jaseur*, of eighteen guns (Captain George Edward Watts commanding) and HMS *Loire*, of thirty-eight guns (Captain Thomas Brown commanding).[1]

With his little flotilla, carrying a total of only thirty-four long guns and carronades, now outgunned by better than four to one, Barney had little choice but to retire from the deep waters under Drum Point, where the enemy could maneuver at will, into a more defensible narrows, adjacent to Point Patience. By early evening, June 7, the British squadron had entered the Patuxent and began preparations for what they hoped would merely be a mopping up effort. Barrie transferred his flag to the shallower-draft *Loire* in preparation for the final push the next morning.[2]

At 7:00 A.M., June 8, much to Barrie's chagrin, the Americans were spotted working up toward St. Leonard's Creek, a shoally waterway into which the great warships dare not enter. Dismayed, Barrie ordered *Jaseur* and *St. Lawrence* off in hot pursuit. *Loire* and seven armed barges would follow in short order. Without adequate charts of the river, the British haste was certain to generate mishaps. *St. Lawrence* was run aground, with only *Jaseur* able to haul her off. The barges pressed on alone in their pursuit, but failed to come up before the Americans entered the creek.[3]

Barney's selection of St. Leonard's Creek as his ultimate sanctuary was an excellent tactical choice, for its narrow confines, "in few places more than a musket shot wide, and in many not above two cable lengths," combined with shoals and sandbars, provided a superb defensive position for his shallow-draft vessels. A long bar spreading shieldlike southward from the creek's northern shore made anchorage off the mouth all the more hazardous. Tall, forest-covered bluffs on either lip of the mouth, upon which musketmen or ordnance could be concealed, could make close-in anchorage untenable. At the head of the creek was the venerable

Port of St. Leonard's, connected by a single roadway to the rest of the Calvert County peninsula, Annapolis, and Washington. It was indeed an admirable defensive position. But it was also a closet from which escape might prove extremely difficult.[4]

Barrie, unable to bring his great ships within the creek, and uncertain of its nature or the American defensive posture or strength two miles upstream, had decided to personally lead the first probing attack at noon with his barges. The British opened with a long-range rocket assault but were unable to lure the Americans down to engage at close quarters. When Barney attacked with his long guns, Barrie adroitly slipped back each time. The engagement quickly became a feeling-out waltz that would be repeated over the next few days with increasing frequency and vigor.[5]

The engagement was renewed later in the afternoon, with additional British barges joining the fray. Once again Barrie relied on his Congreve rockets, which again served to thoroughly terrorize the Americans. "This kind of fighting," Barney later wrote, "is much against us as they can reach us when we cannot reach them, and when we pursue them their light boats fly before us." The rockets, although highly inaccurate, were downright disastrous when they did chance to hit a target. When one of the devices fell on board one of the barges, passing through a hapless flotillaman in the process, the vessel was set ablaze, igniting powder and cartridge barrels. The explosion hurled seamen into the water in every direction, wounding several, setting two magazines on fire, and causing the barge to be abandoned. The vessel was saved from total destruction only by a heroic act of Barney's son, Major William B. Barney, who reboarded the craft and succeeded in dousing the flames.[6]

Despite his rockets and a barge fleet that had now increased to fifteen vessels, Barrie soon despaired of success in a direct assault. But there were other games to play. St. Lawrence had been refloated and was of such draft that she could swim freely in the lower creek while Loire and Jaseur were now equally free to effect a blockade anchorage across its mouth. Barrie resolved "to annoy [Barney] from our boats" and provoke him to chase them within gunshot range of the frigate. Carefully, Barrie worked his great ships closer into the mouth of the creek, tightening the noose ever more securely. Spring lines were run out to facilitate rapid shifts in firing positions from stationary anchorages. A recently captured lumber schooner was stripped of her cargo and armed with a thirty-two-pounder carronade and sent to join the barge squadron. Boats were dispatched to take soundings of the lower creek. If Barrie couldn't get in, Barney certainly wasn't going to be let out—except to fight.[7]

Time and again, Barrie pressed his barges into the creek, firing rockets, and seeking to lure the besieged Americans to within broadside range of Loire and her sisters. The commodore demurred, repelling each attack but never taking the bait, even though provisions were beginning to run low.[8]

On the afternoon of June 9, Barney dashed off a report of the events of the few preceding days and requested that a strong force of regular infantry be sent to the creek to protect his flanks on either shore. Should the enemy secure a strong landing force, the American position would become indefensible. No sooner was the ink on the communique dry than word of yet another British attack was handed to him.[9]

At 4:00 P.M. the enemy was seen moving up with a force of twenty armed barges, this time with *St. Lawrence* in company. Again the battle opened with rockets. And again Barney refused to take the hook. The skirmish of June 9 ended at 6:30 P.M. as had all that had gone before.[10]

It would not be the same the next time.

□   □   □

The morning of June 10 was born with clear skies and a pleasant breeze out of the north. A perfect day for battle. Although a seadog by nature, Barney was a tactician of merit and was anything but ignorant to the exposed position of his shoreward flanks should the enemy attempt to land marines. He thus took precautions to establish strong points on either side of the flotilla by ordering his tiny contingent of seventy-five U.S. marines to bivouac on the heights to his left, and a land battery to be erected on his right, at a narrows in the upper creek. His flotilla, divided into three divisions, red, blue, and white, was then drawn up in a line across the waterway between the two strong points. Although no one knew for certain, reinforcements, it was said, were on the way. The rumors proved to be true. Even as the sun began to rise, several American units, either militia or regular army, which had been rushed down to St. Mary's County, were attempting to cross the Patuxent by boat above the British lines into Calvert County from Sotterley Plantation.[11]

Barrie was not alarmed by the crossing attempt but immediately dispatched armed boat parties to put an end to it. Then, having received yet another reinforcement of barges the night before, he again turned his full attention to Barney. He was determined to either chastise the old wardog in his lair or lure him down the creek and destroy him for good.[12]

Barney was ready and had prepared a surprise counterattack. He was going to willingly take the bait. If the enemy refused to close he would redouble his own efforts. He had already decided that his tiny force would be weened before the battle of all but the fleetest vessels suitable for combat. Thirteen barges, with masts unstepped and propelled by oars alone for greater control, and manned by five hundred men, would form his frontline force. The slower, crankier vessels such as *Scorpion*, the two gunboats, a tiny lookout boat, and *Vigilant* would remain in the rear with the merchantmen or would ferry troops as necessary. Barney maintained his divisional designation, with his own red division of six barges holding the center, Solomon Frazier's blue division securing the left, and John Rutter's white division holding the right with three or four vessels each.[13]

At 2:00 P.M., following a preliminary reconnaissance that failed miserably to discern the American intentions, Barrie ordered every available vessel up the creek "to annoy the enemy." Twenty-one barges and boats, a rocket boat, and two schooners towed by the barges (outnumbering the Americans nearly two to one), armed and manned by six hundred to seven hundred seamen and marines, launched the attack in grand style, with a band of music playing, flags flying, and spirits high. This time, however, Barney had ordered his force to up anchor and fall upon the enemy as soon as it had entered the upper creek.[14]

The American line of battle stretched across St. Leonard's just above the mouth of a small waterway known today as John's Creek, less than two miles below St. Leonard's Town. The British flotilla arrived below the little tributary in three lines, and approached to within a thousand feet of the Americans, bands still playing and flags aflutter. Suddenly, all the guns of both flotillas erupted in a furious explosion, and every vessel present was suddenly and irrevocably engaged in mortal combat. In the very center of it all, Joshua Barney stood completely exposed, directing the fight, from time to time dispatching his son William hither and yon with messages to his commanders. Unlike every previous engagement, the British did not retire, but "kept up a smart fire for sometime and seemed determined to something decisive." An American barge was sunk, but still the unrelenting cannonade, rockets, and small arms fire continued unabated.[15]

Slowly, but perceptively, the galling accuracy of the American fire seemed to be taking its toll. The British began to retire, slowly at first. Then, without warning, the enemy lines appeared to be stricken with panic (or so it seemed to Barney) retreating helter-skelter in total confusion for the shelter of the big ships' guns down creek. The Chesapeake Flotilla brazenly took up the pursuit.[16]

As a measure of security, Captain Barrie had, early on in the game, moved *St. Lawrence* into the throat of St. Leonard's Creek, still under the big guns of the *Loire* and *Jaseur*, but far enough up to offer early protection for his retiring barge flotilla. By 3:30 P.M., as the running battle upstream began to spill towards the mouth of the creek, the wisdom of the move seemed in doubt. Two dozen vessels of the British flotilla, with Barney in hot pursuit, began to skim by in total panic past the big anchored war schooner, leaving her to face the Americans alone. Within minutes the entire American line began to concentrate its fire on the hapless *St. Lawrence*. Stunned by the vigor and ferocity of the attack, her acting commander, Captain Watts, ordered her to beat out of the creek behind the retreating barges. Suddenly, Watts lost control and the schooner grounded with a falling line and lay completely exposed to the fire of the flotilla without being able to bring more than one gun to act against it.[17]

The retreat had become a rout. Barrie's armed gig was cut in half. One of the two small but heavily armed schooners that had been towed up was raked and cleared by shot from her stern as she fled. The rocket barge was shattered by a direct hit. No thought was even given to towing the grounded *St. Lawrence* to safety as barge after barge fled by, seeking the iron umbrellas of *Loire* and *Jaseur*, which had yet to open.[18]

The concentrated fire on *St. Lawrence* was telling. Her boom was practically cut in half, her decks were torn up, her guns dismounted, and her hull holed at the waterline. Many of her crew were killed attempting to flee the point-blank fire. The order to abandon ship was given.[19]

At that precise moment, the big guns of *Loire* and *Jaseur* roared their welcoming broadsides to the Chesapeake Flotilla. It was now the Americans' turn to run for cover from the rain of iron. Yet Barney was unwilling to give up on the capture or destruction of so great a prize as *St. Lawrence* and ordered only a modest retreat to the tree-lined sanctuary offered by the highland lip of the eastern shore bluff of the creek. Without masts to betray its positions, his squadron took on a mantle of invisibility, yet could keep watch with their long guns over the stranded schooner to beat back any rescue effort.[20]

Barrie cooly countered the American maneuver by directing officers in his fighting tops to direct *Loire*'s fire over the point of land onto the flotilla. At the same time, he ordered a detachment of Royal Marines from both *Loire* and *Jaseur* to land and secure the highlands overlooking the American position. Enfiladed by troops that could now fire down on him and bombarded by heavy fire from beyond the bluffs, Barney had little alternative but to retreat. At 7:00 P.M., after half a day of fierce combat, the Chesapeake Flotilla grudgingly retired to its protected anchorage in front of St. Leonard's Town, weary but unbroken.[21]

The three days of engagements that would be collectively dubbed the Battle of the Barges, or the First Battle of St. Leonard's Creek, had ended in a draw. Neither side had achieved its objectives: the Americans, faced with inordinately stronger forces, had been unable to escape from the creek, and the British had been unable to destroy them. Barney had expended over seven hundred shot against *Loire* and *Jaseur* alone, with little or no apparent effect. Both sides had managed to raise and recover their wounded or sunken vessels, making sufficient repairs to return them to their respective lines within two days, thus insuring the resumption of the status quo. Casualties, however, were another issue. Not one of Barney's men had been lost, while the British had suffered numerous dead and wounded, a manpower drain that could be ill afforded, much less replaced.[22]

71

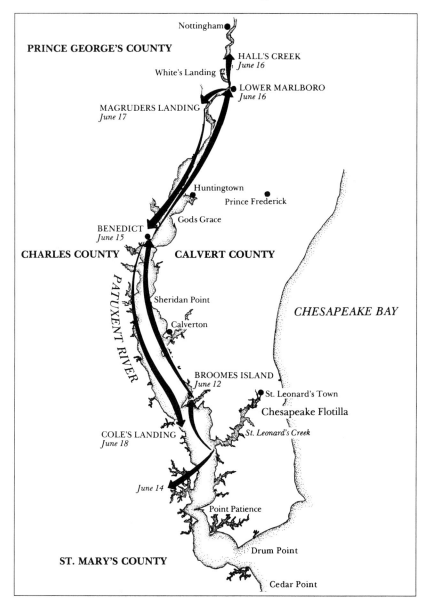

Barrie's raids on the Patuxent.

The British had developed a healthy respect for their foe and made little further effort to "disturb the tranquility of the flotilla, but contented themselves with converting the siege into a blockade, by mooring in the mouth of the creek." Barrie, however, fully intended on doing far more. The Americans, he complained to his superiors, "showed no disposition to again venture from the fastness" of St. Leonard's. He decided that, "by destroying some of the tobacco stores of the region the inhabitants would be induced" to force Commodore Barney to put out and defend their property.[23]

Thus was born a program of wanton pillage and destruction that would leave its cruel scars upon the Patuxent Valley for more than a half century.

□   □   □

Barrie launched the first of numerous attacks on the lower reaches of the Patuxent on the morning of June 11, raiding plantations, tobacco store-houses, and private homes. Warehouses were burned and livestock carried off. Whenever demands upon the local population were not met, landing parties composed of Royal Marines and, for the first time, a detachment of the Black Colonial Corps, plundered and burned at will in retribution. Although the local militia, ill equipped and lacking any form of discipline, frequently turned out, they usually fled before the battle-hardened veterans.[24] "Tobacco, slaves, farm stock of all kinds, and household furniture," it was later reported,

> became the objects of their daily enterprises, and possession of them in large quantities was the regard of their honorable achievements. What they could not conveniently carry away, they destroyed by burning. Unarmed, unoffending citizens were taken from their very beds sometimes with bed and all, and carried on board their ships, from which many of them were not released until the close of the war. . . .[25]

Barrie was soon reinforced by the arrival of yet another warship, HMS *Narcissus*, of thirty-two guns, commanded by Captain John Richard Lumly, along with five more boats and 231 men. Emboldened by the reinforce-ments, Barrie launched a raid on the town of Benedict with 160 marines and the 30-man detachment of the Black Colonial Corps. Though nomi-nally defended by local militia, the town was taken without a fight and plundered. The raiders pressed on upriver and on June 16 took "quiet possession" of Lower Marlborough as the militia and townsfolk fled terror-stricken into the wood. Even as this venerable village was being plundered and torn apart, a small reconnaissance squadron of armed barges pressed northward toward Hall's Creek and menaced Upper Marlborough.[26] The following morning, the tobacco-swollen warehouses at Lower Marlborough were set afire, and $125,000 of the valuable leaf went up in smoke. On the return trip downriver, the British conducted more raids, at Magruders Landing, Benedict, and Coles, Kents, Ballards, and Grahams Landings, where more livestock, slaves, and tobacco were taken off without the slightest opposition.[27]

Barney's situation was critical. Although his flotillamen and marines were obviously more than able and willing to fight, his land support was less than adequate. The Calvert County Militia, under Colonel Michael Taney, were "to be seen everywhere but just where they were wanted —whenever the enemy appeared they disappeared," complained the commodore. The 36th Regiment of the U.S. Army, under Colonel Henry Carberry, which had arrived on June 14 in belated response to Barney's pleas for land troops to protect his flanks, was neither disciplined nor inclined to fight. Moreover, Carberry cared little for Barney, and less for his boats, and felt he and his regiment could be put to better use elsewhere, perhaps in the Canadian theater where they might earn honor and accolades. When Barrie's raiders began to ransack the upriver areas, Carberry rushed off to shadow them—but never came to grips—leaving the flotilla's flanks only weakly defended by the U.S. Marines.[28]

There were additional problems, such as lack of security, which constantly gnawed at the commodore. Much of southern Maryland was against the war, and a few inhabitants were outright sympathetic to the British despite their raids. Many felt that it was the very presence of the flotilla that had drawn the British to the Patuxent in the first place and blamed Barney for bringing the fire and sword of the enemy down upon them. Others proved to be outright treasonous and fed the enemy a constant diet of intelligence regarding the movements of the American forces on the creek and along the Patuxent shores. At least one local spy was taken into custody by Barney and confined.

And as Barney mulled over his seemingly hopeless situation, Captain Robert Barrie continued his stinging depredations. Not all of his efforts, however, were to go unpunished.

The enemy's freedom of action on the Patuxent had caused tremors in Washington. A number of false reports had reached the capital, most noteworthy among them being fictitious accounts of the total destruction of Benedict, Lower Marlborough, and Nottingham. The local militia, which feared inciting the incendiary actions of the enemy if they dared oppose his landings, were obviously not to be counted on. Moreover, rumors and facts had become so entwined that only verification by trustworthy troops could resolve the intelligence gap.[29]

In an effort to clarify the situation, the secretary of war directed Major General John P. Van Ness, commander of the District of Columbia Militia, to dispatch a force of 280 of his men to the fluid Patuxent front, locate the enemy, put some backbone in the militia organizations, and in concert with local forces "stop the progress of the incendiaries and drive them back."[30]

By the afternoon of June 20 it had been learned by advance units of the District Militia that enemy barges had penetrated as high as Nottingham, while others, guarded by the *St. Lawrence*, were again plundering Benedict. The District force was composed of Peter's Georgetown Artillery with six field pieces, Stull's Georgetown Riflemen, the Georgetown Dragoons, Thornton's Alexandria Riflemen, and Caldwell's Washington Riflemen, all under the command of Major George Peter. The enemy, it was decided, must be driven from Benedict. This time, the American militia would fight.[31]

Arriving on the hills overlooking Benedict at 5:30 P.M., the District troopers encountered a small force of local militia under General George Stuart keeping a timid watch from a very safe distance on the enemy below. The British, it appeared, were systematically hauling off hogsheads of tobacco to their barges under the protection of *St. Lawrence*. Buoyed by the arrival of the District Militia, Stuart, the senior commander, determined to attack.[32]

Led by the Georgetown Dragoons, the militiamen swarmed down upon the enemy, who quickly formed into a thin defensive line. The skirmish, however, was over in an instant as English tars and marines were driven into a nearby marsh, with the loss of one seaman and five marines killed or captured. The British response was immediate. Seven bargeloads of seamen were immediately sent from *St. Lawrence* to counterattack, even as the schooner and her gaggle of barges opened with a brisk covering fire of round and grapeshot. The American artillery responded quickly, but it was soon apparent that the Royal Navy gunners were the more numerous and better of the two sides. Yet, dismayed by the American fire, the barges returned to the shipping. Captain Watts, in command of the raiders, quickly ordered anchors weighed, and his whole flotilla to retreat a distance downriver. Ironically, at the same moment, Stuart ordered his own force to retire to a safe distance from the town.[33]

The affair at Benedict, hailed by the militia as a great victory, proved hollow indeed, for the British had soon resumed their depredations with impunity. And Barrie's scheme was, indeed, beginning to bear fruit. Local pressure began to build on the federal government to take concerted action to either vigorously defend the region or cause the removal of the reason for the British presence in the first place, namely, the Chesapeake Flotilla.

Secretary of the Navy William Jones was at his wit's end. With his forces blockaded in Baltimore, Norfolk, and the Patuxent, the Chesapeake was open to enemy attacks in every quarter. Grasping at straws, on June 14, he suggested that the flotilla be dismantled and transported by wagons across the narrow neck of the Calvert County peninsula between the head of St. Leonard's Creek and the Chesapeake, a distance of less than a half mile. Barney was skeptical.[34] The British would surely learn of the move and be there on the Bay side ready to meet him when he emerged from the woods with his barges. And even if he did beat them to the punch, there was no protective inlet on the western shore for many miles northward to offer him shelter if pursued.

Jones was irate. On June 20 Barney received another communiqué from the secretary. This time it was a direct order to destroy the flotilla. Once the barge force was removed, it was reasoned, the enemy would most certainly leave.[35] Barney was stunned. Unable to bring himself to such a drastic action, he kept the order secret for a day or two. Finally, he reluctantly gave the command to dismantle the squadron. Quickly and efficiently, *Scorpion*, the two gunboats, the lookout boat, and six of the thirteen barges were broken down, and all movable components hauled ashore for storage. More than half the flotilla had been thus disposed of when a countermanding order arrived the following day from the fickle Navy Secretary. No doubt grumbling at the bureaucratic bungling, the flotillamen nevertheless set about to restore the squadron to its original status. Within a short time, the entire fleet was again afloat.[36]

As for the enemy, Barney wrote on June 22, Captain Barrie had departed to consult with Admiral Cockburn on "what means they are to take for my destruction, but sooner than they shall do it, I will put the fire to the flotilla and walk off by the light of the blaze."[37]

Barney's plight and tenacity had become the talk of Washington, and not a few plans had been put forward about what should be done. The most competent scheme, however, was suggested by Colonel Decius Wadsworth, commissary general of ordnance for the U.S. Army, who had merely adopted a well-known military maxim: Seize the high ground. Wadsworth suggested that if batteries could be mounted on the opposite bluffs of land at the mouth of the creek, shell fire could be aimed down on the blockading ships. The enemy could thus be driven from his anchorage even before he had time to elevate his own guns, and Barney could escape.[38]

By mid-June, British depredations on the river had become so devastating that Washington was forced to act. Wadsworth's plan was accepted. The colonel was dispatched down to St. Leonard's with a pair of eighteen-pounders, several small field pieces, and a traveling furnace for hot shot. The Second Battalion, 38th Infantry Regiment, was to be brought down from Baltimore, and Colonel Carberry's 36th Infantry was to be summoned from upriver. Both units were to be placed under Wadsworth's command. The secretary of the Navy ordered an additional one hundred U.S. Marines under Captain Samuel Miller, and three pieces of artillery, all twelve-pounders, down to operate directly under Barney's orders.[39]

Upon their arrival on June 24, Wadsworth and Miller were summoned to a war council with Barney to work out their strategy. It was decided that a battery and furnace should be erected on the commanding height on the north shore of the creek entrance, and that on the morning of June

26, before daylight, a simultaneous attack be made by batteries and flotilla upon the blockading forces. Several picked gun crews from the flotilla, under the command of Sailing Master John Geoghegan, were assigned to man Wadsworth's two eighteen-pounders. Miller would man his own guns but act in concert with the flotillamen's battery.[40]

On the evening of June 25, with the arrival of Major George Keyser's 38th Infantry, 260 men strong, after a thirty-mile forced march from the town of Friendship, preparations were begun in earnest. Geoghegan and Miller plunged themselves into the task of building the gun platforms and a hot shot furnace in silence and with the utmost secrecy. Wagons and carts were held up a quarter of a mile from the bluff and all supplies, ammunition, and bricks for the furnace were passed along by hand.[41]

As the emplacement was nearing completion, Wadsworth appeared on the scene and, much to the flotillamen's disgust, disapproved of the battery position as being too exposed to the enemy's fire. The battery was ordered moved behind the summit of the hill overlooking the British anchorage. Geoghegan protested that in the soft sand of the new position, it would be difficult if not impossible to fire with any accuracy. Wadsworth was obdurate. Dutifully, Geoghegan and his men immediately, if grudgingly, began construction at an entirely new position.[42]

In the meantime, Keyser's battalion was brought up on a field behind the battery and was joined by the 36th Regiment. Wadsworth immediately placed Keyser and his exhausted troopers under the command of Carberry. Keyser protested that the position was exposed to the river on its right and to a possible enfilading attack by the enemy ships, but Wadsworth paid little heed.[43] The battle was at hand. There was simply no time to make adjustments.

□   □   □

At 4:00 A.M. the masked American batteries opened with a suddenness that shattered the morning calm. The hulking battleships six hundred yards away were stunned by the American's seemingly point-blank fire. Unable to elevate his own guns, Captain Brown (now in charge of the blockade in Barrie's absence) was in a momentary quandary. Three full rounds were fired by the Americans before even the first feeble British reply could be made. Despite the initial shock of their fire, however, the American guns, though well served, did little damage.[44] As Barney later so bitterly observed, the battery guns,

> being placed on a declevity, must either fire directly into the hill, or be elevated so high in the air . . . they were rendered useless. At the very first fire, the guns recoiled half way down the hill and in this situation they continued to fire in the air at random. . . . [45]

If the American guns could not find their mark, neither could those of the British, whose shot either fell short or was lobbed over the batteries. Brown knew the situation might soon change and immediately dispatched a rocket barge and several launches loaded with Royal Marines to flank the American position on the Patuxent River side. He also began to employ smaller charges to simply lob shells a short way over the crest of the hill, and with some effect.[46]

But where was Barney?

The American flotilla was delayed a full forty-five minutes in coming down the creek by conflicting messages from Wadsworth, and by Barney's own innate distrust of the army's abilities.[47] The stunning effect a combined attack could have made had been seriously impaired. Yet, when he arrived there was no stopping him. Brown, who had just managed to elevate his guns to return the battery fire, had his second surprise of the morning as the Chesapeake Flotilla's line of battle rowed to within four hundred yards of his own ships and opened fire. The British were quickly forced to up anchor and retire to a position further out. They had soon brought their guns to bear on the American's mosquito fleet, which had been forced to attack through the narrows of the creek mouth in a line of only eight barges abreast. The initial onslaught of the flotilla, however, had been costly. *Loire* was hulled seven times, and her small craft were seriously mauled.[48]

Despite the hail of grape- and canister shot that rained down upon the unprotected decks of Barney's barges and literally churned the waters about them into a fine froth, the flotilla gunners returned the enemy fire with interest. The battle, as Commodore Barney later noted, became "a scene to appall the inexperienced and the feint hearted." [49]

On several occasions the British frigates were seen ablaze, set afire by hot shot from the Geoghegan and Miller batteries, but after each report, the flames were extinguished. Then, one of Geoghegan's guns fired prematurely, injuring several of his men. Worse, ammunition supplies were quickly running out. When an eighteen-pound ball collided with a British thirty-two-pound ball in midflight, one of the battery's ammunition boxes was set aflame, exploded, and injured several seamen, including Geoghegan. Still the battery fired. Yet most of the damage was now being inflicted by the flotilla.[50]

When word arrived at the battery that enemy boats and a rocket barge were moving up on its right flank, Miller observed that the U.S. Infantry, and a small three-gun army battery "injudiciously" placed in the rear to defend against just such an event, had failed to respond. His own ammunition stocks were now expended, or nearly so. Thinking his men might be better employed elsewhere to counter the flanking motions of the enemy, and after conferring with Geoghegan, Miller limbered his own guns and sought a position in the rear facing the river. As he moved back, he suddenly found himself immersed in a mass of soldiers retiring in good order from the field. Thinking the movement had been at the instigation of Wadsworth, he and his men joined in the move. Unknowingly, however, it had been Miller himself who had started the retreat.[51]

What had begun as a movement to counter the insignificant flanking move of the enemy had become a flood. When Miller had passed through Keyser's battalion, informing them that he was going to counter the motions by the enemy's rocket barges, the 38th Infantry promptly sought to realign its front toward the river. The complex move, unfortunately, proved too much for the green, untested troops, who had been subjected to the bombardment of the enemy's ships. At the same time, Carberry's force, becoming skittish, began to leave the field at an accelerated rate. Keyser's men, observing the premature retirement of the 36th Infantry, had soon joined in the retirement. The retreat immediately turned into outright flight.[52]

Left alone on the bluff, with the fields behind him abandoned to the British should they seek to land, Geoghegan informed Wadsworth of the obvious. The colonel ordered the guns spiked and the battery abandoned. Barney was on his own.[53]

The fight on the river, however, was as heavily engaged as ever—that is, until the batteries became silent. Now Barney suffered the undivided attention of the British squadron. Three of his barges were seriously damaged, and the commodore was certain that his casualties numbered over a hundred men. He immediately ordered the flotilla to disengage, noting that it would have been "an act of madness in such a force, to contend against two frigates, a brig, two schooners, and a number of barges, in themselves equal to the force that could be brought into action by the flotilla." [54]

Within minutes, the flotilla had retired three-quarters of a mile up the creek, formed in a line, and awaited the inevitable counterattack. Barney then learned of the ignominious retreat of the entire army. His comments, thankfully, were not recorded.[55] Then, incredibly, the unthinkable happened. At the very moment Barney was learning of the American retreat, *Loire, Narcissus,* and the entire British blockading force began to retire downriver. Both frigates had suffered considerable damage. *Loire* had been hulled fifteen times, and was barely able to swim, even with all of her pumps going; *Narcissus* was in an equally bad shape, and both vessels were in danger of sinking. In his official report of June 27, Brown explained his retreat thus:

> Judging we might be harassed by the battery again opening on us, and the ships having been frequently hulled, and part of the rigging shot away I thought it prudent to weigh and drop down the river to a place called Point Patience, where I anchored about three miles below in hopes the flotilla might be induced to follow. . . . [56]

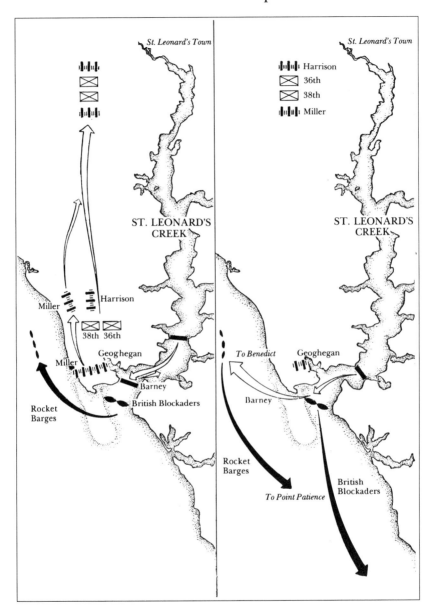

Plan of the Second Battle of St. Leonard's Creek.

It was a blatant excuse, for the Americans now only sought to escape. Barney immediately seized the opportunity he had fought so hard for and ordered his gallant little force out of the creek and up the Patuxent to Benedict. Brown observed the escape with disgust. "I had the mortifica- tion to observe them rowing down the creek, and up the river, the whole consisting of one sloop and eighteen row boats." Embarrassed and frustrated by the American victory, the British took their anger out on the nearest hapless victim. A landing was made at Point Patience and the home of one Dr. Somerville was wantonly destroyed. It was small consolation. [57]

The American escape after the Second Battle of St. Leonard's Creek was indeed a cause for jubilation in Barney's home town. "Thus," reported one ebullient Baltimore newspaper,

> we have beat them and their *rockets,* which they did not spare. You see we improve: first we beat off a few boats, which they thought would make an easy prey of us. Then they increased the number. Then they added schooners. And now behold the two frigates, all, all, have shared the same fate. We next expect ships of the line. No matter we will do our duty. . . . [58]

FIVE

The Only Fighting We Have Had

Joshua Barney wasted little time in pressing his battered little fleet up river. By 8:00 P.M. the Chesapeake Flotilla, injured but intact, sans the two slow gunboats and several slower merchantmen, which had been left behind in St. Leonard's Creek, came to anchor opposite Benedict.[1] Taking count, Barney was pleased to discover that his force had suffered fewer than twenty casualties, and not the five score he had anticipated. His disgust with the infantry, which had fled without facing more than a random bombardment and never firing one of its own guns in anger, was total. For his own men, he had nothing but praise. Yet, the conduct of battle would be criticized in the press for weeks to come, particularly the bungling by Wadsworth, the lateness of the flotilla's arrival on the scene of combat, and the unauthorized retreat of the infantry. Captain Miller would face a court of inquiry about his own movements and would be honorably acquitted. But the public's confidence in the federal government's defense capabilities was seriously frayed.[2]

Back on the creek, a detachment of ten or twelve volunteers led by a young captain named Thomas Carberry, brother to Father Joseph Carberry of St. Inigoes and later mayor of Washington, had retrieved the spiked artillery, furnace, and gear from the battery, along with several wounded who had been left behind in the face of a potential enemy counterattack, which fortunately did not materialize. For his own part, Wadsworth was finally able to stop the flood of troops from the field and return to his former position, albeit only for a very brief time. Geoghegan, hauling his wounded with him, retired to the marine encampment on the creek. Then, agreeable to orders received from Lieutenant Rutter, who had remained behind with him, he proceeded to scuttle gunboats *No. 137* and *No. 138* alongside each other to prevent capture. The American base at St. Leonard's Town was stripped of gear and, for the most part, hauled by schooner, unimpeded by the enemy, down the creek and up the Patuxent on June 30. Then, on July 2, as Geoghegan was loading the very last of the flotilla's gear onto a wagon at St. Leonard's Town, the British reappeared on the creek.[3]

The foe had been reinforced by the arrival of HMS *Severn*, of forty guns, commanded by Captain Joseph Nourse. Nourse, now the senior commander in the area, had immediately ordered *Loire* and *St. Lawrence* to join him in a reconnaissance of the enemy's former position. After all, in his report of the battle of June 26, Brown had made mention that at least one vessel had been observed retreating back up the creek instead of upriver. Perhaps there were more.[4]

Coming to anchor with his squadron off the mouth of St. Leonard's, Nourse dispatched several barges loaded with 150 marines up the creek. At their approach, Geoghegan immediately cast thirteen barge masts, the row galley's yards, and a gun slide, which he had been loading, into the water to conceal them from view. He remained only briefly to harass the oncoming enemy with musket fire and then retreated into the forest. By firing upon the enemy, the sailing master had unwittingly provided the invaders with the excuse to do what they enjoyed the most.[5]

The enemy were thorough in their revenge. Upon their arrival at the town, they set to work burning the few merchantmen and other small vessels lying about. The tobacco stores in the warehouses were plundered, and anything not carried off was burned. The town itself was set afire, with the exception of the doctor's quarters, an adjoining store, and another store immediately opposite. Absolutely nothing else was spared—not even the slave quarters, henhouses, or pigsties. The invaders then boarded the gunboats that had been scuttled level with the water, and attempted to blow up their decks. When the raiders finally departed, there was little left but ashes to signify that there had ever been a St. Leonard's Town.[6]

Immediately after the enemy's departure, Rutter and Geoghegan returned to recover the masts, spars, and gun slides hidden in the water. Without warning they discovered the inhabitants plundering the wrecks of the two gunboats of every piece of copper and iron they could get. The two stunned officers immediately seized all the salvaged goods, which were, after all, still U.S. government property.[7]

Soon after his arrival at Benedict, Barney traveled to Washington to discuss the disposition of the squadron. The flotilla, it was decided, would be removed to a narrows upriver near Nottingham where its guns could easily command the approach to the town and where communications with Washington would be better facilitated. *Scorpion* and her gaggle of barges would remain stationed in the river. Lieutenant Rutter was to be sent to Baltimore to take command of fourteen more barges completed in Barney's absence and which were now charged with the naval defense of the city. As for the British invader, he was to be allowed free reign below the American line.[8]

Admiral Sir George Cockburn's flagship, the majestic seventy-four-gun ship of the line *Albion*, joined Nourse's squadron on the Patuxent on July 6. The admiral had come to personally assess the situation. Barney's flotilla, he quickly decided, was so high up the river that it was no longer a threat. Thus, he ordered *Loire* and *St. Lawrence* on a cruise, leaving *Severn* and *Narcissus* to prevent an American breakout from the Patuxent. He need not have worried. Barney would remain on the defensive.[9] The government had decreed it. But the old commodore had resolved to protect what he could.

On July 10 word arrived that Annapolis was being seriously menaced by the British. An attack on the town was feared. Wadsworth's troops, then stationed at Benedict and the only viable land forces now on the river, were promptly marched off to meet the threat. No sooner had they departed than reports reached Nottingham that the British had again attacked Benedict. Barney ordered the flotilla down to the town, only to discover an empty stretch of river before it. The report, it appeared, had been false.[10]

Four days later, *Loire* and *St. Lawrence* returned to the Patuxent. News for the British was good. Five more warships and two transports filled with troops had arrived on the Chesapeake. The flagship of the squadron, HMS *Asia*, had brought Cockburn the long-awaited news that a powerful army of invasion would soon be available.[11] The new commander-in-chief of the American Station, Vice Admiral Sir Alexander Cochrane, wanted to know just where Cockburn thought a decisive attack on the American coast might be made. "I feel no hesitation in stating to you," replied Cockburn,

> that I consider the town of Benedict in the Patuxent, to offer us advantage for this purpose beyond any other spot within the United States. . . . Within forty-eight hours after our arrival in the Patuxent of such a force as you expect, the City of Washington might be possessed without difficulty or opposition of any kind.[12]

The admiral proposed that if Washington was deemed a suitable objective, that the troops be landed on the Patuxent's shores, and a diversionary expedition be dispatched up the Potomac to distract and divide the American forces and to annoy or reduce Fort Washington. Cockburn's plan was well thought out. The Patuxent had already been sounded as far as Benedict and it was found to be deep enough for the great warships and transports from which any landing must be made. Moreover, any movement up the river would have the added benefit of being initially considered as a move against the flotilla, not Washington. In the meantime, Sir George proposed focusing his own attentions on the Potomac to terrify and distract the Americans from his true plans until the army of invasion arrived. To ensure success, the fleet in the upper Bay would be divided into two squadrons, one under his own command, which would conduct attacks on the Potomac, and the other under Nourse, which would continue its depredations on the Patuxent.[13]

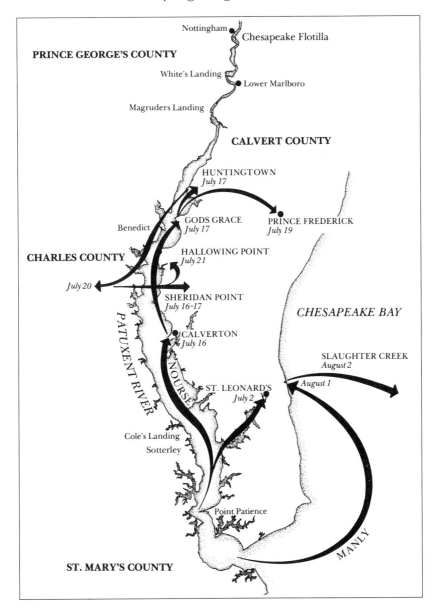

Nourse's raids of July–August 1814.

Nourse's squadron was to consist of the recently arrived *Brune* (thirty-eight guns), *Aetna* bomb ship (eight guns), *Manly* sloop-of-war (twelve guns), and, of course, *Severn*. The captain was encouraged to foster the "emigration" of black slaves from the region while conducting his for-

85

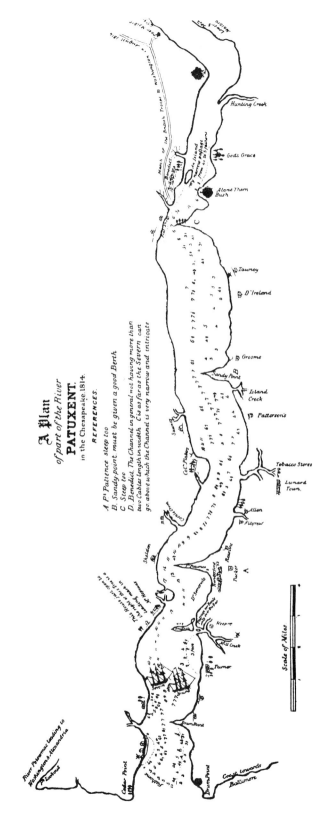

A rough British nautical chart of the Patuxent, probably drawn from data assembled preparatory to the August 1814 expedition against Washington. Courtesy of the Library of Congress

ays, but was not to seem too aggressive lest Washington become overly alarmed.[14] His expedition was to have as its objective the capture of a place called Wilkinson's Store, somewhat above Benedict, "where articles of considerable value are supposed to be deposited." Upon completion of the raid, during which he was to cause "the enemy any other arrogance" that he might see fit, he was to return to the anchorage under Drum Point and dispatch *Aetna* to the admiral with a full report.[15]

Nourse was not slow in following through the admiral's orders. On July 16 he landed at Battle Creek and destroyed the former Calvert County seat of Calverton.[16] Continuing up the river he next put ashore with three hundred men at Gods Grace, above Sheridan Point. From there, he set out on a seven-mile forced march to the town of Huntingtown, on Hunting Creek. The town was taken by surprise, and its warehouse and 130 hogsheads of tobacco burned. The fire, unfortunately, raged out of control, spreading from house to house unimpeded by the hand of man: Huntingtown was burned to the ground. Temporarily satiated, the British returned by the same road, destroying a plantation belonging to the Mackall family at Gods Grace, reembarked aboard their boats with their plunder, and set off for their ships.[17]

Opposition by the American army, now under the command of an inept officer named William Henry Winder and the local militia (scurrying hither and yon with total ineffectiveness) would have added a comic touch to the affair if the stakes had not been so tragically serious.[18] Unfortunately, Nourse was far from finished.

On July 19 Nourse decided on an attack on the county seat of Calvert County, the town of Prince Frederick. Though opposed by a strong force of local militia, the Americans were not inclined to fight and melted into the countryside as the British marched nine miles overland without opposition. At Prince Frederick, the captain ordered the county courthouse, all of its records, and the county jail burned, and then marched back to his ships, again without the least molestation.[19] The following day, he landed two miles below Benedict, in St. Mary's County, marched four miles inland, destroyed the local warehouses and tobacco stocks, and retired again to his ships unopposed. Soon afterward, another landing at Sandy Point and another forced march five miles inland resulted in the destruction of another tobacco warehouse and the plundering of even more local tobacco stocks.[20]

Belatedly, Barney was alerted to the raids and dropped down the river to interdict the invaders, but to no effect. He was a few hours too late. The river was again barren of ships. Nourse was already en route to the squadron anchorage under Drum Point, fat with plunder and full of praise for his officers and men.[21]

The British on the Patuxent again seemed invincible. Then, on July 25, the leveling effects of nature made all men equal. About midday, the sky began to fill with enormous black cumulous clouds blowing in from the northwest. The storm that soon struck was accompanied by violent thunder, lightning, and incredibly powerful winds. One of the frigates was heeled over so far that her main gun deck nearly touched the water. A seventy-ton schooner, tender to *Severn*, with a long eighteen-pounder on deck, was capsized in an instant. Clinging for dear life to their puny warships, the British sailors, certainly no strangers to violent storms, watched in awe as immense trees were ripped up by their roots from the nearby shoreline. The river itself swept all before it as its voracious currents increased a hundredfold. Then, as suddenly as it had begun, the tornado was over. Barely ten minutes had elapsed.[22]

Observing a large raft of debris, timber, and other articles floating down from the upriver reaches, Nourse mistook the flotsam for the American flotilla and immediately moved to prepare his ships for battle. At the last minute before giving the order, however, it was "discovered by means of a spy glass, the approaching flotilla was perfectly harmless." [23]

□   □   □

While Nourse blockaded the Patuxent, and Cockburn raided up and down on the Potomac, Barney and Secretary of the Navy Jones agonized over what to do with the flotilla. Escape past the blockaders seemed out of the question. Jones dusted off his recent idea of hauling the flotilla out by land. Was it possibly feasible to bring the fleet upriver to Queen Anne's Town, and cart the boats overland by wagon to the South River, where they could be refloated, perhaps at the old port of London Town?[24]

Barney thought little of the idea, but dispatched his son William to take soundings of the river from Pig Point to Queen Anne's, the first known soundings of the reach ever recorded. Major Barney returned from his reconnaissance on July 31 and reported to his father. The commodore promptly informed Jones of the findings and added his own computations. The river route seemed doable, but the overland passage was all but impassable. The logistics were enormous. The entire flotilla, he calculated, weighed less than 155 tons. Three horses per ton would be needed to move the entire fleet, not to mention at least sixty-four wagons and fifty-six pair of dray wheels. "Such a thing can be done," he informed the secretary, "but can it be done with safety, if done will we be better off in South River than in the Patuxent? . . ." [25]

Barney was absolutely certain that the next major British offensive would be in his quarter, first for the plunder, and second, "if successful, they can march on the Capitol with as much ease and in as short a distance as from any other place." [26] No, it was better the flotilla remain where it was. Properly supported, he reported confidently, he could put an end to the war in this quarter once and for all. His observations were read, and quietly shelved.

When the gunmetal gray dawn of August 17 broke over Point Lookout, Thomas Swann, manning the government's forward lookout post on the Potomac River, gazed in astonishment at an enormous forest of masts and sails blanketing the Chesapeake. The long-awaited and feared British invasion fleet, at least forty-six ships strong, had arrived. Aboard were 2,814 men of the 4th, 44th, and 85th Regiments, veterans of the Peninsula Campaign in Spain known as "Wellington's Invincibles" for their part in the victory over Napoleon, and who had embarked at Bordeaux, France, with the expressed intention of trouncing old Jimmy Madison into submission. Also aboard were 1,000 men of the veteran 21st Regiment. Together with the Royal Marines and a contingent of trained naval personnel, the invasion of Maryland and the attack on Washington was to be carried out by no less than 4,500 crack troops.[27] Their designated landing point, suggested by Cockburn and approved by Cochrane, was to be at the sad little town of Benedict. At 6:30 P.M. that evening, led by HMS *Tonnant*, the British invasion force dropped anchor off Drum Point. The following morning they entered the river, their line resembling a peacetime sailing regatta more than a heavily armed invasion force bent on the destruction of a national capital.[28]

Joshua Barney learned almost immediately of the British arrival from two lookouts he had posted at the mouth of the Patuxent.[29] On the morning of Friday, August 19, he fired off a confirmation. The force at the entrance of the river had in all seven frigates, seven transports, a sixty-four-gun ship, one razee (or cut down frigate), two seventy-four-gun ships of the line, and two or three gun brigs. Cockburn, it was reported, had vowed nothing less than the annihilation of the flotilla but his actual objective was to "dine in Washington on Sunday." [30]

As Barney composed his communiqué aboard *Scorpion*, the British Army, under the direction of a disciplined, seasoned commander and veteran of the Peninsular Campaign in Spain, Major General Robert Ross, streamed ashore at Benedict and prepared for its long, dusty march toward Washington.[31]

By the early morning hours of August 20, Joshua Barney learned of the successful British landing at Benedict, even then still under way, and at 7:00 A.M. dispatched another urgent report to Secretary Jones. The enemy had committed himself. The commodore was now absolutely certain the British target was Washington.[32]

At the Navy Department, Secretary Jones read Barney's dispatch with alarm. The letter had been delivered from Nottingham in less than five hours. He looked at a map and found to his dismay that there was a very good road from Benedict to the capital. Yet, unlike Barney, he wasn't certain just what the British objective was. There were, unfortunately, also good roads from the head of navigation to Annapolis and Baltimore. One thing was obvious, however: the flotilla was bound to be in the way whatever the enemy's objectives were. He immediately dashed off another order to Barney.

> Should the enemy dash for this place, he will probably take this road from Benedict, unless he should follow the bank of the river to Nottingham with his advance guard to drive back your flotilla and bring off his main body by water. This will have been discovered before you receive this, and you will immediately send the flotilla up to Queen Anns with as few men as possible and a trusty officer to remain there and in the event of the enemy advancing upon the flotilla in force to destroy the whole effectually and proceed with his men to this place. Having given these directions you will retire before the enemy toward this place opposing his progress as well by your arms, as by falling trees across the road, removing bridges, and presenting every other possible obstacle to his march. [33]

An American army almost seven thousand strong was being formed to meet the invaders, and Barney's ragged flotillamen and Captain Miller's redoubtable marines were to join them. Within hours of receiving the secretary's orders, Barney had upped anchor and retired from Nottingham in good order.[34]

The British pressed northward from Benedict by both land and water. Ross's troops marched along, parched and wearied by the unforgiving Tidewater heat, while Cockburn pressed on in a flotilla of armed barges, never knowing just when Barney might appear. At Nottingham, about 5:30 P.M. on the 21st, the British juggernaut briefly collided with a flying squadron of American dragoons under the direct command of Secretary of State James Monroe; the squadron was driven off with little difficulty. Here, the invaders came to rest for the night.[35]

The flotilla and a covey of merchantmen that had retreated with it had retired as far up the Patuxent as it could go, and came to anchor in a single line, bow to stern, a little above a bend at Pig Point. Despite the reported depth of the river, it was impossible for *Scorpion* to proceed any higher than Scotchmans Hole. The order to bring the squadron up to Queen Anne's, with the minor exception of two barges that could swim the distance, was out of the question. The river had silted up and was simply too shallow to traverse. There was little question that in these confines, the flotilla was doomed.[36] Now it was Barney's sad duty to turn over command of the fleet to Lieutenant Solomon Frazier and a small party of flotillamen. Frazier's instructions were simple: destroy the fleet upon the first appearance of the enemy. Barney and four hundred of his men were to leave immediately to join the defense of the capital.[37]

Shortly before 11:00 A.M. on August 22, the British armada neared the American fleet. Cockburn, personally leading the van, later reported on the final moments of the Chesapeake Flotilla:

The Only Fighting We Have Had

I then proceeded on with the boats, and as we opened the reach above Pig Point I plainly discovered Commodore Barney's broad pendant in the headmost vessel, a large sloop, and the remainder of the flotilla extending in a long line astern of her. Our boats now advanced toward them as rapidly as possible, but on nearing them we observed the sloop bearing the broad pendant to be on fire, and she very soon afterwards blew up. I now saw clearly that they were all abandoned and on fire with trains to their magazines, and out of the seventeen vessels which composed this formidable and so much vaunted flotilla sixteen were in quick succession blown to atoms, and the seventeenth, in which the fire had not taken, was captured. The commodore's sloop was a large armed vessel, the others were gun boats all having a long gun in the bow and a carronade in the stern, but the calibre of the guns and the number of the crew of each differed in proportion to the size of the boat, varying from 32 pdrs. and 60 men, to 18 pdrs. and 40 men. I found here lying above the flotilla under its protection thirteen merchant schooners, some of which not being worth bringing away I caused to be burnt, such as were in good condition, I directed to be moved to Pig Point. Whilst employed taking these vessels a few shots were fired at us by some of the men of the flotilla from the bushes on the shore near us, but Lieutenant Scott whom I had landed for that purpose, soon got hold of them and made them prisoners. Some horsemen likewise shewed themselves on the neighbouring heights, but a rocket or two depended them without resistance. Now spreading his men through the country, the enemy retreated to a distance and left us in quiet possession of the town [Upper Marlboro], the neighbourhood, and our prizes. [38]

The tremendous explosions which ripped the Chesapeake Flotilla asunder were heard for miles.[39] At that moment, General Ross's troops were entering Upper Marlboro and sensed the enormous importance of the sounds. Neither was the chilling significance of the blasts lost on General Winder's retreating soldiers.

The British lodged for a while in Upper Marlboro and then pressed on toward Washington. At the little town of Bladensburg, the American forces under General Winder determined to make their stand against a foe of only half their strength. The humiliating defeat of American arms that followed on that grim day of August 25 has been ignominiously referred to ever after as "The Bladensburg Races," in reference to the speed with which the American troops fled from the field. Only the gallant Barney and his flotillamen, together with Captain Miller's valiant marines, stood holding the entire British Army at bay. Charge after charge was repelled by the little party of American seamen and marines, until the defenders' ammunition was finally expended. Barney, wounded in the thigh by a musket ball while directing the fire of his small battery and abandoned by all but his beloved flotillamen, ordered them to save themselves and leave him behind.[40]

Captain John Wainwright, commander of HMS *Tonnant*, was the first British officer to encounter the bleeding American on the field of battle. He immediately went off in search of Cockburn and soon returned with the admiral and General Ross. Both treated the commodore in the most polite and respectful manner and offered him every assistance.

"I am," declared Ross sincerely, "really very glad to see you, Commodore."

"I am sorry I cannot return your compliment, General," replied Barney, in obvious pain.

Turning to Cockburn, the general declared, "I told you it was the Flotillamen."

"Yes. You were right, though I could not believe you," responded the admiral. "They have given us the only fighting we have had."

For a moment the two officers talked between themselves, then turning to the American, Ross spoke softly. "Commodore Barney, you are paroled. Where do you wish to be conveyed?" [41]

□   □   □

The American defeat at the Battle of Bladensburg doomed Washington.[42] On the Patuxent, the British invasion fleet lay at Benedict awaiting the return of its warriors when another violent storm lit the sky with lightning. As before, the tempest soon passed, leaving behind a moody, darkened afterglow. Then, at 9:00 P.M., a significant entry was scribbled in HMS *Albion*'s log: "Observed a great fire in the direction of Washington." The capital of the United States was in flames.[43]

□   □   □

Of the sixty Americans killed in action at Bladensburg, fifty had belonged to Joshua Barney's tiny command. The commodore was soon repatriated and returned to his home at Elk Ridge in Anne Arundel County to convalesce even as the world turned topsy-turvy. The invaders had turned their attentions on Baltimore. But at the city on the Patapsco, unlike at Washington, the story had been different. There the flotillamen had manned the big guns at the Lazaretto, the city battery, and Fort McHenry and had saved the day by repelling a landing attempt at Port Covington. On the Potomac River, they had served valiantly with Captains David Porter and Oliver Hazard Perry in harassing the retreat of an enemy fleet under Captain James Alexander Gordon, which had just captured Fort Washington (Warburton) and Alexandria.[44]

For his own heroic stand, the commodore was awarded a handsome sword and the thanks of the city of Washington. When he sought remu-

The British Invasion of America, showing the destruction of the Chesapeake Flotilla (lower right), the Battle of Bladensburg (upper right), the burning of Washington (center), and the destruction of the Washington Navy Yard (left). Courtesy of Greenwich Hospital Collection, Royal Maritime Museum, Greenwich, England

neration from Congress, however, for the loss of all the personal effects and clothing of his men at the abandonment of the flotilla, certain members of Congress alleged the flotilla had been blown up too soon, and that the commodore had, out of stupidity or cowardice, abandoned it prematurely. Barney persisted and was eventually able to secure compensation for his enlisted men, but not for the officers.[45]

In the meantime, the flotilla wrecks, lying in the shallow waters of the Patuxent, had become the subject of indiscriminate salvage by local inhabitants. The government quickly contracted with a local salvor named John Weems to raise the vessels, if he could, and salvage the government's effects on them. Weems went to work immediately and recovered at least two of the craft, but found the flagship *Scorpion*, though very valuable, impossible to raise. When the government failed to pay him for his ongoing efforts, he responded by giving one of the boats away and refusing to do any more work.[46]

By October 10, Barney had recovered enough to resume command and was instructed to raise the flotilla. In November his men "went with pleasure to the Patuxent . . . and there saved from the bottom of the river all the guns, gun carriages, cambooses, anchors, cables, shots, etc. belonging to their late flotilla which had been destroyed. . . ." But the majority of the vessels remained where they had been scuttled, their battered and charred remains gradually being covered by the Patuxent silts.[47]

□   □   □

The bullet in Barney's thigh had been buried so deeply that it could not be removed. It traveled with him for the next three years, to London, to Paris, to Stockholm, to Kentucky, and finally to Pennsylvania. On December 1, 1818, the commodore finally succumbed to a "bilious fever" resulting from his wound and died at age fifty-nine. He was a hero unrecognized by his own state, and castigated for a defeat that he had not caused. But he lay in peace.[48]

And on the bottom of the Patuxent River, more than two hundred miles away, the bones of his gallant little flotilla also lay in quiet repose, ignored and forgotten by the nation and history.

S I X

Not Worthy of Further Improvement

At the close of the War of 1812 the Patuxent region lay in ashen ruins. Few, if any, plantations or towns along its banks had escaped destruction or plunder at the hands of the British. Capital had flown and the infrastructure of social order was in shambles. The little urban life that had once existed had been all but snuffed out. Reconstruction was to be a slow, arduous process, and in many cases outright impossible. One of the principal influences on redevelopment of the region, however, was the introduction of the steamboat to the Maryland Tidewater. Its impact upon the people and life along the Patuxent drainage was enormous.

Within three years after the destruction of Joshua Barney's oar- and sail-powered flotilla, the Patuxent River was treated to the sight of the first of many steamboats to skim her surface. The vessel was called *Surprise,* and she was owned by a native Marylander, Captain George Weems, founder of a steamboat dynasty that would dominate Patuxent River travel and commerce for nearly a century. *Surprise* had the distinction of being propelled by a rotary steam engine, a forerunner of the great turbines used on ocean liners today. In 1817 Weems initiated Maryland into the Steamboat Age by thrusting *Surprise* into regular service on runs from Baltimore to landings on Maryland's western shore, with terminal points in the Patuxent River. Four years later he replaced *Surprise* with another vessel named *Eagle.*[1]

Eagle was perhaps one of the most historic steamers to ply the Patuxent. Built in 1813 at Philadelphia, she was one of the first steamboats to operate on a regular run on the Delaware with a route between the aforementioned city and the port of Trenton, New Jersey. In 1815 Captain Weems acquired *Eagle* for operation in Maryland waters and proceeded to have her brought, under the command of Captain Moses Rogers, from the Delaware to the Chesapeake. In so doing, the little vessel made the second oceanic steamship voyage in history. *Eagle* arrived at Norfolk, Virginia, on June 19, 1815, after a passage of twenty-five hours from the Delaware capes. Following a short layover, she proceeded on to Baltimore, arriving there on June 25 after a twenty-nine-hour voyage up the Bay. She again made history soon afterward by becoming the first steamer to

95

traverse the full length of Chesapeake Bay.[2] She was soon placed on the Patuxent River–Annapolis–Baltimore run.

Then, on April 18, 1824, her boiler exploded, killing one Henry M. Murray, and injuring a number of others, including Captain Weems. As a result of this catastrophe, *Eagle* had once again achieved another first—the first steamboat fatality in the Tidewater.[3]

Weems recovered from the loss of *Eagle* and in 1827 organized a company and contracted for the construction of another steamboat, to be called *Patuxent*. This vessel was to run from Baltimore to Herring Bay and then to landings on the lower Patuxent River, Rappahannock River, and ultimately to Fredericksburg.[4] *Patuxent* remained in service until 1858 when she was sold and replaced by a 447-ton side-wheeler called *George Weems*. Two years later the Patuxent Steam Express Company opened for business and began to compete with the Weems Line for the Patuxent River trade, and was to employ the 275-ton steamer *Express* on this mission. *Express* was a side-wheel steamer built in 1841, and though her initial operations on the Patuxent were short-lived, she continued in Tidewater service until 1878 when she was lost in a violent storm off the mouth of the river.[5]

The flourishing steamer traffic of the Patuxent region was, unfortunately, slowed considerably by the outbreak of the Civil War in 1861. Calvert, Charles, and St. Mary's Counties were particularly strong in their sympathies toward the Confederacy, and many young men from these areas enlisted in the Confederate Army.

Early opposition to the federal government was noted in several areas. One such instance occurred on February 9, 1861, in St. Mary's County, with the formation of a milita unit called "Smallwoods Vigilantes."[6] Outright opposition movements, however, soon gave way to hidden resentment when Union military forces were sent to maintain federal control in potentially rebellious areas. On September 9, the First Massachusetts Regiment would be the first to project Northern power into southern Maryland. From the regimental base at Camp Union, in Bladensburg, regular army units set off to disrupt supplies being sent across the Potomac by Confederate sympathizers. After establishing a forward bivouac at Upper Marlboro, units were dispatched as far south as Prince Frederick; en route they talked to black men and the few Unionists encountered along the way to locate hidden contraband destined for the South.[7] On October 7, the troops returned to Bladensburg with a full wagonload of confiscated guns, swords, uniforms, and even a rebel flag.[8]

On November 3, 1861, Union infantry brigades under Generals O. O. Howard and George Syckes marched from Washington to occupy polling stations in Prince George's, Charles, St. Mary's, and Calvert Counties to enforce open elections.[9] It was a significant demonstration of Union will and military might conducted in a hostile land. Federal units marched as far south as Lower Marlboro in Calvert, and Charlotte Hall in St. Mary's to impose the Union's authority in the most forceful manner possible.[10]

Federal control over southern Maryland was demonstrated time and again, frequently with ruthless determination. In St. Mary's County, a small army of occupation, composed of roughly 150 soldiers (excluding garrison forces at the giant prisoner-of-war camp at Point Lookout) maintained order and quelled uprisings before they could begin. On March 15, 1863, for instance, J. S. Downs, editor of the *St. Mary's Beacon*, was arrested for publishing anti-Lincoln editorials and was incarcerated at Point Lookout for his loyalty to the Confederacy.[11]

Naval patrols were regularly conducted on the Potomac River to counter the danger of Confederate naval invasion from Virginia. To back up control of the Patuxent region, Union military camps were soon established throughout southern Maryland, and two were situated directly on the river. One of these was erected at the mouth of Battle Creek where an arsenal was constructed, as well as a place for the temporary confinement of Confederate prisoners of war. A second military establishment was situated on the western shore at Benedict. The Benedict encampment was erected on October 21, 1863, and is referred to in official records as Camp Stanton. This site was garrisoned by two companies of the Seventh Regiment of Infantry, United States Colored Troops, Maryland Volunteers, under the command of Lieutenant Even White, and was composed entirely of black Marylanders. These troops were to spend the winter of 1863 drilling, recruiting, and preparing for active field duty.[12] "The location of the camp turned out to be an unhealthy one," noted one historian, "and many of the volunteers died during the winter season." The unit, however, was far from inactive. In late November 1863, a detachment under Lieutenants Thompson, Mach, Cheney, and Califf boarded the steam tugs *Balloon* and *Cecil* at Benedict. On November 29 the troopers raided the oyster fleets operating in the mouth of the Patuxent and in Tangier Sound, and returned ten days later with 130 "recruits." The regiment was finally activated in 1864 and fought in all of the subsequent campaigns of the Army of the Potomac, suffering innumerable casualties.[13]

During the war a settlement of contraband blacks was established on the banks of the Patuxent River at Cole's Farm, in old De la Brooke Manor. The camp seemed forever in need of supplies and equipment. On June 11, 1864, and again ten days later, expeditions were led by Colonel A. G. Draper, USA, to Popes Creek, Virginia to remedy the situation. Draper's force of 600 troopers was made of 475 men of the 36th Colored Infantry and detachments from the 2nd and 5th Cavalry. Their objective was to procure horses for the Quartermaster Department and farming implements, wagons, and the likes, for "the contraband settlement" on the Patuxent River. The expeditions were successful and Draper returned to Maryland with 160 horses and mules, 375 cattle, and 600 more contrabands, including 60 to 70 who wished to join the U.S. Army. Also captured were a large number of plows, harrows, cutwaters, wheat drills, corn shellers, harnesses, carts, carriages, and sundry other goods. The plunder was so great that it required two transport ships to carry it off.[14]

The Patuxent remained relatively peaceful during the war despite the occupation, though some spy activities were reported in the vicinity of Battle Creek and Milltown Landing. However, near the end, Confederate guerillas began to wreak havoc on Union commerce in the Bay and near the mouth of the river. On March 31, 1865, the 115-ton schooner *St. Mary's*, out of St. Mary's City, loaded with an assorted cargo valued at twenty thousand dollars, was boarded and captured off the Patuxent by a Confederate raiding party of twenty men led by Master John C. Braine, CSN. The disguised rebels were in a yawl and had come alongside the schooner on the pretext that their craft was sinking. Braine successfully carried the schooner, took her to sea, and employed her in the capture of the New York-bound schooner *J.B. Spafford*. *Spafford* was released after the rebels placed the *St. Mary's* crew on board and plundered them of their personal effects. To confuse possible pursuers, the rebels indicated to their captives their intentions of taking the *St. Mary's* to St. Marks, Florida, but put into Nassau instead.[15]

By the onset of spring 1865 the closing days of the war were finally at hand. Then, on April 14 President Lincoln was assassinated. Secretary of the Navy Gideon Welles warned the Potomac Flotilla that John Wilkes Booth, the assassin, had been reported near Bryantown on April 15. His ankle had been broken in a fall from the president's box at Ford's Theater, in Washington, where the president had been shot. The killer had apparently made his way into southern Maryland, where his leg was set by a certain Dr. Samuel Mudd. Welles urged strict vigilance in both the Potomac and Patuxent regions and ordered that on both rivers "all boats should be searched. . . ."[16] Overzealous occupation troops, however, not only searched and secured every vessel afloat on the Patuxent, but sank nearly a dozen watercraft merely to spite rebel sympathizers along the river. The alert remained in effect until April 26, when word of the assassin's death in Virginia was received in Washington.

In May 1865 occupation of the Patuxent region by federal troops came to an end. Camps along the river were quickly dismantled and southern Maryland began the agonizing return to normalcy, a healing process that would take nearly a century of adjustment to be accomplished.

       □   □   □

In many ways, the Civil War had left the Patuxent Valley even more prostrate than the War of 1812 had, though few actual military incidents had marred the countryside. The loss of great portions of the plantation labor force, the former slave population, and the incumbent depletion of wealth, had brought unending difficulties to the river people. Few of the counties bordering the waterway possessed capital to develop industry, and, like the rest of the South, most were obliged to fall back on agriculture. Yet migration of farm workers to the cities caused increasing hardship to the planters, and depression and economic suffering plagued the region. For Charles, St. Mary's, and Calvert Counties, there was yet one more expedient—fishing and oystering.

The early colonists of Maryland made little use, except for local consumption, of the vast seafood supply right at their fingertips. Indeed, it was not until the early nineteenth century that commercial harvesting of oysters and a fishing industry of any note took root in the state, and then it was only after the major oyster beds of Long Island and New Jersey had been worked out. Fishing had primarily been for subsistence, but when the first oyster fleets began to work the Bay and its rivers, fishing as an industry soon followed. Though not on a large scale at first, the industry took hold about 1811 with the arrival of a small flotilla of oyster dredge boats that had headed south to the Chesapeake from Fairhaven, Connecticut.[17]

It was not until after the Civil War, however, that commercial fishing and oystering was firmly seated in the Patuxent region. In 1867 the first major commercial fishery on the river was established by one Isaac Solomon of Philadelphia. Solomon chose to settle on an island near the mouth of the river and just below Point Patience. This tidy little piece of land had originally been known as Bourne's Island, but after the settlement of a family by the name of Somervell it was referred to as Somervell's Island. Solomon wisely married into the Somervell clan, purchased and occupied a house on the island, and commenced construction of the first oyster canning establishment on the river. Within a short time, Patuxent River oysters were being shipped up and down the Eastern Seaboard.[18] The once tiny oyster fleet grew rapidly in number. Mariners and cannery workers arrived from the Eastern Shore and helped establish a distinctively maritime community on the island, whose sole source of revenue was now being derived from the water. In 1869 Solomon established the first shipyard on the island, apparently a rather small affair, which was later to become the M. M. Davis yard, famed throughout the Tidewater for its boat production.[19]

It was a splendid time for the Somervell's Islanders. After the Civil War the Maryland oyster fishery, rich from several years of little fishing and with prices mounting every day, faced the pleasant prospect of prosperity. Hitherto, the fishing had been carried out by scraping with tongs from log canoes and small sailing craft such as pungies and sloops. But now, a change in Maryland legislation permitted the dragging of dredges to scrape the oysters off the beds. The dredges were relatively simple, though bulky, affairs—little more than baskets made of chain, iron and rope—but they were effective. To drag these heavy dredges, bigger and more powerful sailing craft were needed, but there was little capital available to build them.[20]

To construct a traditional frame and plank vessel was a major shipwrighting job. The oystermen knew only the traditions of edge-joining and hewing. The log canoes employed and produced by many of the oystermen were direct descendents in type of the primitive Indian dugouts and were constructed by bolting together shaped logs to create a massive, frameless boat. The major part of the shaping of this craft had been with an axe or adze cutting and modeling from the solid mass of timbers bolted together. It was, in essence, more of a carving job than a construction process.[21]

The need for a more powerful boat was met by the development at Somervell's (Solomons) Island and elsewhere on the Bay of the log "bugeye." It has been said by some experts that the name bugeye, or buck-eye, had been derived from the ease with which the vessel could be "turned in a bug's eye." Some maritime historians claim that the origin of the term was from an archaic Scottish term for oyster boat. Yet the boat itself was a simple affair. In the words of historian Marion Brewington: "Some person added a couple of extra wing logs, put a deck on his dugout, and with that the bugeye was born." In point of fact, the bugeye had massive solid edge-bolted bottoms of shaped logs with no floor timbers, frames fastened to the made-up bottoms which were planked up in the ordinary way, and ordinary decks and low bulwarks. It was quite a distinctive vessel in appearance with clipper bow, long trailboards, and a very simple two-masted rig.[22]

In a compilation of all craft definitely identifiable as bugeyes, Chesapeake historian Brewington lists a total of 627 vessels, though there were undoubtedly many more that have gone unrecorded. The earliest listed vessel of this construction was the *Coral*, built in Somerset County in 1867. A total of 21 bugeyes, in fact, are listed as having been constructed elsewhere before the first Solomons Island bugeye, the *Clytie*, was built in 1876.[23] Yet Solomons Island truly deserved the sobriquet "home of the bugeye," for in 1872 there arrived at the little fishing village a thirty-three-year-old New York ship carpenter by the name of James T. Marsh. After having received early apprenticeship training at the Brooklyn Navy Yard and working a bit at several shipyards on Long Island, Marsh had decided to set out on his own. Sailing south in a sloop of his own construction, the *Mystic Shrine*, the ambitious young shipwright landed at Solomons and opened his own shipyard. Business was good and demands for Marsh-built craft grew rapidly. His first vessel, the schooner *Lillie Hellen*, was followed by numerous sloops and schooners.[24] "Schooners and sloops," according to Brewington, occupied Mr. Marsh's attention until, in 1879, he was asked by one of the Solomon family to build a bugeye. He agreed, provided Solomon would allow the vessel to be designed and built according to his own ideas. The result was what is thought to be the first regularly framed and planked bugeye to be launched, the *Carrie*. She proved to be such a success that orders came into the Marsh yard so quickly that its ways were devoted almost exclusively to the construction of that one type and in some years as many as four bugeyes were on the stocks at one time.[25]

Marsh continued to improve the design of the bugeye, the most notable improvement being the "ducktail" stern, fitted for the first time on the bugeye *Alexine* in 1880. It was a feature adding substantial deck space to the vessel, making it far more profitable to operate in the oystering trade than other vessel types. Although the Marsh specialty was bugeye construction, his yard produced a wide range of other craft as well, ranging from the hardy sloops and workboats to elegant three-masted schooner yachts. All of the Marsh vessels were notable for their speed and solid construction.[26]

Oystering spurred other developments besides those of the shipwright's art. Among the more significant technological advances produced by Patuxent River watermen was that of the deep-water oystering tongs, invented by Charles L. Marsh in 1887, which were a distinct improvement over the hand tong in common use throughout the Tidewater. In 1903 it was noted that the use of the deep-water patent tongs was confined primarily to Kent, Calvert, and St. Mary's Counties. The invention had the effect, however, of opening up the deepest recesses of the Chesapeake to oystering, leaving no areas totally free of the oysterman's incursions. "The use of this type tong," it was noted in the Baltimore *Sun*, "is confined principally to the mouth of the Patuxent River, where they are especially advantageous owing to the depth of water being too great in most places for commonly used shaft tongs."[27]

The Isaac Solomon Oyster Canning Company became a mainstay of the local economy at the mouth of the Patuxent. And it became a common phrase heard on the waters where oystermen conducted their work to say: "I am going to Solomons to sell," meaning to the Isaac Solomon canning operation on the island. Soon the phrase "going to Solomons" was given to mean going to the island, which soon acquired the good captain's name. Solomon was soon handling ten thousand bushels of oysters per month, with some months averaging as many as forty thousand bushels.[28]

Solomons served as a magnet to the oystering trade throughout the region, and it was a rough and tumble lot of men who were employed in this arduous enterprise. In the recollections of one of the latter-day breed of oystermen, Captain W. E. Northam, an interesting picture of Solomons Island at the onset of the 1880s is colorfully provided:

> I have been told that period compared favorably with the pioneer mining in the West. It was 'wild and wooly,' here at Solomon's, caused by a great influx of as motly polyglot a crew as ever garnished the Spanish Main. The vessels were small and poorly equipped, and dredging so young, necessary regulations had not been perfected for governing the industry.[29]

Consequently, considerable conflict arose over territorial rights to the oyster grounds. During the Oyster Wars, as these conflicts were often termed, the Patuxent was usually—but not always—a relatively quiet backwater. However, the area served as a frequent staging ground for oyster hijackers who provided themselves with whiskey and goods at John Hack's store at Drum Point before setting off on their nefarious endeavors.[30]

Oystering in the river was extremely productive. In the spring of 1879 the Calvert County take of oysters from the Patuxent alone totalled 150,000 bushels, which brought a price of seven cents per bushel. And the new bugeyes, being employed more and more frequently, brought in a commensurately larger and larger share of the take each year simply because they were far better equipped to do the job. One vessel, the *Clytie*, the first bugeye built at Solomons, had a carrying capacity of 800 bushels of oysters.[31]

Almost all of the land in the eastern section of Solomons Island was under the ownership of the Isaac Solomon Oyster Canning Company. The potentials for great profit in the Patuxent region did not go long unnoticed, particularly by the larger firms such as J. S. Farrar & Co. of New Haven, Connecticut, which were eager to secure a stake in the rich, untapped bounty of the Chesapeake. Farrar's interest in the Solomon company was considerable. The Connecticut-based firm already operated one cannery in Maryland, at Baltimore, and had decided to open another somewhere else in the state. Solomons Island fitted the bill. Thus, it was not long afterward that John S. Farrar joined forces with Captain Thomas Moore of Dorchester County, owner of a large oyster fleet, and bought out the Solomon operation for the princely sum of $6,225.[32]

In 1880 Moore, who owned and managed the largest workboat fleet on the Bay, well over a hundred boats, arrived at Solomons, started up a shipyard on Back Creek, and with a one third share of the Farrar-Moore concern under his belt, proceeded to superintend the Patuxent oystering operation. Unfortunately, the concern failed to show a profit and within two years was forced to close.[33]

The fin and shellfish fishery apparently suffered little from the Farrar-Moore failure. In the period 1890-91, for which the first reliable records exist for Calvert County, the largest fishery county on the Patuxent, the total take was $188,572 for fish, and $203,68 for shellfish, or 3 percent of the total for the entire state. Of the total effort devoted to the Patuxent fishery, 89 percent of the value was derived from the shellfishing industry, and the remainder from the fin take. The most predominant fish sought were alewives, menhaden, white and yellow perch, shad, and striped bass. In 1890 a total of 1,309 men were employed in the Calvert County fishery industry, and in 1891 the number reached 1,383, or 3 percent of the total manpower of state watermen.[34]

In 1883 navigation of the Patuxent was given a boost when a lighthouse was constructed at the entrance to the river at Drum Point. The lighthouse, first proposed in 1853 but delayed for three decades, replaced a single red buoy at the river entrance. This structure, now preserved and restored at the Calvert Marine Museum, was erected a sixth of a nautical mile offshore in ten feet of water, and was one of sixty screw-pile cottage-type lighthouses in the Chesapeake (of which only three survive). Her first keeper was Benjamin Gray.[35]

During the Gay Nineties the U.S. Navy was much in evidence in the Patuxent. Here was stationed the training ship USS *Severn*, a magnificent white-painted, fully rigged sailing ship commanded by one Captain Seales. Solomons Island was to see much of the U.S. Navy in days to come, especially during special speed trials for the infant U.S. Torpedo Flotilla. The flotilla frequently employed the anchored *Severn* as a base in crossbay speed performance races. These contests were only the forerunner of many naval testing activities to be visited upon the Patuxent. Yet, it was still the commercial fisheries that provided the lifeblood of the region, where many worked the water in the winter and the fields in the summer.

In 1906 the laws of Maryland relating to oyster culture provided that "no person shall be permitted, by lease, assignment, or any other manner, to acquire a greater amount of land than ten acres situated within the territorial limits of the counties, or one hundred acres in any other places." The laws further required that a true and accurate delineation of all natural oyster bars be made in order that oyster culture areas be opened up for leasing. Thus, the Patuxent River oyster beds came up for governmental scrutiny, and their full extent was recorded for the first time. In May 1906, survey units of the U.S. Coast and Geodetic Survey, in concert with the U.S. Bureau of Fisheries and the Maryland Shell Fish Commission were instructed by the chief of the Coast and Geodetic Survey to plot and survey the extent of the oyster bars in the Patuxent River.[36]

As a result of the Patuxent River oyster culture survey, a total of 12,303 acres of natural oyster bars in the Patuxent were surveyed in the territorial waters of Calvert, St. Mary's, Charles, and Prince George's counties. By comparison, the natural oyster bars for the entire state of Connecticut, the birthplace of commercial oyster harvesting in the United States, totaled only 5,770 acres.[37]

As a major commercial offshoot of the fishing industry, one of the few profitable maritime endeavors along the Patuxent was boat construction. Solomons Island shipbuilders ultimately produced nearly 14 percent of all known bugeyes built, the largest of any shipbuilding center in the entire Tidewater region. In 1901 the town of Solomons Island was described as "a perfect nest of little ship-yards, where the bugeye is created in all its glory." Until 1910 the Solomons yards sent an average of two bugeyes per yard each year into the oyster fishery, and many vessels of traditional construction as well.[38]

The days of the bugeye, however, were numbered. Local timber suitable for employment in bugeye construction was growing scarce, and overfishing of the oyster grounds, encouraged by mechanized power equipment, began to deplete the shellfish stock. Many of the shipyards were obliged to turn to recreational boat building and private requests for nonfishing needs. Within a decade the Age of the Bugeye had drawn to a close.

But the steamboats remained.

□   □   □

Before the Civil War the Weems Steamboat Company possessed a veritable monopoly of steamboat access to the Patuxent River. The company had developed and owned or leased many of the landings, as well as the control over who was permitted to use them. In 1861, company vessels (the steamers *Mary Washington*, *Planter*, and *George Weems*) made four trips a week from Baltimore to the Patuxent. With the outbreak of war, however, federal authorities brought chaos to company operations by seizing several steamers, including the *George Weems*, for military service.[39] Despite hindered operations, the Patuxent appears to have remained open to steamer activity, and service by the Weems Line continued, though irregularly. In 1865 the company permitted the *Harriet De Ford* of the Eastern Shore Steamboat Company, and the *Commerce*, an independent operation, to use its Patuxent wharves.[40]

At the close of the Civil War, the steamboat lines of the Chesapeake resumed their full roles in the peacetime transportation operations of the Chesapeake region. The Weems Line was among those capable of successfully returning to full service. There were, unfortunately, many setbacks inherent to the trade. One of the worst occurred on June 10, 1871, when *George Weems* was accidentally destroyed by fire at her Baltimore dock. She was replaced the following year by *Theodore Weems*, built by William H. Skinner and Sons, of Baltimore. The old *George Weems*'s engine was salvaged and placed in the new steamer by Charles Reeder and Sons.[41] By 1879 three of the Weems Line vessels, *Wenonah*, *Planter*, and *Matilda*, sailed from Pier 8, Light Street, Baltimore, for points on the Patuxent as high as Hills Landing.[42]

The river had much to offer in the way of maritime commerce. Henry Williams, agent for the Weems Line, reported that in 1887 there were thirty grist mills, four canning factories, and at least fifty general stores on or near the river which were entirely dependent on the Patuxent for transportation and supply. The value of goods shipped on his line was substantial, $907,500 in that one year alone, and the total value of receipts was estimated at $462,500. The annual trade for the entire river for the previous year was reported at well over half a million dollars, and was termed by federal authorities as "significant." Though most of the river's commerce was conducted primarily with the city of Baltimore, generally funneled through the Weems Line, there was considerable trade with the ports of New York and Philadelphia as well.[43]

Most outward-bound trade items consisted of tobacco, twelve thousand hogsheads in 1886 alone (two-thirds of which was carried by the Weems Line), corn, wheat, poultry, fruits, oysters, and fish. Incoming cargoes usually consisted of farming implements and agricultural necessities which were dispersed through the general stores at ports such as Solomons, Lower Marlborough, Nottingham, Bristol, and Upper Marlboro. There was even a novel industrial development on the river, opposite Nottingham. "A new article has recently been mined upon the banks of the river," reported a federal engineer in 1886, "and the value of the plant engaged in its preparation and shipment amounts to about $10,000. This is silici [silica], which is employed as a filling for bank safes and as a non-conducting covering for boilers and hot air pipes."[44]

By 1888 silting in of the channels at several points in the river was beginning to cause severe navigational problems for steamboat traffic, particularly in the upriver region. Hills Landing, formerly the head of steamer navigation, had to be abandoned in 1885 as a result of the filling in of the main channel approach. By 1888 only lighters and scows could be employed in servicing the landing and the new terminus for the Weems Line's Patuxent run became Bristol Landing. "The pilots," it was regretfully reported, "seem willing to make Bristol the head of navigation." But even Bristol Landing's days were numbered.[45]

Local, state, and federal concerns over the shoaling of the river had seldom been expressed prior to any in-depth examination of the situation. But on September 27, 1886, a U.S. Army engineer, S. T. Albert, was ordered by the Army chief of engineers to conduct a preliminary examination of the river between Hills Landing and the port of Benedict, a distance of twenty-seven miles, to determine "whether the river is worthy of improvement."[46]

Albert recommended that at least four major bars be surveyed for possible consideration for dredging operations: Bristol Bar, opposite

Bristol Landing, which delayed steamer traffic until high water; Swanns Point Bar, three miles below Bristol; Warrens Reach Bar, three miles from Nottingham and fourteen miles above Benedict, which often obstructed passage at low water; and Popes Shoal, three miles above Benedict and opposite Hunting Creek. Although action was ultimately forthcoming, only two of the bars were to receive intense evaluation and excavation. By January 31, 1888, surveys of Bristol Bar and Swanns Point Bar, the most serious obstructions between Benedict and the head of navigation, had been completed, but examinations of Warrens Reach Bar and Popes Shoal were dropped from consideration owing to a lack of funds.[47]

Dredging was imperative if Bristol Landing was to remain open to steamer traffic and keep the lifeblood of commerce flowing down the river. The Weems Line steamer *Westmoreland*, which served the upriver ports, was a vessel of 600 tons and a length of 210 feet (200 feet at the keel), a beam of 32 feet, and a draft of 7 feet unloaded and 8 feet fully laden. Without channel clearance it was obvious that a vessel of this size would soon be cut off from operating up to Bristol.[48]

Albert's report was transmitted to Congress on February 14, 1888, and a watered-down plan calling for the removal of 12,500 cubic yards was approved and a partial appropriation of five thousand dollars granted.[49] The work was deemed necessary and the five thousand dollars appropriated in 1888 was quickly expended. A total of 18,295 cubic yards of mud was removed during the work, and a channel 794 feet long and 12 feet deep was cleared. But further work was necessary. In 1889, one Thomas P. Morgan was given permission to dredge and deposit the spoils from a half mile to two miles north of Bristol Landing. In 1890 the project was continued, with modifications to provide a smaller channel of 120-foot width and 12-foot depth at Bristol Bar, and one of 100-foot length and 9-foot depth at Swanns Point Bar.[50] The work undertaken between 1888 and 1891 was unfortunately to be entirely fruitless, for on May 1, 1899, another examination of the channel at Bristol Landing was required and carried out by Assistant Engineer F. C. Warman, at the direction of Lieutenant Colonel Charles J. Allen, U.S. Army Engineers. More work would be required.[51]

In his report, Warman noted that Bristol Landing was still the head of Patuxent navigation "and consequently is the outlet for produce of quite a large section of the county." There were still two wharves at the landing, although only the steamboat wharf was operative. The steamboat line was still running one boat a week to this wharf regularly during winter and spring, and two boats during the summer and fall. But commerce was drying up. "Very little freight," Warman noted, "is shipped from the landing except by these steamers," although approximately 200 tons of coal, 10,000 bushels of lime, and 200,000 feet of lumber were still being received at the site annually. During the 1898-99 season more than 400,000 feet of

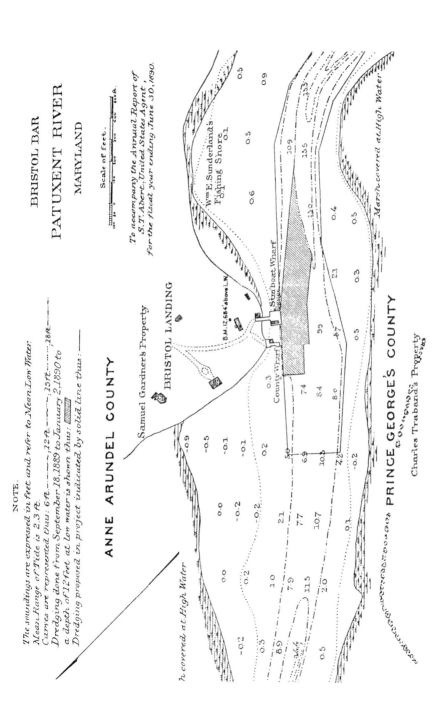

The Patuxent River at Bristol Landing in 1890.

lumber had been received, but this was primarily because of the ongoing construction of the Chesapeake Beach Railroad nearby. "The steamers have no trouble from shoals in navigating the Patuxent River," Warman reported, "until they get to within about 300 feet of the wharf at Bristol Landing."[52]

The Weems Line was anxious to keep the river open for obvious commercial reasons, despite the downturn in trade, and served as the primary source of information for the Corps of Engineers studies, which, as a consequence, frequently appeared to be less than objective. In 1899, Henry Williams, then president of the line, described the business at the landing:

> The business done at that port [Bristol Landing] is quite large [and] for 5 or 6 miles around the people have all their supplies landed at this place and ship all of their crops, etc., from here. The business is mostly done from Baltimore, and I suppose that the value of the goods landed there, which consists of groceries, dry goods, and other articles consumed through the county, is fully $75,000. The shipments consist of tobacco, corn, wheat, poultry, eggs, fruit, and other commodities produced in this section of the country.[53]

Pressure on the government from shippers and carriers to keep the landing open to traffic continued. On June 13, 1902, another evaluation of the Bristol Bar and another review of the commercial reliance on the river was made. But now there was another factor to contend with: the Chesapeake Beach Railroad. Much of the commercial flow from the region was now being siphoned off by the railroad as more and more river traffic was curtailed because of siltation. It was clear that Bristol Landing's days as a commercial crossroads were limited at best.

> There are many other landings on the Patuxent below Bristol Landing, and the commerce of the river, taken as a whole, is considerable, but that at Bristol Landing is very small. Accurate commercial statistics of the business done at this point are nowhere in print: but it transpired at the public hearing that practically all of the business is done by the Weems Steamboat Company, of Baltimore, and amounts to about 2,000 tons annual.[54]

There were now barely 150 departures and arrivals of steam vessels a year and only 40 departures and arrivals of sailing vessels drawing less than ten feet.[55] Commerce declined dramatically.

The 1902 Corps of Engineers assessments noted the sad state of affairs that river traffic at Bristol Landing had come to: "The merchandise received is hauled by carts to two or three county stores, from which the rural population within a radius of 4 or 5 miles is supplied. It is believed that this population is gradually diminishing, as the soil becomes less productive and farm labor more difficult to obtain."[56]

Yet another scheme to dredge the channel was offered up and a contract let to the Maryland Dredging and Construction Company. In 1904 the work was completed. The battle, however, was inevitably going against man. In June 1905 it was reported that the draft at Bristol Landing was barely 9.5 feet and the silt continued to settle. [57]

While the federal government battled the silt, the Weems Line continued to prosper, but not without some difficulties. In 1889, as dredgers diligently cleared the muck from the Patuxent's main channel at Bristol Landing for the first time, *Theodore Weems* was all but destroyed by a fire at her Light Street wharf in Baltimore. The company, fortunately, managed to salvage her hull and the vessel was rebuilt and rechristened as *St. Mary's*. In January 1905 the decision was made to sell the line. Thus, the company's six screw and four side-wheel steamers, all of the company wharves, including twenty-four on the Patuxent, and all other miscellaneous property were disposed of. The line was purchased by the Maryland, Delaware and Virginia Railroad Company, a firm backed by the Pennsylvania Railroad. The MD&V supported by Pennsy money, was able to swallow up three other steamboat lines as well, but had determined quite early to maintain the once profitable Patuxent run. *St. Mary's* would make the regular daytime runs to the lower river, with the fast side-wheel night steamers making the weekly runs to the head of navigation.[58]

The change of ownership for the steamboat line and the consequent alteration in the quality of service had considerable impact on the Patuxent region and was to influence the destiny of commerce at all of the landings serviced. In 1906 only 143 passengers were taken aboard at Bristol Landing. Combined with the notably inferior steamer service, the siltation was making it even more difficult to carry commerce to the head of navigation. Full laden steamers leaving Bristol were drawing up to eight feet, but clearance over the bar was now only eight feet. Obviously, this limited the amount of produce that could be carried aboard from the landing if the ships were to depart in safety. Nevertheless, two boats a week made the run, except between January and March, when only one was provided. Between August and September three boats a week were employed on the run. But the schedule was not rigidly adhered to as in the days of the Weems ownership.[59]

Federal authorities hinted at MD&V inefficiency, and the impact of the irregular schedule on those serviced by the line was significant. "A delay at Bristol Landing," wrote one investigator in 1907, "affects the schedule on the entire river, and uncertainties of delivery have recently compelled merchants and others to ship perishable articles by rail at much higher rates or to haul long distances to wharves on Chesapeake Bay."[60] MD&V's intransigence regarding the merchants' difficulties helped little and the line refused to alter its schedule to improve service. The company's displeasure with the run to the head of navigation, considering the navigational hazards, seemed, however, quite natural. Even the number of light-draft sailing vessels calling at the recently reopened county wharf at Bristol Landing had fallen off considerably. Fewer than ten of these craft now called each year, and the number continued to dwindle. In earlier times, the Weems Line had managed a large fleet of scows between Bristol and Clagetts Landing, a distance upriver of some ten miles, with efficiency. Now, upriver shippers were obliged to haul their stocks over roads to Bristol Landing or Upper Marlboro, both of which were, themselves, being strangled by siltation.[61]

Yet, riverborne transportation was still a necessity. The little community at Bristol alone numbered only several hundred persons, and the regional estimate of the upriver population dependent on waterborne supply numbered over a thousand individuals, 120 of whom were shippers. "This landing," stated one account, "is the outlet for the produce of a fairly large section of the country, and is said to be, next to Lower Marlboro, the most important shipping on the river." Still, at least six general stores were now supported by the landing, all of which were affected by the slackening of steamboat service.[62]

The service of the MD&V, unfortunately, was becoming impossible to maintain at Bristol Landing. People residing within five miles of the landing were beginning to ship more and more of their freight for Chesapeake Bay landings, though most living directly on the river still used the MD&V. Chesapeake Beach Railroad's nearest station was at Pindell, two miles from Bristol Landing, but roads to the station were poor and often impassable, and freight rates were high. Consequently, the diminishing commerce from the landing, more than a thousand tons a year and valued at $125,000, began to find other outlets. By 1907 it was noted that the "commerce of Patuxent River in the aggregate is considerable, but that of Bristol Landing is comparatively small."[63]

On July 15, 1907, Major Spenser Cosby, of the Army Engineers, sounded the death knell for the port of Bristol Landing by recommending that efforts at keeping the channel open to that place be given up.

It will be possible, when the shoaling has made navigation by large steamers impracticable, to abandon Bristol Landing as a wharf on the schedule of the regular line steamers and make Lyons Creek wharf the head of navigation for such boats. A light-draft steam or gasoline lighter could easily and economically be operated from this point to Bristol, Hills, and other landings above. The schedule could also be enlarged to accommodate shippers even better than at present. In view of these facts I am of the opinion the Patuxent River, Maryland, is not worthy of further improvement by the General Government.[64]

Cosby's opinion was heeded.

The MD&V had occasion to experience yet another major catastrophe on the Patuxent not long after Major Cosby's fateful opinion was issued. On December 5, 1907, disaster struck the line when the steamer *St. Mary's* burned while aground in the Patuxent, on Holland Bar. It was later claimed in legend that when she made her last landing before burning, a cat that was carried aboard as ship's mascot jumped overboard and did not return. The steamer *Potomac* was soon afterward scheduled to replace the destroyed steamer.[65]

Still, the company persevered. In 1910 the MD&V purchased the side-wheeler *Three Rivers*, built at Sparrows Point by the Maryland Steel Company for $125,000. Named for the three rivers serviced by the line, the Patuxent, Potomac, and Rappahannock, she was the first steamer to have staterooms on her top deck, and was initially placed on the Potomac River run with the *Northumberland*. The steamer *Anne Arundel* was shifted to the Patuxent run and the *Potomac* moved to take on the Rappahannock operation.[66]

In 1921 an average weekday scheduled run to Patuxent River left Pier 4, Light Street, Baltimore, on Tuesdays and Thursdays at 2:00 P.M., weather permitting. Four stops, at Fairhaven, Plum Point, Dares Beach, and Governors Run, were made before entering the river. The first landing on the Patuxent was made at Millstone Landing. After Millstone, stops were made at Solomons, Spencers Wharf, St. Cutherberts (which had been "temporarily" abandoned by this date), St. Leonards, Sollers, Cashners, Parkers, Forests, Dukes, Holland Point, Benedict, and Lower Marlboro. The return trip left the following morning at 9:30 A.M. and stopped at Magruders Ferry, Hollands Cliffs, Deep Landing, Truemans Point, Leitchs Wharf, and Holland Point again. At 11:30 A.M. the steamer left Holland Point, landed at Benedict, and then departed that wharf at noon for Dukes Wharf, Forests Wharf, Parkers Wharf, Cashners Wharf, and Sotterley. At 2:30 P.M. she left Sotterley for St. Leonards Wharf and Sollers Wharf, in St. Leonards Creek. More stops were made again at St. Cutherberts, Spencers, and Solomons Island. At 5:30 P.M. she left Solomons for Millstone, and after a brief visit there of approximately a half hour departed the Patuxent for several more stops on the Bay at Cove Point, Governors Run, Dare's, Plum Point, and Fairhaven. The steamer then proceeded north to Baltimore, arriving there early the next morning. A weekend run to the Patuxent was made on Saturdays but with additional stops being made on the upriver leg at Whites Landing, Ferry

Landing, Nottingham, and Lyons Creek. Occasional runs were still made as far north as Bristol Landing, but these became more infrequent as time passed, and by the 1920s had all but ceased.[67]

Under the direction of the Pennsylvania Rairoad, the MD&V was increasingly unable to function profitably. Finally, in 1922, the president of the Pennsy stated in a speech that two of its major subsidiary operations, the Baltimore, Chesapeake and Atlantic Railway Company, and the MD&V would have to be abandoned because of stiff competition with ferry lines and overland motor trucking firms. He pointed out that the MD&V in particular, had been losing money since 1913.[68]

On May 7, 1923, the MD&V was dismembered into three parcels at a foreclosure sale. The second included the company's Chester River route, the Patuxent River route, and the steamers *B.S. Ford*, *Corsica*, and *Westmoreland*. *Ford* and *Westmoreland*, the most familiar steamers of all to folks along the Patuxent, failed to attract buyers at the sale and were eventually acquired by another Pennsy subsidiary and sold. By 1924, steamboat operations on the Patuxent had been materially curtailed by the new owners of the route, the Baltimore and Virginia Steamboat Company, another Pennsy subsidiary, partially as a result of another major disaster, the burning of the *Three Rivers* off the mouth of the river on July 5,1924.[69]

Between 1924 and 1929 several of the line's Potomac River steamers, including the *Calvert*, made frequent but irregular calls at these same ports. Harder times lay ahead.[70] In 1929 economic tribulations befell America, and the Baltimore and Virginia Steamboat Company was soon cast, as were thousands of other businesses, into the vortex of the Great Depression. By the middle of 1930 the line had nine steamers, although there was but a single weekly trip to the Patuxent. There were, however, irregular stops made by the steamer *Piankatank*, whose regular run was to the Great Wicomico and Piankatank Rivers. This craft is known to have called on occasion at Solomons and Millstone Landing with excursionists. Despite every effort to maintain service, however, the line could continue no longer. By 1932 the line had been declared bankrupt in the U.S. District Court of Maryland, and on March 1 of that year all of its steamer operations on the Chesapeake and its tributaries, with the exception of the Love Point Ferry to Kent Island, were suspended.[71]

Almost immediately, two independent companies were formed from the bare bones of the Baltimore and Virginia line. These were the Western Shore Steamboat Company (WSSC) and the New Castle Terminal Company. The WSSC was backed by a group of produce dealers and merchants in Baltimore specifically to continue the needed steamer operations down the Bay upon which their businesses depended. The steamers *Potomac* and *Virginia* were among the vessels employed, though now only weekend excursions to the mouth of the Patuxent were being carried out. But overland vehicular and ferry operations were cutting deeply into WSSC business and by 1938 the company, strapped with the dinosaur of another era, was forced to close down.[72]

The end of the Steamboat Age on the Patuxent had arrived.

❑   ❑   ❑

The demise of regular steamer navigation on the Patuxent River sounded the death knell to the role of the river as a major communication and transportation arm of Maryland commerce. Activities dependent on water transportation or support, with the exception of ferry operations, either collapsed or found other outlets. The few remaining towns and landings along the river shores shriveled and died. Nottingham, Lower Marlboro, Benedict, and a few others were mere skeletons of their former selves. Others, such as Upper Marlboro, had long since been weaned from dependence on the water but were now little more than sleepy hamlets.

Yet, at Solomons, that wonderful deep-water fishing village at the mouth of the river, some notable events occurred. In 1892 the U.S. Weather Bureau had established a station on the island under the direction of Dr. Henry Marsh. In 1905 the U.S. government selected the mouth of the Patuxent as the best site in the Tidewater to test the famous *Dewey* floating dry dock, which had been constructed in part at Sparrows Point, near Baltimore, and completed at Solomons by the Maryland Steel Company. This mammoth sixteen-thousand-ton vessel, which was five hundred feet long and one hundred feet wide, was unique in that it did its own docking and interlocking of ships. Deep water was a prerequisite for the test, and the waters off Solomons Island fitted the bill. The final test for the *Dewey* was the placement of the battleships *Iowa* and *Colorado* upon the craft to gauge its strength, a feat passed with flying colors. The great vessel was then hauled halfway around the world to the Philippines, where it was placed in full operational service for the American Pacific Fleet.[73]

With American entry as a combatant in World War I, several luxury liners then in American ports and belonging to the German Lloyd Line were impounded by the U.S. government. These vessels *(Kronprinzessin Cecelie, George Washington* [a recent acquisition from America], *Kaiser Wilhelm II,* and *Vaterland)* were, after much deliberation, dispatched to a permanent anchorage southwest of Point Patience and put in mothballs. The ships eventually became known as the Ghost Fleet of Solomons, although one of the vessels, the *George Washington,* was eventually refitted and given the honor of carrying President Woodrow Wilson to the peace conference at Versailles.[74]

In 1922 the Chesapeake Biological Laboratory was established on the island under the direction of Dr. R. V. Truitt. Yet, progress on the lower Patuxent was slow in coming. In 1925 the elementary school system of lower Calvert County was consolidated into a single school at Solomons.

At this time a forty-two-foot boat, *James Aubry,* originally a log brogan employed in the fishing and oystering trade, was taken into service by the county to serve as a schoolboat to carry children, isolated by the myriad waterways converging behind the island, to and from the school. *Aubry* remained in continuous service from September 1925 to June 1935, the only vessel east of the Mississippi serving in such a capacity at that time.[75]

The schoolboat was not the only ferry service available on the Patuxent. Indeed, a considerable amount of cargo and passenger service noted in river traffic statistics from the 1920s onward was attributable to ferry operations—operations that had, in fact, helped drive the steamboats out of business. With the reestablishment of ferry service across the Patuxent between Solomons and Millstone in about 1915 and between Benedict and Hallowing Point in the late 1920s, the two shores of the lower Patuxent were again loosely linked for the first time in decades.[76]

At Solomons, Captain Ed Swift, a Virginian who came to the island in about 1915 to fish pound nets, established the Solomons–Millstone Ferry when fishing declined. The service was admittedly primitive. Employing his sharp-ended fishing boat, Swift simply towed a small scow on which he could load a single automobile. About 1925 this operation was improved when a larger boat was built at the M. M. Davis and Son yard at a cost of $1,106.16. This vessel was constructed along the lines of a small tug. Swift christened her *Otho,* after his son. Passengers could now be conveyed across the river in comfort under a canopy cover while their cars were towed behind aboard a larger scow. Fares were a dollar per car and passenger. There was no schedule; service was provided on demand. [77]

Swift's ferry operation was to continue until 1933 when a hurricane drove his vessel, along with many others, up the Narrows behind the island. The destruction wrought by the storm, which flooded the entire island, was terrible to the Solomons shipping interests, and service vessels such as the *Otho* were among the hardest hit. Many never saw service again. In 1934, Captain John Quincy Adams of Colonial Beach, Virginia, opened a new ferry link between St. Mary's and Calvert Counties with the ferryboat *Miss Constance,* a barrel-sided, square-ended vessel built to accommodate both passengers and vehicles. This craft was 59.8 feet long, and 25.1 feet abeam. Unlike *Otho,* her deck was capable of carrying several vehicles at a time. Scheduled runs were made between Millstone, in St. Mary's County, and Captain Rodie Langley's dock at Solomons for a fare of $1.25.[78]

Another ferry service, home ported at Benedict, was opened in the late 1920s when Captain Perry G. Henderson began employing a motorized scow to ferry automobiles and passengers across the river to Hallowing (now Hollowing) Point. Henderson, unlike Adams, did not run on a regular schedule, but responded to signals from the Calvert County side when service was required; by day the sounding of the automobile's horn, at night the blinking of the auto headlights. Although service was neither speedy (and perhaps not the most efficient), it was always there. Captain Henderson's operations were finally terminated in 1951 when the Patuxent River Bridge was constructed between Benedict and Hollowing Point.[79]

Small boat operations, despite the peaks and valleys of national and regional economics, continued on a day-to-day and year-to-year cycle almost without fail. Typical of such operations at the end of each year's oyster season were those of James Webster Dixon. "Cap'm" Dixon, from the time the herring run began in March until late in May, was in the fish running business. A heavy demand existed among the farmers of St. Mary's County, from Cuckholds Creek all the way upriver to Trent Hall, for fish to feed their tenants and hired field laborers. Captain Philip Vail of Solomons, who regularly fished ten- to twelve-pound nets stretched from Cove to Cedar Points, supplied the fish. Captain Dixon, among others, engaged in supplying the fish to the Patuxent River farmers.[80]

Leaving home on Mill Creek in complete darkness, Dixon arrived at Vail's pound nets by dawn where he loaded his log canoe *Laura* with as many as twenty-three thousand herring for which he paid $1.00 per thousand. The route up the Patuxent along the St. Mary's side included stops at Cuckholds Creek, Sotterley, Sandgate, Horse Landing, Persimmon Creek, and Trent Hall. Sales were made at these stops on designated days. Farmers, alerted to the day for their landing, arrived by ox cart or wagon, and filled up every conceivable kind of container with herring at $2.50 per thousand. At Persimmon Creek, Thomas Holton acted as agent for Dixon, drumming up trade among the inland farmers. During the season an individual farmer may have bought as many as fifteen thousand herring, salted them down and stored them for later consumption. No other kind of meat could be supplied to large numbers of people so cheaply. Herring was cheap; the more expensive shad and rockfish were boxed in ice and shipped three times a week by steamboat to Baltimore's fish markets.[81]

When the herring run was over, it was time for the strawberry season to open on the Eastern Shore. Large numbers of pickers were needed for the harvesting of the fragile fruit at the moment of ripeness, and the western shore of the Chesapeake provided much of the manpower. The cheapest, quickest, and easiest way to get over there was by boat, and soon the *Laura* was crossing the bay to Crisfield with men and older boys from the Coster area of Calvert County to pick berries in the fields around Marion and Hopewell.[82]

The harvesting season lasted two or three weeks, but Captain Dixon did not stay in Crisfield for the duration. The trip back home was not wasted, nor could it be an empty one, so he loaded ice in the hold of his log canoe and delivered it to the icehouse at Solomons. Since, at this time, almost all of the ice in this region was imported from Maine by the schooner trade, that arriving from Crisfield was heartily welcomed.

By the 1920s bugeye construction had long since ceased, but the production of skipjacks and other fine sailing craft in the Solomons yards continued unabated. The M. M. Davis Yard, earlier famed throughout the Tidewater for its sturdy schooners and workboats, had also turned to the production of special order yachts and racing boats. In 1937 the Davis Yard built the sleek racing boat *Manitou*, which had been designed by the firm of Sparkman and Stephens, Inc., of New York. The *Manitou* became internationally famous and won no fewer than three of the esteemed Mackinac, Michigan, races, and was later sailed by President John F. Kennedy. In 1968 the vessel was sold by the Defense Surplus Agency to her present owners, the Harry Lundeberg School of Seamanship at Piney Point, Maryland.[83]

With the onset of the Great Depression, Calvert was still the largest of the counties bordering on the Patuxent to be involved in the fishing industry. It was thus not surprising that the presence of many game fish began to draw the attentions of sport fishermen to the lower river. By the 1940s it was common among sport fishermen to say that "once you get the Solomons habit you never shake it." In 1941 it was reported that "Solomons has become a Summer resort for fishing enthusiasts, and on the land side the harbour serves as an anchorage for a large commercial fishing fleet. The deepest water is nearly one hundred feet and averages fifty feet deep on much of the river near the town, and the island boasts a harbour two miles wide."[84]

The U.S. Navy was well aware of the deep waters of the lower Patuxent, and when World War II threatened to engulf America in its turmoil, the river was viewed as a superb location for a naval establishment. In 1941-42 the Patuxent Naval Air Test Center was constructed on the site of old Fort Mattapany, and the following year an amphibious training base was constructed at Solomons. Soon, there was also a Navy mine test station erected at Point Patience. Unfortunately, as a result of security measures required by the war, much of the lands and waters of the region about the lower river were turned to military needs such as weapons testing and were all but closed to commercial fishing. Party boat operations ceased. Damage to the fishing industry was severe. It was later reported in the Washington press: "Dredging and bombing during construction and operations of the bases resulted in permanent destruction of many acres of oyster bottom near Solomons..." and as late as 1949 limited restrictions on fishing activities remained in effect.[85]

The war years, however, did bring about the revival of the ferry services on the lower Patuxent. With the construction of the Patuxent Naval Air

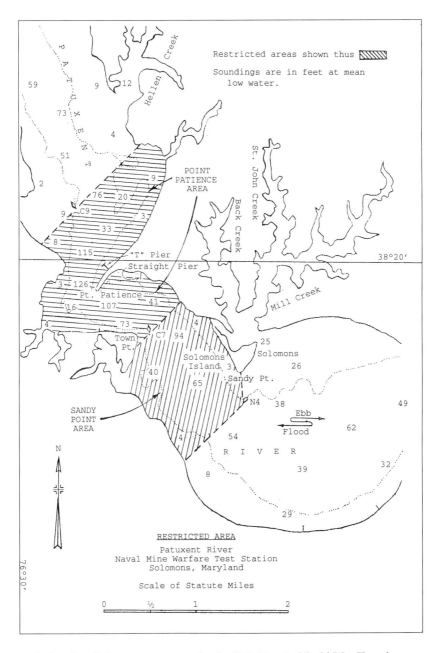

Restricted areas shown thus ░░░░░

Soundings are in feet at mean low water.

A flyer handed out to watermen by the U.S. Navy in World War II to show
restricted areas of the Patuxent reserved for naval mine warfare testing.
Courtesy of the Calvert Marine Museum

Test Center, much of the work force was provided by Calvert County, and transportation across the two-mile-wide river was essential. Captain Leon Langley provided that transportation with his forty-eight-foot bay-built boat, *Miss Solomons*. Capable of carrying up to forty-nine passengers, this vessel made one round trip to Patuxent Naval Center nearly every day for thirty-five years, despite rain, wind and fog. When weather absolutely prohibited transit, workers were obliged to make the hour-long trip by car.[86]

The military activities about the mouth of the Patuxent were not the only villains to wreak destruction on the river. The forces of nature herself were just as evident. Erosion had become a serious problem. Between 1866 and 1949, one shoreline area between Chalk Point and Black Swamp Creek had eroded a maximum linear recession of up to 100 feet in spots. Between Milltown Landing and Rock Creek there were areas of linear recession of up to 300 feet. Shore Point had been cut back 120 feet, and numerous other areas had lost 100 feet or more. The lower half of the river seemed to have a higher rate of annual loss than the upper reaches. Yet, in other areas, the continued siltation had begun to establish new shorelines through accretion. South of Black Swamp Creek, for instance, there had been a maximum linear building out of 150 feet. Between Chalk Point and Truemans Point a new shore had been constructed out 100 feet. Between Short Point and Magruders Landing there had been a maximum linear building out of over 120 feet. And the river had only begun to experience the harrowing impact of urbanization.[87]

By the 1960s southern Maryland had been included in the outer orbital fringes of an ever enlarging metropolitan complex composed of the cities of Washington, Baltimore, and Annapolis. Urbanization was sweeping in on the upriver areas with developments at Laurel, Bowie, and near Upper Marlboro. Development and utilization of the Patuxent drainage for the benefits of these and other urban centers had been considered years before, but were now becoming a reality. Pollution and abuse of the upriver areas, from gravel mining, housing developments, sewage treatment, and many other causes soon began to have their effects. Downriver, the onslaught was not as dramatic, but was felt nevertheless. The construction of a massive power station at Chalk Point had debatable effects on the river's ecology, and the recent subdividing of land for housing developments on tributaries such as Battle Creek and St. Leonard's Creek heralded the wave of the future.[88]

On the morning of December 17, 1977, one of the most significant engineering accomplishments ever undertaken on the Patuxent River was dedicated at a formal ceremony and opened to the general public. This singularly important achievement was the completion of the Governor Thomas Johnson Memorial Bridge, constructed at a cost of $26 million and spanning the deepest portion of the Patuxent River just below Point

Patience on the Calvert County side to the Town Creek vicinity on the St. Mary's County side. More than twenty-two thousand citizens of Calvert County and forty-seven thousand citizens of St. Mary's County were now linked, and modern urbanization of a once sleepy backwater was assured.[89] At quiet little Solomons, spacious marinas were built to host the multitude of plastic sailboats and pleasure yachts that had arrived to replace the grimy fleet of workboats that had once dominated the scene. Elegant hotels, restaurants, "tiki bars," fast food joints, and other accoutrements of modern urban culture were not far behind. Nearby, the land was parceled out, divided, subdivided, sold, and turned into vast housing tracts for many who sought to own a piece of tranquility far from the maddening crowd. And in the doing, the tranquil and once bountiful Patuxent became an open sewer. The pitiful remnants of marine life that survived in its now chocolate-brown waters were condemned by state health authorities as too poisonous to eat. Oysters served in restaurants at Solomons were now frequently imported from as far away as Louisiana.

The evening before the dedication of the magnificent new bridge, the stalwart little ferryboat *Miss Solomons* tied up at her dock at Solomons for the last time, a relic of a vanished and simpler age.

SEVEN

Survey

My meeting with Dr. Ralph Eshelman in the quaint little schoolhouse-turned-museum at Solomons on that cold December day in 1977 proved to be more than I or my colleague, Nicholas Freda, who had arranged the conference, had hoped for. Eshelman, the young head of the new Calvert Marine Museum, indeed its first director, was a rangy-looking fellow, a vertebrate paleontologist by training from the University of Michigan. The institution he managed was barely five years old and, at first glance, seemed an odd place for an "old bones man" to be administering. Yet, upon his arrival in 1974 he had launched into the job with unparalleled vigor. In the few years he had been there, his achievements had garnered statewide attention. Although armed with little capital, one of Eshelman's and the museum's first miracles had been to rescue the condemned Drum Point Lighthouse, one of the last screw-pile lighthouses left in America, from demolition. The success of the project was largely due to the director's limitless zeal, ability, charisma, organizational talent, and considerable community support. Built in 1883 and decommissioned in 1963, the lighthouse was indeed an historic treasure. After great effort, the light was moved to the museum grounds and fully restored. It was eventually adopted as the unofficial symbol of southern Maryland. Eshelman had also built the museum's historic watercraft collection into one of the finest in the Tidewater and had expanded the tiny museum library into one of the best marine reference collections in Maryland. But most important, he had given the museum an institutional philosophy and a mission: to collect, research, and interpret the estuarine, paleontological, and historic maritime record of the tidal Patuxent River for the education and benefit of the people of Maryland and the nation.[1] Considering the extent and richness of the river and region, the mission might have been, for anyone less dedicated, overwhelming. For Ralph Eshelman, it was a challenge of unparalleled opportunity.

The Patuxent River is the largest intrastate river in Maryland, having a length of approximately 110 miles and draining 9.5 percent of the landmass of the state. In 1976 the river basin was 50 percent forested, 35 percent cultivated, and the remainder, the fastest changing section of all, under intensive urban development. With its slender, meandering trunk

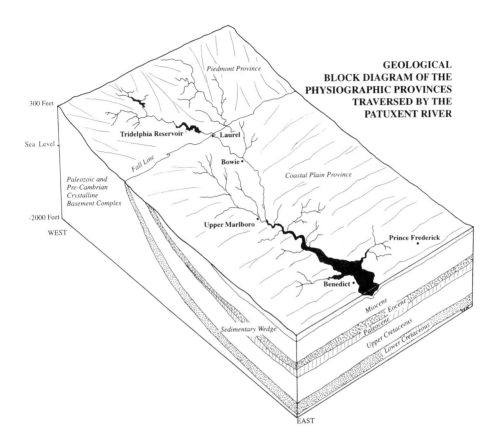

**GEOLOGICAL
BLOCK DIAGRAM OF THE
PHYSIOGRAPHIC PROVINCES
TRAVERSED BY THE
PATUXENT RIVER**

Geological provinces traversed by the Patuxent River.
Drawing by Ralph E. Eshelman

and myriad tributaries weaving through Montgomery, Howard, Prince George's, Charles, Calvert, and St. Mary's Counties on its way to the Chesapeake Bay, it is a linear estuary with the head of tidal influence reaching a full fifty-six miles above its mouth. Early on, naturalists and scientists had been attracted to the region because of the extensive fossil deposits and fine geological exposures lacing its banks, ranging in age from 10 million to 135 million years old.

The navigable portion of the river basin lies entirely within the Atlantic Coastal Plain, a geologic province characterized by a sedimentary wedge of clays, silts, sands, and gravels eroded from the Appalachian Mountains and representing the product of marine transgression from 150 million years ago to the present (Table 1). During the last glaciation, 25,000 to

Table 1

Essential Characteristics of Formations of Outcropping in Patuxent River Basin

System	Series	Group	Stratigraphic Unit	Thickness (feet)	Lithologic Character	Economic Potential
Quaternary	Pleistocene		Lowland Deposits	0–150	Interbedded quartz gravel, medium to coarse sand, and silt-clay; grayish white to dark greenish gray; peat, and sparse molluscan fauna.	Sand and gravel.
	Pliocene		Upland Deposits	0–70	Quartz gravel and medium to coarse sand overlain by massive silt; orange to reddish brown where oxidized, otherwise pale gray; rare plant fossils.	Sand and gravel.
		Chesapeake	St. Mary's Formation	0–80	Interbedded bluish gray silt-clay and fine argillaceous sand, glauconitic in part; fossiliferous.	Lightweight aggregate.
	Miocene		Choptank Formation	0–55	Interbedded bluish gray to gray green silt-clay and abundantly fossiliferous fine to medium sand.	
Tertiary			Calvert Formation	0–150	Olive-gray to olive-brown, fine argillaceous sand, silt and clay; diatomaceous silt near base; some beds abundantly fossiliferous.	Diatomite.
		Pamunkey	Nanjemoy Formation	0–120	Dark greenish gray, argillaceous, glauconitic sand and silt; minor dark gray silty clay; fossiliferous.	Glauconite.
	Eocene		Marlboro Clay	0–30	Pale red to silvery gray plastic clay with thin lenses of pale gray silt; sparingly lignitic.	Brick clay.
			Aquia Formation	0–100	Dark greenish gray, fine to medium glauconitic sand and silt; sporadic calcite-cemented sandstone; fossiliferous.	Glauconite.
	Paleocene		Monmouth Formation	0–40	Dark greenish gray to black, fine micaceous clayey sand and silt; quartzose gravel at base; fossiliferous.	
Cretaceous		Potomac	Patapsco Formation	0–200	Red and gray mottled silty clay and fine to medium, gray to yellow sand; rare plant fossils.	

12,000 years ago, the river basin was heavily forested by spruce, pine, fir, and birch, and later beech hemlock. By the time sea-level inundation began as a result of glacial melt, freshwater streams draining the area had already begun to form the proto-Patuxent drainage, with the ancient paleochannel eventually reaching its maximum depth of 140 feet at Point Patience. As early Holocene sea levels continued to rise, the Patuxent and its tributaries near the mouth were drowned, and about 8,000 years ago great inland swamps were created. Vegetation along the uplands soon changed to forests of oak, chestnut, and hickory. By 6,000 B.P. (before present) the river had become saline enough to support oysters. Anadromous fish species pressed their freshwater spawning grounds further upstream as sea levels continued to rise and brackish waters began to penetrate the river's lower reaches. By 3,000 B.P. oysters had reached their uppermost limits in the river near present-day Mount Calvert.[2]

When the first colonists arrived in southern Maryland, they discovered a vast expanse of unbroken hardwood forests dominated by chestnut, hickory, birch, and sweet gum. It was a most dramatic vista that had greeted the early settlers. "Fine groves of trees appear, not choked with thorns or undergrowth," reported a delighted Father Andrew White, "but growing at intervals as if planted by the hand of man, so that you can drive a four-horse carriage wherever you choose through the midst of the trees." The many hickories, the oaks "so straight and tall that beams sixty feet long and two and a half feet wide can be made of them," and the cypress trees, "growing to a height of eighty feet before they have any branches around their trunks" all excited the wonder of the colonists.[3]

Yet it was not to be from the verdant forest that colonial prosperity was derived, but from the fertile soils beneath it and from the excellent natural deep harbors of the Patuxent and neighboring waters. With few settlements over five miles from a good landing, the river provided cheap and easy communications and transportation. The white settlers' deforestation and poor agricultural practices, however, had soon transmogrified the region. Within but a few years none of the original virgin forests remained, nearly all having undergone at least one cycle of clearing for agriculture, and in some cases abandonment and reforestation. With land clearance, runoff increased siltation in the river system dramatically. Before the Revolution, vessels of 300 tons could travel fifty miles upstream, and the waters above Queen Anne's Town were navigable by flat-bottomed boats for another twenty-five miles. By 1824, navigation for seagoing vessels of up to 250 tons ended at Nottingham, forty-six miles upriver. By 1945, navigation of any sort had ended beyond Lyons Creek. Although the shallow-draft steamboats had continued to operate, albeit with difficulty, until the 1930s, seagoing commerce was at an end.

The damage was irreversible. In 1966, a Johns Hopkins University study estimated that 235,000 tons of sediment per square mile was annually

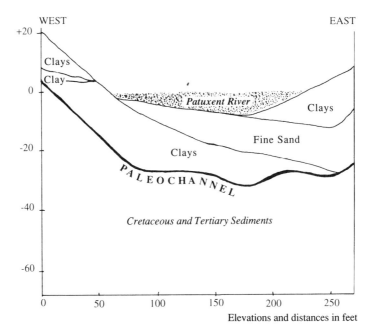

WEST

EAST

+20

Clays

Clay

0

Patuxent River

Clays

Fine Sand

-20

Clays

PALEOCHANNEL

-40

Cretaceous and Tertiary Sediments

-60

0   50   100   150   200   250

Elevations and distances in feet

Geological cross section of Patuxent River at Hills Bridge.
Drawing by Ralph E. Eshelman

running into the river from its onetime navigable head at Queen Anne's to Solomons, with an overall sediment load for the entire basin estimated at 193,000 tons per square mile. At one test area, between Hellen Creek and Broomes Island, the waterway had been reduced in depth five to ten feet between 1859 and 1944.[4] But worse degradation was to follow. After World War II, urban, commercial, and industrial development, resulting in even further land clearance, pollution, and blight along great reaches of its upland shores, began to spread at an alarming rate, impacting the natural and historic resources even more severely. By the mid-1970s, entire sections of the river were declared biologically dead, and in some areas the waters had become little more than open sewers.[5]

Clearly, any effort to locate and assess the physical remnants of the river's rich history lying beneath its waters and muds and along its convoluted shorelines was likely to prove a most formidable task indeed.

The project design that I suggested was to be, with little in the way of monetary support or sophisticated technical capabilities available, flexible enough for the resources readily in hand. As the work proceeded, an increase in funding would be necessary during each successive stage and would be jointly promulgated through grants and museum fund-raising efforts.

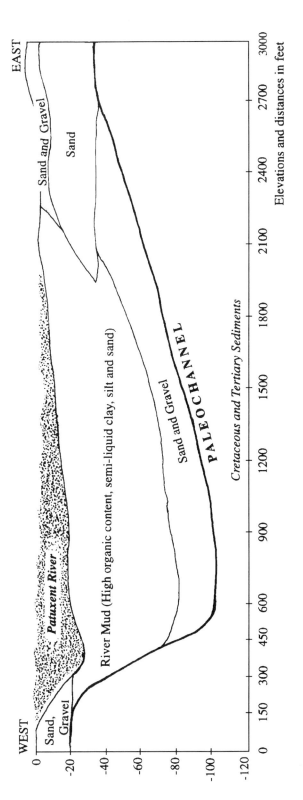

Geological cross section of Patuxent River at Benedict Bridge. Drawing by Ralph E. Eshelman

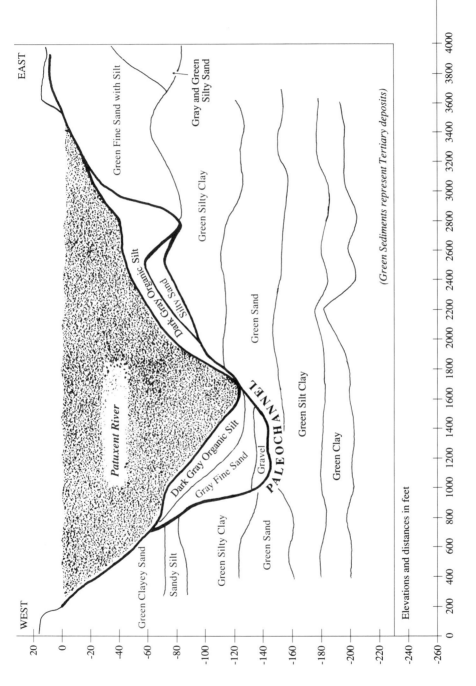

Geological cross section of Patuxent River at Thomas Johnson Bridge. Drawing by Ralph E. Eshelman

The project, as envisioned, would pass through three distinctive stages. The preliminary reconnaissance phase during 1978-79 would consist of archival research; the gathering of oral history and folk traditions relative to the maritime heritage of the river and its people; examination of locally known shipwreck sites, inundated sites, and related land sites of an archaeological or historical nature; field evaluation of the estuarine environment of the Patuxent over the colonial era stretch of navigable water as far north as Queen Anne's Town; and the construction of a foundation suitable for forwarding the next stage of survey.[6]

Phase 1 would begin during the summer of 1979 and be completed by the fall. The phase was to consist of an intensive remote sensing survey of four environmentally and historically representative transects of the river to locate and identify unknown submerged cultural resources lying beneath its waters and silts (See Table 2). Phase 2 would be conducted during the summer of 1980 and would focus on the testing of specific sites in each of the four transects, the excavation of significant sites, and the limited recovery of representative cultural materials lying beneath the surface. The post-survey efforts would focus on the stabilization and mending of artifacts recovered, reporting on the survey

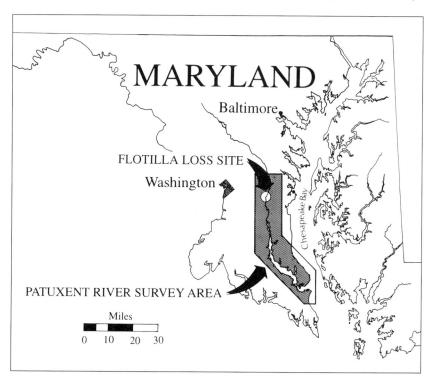

The Patuxent River Project survey area.

Table 2

Environmental Variables Considered in Transect Area Selection

Factor	Point Patience Test Area	St. Leonard's	Nottingham	Lyons Creek	Selby–Spyglass
Maximum channel depth	135 feet	25 feet	30 feet	6 feet	30 feet
Minimum channel depth	125 feet	4 feet	6 feet	1.5 feet	5 feet
Bottom composition (channel)	Mud	Mud/sand	Mud/sand	Mud	Sand/mud/organic matter
Bottom composition (nearshore)	Sand/shell	Sand/pebbles/shell	Pebbles/sand	Mud	Sand/clay
Salinity	Salt	Brackish-fresh to heavy brackish	Brackish	Fresh	Slight brackish to fresh
Eroded areas	0	2	1	1	1
Tributaries (within transect area)	0	14	4	0	15
Maximum current flow	4 knots	Minimal	2 knots	Minimal	1–2 knots
Length of transect		4.3 miles	0.7 miles	1 mile	6.5 miles
Prevalence of wetlands in transect geography	0%	25% or less	50%	50%+	75%+

Table 3

Historic Variables of Transect Areas

Factor	Point Patience Test Area	St. Leonard's	Nottingham	Lyons Creek	Selby–Spyglass
River Ports	0	1	1	0	2
Tobacco Inspection Stations	0	1	1	0	1
Aboriginal Sites	0	2	8	1	7
Military Establishments and Fortifications	1	6+	2	0	0
Battle Sites	0	2	0	0	1
Known, Reported, or Conjectured Shipwrecks and Abandoned Vessels	1	6+	3	1	23+
Ferry Landings	0	0	1	1	2
Steamboat Landings	0	2	2	1	4
Colonial Harbor and Landing Facilities	0	2+	1	1(?)	4
Bridges	1	0	0	0	2

findings, and exhibition of select materials in a display on the maritime history of the river.[7]

Eshelman was more than game. To mount any project to inventory and evaluate the submerged cultural resources of the Patuxent River basin would directly address one of the primary missions of the museum, namely, the development of an understanding of the history of the Patuxent. He enthusiastically promised to throw the full resources of the Calvert Marine Museum behind a holistic archaeological survey of the waterway in a joint effort with Nautical Archaeological Associates, Inc. It was a leap of faith for a man I had never met before to commit himself and his young museum to a project that would last more than three years, cost an undetermined amount of money, and be undertaken by a company of unproven abilities. Moreover, the end objectives were anything but modest, for we would be conducting the first underwater archaeological survey of an entire river system in the United States in a pure research effort searching for and documenting such diverse resources as inundated aboriginal and historic sites, colonial tobacco inspection stations and landings, wharves, piers, ferries, plantation landings, bridges, harbors, military establishments, anchorages, battle sites, shipwrecks, and derelicts, and, of course, the final resting place of the U.S. Chesapeake Flotilla (See Table 3).[8]

The 1978 survey team was to consist of both museum and NAA personnel. The lion's share of archival and actual field investigation, however, would fall upon my colleagues in NAA, a multidisciplinary group of scientists, historians, and professionals in numerous fields who had participated in many of the early underwater archaeology projects in the United States and Central America. Our organization, incorporated and chartered in Maryland in 1973 as a nonprofit marine archaeological research corporation (the first of its kind on the mid-Atlantic seaboard), was small, consisting of only seven men, all with different professional backgrounds: Dr. Fred Hopkins, Jr., our principal researcher, was dean of the Graduate School at the University of Baltimore, a professional historian and an author, and one of the most adept men I had ever encountered at plumbing the mysteries of an archives; Kenneth Hollingshead, a marine environmental affairs expert, marine biologist with the National Oceanic and Atmospheric Administration, and veteran diver, had cut his teeth on archaeological projects in Mexico and Belize; Larry Pugh, a senior oceanographer with NOAA, was an amateur archaeologist of more than ten years' diving experience; Nicholas M. Freda, a professional photographer and designer, was also a veteran archaeological diver whose work had taken him from the water of New Jersey to the Yucatan; Eldon Volkmer, a senior communications engineer with the National Aeronautics and Space Administration (NASA), and amateur archaeologist, was also a diver with nearly two decades of experience on three continents.

Survey

My brother Dale Shomette was an ex-Coast Guard diver and amateur archaeologist; and there was also myself, a maritime historian and staff member of the Library of Congress.[9]

□   □   □

Within days of the meeting with Eshelman, preliminary archival research on the history of the river, with a special accent on the War of 1812, had begun. Fred Hopkins began immediately to systematically address the thousands of feet of microfilmed war records in the National Archives to extract the official unpublished documentation of the U.S. Chesapeake Flotilla, the progress of the conflict on the Patuxent, the loss of the fleet, and the subsequent salvage records, if any. His research, despite a seemingly unending chain of dead ends, proved wonderfully fruitful; everything from muster lists to armament specifications began to turn up.

At the same time, I launched into researching the campaign from British resources, such as ship logs, captain's reports, and admiralty communiqués, primarily from the Admiralty Records Collection in the Public Record Office in London. It was a wonderful vein of data to mine, one that revealed not only the untold—and unpopular—side of the war on the river that had never seen the light of publication, but the story from the side of the enemy. Yet Admiral Cockburn's own personal reports of the affair, those that provided the eyewitness specifics and precise location of the flotilla's loss, were missing from the Public Record Office.

Incredibly, I found his critical correspondences regarding the Patuxent campaign and the destruction of Barney's barges not in England, but in Washington, D.C., housed in the Manuscript Collection of the Library of Congress, right across from my office! Upon investigation I soon learned that all of the admiral's manuscripts, including logs, journals, fleet orders, correspondences, and miscellany, spanning his entire naval career, had been purchased by the library in 1909 from the holdings of one Karl Hiersemann of Leipzig, Germany, and in 1912 from the collections of one Francis Edwards of London, and totalled eighty-two volumes. Combined with Fred's findings, the manuscripts were to prove pivotal in our search for, and interpretation of, the remains of the flotilla.

Research on Barney's barges, however, was but a small portion of the archival work that would be undertaken over the next three years. The historic record of the development of the river's contact-period occupation (namely, the period following the arrival of European explorers, traders, and colonists in which the natives began to embrace a dependent culture), as evidenced by no fewer than seventeen Indian towns and villages noted by Captain John Smith during his visit in 1608, would be sought and documented, as would that of forty-two riverfront colonial plantation sites, fourteen townsites, and twelve tobacco inspection stations along the navigable Patuxent drainage. We would ultimately docu-

131

ment the location, development, and demise of no fewer than fifty ferry operations, bridges, wharves, and landings erected between 1650 and 1976, thirteen military establishments, fourteen military engagements and naval battles, and finally a total of 142 known or reported shipwrecks, naval losses, or derelicts lying in the river or in adjacent waters. For the first time in its long history, the archival record of the Patuxent River and the people who flourished along its banks, traversed its waters, and thrived upon its bounties would be explored as never before.

And then, and only then, we would seek out the remnants of that which had never been recorded, the shrouded bones of history itself.

EIGHT

Shipwrecks and Saturday Night Specials

Field work on the Patuxent, buttressed by an ever-growing compendium of archival data, largely researched by Fred Hopkins and reinforced by an ongoing program of oral history, began in April 1978 with an in-depth reconnaissance of St. Leonard's Creek. Utilizing several small craft, including a diminutive pram dubbed *Sneaky Seaweed,* a larger service boat called *Muskrat* (loaned to the project by the state-run Patuxent River Park at Jug Bay), a small Boston Whaler, and a strip chart fathometer provided by the Naval Weapons Test Center at Solomons, the survey began.

Our initial efforts focused on conducting a hands-on underwater investigation of known or reported shipwreck sites on the creek. Some sites, such as a charted wreck noted as lying off a wharf near Fort Hill (the site of one of Barney's marine batteries), no longer existed, having been removed by a special state-funded operation called the Maryland Derelict Boat Removal Program![1] Others, such as a wreck lying in a shallow-water cove well up the creek and noted by a local eel fisherman as having been visible a quarter century ago, were more speculative. The latter, consisting of little more than keel and keelson and a few strakes, ceiling planks, and framing timbers, and situated directly adjacent to the site of another of Barney's land batteries, seemed like a prime candidate for one of the two gunboats scuttled to prevent capture on June 26, 1814.[2]

A third vessel site, noted on nautical charts in recent years as an abandoned derelict, but now as a submerged wreck, was well known to local watermen and became our first target. She was identified by several elderly local residents as a late nineteenth century schooner called *Henrietta Bach.* Lying in an isolated cove near the entrance to St. Leonard's, in waters ranging from four to ten feet deep, with her starboard side less than fifteen feet from shore, the *Bach* was a vessel whose history of service was typical of many in the Tidewater. Built in 1883 at Cambridge, Maryland, her tonnage was officially listed as thirty-two net and forty-four gross. Schooner rigged, and entered on the register of merchant vessels as number 95785, she was 66.5 feet long, 22 feet abeam, and 5.7 feet deep in hold.[3] In 1909 she had been brought to the Patuxent by Captain William E. Breeden, who had purchased her to serve as an oyster buyboat. For years she had remained in the Breeden family, which kept her busy

133

in the oyster trade during the winter and hauling fertilizer, wheat, and pulpwood in the summer. Sometime near the end of the 1920s, while sailing in the Elk River in the upper Bay, the *Bach* capsized during a freak storm but was somehow righted and saved. The accident had nearly ended the career of Captain Breeden, who lived on Sawpit Cove on St. Leonard's Creek, but the old boat's heyday was definitely over. Not long after the disaster, it was said, she was either sold or salvaged by a black waterman named Butler, who hauled her back into St. Leonard's and finally abandoned her. For years thereafter, the hulk remained the objective of Sunday outings by the Breeden children, among them Laura Breeden, the daughter of George L. Breeden, who shared her recollections of the old vessel and its gradual collapse with us.[4] In the years that followed, the wreck was visited often by local watermen as her frames gradually sagged and finally collapsed. A number of souvenirs and relics such as her navigation lights, chain plate with deadeye, and broken stoneware were saved, some of which would eventually find their way into the collections of the Calvert Marine Museum.

When we first examined the *Bach* on a late spring morning in 1978, it was found that she had completely collapsed along her keel with both sides falling outwards and now lay entirely submerged. Close inspection of the remains, however, proved instructive. She had, at the time of her

The schooner *Henrietta Bach* under sail.
Photograph courtesy of Laura Breeden Elseroad

134

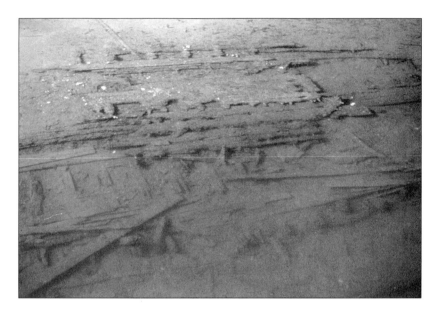

The bones of the schooner *Henrietta Bach.*

abandonment, been a heavily repaired vessel. Concrete had been poured between several frames and ceiling planks as a quick fix to prevent leakage without having to haul her into drydock for repairs and caulking (a technique once widely employed in the Chesapeake although no longer acceptable under Coast Guard regulations). The concrete slabs or "castings," with a clean impression of the planking they had been used to seal were, in many instances, all that remained of an afflicted area.

A large anchor was discovered beneath the bones of the port bow, a small tip of its fluke being the only part exposed above the silt to reveal its location. A heavily encrusted windlass, an iron bowsprit collar, a small boiler possibly used for a small stove, a pair of iron gudgeons, and a small lignum vitae sheave with a brass axle bearing a patent date of 1871 were also found. A single gudgeon and the sheave were removed to the museum. The big five-foot anchor was eventually recovered with the assistance of the University of Maryland's research vessel *Aquarius* and carried to Solomons for stabilization and documentation. After a preliminary mapping of the site was completed, the remainder of the movable artifacts as well as prominent architectural features of the wreck itself were left *in situ*, because of a complete lack of conservation facilities in the state capable of preserving large-scale waterlogged materials.[5] After all, we reasoned, who would be interested in the well-known bones of an old workboat, already largely stripped, that had been lying there for more than half a century? It was, unhappily, an assumption that proved to be

The University of Maryland research vessel *Aquarius* recovers the *Henrietta Bach*'s anchor from St. Leonard's Creek.

utterly mistaken. Within a month of our initial examination of the site, news of the survey had been widely circulated by word of mouth, and then by reportage in the local press. Within a year the wreck was completely stripped of all removable artifacts by relic hunters.[6]

It was abundantly clear that our reconnaissance would have to be carried out more discreetly than we had anticipated. Yet the survey would continue unabated, even though secrecy was next to impossible, as local informants, primarily watermen, continued to serve as an important component of our research effort. Their reports of sites, some factual, some fictitious, were all treated with the same degree of credulity. Many accounts of potential sites were merely stories handed down from father to son. Others who had actually encountered features of wrecks or had recovered artifacts while dredging provided information of greater substance. No reports were ignored, and many would bear inordinately sweet fruit.

A survey of the waters at the mouth of the creek, below modern Mackall's Cliffs, was initiated with considerable optimism. Here, the engagement between Barney's flotilla and the Royal Navy had been brought to one of its most heated moments as both sides contended over the grounded British warship *St. Lawrence* on June 10, 1814. On the cliffs themselves, Geoghegan's and Miller's batteries had been erected to initiate the surprise attack that had driven the British from the creek during the decisive Second Battle of St. Leonard's Creek. And it had been

136

on the fields beyond that the American Army had mustered, only to flee in disarray during the height of the battle. Moreover, based upon John Smith's famous map of his 1608 visit, we had conjectured that it was somewhere in the vicinity of the north shore cliffs that the Patuxent Indian village of Quomacoc lay. And somewhere nearby, on the south shore, had been the site of the village of Opament.[7]

Could we find evidence of any of these sites, events, or features? Prehistoric relics had been found by many local inhabitants and there were, of course, many stories afloat relative to the most important historic events on the creek, the battles of 1814. Indeed, few local residents had not heard of the many cannonballs that once allegedly lay in profusion in the waters and along the creek's shores. Many, it was said, had been picked up by watermen on both sides of the waterway, especially around

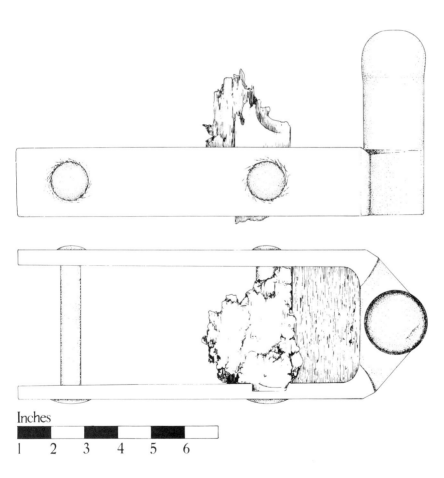

Gudgeon recovered from the wreck of the *Henrietta Bach.*

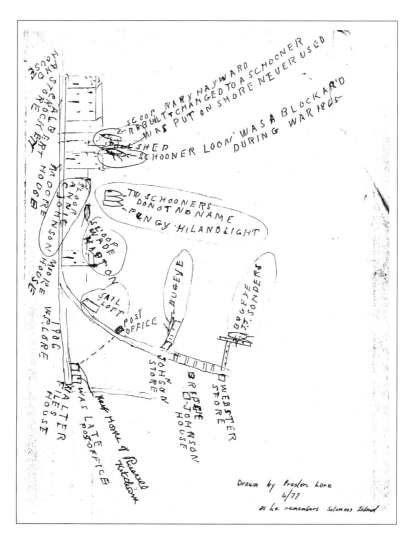

The text within the sketch map reads:

MOORE STORE
CALVERT HOUSE
SCOOP MARY HAYWARD SCHOONER REBUILT CHANGED TO A SCHOONER WAS PUT ON SHORE NEVER USED
SHED
SCHOONER LOON WAS A BLOCKAR'D DURING WAR 1865
SLOOP ANNIE JOHNSON MOORE HOUSE
TW SCHOONERS DO NOT NO NAME
PUNGY "HILAND LIGHT
SLOOP WADE HAMPTON
1906 W.P.LORE
SAIL LOFT
POST OFFICE
BUGEYE
BUGEYE N. SONDERS
JOHNSON STORE
BUGEYE R.T. JOHNSON HOUSE
WEBSTER STORE
WAS LATE POSTOFFICE
WALTER LESTER HOUSE
WAS HOME OF Russell Kitchen

Drawn by Preston Lore
6/77
as he remembers Solomons Island

Drawings and oral traditions of many long-time residents of the Patuxent drainage were important sources of information to our early investigations of the river's maritime resources and heritage. This sketch map of the early 20th-century anchorage, facilities, and shipping along a portion of the Solomons Island waterfront produced from memory by Preston Lore was typical of the important descriptive data that enriched our research. Courtesy of the Calvert Marine Museum

its mouth. Others told of the bones of gunboats, and even those of a British warship, still sleeping undisturbed in the waterway. Yet, aside from a few prehistoric points and scrapers picked up at long-forgotten locations in nearby fields, there were few actual pieces of evidence put forth to substantiate most accounts. A walkabout of the creekside beach below

Mackall's Cliffs and then on the plain above, however, produced a tantalizing preview of the validity of some claims.

The beach was littered with ceramic fragments, stoneware, and creamware dating circa 1870-1900, which was eroding from trash pits at the edge of the bluff. Unhappily, there was no evidence of either historic or prehistoric occupation or of the dramatic battles that had been fought here.[8] A preliminary reconnaissance on the plain above at first also failed to produce any positive evidence of the batteries or military occupation of the area in 1814. At first glance the fields appeared barren of any cultural materials.

Then, like the wonderful discovery of gold in that remote creek in California, we struck pay dirt, the first hint of something that would even-

Dr. Ralph Eshelman examines a shallow unidentified earthen mound on the plateau overlooking St. Leonard's Creek during the reconnaissance phase of the Patuxent Project.

139

tually prove of great importance. Amidst the rolling fields and ravines, heavy briars and brush, we detected several burrow holes. Incredibly, the earthen spoil at the mouths of every burrow was flecked with oyster shells. Upon closer examination of the nearby unplowed fields we soon discovered great spreads of shell material, formed into numerous concentric circles, as well as brick fragments, pieces of kaolin smoking pipes common to the seventeenth and eighteenth centuries, badly corroded pieces of iron, and pottery sherds of various eras, from the seventeenth through nineteenth centuries. Along one edge of the cliff overlooking the Patuxent, the remnants of a small earthen embankment, badly eroded and less than 2 feet in elevation but running more than 360 feet in length, was also detected. The embankment was far too long to have been an emplacement for the American batteries of 1814, but, together with the strong evidence of prehistoric and colonial occupation on the plain, it was definitely a feature of significance.[9]

During subsequent visits, with an archaeologist from the Maryland Historical Trust in company, the importance of the find was soon confirmed, and the foundations for one of the most significant long-term archaeological programs in Maryland history would soon be given birth. But that is getting ahead of the story.

As our investigation proceeded to expand, so did the types of sites we encountered. In the waters off Sollers Wharf, where the ruins of a

The ruins of Sollers Wharf, once an important Patuxent steamboat landing, as they appeared in 1978.

140

steamboat landing, general store, post office, and warehouse edged up to, or projected out over, the creek, we began to probe an anchorage favored by shipping from the seventeenth through the early twentieth centuries. Beneath the shadow of a rambling eighteenth century manor house known as Spout Farm, it was said, slavers and merchantmen alike had regularly stopped to take on fresh water from the bountiful spring that gave the plantation its name. Here, Barney's little flotilla had retired to evade the deadly bombardment of the British fleet in the First Battle of St. Leonard's Creek. And here, too, the majestic steamboats of the nineteenth and early twentieth centuries paid scheduled visits to take on the bounty of Calvert County and to offload the much-needed merchandise that kept rural southern Maryland productive.

Yet the romance of the setting belied its apparent archaeological sterility. Once more we failed to find evidence of the events that had transpired here, other than the ruins of the collapsed early twentieth century building complex which once supported the steamboat landing and the Sollers and Dowell Oyster House. Rotten, creosoted pilings and modern bottles and little else littered the river bottom.[10] But again, survey of the majestic elevations overlooking the site and running to the creek's lower lip at Rodney Point revealed more interesting features. Evidence of prehistoric shell middens could be observed eroding along the upper edge of the cliff terrace, thirty to forty feet above sea level, and extending in weathered exposures all the way around the point and along the Patuxent shore. Tapering off nearly half a mile below the point, the exposures again appeared well to the south between two waterways known as Mears and Hellen Creek. The prehistoric presence of Native American peoples along the Patuxent drainage seemed to be in evidence everywhere we turned.[11]

One typical informant, the owner of a prominent estate on the point, a delightful octogenarian named G. Gordon Bennett who offered us tea and cookies, hinted at what lay beneath his property, a tract cryptically noted on early maps as Windmill Point. A review of artifacts found on his property, primarily lithics such as projectile points and a few cannonballs from the June 10, 1814, battle, and a walk-over of his estate, during which several possible foundation sites were noted, suggested to us that there were potentially greater archaeological resources here than met the eye. Yet Bennett's tract was but one of many that would be visited, albeit all too briefly, and recorded before we moved on to the next.

Day after day, St. Leonard's Creek continued to reveal her secrets to us. One day we would explore the conjectured location of St. Leonard's Town, destroyed by the British in 1814, and the next it would be a small wreck, steamboat wharf, colonial landing, gun battery, or shell midden. At the site of St. Leonard's Wharf, a possible colonial site which later hosted the steamboat era and is known today as Mackall's Wharf, we

Nicholas Freda photographs the remains of a log canoe in Sawpit Cove.

found the remains of what we believed to be a T-shaped nineteenth or early twentieth century steamboat wharf, replete with a small boiler and two large flywheels, overlaying the colonial site. Not far from Sollers Wharf, in a small, dimpled recess of St. Leonard's Creek known as Sawpit Cove, the survey team documented yet another small wreck site. Sheltered by a sand spit that divided it from the main creek, the cove could only be described as serene, and certainly one of the most beautiful unknown corners of the Chesapeake Tidewater. Receiving information from a local informant named Jim Buys that the remains of a small log canoe lay on the spit amidst a heavy growth of underbrush, we descended on the little enclosure to briefly violate its tranquility with camera, tapes, and transit.

The vessel in question proved to be a very poorly preserved derelict three-log canoe, nearly thirty-one feet long, fitted with both iron and wood, and lying in pieces entirely overgrown by shrubs. Modern rubber gaskets had been employed for through-hull components, indicating the life of the boat lasted to a relatively recent period. Although the remains of the diminutive little craft (a type common to the seventeenth through early twentieth centuries and one that could be found in most maritime museums throughout the Chesapeake) were far from spectacular, the find was duly documented and photographed. It wouldn't be our last.

□   □   □

It was well known that Joshua Barney sunk two of his gunboats, *No. 137* and *No. 138,* somewhere in the upper reaches of St. Leonard's Creek after the pivotal battle of June 26, 1814. The two vessels, considered too unwieldy and slow to participate in the battle in the narrow confines of the little waterway, or possibly because of damage suffered during earlier engagements, had been stripped of their valuable rigging, naval gear, and furniture in anticipation of abandonment. Following Barney's escape from the creek, the two gunboats, along with several merchantmen, were scuttled to prevent capture. On July 2, 1814, when a British naval foray up the creek resulted in the destruction of St. Leonard's Town, the enemy also took the two gunboats, lying in shallow water with their gunnels awash, and tore up their decks. Later, the two warboats would suffer even further indignities when local scavengers descended upon them to pick their bones clean. Because no records had been found to suggest the wrecks had been raised, and a strong folk tradition survived that at least one of the sites still lay in a small cove in the upper reaches of the creek, we were optimistic that the two sites still remained, quietly awaiting discovery.[12]

Exploration of a small indention on the northern shores of St. Leonard's produced the perfect candidate. The cove was fed by a small creek and surrounded by rising uplands on all three of its landward borders. Except for a small home and private dock on the southern lip of the indent, the shores appeared largely devoid of human habitation. The cove itself was barely five feet deep, and two hundred yards across at its widest point. Moreover, it was situated just above the upper picket line Barney had maintained across the creek from June 11 to June 25, 1814, within artillery range of the batteries across the creek, and small arms range from the U.S. Infantry works on the heights above. (A reconnaissance ashore by Eshelman and archaeologist Michael Smolek, several years after the initial surveys in the creek, established the location of the infantry's earthen

143

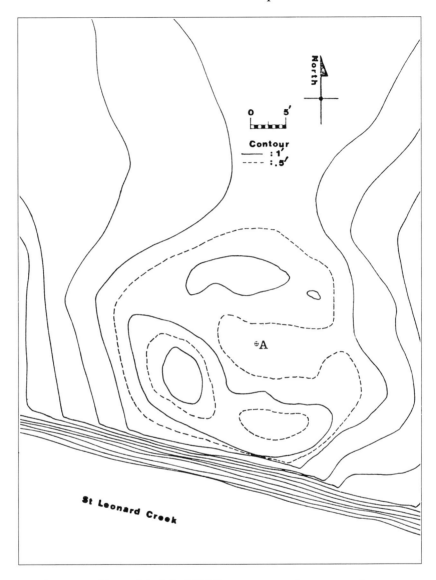

A topographic model of the 1814 Barney gun emplacement or lunette commanding the upper reaches of St. Leonard's Creek. Soon after this survey was completed, the area was bulldozed to make way for a housing tract.
Courtesy of the Calvert Marine Museum

works only a few days before the remains were bulldozed into oblivion for a housing development. The battery on the opposite side of the creek, at Fort Hill, had already been largely destroyed during construction of a private home.)[13]

144

Shipwrecks and Saturday Night Specials

Investigation of the cove by volunteer divers, spurred on by local tales of cannonballs being found here amidst several wrecks, was almost instantly rewarded. A badly worm-eaten shipwreck, lying in a northwesterly orientation and terribly disarticulated, was discovered in the center of the cove. Despite heavy sediment cover, zero visibility, and the poor condition of the few remains encountered still lying above the porous sediments, a brief survey was undertaken. Measurement of the keelson suggested a

NAA divers Larry Pugh and Dale Shomette examine a futtock temporarily removed from the "Gunboat" Wreck in St. Leonard's Creek. Once drawn and photographed, the piece was returned to its original position on the site.

145

minimum length vessel of sixty-four feet, but only four feet of the conjectured sixteen-foot beam remained. The fittings were both iron and wood. Few ceiling planks or strakes had survived the rot and worm damage or the destructive forces of man. The few frames that were found were generally four inches wide and irregularly spaced at one to two feet apart. Sadly, no datable diagnostic artifacts were discovered. Only a single heavily corroded iron pin, a lead sheathing strip with nail holes in it, an iron strap, and a single futtock were removed for later evaluation.[14]

It was scant data to go on, yet the desire to accept the site as the remains of one of the gunboats was tempting and the hulk was promptly dubbed the "Gunboat" Wreck. The length of the vessel was certainly close to the proportions of the gunboat series designed by Commodore James Barron in 1806 in which *No. 137* and *No. 138* had been built. Geographically the wreck was clearly in the correct area. It had suffered considerable teredo (shipworm) damage, which suggested that it had spent a good bit of time in the warm salt waters of the Bay or ocean before coming to rest for all eternity in the brackish waters of upper St. Leonard's. Yet, artifactual data suitable for assigning a period of construction or deposition was entirely lacking.

Was there enough circumstantial evidence to say that the vessel was indeed one of Barney's own? "A definitive conclusion as to the identity of

The bowsprit assemblage of a vessel sunk in St. Leonard's Creek and once believed to have belonged to the Chesapeake Flotilla. The artifact was reportedly saved from destruction at the hands of a state sponsored Derelict Removal Program by local antiquarians.

146

the wreck from the information available," Eshelman and I would later write in our final report to the Maryland Historical Trust in 1981, "is not possible. . . . Despite the circumstantial data and local traditions suggesting that the site is one of the Barney gunboats, actual evidence relating to the identity of the wreck is far from conclusive."[15]

Not long after our reconnaissance, we discovered exactly why the remains had been so poorly preserved and scattered. During the final days of the reconnaissance phase in St. Leonard's Creek, Eshelman and I visited the grounds of the White Sands Marina, not far from the site of the "Gunboat" Wreck (1-GBW). On a scenic, well-kept, emerald-green sward overlooking the creek, we discovered an intact but poorly preserved bowsprit and collar assemblage from an ancient sailing ship. The aggregation was being employed as a yard decoration beside the marina restaurant. Inquiry at the restaurant revealed that the assemblage had been saved, only a few years earlier, from 1-GBW. Further investigation led to the discovery that the wreck itself had been broken up and largely destroyed by wrecking contractors working under the auspices of Calvert County and funded by the Maryland Department of Natural Resources. The program had been part of a national waterways beautification project promoted by none other than Lady Bird Johnson and aimed at removing unsightly derelicts and obstructions from public waterways. It was, on the surface, a well-intentioned agenda. But without an archaeological review process, it was an agenda that would likely produce great destruction of potentially important historical resources or, at the very least, as with 1-GBW, render them unidentifiable.

Eshelman soon learned from the contractors who had actually conducted the operation for the county that nearly a score of wooden wrecks, both visible and sunken, had been ripped from the creek, broken up, and destroyed in "burn boxes" aboard the salvage boats—including figureheads, decorative trailboards, and carved mastheads. Our own 1-GBW had not been spared. What other potential historic shipwrecks had also been destroyed in the statewide program was anyone's guess.[16]

Final confirmation that 1-GBW had indeed been the subject of a derelict removal effort came several years later. During a University of Baltimore field school in underwater archaeology being taught by NAA's Ken Hollingshead and myself, we discovered the remains of a woven iron BX cable still wrapped around some of the wreckage—cable once employed to lift the hulk from the water for the wrecking process. It would not be the last sad discovery made during the Patuxent Project.

□   □   □

The reconnaissance of St. Leonard's Creek continued off and on throughout the spring and early summer of 1978. In August, however, the focus of investigation began to shift upriver to Broome's Island, Battle Creek,

147

and a three-mile reach of river between the town of Benedict and Hunting Creek. They were indeed areas rich with potential.

Broomes Island, not really an island at all but a peninsula, is located on the west side of a little waterway in Calvert County called Island Creek. It had been granted to one John Brome in 1651 as part of a two-thousand-acre tract called Brome's Manor. Despite a superb location on the river, actual settlement on the peninsula did not begin in earnest until the late nineteenth century, when a small maritime community was established to tap the bounty of the Bay and river. At least two historic vessel wrecks had been reported to be lying in the waters surrounding the peninsula.[17]

The shores of Battle Creek had, of course, hosted the site of Calverton, erected in 1669 as the first county seat of Calvert County and destroyed by the British in the War of 1812. The townsite was probably located at or near Prison Point, on the north shore lip of the waterway entrance, possibly even overlying the remains of the American Indian village of Onan-tuck, the location of which had been conjectured from the John Smith map of 1612. A larger, lambchop-shaped peninsular protrusion guarded the south shore approach to the creek and formed a small embayment known as Jacks Bay. From the Smith map, we had also conjectured that this could be the possible location of one of the most important contact-period Native American settlements on the river, indeed the village that had given the river its name, Pawtuxunt. And in the waters surrounding the point lay at least one wreck site, that of the schooner *James E. Trott,* which had been lost in 1928.[18]

Benedict had, of course, also been a river port of great importance during the eighteenth and early nineteenth centuries, and as such became the subject of loyalist seaborne guerilla raids during the Revolution and the invasion site for the British march on Washington during the War of 1812. After the war, the town became one of the more important steamboat ports and commercial centers on the river. During the Civil War, it had served as the site of a Union training and marshalling center for Union troops in southern Maryland.

The waters between Benedict and Hallowing Point offered the prospect of many potential submerged resources, both historic and prehistoric. The opposite shoreline, despite some development, still bore signs of shell middens, which were first noted by the well-known Maryland archaeologist, Richard E. Stearns, during his explorations of littoral sites along the Patuxent drainage system in 1950, and which may have been associated with the site of the village of Wascocup, noted on the 1624 Smith map. Benedict, possibly the site of the contact period village of Wasmacus, was itself located immediately north of a waterway known as Indian Creek, where evidence of prehistoric occupation had been noted by Stearns.[19]

Shipwrecks and Saturday Night Specials

Of great interest to us was the purported wreck site of the Maryland, Delaware and Virginia Line steamboat *St. Mary's*. Originally built in 1872 as the *Theodore Weems* by William H. Skinner and Sons at Baltimore and rebuilt *St. Mary's* in 1881 after burning down at her Light Street Wharf in Baltimore, the old steamer had been the most popular boat on the Patuxent run. Her chivalric commander, Captain James Russell Gourley, was once deemed "the most gallant mariner that ever trod a deck." On December 4, 1907, while approaching Hallowing Point, opposite Benedict, in a howling gale, the popular steamer was run aground because of misplaced lantern markers ashore. The following morning, fire was detected in the areas of the smokestack and engine room casing, and within a short time the entire ship was consumed, along with the life of the ship's steward, Thomas A. Thompson. A table, a clock, a decorative eagle paddlebox housing, and several documents were all that are known to have been saved from the blaze, all of which eventually found a home in the Calvert Marine Museum.[20]

Further upriver lay Gods Grace Point, on the southern lip of Hunting Creek Bay, where the British under Captain Joseph Nourse had landed in 1814, marched further up the creek and burned the warehouses at old Huntingtown, returned down creek, burned a plantation at Gods Grace, and reembarked. Somewhere on the creek itself lay the remains of old Huntingtown. And in the waters of the creek and off adjacent Potts Point, on the north shore, lay the remains of several unidentified wrecks that were indicated on nautical charts or reported to us by local informants.

As in St. Leonard's Creek, we set off on this phase of our reconnaissance with little more than bottom sounder, grappling hooks, diving gear, and considerable optimism. At Broomes Island, our investigation yielded nothing. Neither of the wrecks reported to lie in the adjacent waters could be found. A dragline search for the *James R. Trott,* in Jacks Bay, proved equally disappointing. Had these wrecks also fallen prey to the Maryland Derelict Removal Program? Our investigations, however, were not entirely in vain. An examination of the eroded shores of Prison Point and the upland terrace revealed an extensive shell midden and even some evidence of the seventeenth and eighteenth century occupation of the site—just enough to titillate us even more. Yet, as we would soon discover, they were features that would be encountered at numerous other historic sites on the river with almost numbing frequency.[21]

At Benedict, the eroded shoreline near the old town and the gentle sloping fields about it were thick with the detritus of former centuries, potsherds, green bottle glass, nails, kaolin pipe fragments, and even a few stone flakes of prehistoric origin. But it was the steamboat that held the most interest for our dive teams. Interviews with elderly residents of the area suggested that sections of the wreck still remained intact and that from time to time watermen dredging for oysters had even recovered artifacts. Several informants claimed that the wreck had been completely broken up by channel dredging. Still others went so far as to provide a precise location for the site.

Our search for *St. Mary's* was conducted with a bottom sounder, grappling hooks, and by hands-on underwater radial searches by divers. The swift, chocolate-colored waters flowing between Benedict and Hallowing Point permitted absolutely no light penetration below a depth of three feet. The black ooze of the river bed was so porous and liquid that the inside of one's wetsuit was usually as slimy as the outside after but a few minutes of work on the bottom. Indeed, a grapple hook might penetrate several feet of silty sediments before meeting anything resembling a hard bottom. Still, we persisted, following up on every lead provided by local informants, suggested by the historic record, or indicated on early or contemporary navigational charts. Aside from debris resulting from the construction of the modern bridge connecting Benedict with Hallowing Point and an occasional cluster of oyster shells on a muck-covered bar, the bottom of the Patuxent seemed as devoid of evidence of human activity or animal life as the deserts of Mars. If the remains of *St. Mary's* were there, it seemed altogether likely that they had been swallowed by the river's ever-increasing sediment load and would probably not be found without the assistance of remote-sensing instrumentation.[22]

The survey now pressed northward, passing Gods Grace Point and into Hunting Creek Bay. A foray into the headwaters of navigation on the creek to search for several reported derelicts of unknown vintage yielded three disappointing wrecksites. One of the craft was an abandoned cabin cruiser. The other two sites were larger wooden barges, in an almost total state of collapse, which, according to local informants, had probably been employed in the construction of the Benedict Bridge in 1951 and abandoned soon after its completion in this scenic but isolated backwater. A hike along the shoreline, accelerated somewhat by the appearance of a pack of wild dogs, yielded no evidence of either the prehistoric or colonial occupation. Equally disappointing was a fruitless grapple and diver search for the reported remains of the Potts Point Wreck. Disappointed but undaunted we moved on.

□　　　□　　　□

Less than three miles above Potts Point, the Patuxent River narrows appreciably at Hollands Cliffs, a strategic choke point upon which batteries had been erected during the Revolution by the Board of Patuxent Associators, and not overlooked by Joshua Barney as a possible defense position after his retreat upriver in 1814. Above the cliffs lay the sites of many of the river's most important colonial landings, tobacco inspection stations, steamboat wharves, and seventeenth and eighteenth century ferry operations, as well as such ports as Lower Marlboro, Nottingham, Pig Point, Upper Marlboro, and Queen Anne's. And here also lay the remains of one of our most important targets—the U.S. Chesapeake Flotilla. We had cut our teeth examining reported and conjectural locations of sites on the lower reaches of the river, but it was to be in the twenty-five mile stretch between Hollands Cliffs and old Queen Anne's Town that some of the most significant finds awaited discovery.

The first serendipitous hint of what lay ahead had already been discovered quite by accident on a bright summer day in 1976 by several young boys wading in the river at the base of steep cliffs a half mile below Lyons Creek, in the shadows of a colonial plantation house known as Archer Hays. Erected on a fertile tract of land overlooking the Patuxent by Peter Archer, who had arrived in Calvert County around 1663, the plantation had indeed seen a great deal of history pass along the river below.[23]

When Ralph Eshelman called to inform me that we had been invited to examine the boys' find, a clutch of more than half a dozen handguns found in the river bottom in three to four feet of water, several of which had been held in place by a long stick run through their trigger guards and planted firmly in the mud, I wasn't exactly prepared for what came next. An inspection of the weapons, recovered by the children over a period of several visits to the site, revealed a set of side arms from the eighteenth and nineteenth centuries in a marvelous state of preservation. Six of the seven weapons were made available to us to photograph and record. The photographs were sent off to several experts on early side arms, James Knowles, Craddock Goins, and James Tearman of the Smithsonian Institution, for positive identification and dating.[24]

All of the arms were of cheap manufacture, produced between 1790 and 1840, and could have been employed as military side arms. All were believed to be of European fabrication except two, which may have been of American origins but copied from French models. One was definitely of French manufacture, two others were Belgian, and another was German. The earliest piece was produced between 1790 and 1820, whereas the latest was a single-shot percussion cap pistol dated circa 1840–80. Several of the weapons were commonly referred to as saloon pieces, the equivalent of the "Saturday Night Specials" of a later age. Two of the pistols, both naval flintlocks, were believed to be of French design and intended for use by either naval or land forces.[25]

The identity of the weapons and the reason for their insertion into the marine environment was pure conjecture. The place where they had been found was inaccessible except by boat, or by descending down a dangerous, almost vertical cliff. The pistols had obviously been intentionally placed in the bottom and were in such a superior state of preservation

Six of seven pistols, recovered from the Patuxent by several youths, are believed to have been hidden in the river during the Civil War by Confederate sympathizers to avoid confiscation by Union troops. The guns would wait for more than a century before being retrieved. Photograph by William Tearman, courtesy of Calvert Marine Museum

that Tearman could not at first believe they had been long submerged. Perhaps they had been stolen from a private collection and disposed of, he suggested, or maybe they had been hidden during some municipal action to disarm civilians or the military.

That the preservation of such items beneath the river muds was possible would soon be proven. That the weapons might have been disposed of to prevent confiscation seemed the most likely reason for the insertion into the river bottom. The time period in which the pieces had been manufactured indicated that the pieces could not have been deposited in the river earlier than 1790. The only major confiscation of arms in the region had been during the Civil War when southern Maryland, considered a hotbed for Confederate sympathizers, became a virtual occupied territory by federal forces. Had the guns been hidden to prevent their being taken by the occupying forces of the U.S. government? It seemed a reasonable bet (albeit one that might never be proven) and a delicious prognostication of what might lie ahead.

□   □   □

The next focus of investigation was at Magruders Landing, once the site of a bustling colonial tobacco station known as Hannah Browns Landing. Though little urban development had occurred here, the site had, for a period during the eighteenth and nineteenth centuries, served as the seasonal hub of vigorous commercial activity because of its inspection station status, and as a transshipment point for tobacco destined for foreign markets. The heyday of Magruders Landing ended as a result of the War of 1812, when warehouses containing nearly two thousand hogsheads of tobacco awaiting shipment were burned by British raiders. Yet the site had continued to serve as an occasional steamboat landing well into the twentieth century, until, like the maritime importance of the river itself, it subsided and then slipped into utter obscurity.[26]

The site seemed rich with potential. Local informants reported to us that a cannon had been recovered from four feet of water off the landing, and that numerous artifacts of all kinds, from prehistoric lithics to colonial era pottery, had been picked up in the surrounding fields and at the water's edge during low tide. Although the owner of the cannon was not willing to provide his find for examination, another collector, a soft-spoken fellow named Joe Richards, was persuaded by Eshelman to donate some of his finds, recovered from the near shore, to the Calvert Marine Museum. The artifacts included an iron boat hook and pole ring of undetermined age, but of a type common to the eighteenth century, and a large iron ballast pig bearing the raised inscription "Patapsco 1760," possibly the name of an iron foundry or of a ship and the date of her commission.[27]

153

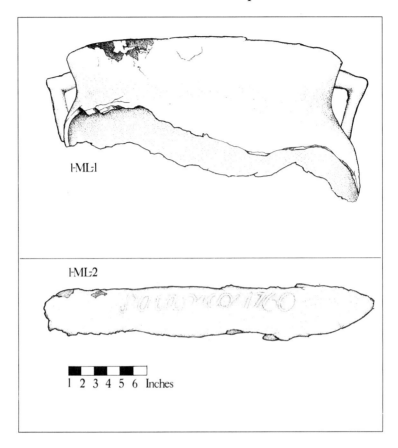

Artifacts recovered from Magruders Landing included half of an iron
cooking or rendering pot of the period 1776-1850 (top) and a large iron
ballast pig bearing the inscription "Patapsco 1760" (bottom).

Guided by Richards to the sites of his finds, we began an extensive
underwater reconnaissance of the shoreline. The rotting remains of the
old steamboat landing were encountered almost immediately. An examination of a three-hundred-foot-long stretch of nearshore below the landing quickly produced a concentration of late eighteenth and early nineteenth century refuse, primarily fragments of green "rum" bottles, half of
an iron cooking or rendering pot of the period 1776–1850, clusters of
ballast stone and bricks, and a few late eighteenth century potsherds.
Examination of the plowed fields ashore produced sherds of gray stoneware of the mid-nineteenth century and kaolin pipe fragments, but
neither prehistoric lithics or pottery as we had been led to believe had
been found there.[28]

Shipwrecks and Saturday Night Specials

The intensive usage and maritime activity at Magruders Landing, as evidenced by the variety and distribution of artifacts, was more than we had anticipated. But was the site typical of what might be expected at other such landings on the river? We would soon find out as our reconnaissance pressed ever northward.

□   □   □

The townsite of Lower Marlboro, situated on the east bank of the Patuxent less than a mile above Magruders, was of considerable significance to the early history of the river. Originally known as Coxtown, the town was one of the most important colonial urban centers in southern Maryland, a major commercial hub, tobacco inspection center, and port. It, like many other nuclei of commerce on the river, had been the subject of raids during the American War of Independence and the War of 1812, and had served as Calvert County's most prominent tobacco port from its very foundation through the 1930s.

Like Magruders, Lower Marlboro was a potentially rich archaeological sector of the river. Indeed, Stearns, in his survey work in the Patuxent Valley, had discovered a large prehistoric site on Coxtown Creek, immediately south of the town, and had recovered over five hundred sherds of pottery, a number of lithics, and bone implements. Many finds were made by local residents. A large grinding stone of the Middle Woodland period, recovered by a local resident and used for years as a doorstop in the town, had even been donated to the Calvert Maritime Museum.[29]

There were yarns aplenty to fill our notebooks and tape recorders during our numerous visits to the town. Oral tradition suggested that a sunken vessel dating from the War of 1812, believed by locals to have been a British gunboat or barge, lay west of town near a wetlands known as Hills Marsh. One informant, Cecil County Historical Society archivist Genevieve Frazer Cockey, who had been born in the town in 1901, recalled the presence of a submerged wreck above the town, "somewhat above the creek which flows through the marsh above Plummer's plantation," and even provided us with a drawing indicating its location. She also related tales of British grave sites below the town, occupied by soldiers who had died of "swamp fever" during the war.[30]

The traditions and folklore of Lower Marlboro and, indeed, along the waterway as far north as the hamlet of Hardesty (colonial Queen Anne's Town), however, were more steeped in the War of 1812 and Barney's barges than anywhere else on the waterway—including St. Leonard's Creek. Every wreck in every tributary, marsh, and channel was one of Barney's barges. Cannonballs along the water's edge, we were repeatedly told, were once so plentiful that almost everyone had one (although only two were ever shown to us). Every snag and obstruction in the river was chalked up as a flotilla wreck. Every waterman interviewed claimed to have recovered anchors from the fleet (all of which had conveniently been sold as scrap). And British dead were apparently buried along the river banks from St. Leonard's clear to Upper Marlboro, although no one could ever pinpoint the location of their grave sites. Clearly, folklore, fiction, and fact had become so intertwined that truth would be difficult to extract from the weave. There was little choice but to follow every thread.

At Lower Marlboro, we used the Cockey map and information provided by several local informants to make a systematic search for the purported British gunboat wreck. In zero visibility with a bottom that can best be described as sludge, our search yielded nothing, save the documentation of several derelict fishing boats of recent vintage abandoned near the town. A hazardous underwater investigation beneath the modern town wharf to locate the remnants of the steamboat landing proved equally unproductive. If there was anything to be found, we decided, it must lie beneath the many feet of goop that had come to settle on the bottom in recent years.

We had begun our recon here with considerable zeal, but the negative findings had left us temporarily demoralized. It was becoming increasingly clear that with the heavy silt cover on the river bottom, it would be necessary to utilize remote-sensing technology before most early sites were likely to be found. Yet, the brackish waters and deep sediments offered the intriguing possibility, as evidenced by the state of preservation of the side arms recovered near Archer Hays, that cultural materials likely to exist further upriver would also be in a good to excellent state of preservation.

Moreover, our next reconnaissance objective, although we could not have foreseen it, would more than compensate for the paltry findings at Lower Marlboro.

N I N E

Nottingham

Thirty-six miles up the Patuxent River, on the eastern edge of the rolling plains of southern Prince George's County, lay the remains of a once-thriving river port known as Nottingham. There is little to see there now, save for a few modest farmsteads set against the backdrop of broad tobacco fields. Yet, it is a place where the imprint of the past, as rich as any in the Tidewater, lies thick beneath the substratum of the plow zone and submerged in the murky river waters beyond. Based upon the 1612 Smith map, here or in the immediate vicinity, we had conjectured, probably lay the contact-period Native American village of Wosameus, in a district the Europeans would designate in 1696 as Mattapany Hundred.[1] Here, too, in 1706, on lands belonging to Thomas Brooke, Esquire, at a site called Mattapany Landing, the Maryland government chose to formally establish by legislative edict the port of Nottingham.[2] Unlike many so-called paper towns of Maryland, supported almost entirely by the tobacco culture that kept the colony afloat, Nottingham grew and flourished. Within but a few years after the town's creation, inns, warehouses, and dwellings began to appear. By 1716, stocks and a whipping post had been erected in the town center by order of the county court.[3] In 1747 the village had become important enough to warrant a tobacco inspection station, and within a quarter century had grown enough in population to be designated as a Hundred on its own.[4]

Nottingham's new-found prominence in Maryland as a center for international commerce was rivaled only by its reputation as a hub for one of Maryland's greatest pastimes, horse racing. In 1773 the first races were organized and run, with healthy purses promised to winning entries.[5] During the revolution, in 1781, Nottingham had served as the command center for the Board of Patuxent Associators, which had convened there to organize the naval defense of the river by erecting batteries on strategic points along the waterway and by purchasing, arming, and fielding the ship *Nautilus* to patrol against enemy raiders.[6] By the beginning of the nineteenth century the town had become the sixth most important port of entry in the entire state and the home of Governor Robert Bowie.[7]

In 1814, when Barney selected Nottingham to serve as his base of operations for two months, the town's population was estimated at nearly fifteen

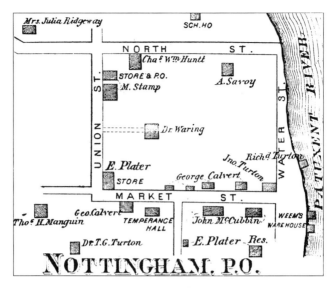

G.M. Hopkins's map of Nottingham, 1878. *Atlas of Prince George's County, Maryland, 1878,* originally compiled by G.M. Hopkins and edited by Frank H. White, Jr.

hundred inhabitants.[8] After Barney's retreat upriver, the British Army marched into the town after sparring briefly with a troop of dragoons led by Secretary of State James Monroe.[9] Unlike other commercial centers on the river, Nottingham was spared by the invaders, but the impact of their desecrations had thoroughly devastated the Patuxent Valley.[10] During the steamboat age, the town drifted into decline, awakened only by the whistle of the steamers that came to call or by the shouts of the black ferrymen who operated the old double-ended scow that carried passengers to and from the landing on the opposite shore.[11] Like many of the villages on the river, Nottingham had struggled on but could not long compete with the rise of the great Tidewater ports of Baltimore and Norfolk or the proliferation of the highway and rail systems that doomed the steamboat and the river ports that depended upon it. By the 1940s, the little port of entry had become a veritable ghost town, inhabited by only a handful of farming families, and remembered only as a footnote of history.

Yet, from time to time, the past had bubbled up from the waters fronting the old town or had emerged from the plowed fields nearby. In 1932 Mrs. Norris Harris, a native of Nottingham, who had been informed of the location of several shipwrecks in the area, all, of course, said to have belonged to Barney's flotilla, convinced her husband to assist in a scheme to recover them. The Harrises not only proceeded to locate a wreck near the shores of the town but, using a block and tackle and a crew of well-muscled laborers, managed to raise seven frames and a number of

158

This aerial photograph of the Nottingham region, taken in the spring of 1938, clearly reveals the superb strategic location of the town, at a narrow bend in the river formed by wetlands on the eastern shore, and above and below on the western shore. Courtesy National Archives and Record Service

smaller pieces from the site. In 1958, it was later reported (although there was no positive identification linking the wrecks to the Chesapeake Flotilla or even to the War of 1812) that three of the frames were placed on display at Fort McHenry. That they had lain on the bed of the Patuxent seemed proof enough for the Harrises.[12]

The year the pieces were said to have been placed on display, several individuals, inspired by the 1932 recovery efforts, vowed to locate the flotilla and recover an entire ship. The first to try, using the relatively new technology of scuba, would be a team of sport divers: Joseph E. Besche, a Baltimore department store executive; Carl DiJulio, owner of a dive shop in Towson, Maryland; Charles Mills, Jr., a plumbing and heating contractor; and Joseph Hollan, a construction foreman. The team arrived on the river well equipped with probes, surplus World War II mine detectors, dive gear, and a "mud hog" (to excavate potential "hot spots") to hunt for Barney's flotilla. Their search covered miles of the muddy waterway with little luck. Finally, in March 1958, they were informed by an elderly farmer

159

at Nottingham of the exact location of the wreck worked on by the Harrises in 1932. "He pointed to the spot," recalled DiJulio. "We waded out and walked right into it."[13]

In the mucky bottom, in waters less than twenty feet deep, the four divers discovered what appeared to be a jumbled pile of frames and planking running parallel to the shore. Operating strictly by touch, they began to explore, searching for artifacts and loose pieces of the hull that might be salvaged. Then, as a small band of local onlookers watched, the team tied a stout rope to several frames and then to their car and pulled them loose.[14]

Reflecting the wishful thinking of the salvors, the Baltimore *Sun* reported that it was conceivable, even likely, that the wreck was one of Barney's boats. "It is even possible that it is the commodore's flagship, the *Scorpion*." Yet, proof was elusive, as none of the hull fragments provided sufficient diagnostic data to confirm the divers' hopes. Officials at the Peabody Museum, the Smithsonian, and the Mariners' Museum, the salvors reported, had examined the finds but could come to no conclusion. Unfortunately, an archival search in all three institutions by NAA's Fred Hopkins failed to locate any mention of such an examination having ever been conducted.[15]

The DiJulio–Besche party would prove to be but the first of many to dive on the Nottingham wreck. In the years to come, many others would also attempt to collect artifacts and remove pieces of the wreck for their personal collections. Indeed, over the next two decades, the site would contribute its own colorful patina to the growing folklore of the Barney flotilla. One unabashed treasure hunter, Donald S. Stewart of Baltimore, even claimed to have recovered a two-pounder cannon from the site. The piece was purportedly donated to the city of Baltimore and mounted at Monument Circle (although intensive research in 1979, again undertaken by Hopkins, failed to locate either the gun or any record of the donation). By the late 1960s the site had been adopted as a training ground for the rescue squad of the Baden, Maryland, Fire Department.[16]

The Nottingham wreck was not the only wreck purportedly dating from the War of 1812 said to be in the area. One local property owner, Edgar Merkle (who would later donate his lands to the state of Maryland, which became the Merkle Wildlife Refuge), reported that there were a total of three wrecks lying in the river between a point north of the town known as Deep Bend and the town landing near Kings Creek. He also informed us, much to our disbelief, that a substantial earthen military fortification built during the war lay partially intact on the bluff overlooking a small stream called Lookout Creek, adjacent to the old town site.[17]

Despite the repeated visitation by relic hunters, the area had also attracted the attentions of serious archaeological investigators. Indeed, the first major survey of the prehistoric and historic potentials of the old town area had been undertaken in 1950 by Richard E. Stearns. Its archaeological riches, he quickly discerned, were indeed enormous. Beginning on a twenty-foot terrace and running for nearly sixteen hundred feet along the river and extending inland for nearly three hundred feet, evidence of nearly forty-five hundred years of occupation was discovered. Here, he reported, lay buried beneath the fields and exposed along the shoreline, a massive concentration of prehistoric cultural materials dating from the Late Archaic to the Woodland periods, with some components of early historic occupation as well.[18]

During his explorations, in one sector Stearns discovered that a twenty-five foot strip of land had been bulldozed and deep-plowed, exposing a dark, rich layer of earth. In this layer, he found an undisturbed prehistoric shell midden, pottery, a broken pestle, several celts, bone awls, and other materials. Limited excavation produced Potomac Creek and Rappahannock Fabric Impressed type pottery sherds, triangular green jasper projectile points, and even worked deer antlers. Fragments of historic artifacts, such as European China, glassware, and kaolin pipes, were also found in a nearby area believed to have been the site of a colonial farmstead. For an investigation that took only a few days, Stearns had produced a major, albeit unheralded, discovery and a foundation for those who would follow to build upon. Many archaeologists, such as Howard MacCord, Thomas Mayr, and Wayne E. Clark, spurred by Stearns's exciting discovery, would later visit the site to conduct further investigations and to contribute their own findings to help sort out the puzzle that was prehistoric Nottingham. By 1974, Clark, in a synthesis of all archaeological evidence produced to that time, along with the historical record and deductive reasoning, was ready to affirm Stearns's assertion about the identity of the site. Pointing to its size, the terminal components of artifacts found therein, lack of comparable sites in the vicinity, and documented sources which suggested it might be the village of Mattapament noted by Captain John Smith, he nominated the site to the National Register of Historic Places.[19]

If we had any doubts about the validity of the earlier archaeological work done, or even of the local tales and press reports about the finds at Nottingham, they were immediately dispelled upon our arrival. The plowed fields adjacent to the old townsite, vigorously protected from relic hunters by the local landowners (who were not opposed to brandishing firearms if necessary), were rich with artifacts, both colonial and prehistoric. Examination of collections of lithics and pottery assembled by local area residents revealed artifacts numbering in the thousands, most of which had been collected in the fields adjacent to and within the boundaries of Nottingham itself. Still, it was a deceiving visage presented by this formidable site. The main road leading to the water's edge, fronted by several modest dwellings (all that remained of this once prominent port

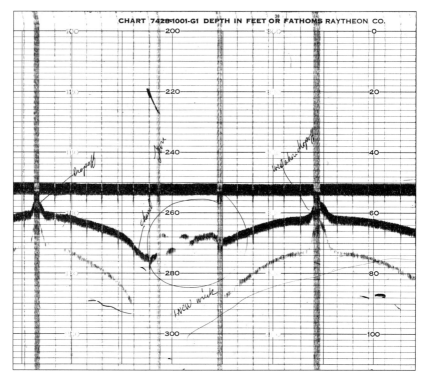

Fathometer record of the Nottingham Cannon Wreck that led to the site's relocation in 1978.

of entry), ended at the ruins of the old steamboat landing. Nottingham, the site of human occupation and industry for literally thousands of years, was now a ghost town in almost every sense of the word.

The reconnaissance of the river front of the old town was initially carried out by Eshelman, Hollingshead, my brother Dale, Sharon Gosnell (a volunteer), and myself, utilizing a borrowed U.S. Navy bottom sounder. With a general location provided by local informants (who claimed the wreck was still armed with cannon) and more precise data provided by our instrumentation, the site was quickly located.

A diver reconnaissance of the wreck, designated 1-NCW and dubbed the Cannon Wreck, revealed the remains to be lying in waters of thirteen to thirty feet deep on the edge of the channel dropoff and running parallel to the beachfront. The landward side of the hull lay almost imbedded in the bottom, while the seaward side had long since been swept away. On-site visibility was less than two inches, and the current was awesome. It was, in fact, impossible to make a direct, unassisted descent to the wreck without being carried a hundred yards or more downstream

162

before hitting the bottom. Our small anchor provided only minimum purchase in the soft muds of the riverbed, and dropping it into the wreck where it might cause further damage to the site was out of the question. Thus, downlines, tied to a tree near the beach, were run out to the wreck itself and secured, thereby allowing divers to pull themselves along hand over hand to the site without being swept away.

Our preliminary findings were both exciting and disturbing. It was immediately apparent that two gaping holes had been torn in the fabric of the well-preserved and still-strong hull remains, undoubtedly by the recovery efforts of relic hunters in earlier times. No evidence of the alleged cannon was found, only a small anchor of recent vintage. A total of five green bottle fragments, all basal ends, were the only datable artifacts recovered, but provided a mean date of circa 1760–1800. If the bottle fragments were, in fact, directly associated with the wreck and were not harbor debris or eroded materials washed into the site during or following the colonial–federal period of occupation, the wreck was of a pre-War of 1812 vintage.[20]

Yet, as exciting as our find was, the shipwreck wasn't the only target of interest in the immediate area. At first glance, the narrow beach along the western shore, terminated at both its northern and southern extremi-

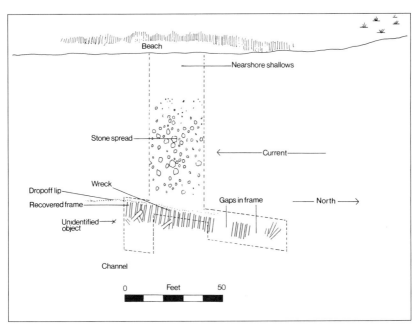

A preliminary sketch of the misnamed Nottingham Cannon Wreck site examined in 1978.

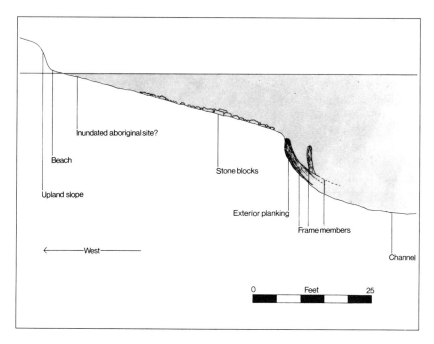

A lateral view of the Nottingham Cannon Wreck site examined in 1978.

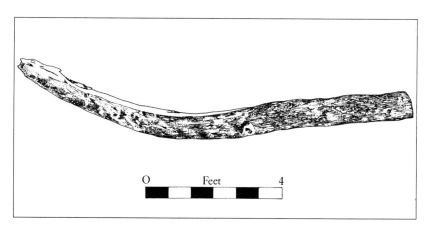

A single frame was recovered from the Nottingham Cannon Wreck for further study and speciation analysis. Wooden treenails were still in place when the sample was removed from the site.

ties by marshland and creeks and backed by a ten-foot embankment sloping from the upland terrace beyond, seemed unimposing. Signs of erosion, like elsewhere along the river, were abundant. One of the local

164

area residents, the congenial son of the farmer who had escorted Stearns about in 1950, reported that despite efforts to stabilize the shores, little had been or could be done to counter nature's depredations.

As we walked the beach, it became evident that there was more than fertile soil being lost. Reexamining the tract reported upon by Stearns, amidst innumerable gouges caused by erosion, we observed sherds of prehistoric pottery fully exposed, all of which were also found on the beach and, as we soon discovered, in the nearby waters. Underwater examination of the beach nearshore to a depth of nearly three feet revealed even more pottery amidst a liberal scatter of gravel and stone. Here, for the first time, we actually observed, during a sudden rainstorm, the dynamics of erosion converting littoral archaeological sites into inundated ones.[21]

For the next few days, as we continued our investigations in the waters, along the shores, and in the fields of Nottingham, reconnoitering the remains of harbor, wharves, building foundations, prehistoric and colonial sites alike, our expectations continued to be dwarfed by the archaeological realities of the area. No site, in either water or on land, however, quite prepared us for the largest single intact archaeological feature we were to encounter during the entire project: a man-made earthen mound wall, in places nearly six feet high, with great ditches on either side, and nearly a quarter mile long.

The mound wall was first brought to our attention by Edgar Merkle, and again by Rich Dolesh, of Patuxent River Park. It lay on the lip of the

The eroding shoreline at Nottingham has yielded important traces of prehistoric man's occupation of this fertile region of the Patuxent drainage.

165

south shore embankment of Lookout Creek, a short distance north of the old townsite, and extended westward from the banks of the Patuxent. The mound line itself was, for the most part, masked by heavy forest cover and was virtually invisible from either the air or nearby fields, and had been entirely overlooked by previous archaeological investigators. Lying just beyond the edge of the borderline of a recently plowed tobacco field, the line had formed a runoff barrier between the field and the creek and had apparently been left in place for that purpose by local landowners. A trench, now two feet deep but once undoubtedly much larger, ran along the north side of the mound, while a shallower, one-foot trench skirted the length of its southern side. Ancient oak trees, some estimated by Dolesh to be 150 years in age or older, grew from the sides and crown of the mound line along its entire length. In one section, a large gap of recent origin had been cut in the works, possibly to provide fill dirt or gravel for construction, land grading, or some other unknown purpose. At another point, a full 125-foot length of the line had been completely removed. At still another point, we discovered an earthen ramp that crossed the ditch on the southern side of the mound to the earthwork itself. At several locations, where the line was intersected by natural ravines or declivities, the mound ended abruptly only to be continued on the opposite side.[22]

Although permission to conduct a test excavation in the mound itself could not be secured from the property owner, we were permitted to walk the fields immediately adjacent to it. Here, surface collection in the plow zone produced a mixed assemblage of prehistoric lithics such as projectile points of quartzite and chert, fragments of bottle glass dating circa 1765, sherds of Rhenish stoneware, gray stoneware of the nineteenth century, numerous pipe fragments, iron slag, a tooth from a cow, and a scatter of oyster shell. The data, on its own and without provenance, provided little assistance in determining the nature and origins of the earthworks.[23]

What purpose had the earthworks served, when were they constructed, and who had built them? Myriad theories about the origins of the works asserted by local inhabitants ranged from defenses constructed by Barney during his two-month-long occupation of the town to the handiwork of prehistoric moundbuilders. Barney, however, was immediately ruled out on several counts, not the least of which was a total lack of archival data even vaguely supporting the theory. Moreover, as the works were facing north, on the south side of a deep valley, and above the north side of the town rather than on its south side, it would have served little purpose against an enemy ascending from the lower Patuxent.

Had the mound been erected by the British during their occupation under General Ross, possibly to defend the Nottingham anchorage? British records of the march on Washington and the occupation of the town, including drawings by Ross's chief engineer, failed to make mention

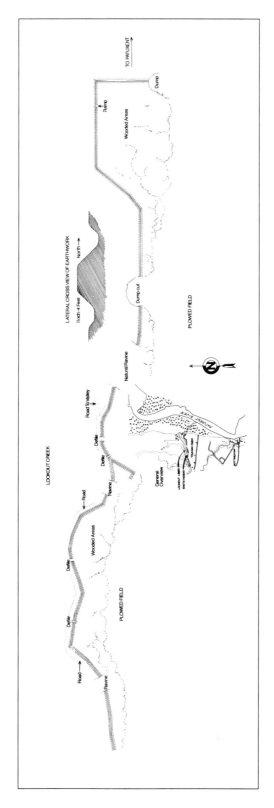

Plan of the Lookout Creek earthworks.

of any such works at or near the town. The time and effort necessary to erect such a structure, even by his four-thousand man army in the few hours they were camped here, would not have been overlooked by the numerous diarists who recorded the historic march. Had the works, perhaps, been erected during the Revolution, when Nottingham had served as the command center for the Board of Patuxent Associators? Again, a total lack of documentary evidence, and the northerly orientation of the works themselves seemed to preclude such a possibility.

Here, indeed, was the proverbial riddle wrapped in an enigma.

An extensive examination of the land title and probate records covering the tract upon which the mound and ditch line stood was begun in the Maryland Hall of Records to determine if there was any mention of the features during the colonial era or later. Any and all colonial newspaper accounts referring to Nottingham were sifted through in the colonial newspaper collections of the Library of Congress. Early aerial photographs of the area, most of which had been taken by the Department of Agriculture during the 1950s and housed in the National Archives, were closely scrutinized for any clues. Finally, after months of research, much of it promulgated through the generous assistance of county historian John Walton, we had our first solid clues into the origins of the mounds.

The tract upon which the mounds had been built was originally part of a 440-acre estate called Twiver, or Twyford, which had first been granted to and surveyed for one George Collins on August 1, 1673, not long after the departure of the last native inhabitants of the region.[24] In 1725 the tract was resurveyed for Richard Reed (or Read) and became known as Reed's Farm. Its northernmost boundary was a small waterway, now called Lookout Creek but then known as Patuxent Creek.[25] In 1731 a petition by several Nottingham merchants, Richard Lee, Alexander Contee, and James Russell, submitted to determine the bounds of lots in the new town nearby, mentioned for the first time an oak tree employed as a boundary marker and a house "to the southward of a ditch drawn by Capt. Richard Read" and "near a ditch drawn by Capt. Richard Read."[26] But of equal importance, the specific survey boundary lines of the northern terminus of the Reed tract coincided almost precisely with the mound line that we had surveyed ourselves. Yet, there were serious problems with the data, for the actual location of the aforementioned ditch was on the western periphery of the property and not on the north. Still, it was a most important piece of data, for it was the earliest documentation of an earthen excavation along the property line and offered a probable early colonial context for the mounds. Additional research soon confirmed the hypothesis.

During the colonial era, it had been a common practice for great landowners and farmers alike, often employing slave labor, to cut ditches to designate property lines, that is, to make visible borders between their lands and those of their neighbors. The resultant piles of earth dug from the ditches were sometimes hauled away but, as at Nottingham, not always. During the seventeenth century, ditch works on great estates such as at Wye House on the upper Eastern Shore were known as *hahas*, an archaic term of medieval English origins, used to denote a sunken wall. On occasion, worm fences were erected along or on top of the ditch mounds to enclose crop-producing fields and to keep out livestock, which were allowed to forage in the adjacent woods and marshes.[27]

For the next 130 years the Reed (or Read) Farm tract, though subdivided and reassembled numerous times, was passed from owner to owner, many of whom were Nottingham's most prominent citizens.[28] In 1764, Thomas Campbell, a prosperous factor for the Glasgow firm of Shortridge, Gordon and Company, owned a large plantation that had been erected on the Reed Farm acreage. His estate included a substantial two-story brick gable-ended house, a great stable paved with Dutch brick, a cook house, and slave quarters, all of which were reported as "newly paled [fenced] in." The whole plantation, replete with "one of the best landings upon Patuxent," when advertised for sale in the *Maryland Gazette,* was noted significantly as having "a good deal of ditching" around it.[29] By 1773, the new owner, David Carcaud, had even added a wharf to the riverfront side of the estate to facilitate his own mercantile interests.[30]

Ditching and mounds were mentioned, albeit infrequently, in the various title and probate records pertaining to property transfers thereafter. In 1917 a lease on a section of the tract to a tenant farmer mentioned for the first time "a ridge of earth in the N[orth] line of the tract," along Lookout Creek, a boundary description that was repeated in a 1942 deed.[31] Then, in 1969, a deed of sale reported the existence of "an ancient earth mound in the same location."[32]

The historic record, unfortunately, provided little address to the mystery of just why the ditch-mound line on the western border of the tract no longer existed. It seemed likely that the northern line had been ignored in the title and probate records until quite late simply because the natural boundary formed by the creek itself was quite suitable for descriptive purposes. But where was the western line? Had it been plowed under, or had it served as a massive borrow area for local construction? If the whole tract had been surrounded by a ditch-mound-fence line, as Thomas Campbell's advertisement in the *Maryland Gazette* in 1764 suggested, why had only its northern side survived? The discovery of a 1955 Department of Agriculture aerial photograph of the sector provided the answer.

Close examination of an enlarged version of the black and white photo, discovered in the National Archives, revealed a faint intimation of a second line, running southward along the western border of the tract. When the 1725 survey description was redrawn to scale on clear acetate and overlayed with the aerial photo, there was no question that it was one and the same as described in the various property records. Though the mound-ditch scar was no longer evident either from the air or on the ground, the photo was evidence enough to jar the memory of several local landowners. When presented with the data, they recalled that a slight mound had indeed once run across the field, but because it formed an obstruction to plowing, the mound line had been entirely removed by excavation. Nor had the Lookout Creek Mounds escaped unscathed. As we conjectured, certain sectors of the earthworks, informants then told us, more than once had served as borrow areas for fill dirt. Suspecting that the mounds had been built by Native Americans as burial mounds and unaware of their actual origins, others had even attempted several unsuccessful excavations to recover artifacts believed to be lying within.[33]

The dusty archives had provided an answer to the origins of the mysterious mounds. Though less than dramatic in purpose, the last vestige of the physical boundaries erected by Richard Reed, probably between 1725 and 1731, to define the limits of his plantation and to enclose his croplands, had survived as the most durable and largest intact remnant of one of Maryland's most prominent colonial towns, the one-time port known as Nottingham.

T E N

Frames, Flatties, and Trivets

By the late summer of 1978, the reconnaissance effort again pressed upriver, this time to examine the remnants of a small boat, cannonballs, and other artifacts dredged from the waters of Lyons Creek, on the border between Calvert and Anne Arundel Counties. It was a site that Ralph Eshelman was already quite familiar with, as it had been brought to his attention soon after he had assumed the directorship of the Calvert Marine Museum, but one that had yet to be fully examined.

The wreck was first discovered in 1974 when a local property owner on the creek named Olga Schwenk hired a local farmer to dredge and deepen a small portion of the shallow streambed adjacent to her land for a boat slip. The contractor, using a clam-bucket operated from the shore, was soon at work scooping the muck from the creek and depositing the spoils on the shoreline. All proceeded without incident until at a depth of ten feet into the silt bed he repeatedly hit a solid obstruction and was obliged to halt the operation to prevent injuring his machinery. The project was abandoned. Not long afterward, heavy rains began to erode the spoil piles, revealing several heavily corroded cannonballs, which were discovered by Mrs. Schwenk's son Peter. Further examination of the spoils produced not only more cannonballs, but fragments of a wooden boat, seventeenth century glassware and pottery, nearly intact kaolin smoking pipes, bones, and sundry other artifacts.[1]

The Schwenks, aware that something of historical importance might have been uncovered, immediately notified local historian Betty Briscoe who, in turn, informed Eshelman. With the assistance of a local sport diver, Charles "Buckie" Dowell, the young museum director attempted to further explore the site using a waterjet but because of the porosity of the sediments, enjoyed little success.[2]

When Nautical Archaeological Associates arrived in August 1978 to examine the site and the artifacts in the Schwenk collection, it was apparent that the Lyons Creek Wreck, as we soon dubbed it, was indeed likely to be one of the more important sites discovered on the river. With Peter Schwenk's assistance, a systematic effort to probe, but not excavate, the site was carried out from a boat and by divers. Ashore, Ralph Eshelman and his wife Evelyne, assisted by Nick Freda and Ken Hollingshead, began

Evelyne and Ralph Eshelman sift through spoils from the Schwenk site for artifacts.

The NAA survey team feeds a dredge hose to a diver working underwater at the Schwenk Site in Lyons Creek.

to thoroughly excavate and sift the previously made spoil pile in search of even the most minute artifacts that might have been overlooked by the Schwenks.

In the creek, using an open-bore rod, we quickly located an obstruction beneath ten feet of bottom soil, and a plug of wood, later determined to be white oak, was retrieved. Though it was impossible to directly associate the plug with the vessel remains as yet, the spoil pile more than compensated by yielding a wealth of artifacts, including more fragments of a wooden boat, cannonballs, potsherds, pipe stems, and sherds of green bottle glass, as well as gun parts, pieces of brick, coal, and even a battered copper pot. Most of the artifacts were promptly loaned by the Schwenks to the museum for further study. Eshelman made immediate arrangements to stabilize the waterlogged boat remains with polyethylene glycol, a microcrystaline wax used to fortify the cellular structure of waterlogged fibers and to prevent their collapse.[3]

The site was definitely intriguing. As I drove from Lyons Creek to the museum with over six hundred pounds of cannonballs in the trunk of my sagging compact car, I was certain we would be back.

□   □   □

Peter Schwenk was well aware of the historic importance of the Lyons Creek sector of the Patuxent Valley. He soon became a most valuable informant, assisting us in our efforts to document the sector's resources by directing us to numerous sites. One of the more important sites to which he prompted us, a derelict vessel, lay immediately below the ruins of the Lyons Creek steamboat wharf on a mud bank that was exposed only at low tide.

The wreck was badly deteriorated and lay broken in two separate pieces. One component consisted of frames, sections of fore and aft ceiling (floor) planks, a mast step, and a centerboard well. A second section, primarily composed of a portion of the starboard hull, lay nearby. Though shattered, and with lesser parts spread about a wide area of the mud bank, enough of the two main sections remained to allow a tentative and partial reconstruction.[4]

The boat was flat bottomed, with an overall length of 26 feet and an extreme beam of 10 feet 4 inches. Her stern appeared to have been square rather than rounded, and her extreme beam lay more than two-thirds of the length abaft of the bowstem. The bow itself was quite sharp and extremely tapered. The boat's frames were spaced at 16-inch intervals. A single mast step, which was eventually removed to the museum for preservation, was located 7 feet abaft the bow. The centerboard trunk, 9 feet in length, began 3.5 feet abaft the mast step and rose 3 feet above the apron. A small sapling had taken root in the center of the trunk and had

173

Tidewater Time Capsule

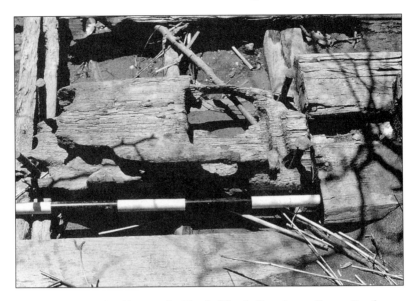

The mast step of the Chesapeake Flattie Wreck, found near Lyons Creek, was removed from the site soon after this photo was taken and entered into the collections of the Calvert Marine Museum.

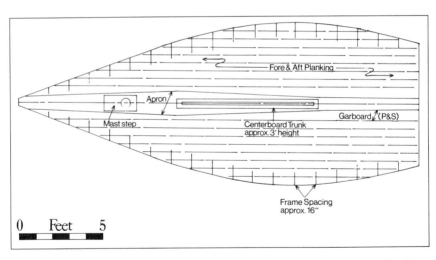

A deck reconstruction of the Chesapeake Flattie Wreck found near Lyons Creek.

already begun splitting the section apart as it grew. Despite nature's incursions, the remnants of an apron and garboard strakes could still be identified and measured. The boat had been entirely fitted with iron.[5]

Once the architectural data had been assembled, a composite plan drawing was made. The plan was then compared to known vessel types

174

with similar characteristics. The boat, we soon discovered, was a type known as a Chesapeake flattie, a short-lived, now-extinct watercraft whose development and tradition was entirely regional in character and evolution. It was a distinctive-looking vessel, with a sloop-rigged sharpie hull design with some dead rise aft. The origins, rise, and decline of the flattie had been documented by Howard Chapelle, the noted Smithsonian maritime historian, to the period shortly before the Civil War in Virginia, with variations appearing briefly in the Carolinas, Florida, and the Gulf states by the early 1880s. Also referred to as a Hampton flattie, the type was usually employed by black watermen in hauling produce in the streams and rivers of the Chesapeake Tidewater, and occasionally in oystering, crab scraping, and duck hunting on the Eastern Shore. Chapelle reported that the flattie did not last long in the Chesapeake, perhaps less than a few decades after its introduction, and had gone out of general usage by the 1890s, although a few remained in service until the first decade of the twentieth century. Unfortunately, owing to its extremely mundane service and brevity on the Tidewater scene, little documentation of the type or its genealogy existed. Chapelle himself had been forced to rely upon lines taken from several disintegrating hulks that he had found during the 1940s at Bishops Head, on the Nanticoke River, in Fishing Bay, and at Elliot, Maryland. None were known to exist on the western shore of the Chesapeake.[6]

The lines of one flattie had been taken in 1940 at Elliot; the vessel dated circa 1880–90 had been used primarily as a "handscrap oyster dredger."[7] The Elliot flattie was intriguingly similar to the Patuxent River flattie, although our find possessed a sharper plane, a bulkier beam aft central midships, and a mast stepped further forward.[8]

Here was a find indeed, a boat that may have served as a small freight hauler between upriver landings such as Hills and Bristol. By the time the craft appeared on the scene, the commerce of these landings had already begun to slowly strangle from the effects of siltation. She must have been a sight to see, tacking on the narrow river, this gawky-looking vessel whose evolution and all-too-brief appearance on the stage of Tidewater history was all but forgotten. Yet she was important to our growing comprehension of maritime development and decline on the river. The flattie's adoption on the upper waters of the Patuxent had undoubtedly been influenced by the radically changing environment, which was growing shallower and ever more impenetrable to the deep-draft vessels of earlier times with every passing year.[9]

Not surprisingly, all of the wrecks that were to be encountered above Nottingham, like the Chesapeake flattie, proved to be flat bottomed, despite their often imposing sizes. One such ship, named *Peter Cooper,* whose location several hundred yards south of Selby's Landing had been pointed out to us by a local youth, was typical. The *Cooper,* named after the famed builder of the first steam locomotive in America, the "Tom Thumb," was a wooden, flat-bottomed steam scow of 96.94 tons built in 1874 and registered at Philadelphia. Owned by one M. Dempsey, and captained by L.A. Dempsey, both of Philadelphia, she had been valued at eight thousand dollars at the time of her loss in 1887 and had apparently spent much of her career working in the Chesapeake, hauling freight. The *Cooper* was no stranger to maritime disasters, having experienced several nearly fatal mishaps before making her last trip to the Patuxent.[10]

On July 17, 1887, *Peter Cooper* had embarked from Washington, D.C., bound for Lyons Creek on what was destined to be her final voyage. She had sailed empty, intending to take on a cargo of diatomaceous earth, which was being mined from the cliffs below the creek and processed by a plant near Nottingham. Arriving off Lyons Creek on the evening of Tuesday, July 19, she suddenly took fire and within a short time had been entirely consumed to the waterline. Fortunately, her crew was saved by workers from the nearby diatomite works. The vessel itself, insured for five thousand dollars, was declared a total loss and her remains abandoned.[11]

When we first encountered the *Peter Cooper,* with her bow firmly lodged in the marshes of the western shore and her stern in fifteen to twenty feet of water in the river channel, her identity was entirely unknown to us. All we had been told was that there was a great obstruction, said by some watermen to be a wreck, lying below Selby's Landing. Rich Dolesh, of Patuxent River Park, believed the wreck to be that of the sloop *Lafayette,* which had been crushed by river ice and lost with a lading of building plaster in 1855 near Half Pone Landing, on the southern periphery of the park's southern border.[12] It was a good guess, but the wrong boat.

Close examination of the site by divers revealed that the wreck was definitely not a sloop. Indeed, the hulk was over 119 feet in length, 22 feet abeam, flat-bottomed, and round ended. Twenty-five feet from the stern we discovered small concentrations of broken whiteware and other debris, all fire-scarred and dating from the 1870s to the 1880s, and fragments of highly corroded eating utensils, probably from a small cabin topside which had collapsed into the hold as the fire burned the ship down. Fifteen feet further, the remains of 6-inch-wide planks covered by a well-laid bed of thin firebrick, with a collapsed brick wall to one side were discovered. It was all that had survived of the firewall insulation upon which the ship's steam engine had been mounted. A few feet beyond, the sternpost jutted up sharply, penetrated by a 4-inch-diameter shaft hole. Two feet further stood the rudder post, gudgeon, and remains of the rudder itself, listing to one side and swaying lazily in the current. The steam engine complex and propeller, valuable components on any vessel, had obviously been salvaged long ago, leaving only the burnt-out carcass of the vessel's hull guarded by a few diamondback snappers and water snakes.

Frames, Flatties, and Trivets

The wreck possessed numerous features suggesting that she had been a steam scow or barge, such as her flat-bottomed six-to-one length-to-beam ratio, the proximity of her steam engine firewall and deck cabin close to the stern, and her inordinately large cargo space—sans any evidence of cargo. Yet, her identity would remain a mystery for another two years. Then, in 1980, while examining an enormous collection of late nineteenth century wreckmaster reports from the port of Philadelphia for another project, I chanced upon the official report of the loss of the *Peter Cooper* in the Patuxent River, near Lyons Creek, and knew instantly that this was our ship. Everything matched.[13]

□   □   □

By early September the survey was again ready to move upriver. Our next major objective was to investigate the waters surrounding the conjectured site of the first county seat of Prince George's County, a lost town known as Charles Town. Here, on a thousand-acre tract of land surveyed in 1657 for Philip Calvert, brother of Lord Baltimore, and granted the following year, had been erected Calvert Manor, at or near the confluence of the Western and Charles Branches and the main trunk of the Patuxent. In 1683, by an act of the Maryland General Assembly, at the behest of the lord proprietor, a hundred-acre segment of Calvert Manor had been officially set aside for the erection of Charles Town. The following year, another act of the assembly declared the new town an official port of entry.

It had been, all things considered, a logical choice of location for a town, at the strategic fulcrum of the two creeks and the river, where a ferry to the opposite shores of the Patuxent had already been established. Unfortunately, like many "paper" towns, erected by legislative action and wishful thinking, it was a town whose star was destined to shine only briefly before flickering and dying. Yet, development had gotten off to an early and positive start as stores, ordinaries, warehouses, a church, and even a physician's office began to appear. In 1696 the justices of the newly erected county of Prince George's convened for the first time in Charles Town, which had been chosen as the county's first seat of government. The following year, a courthouse and jail were built, and a cage, whipping post, and stocks were put up, providing all the trappings of government, law, and order. It was, sadly, to be a short-lived residency.[14]

In 1706 the town of Marlborough, later to become Upper Marlboro, was founded by another act of assembly at the head of navigation on the Western Branch. Closer to the central core of the county for shipping than Charles Town, Marlborough soon began to compete with and then totally eclipse the county seat. By 1710 trade at Charles Town had begun to decline dramatically. In 1717 the official county weights and measures were moved to Marlborough, and the following year county residents

177

petitioned for the removal of the court as well. Public pressure could not long be ignored. On March 28, 1721, the county justices met for the first time in Marlborough, and thereafter, Charles Town slipped rapidly into obscurity.[15]

Today, a single large brick house, known as Mount Calvert, the sole surviving remnant of colonial Charles Town, sitting on a scenic promontory overlooking the confluence of the Western Branch and the Patuxent, is a place that reeks of untold history. From the owner of the old estate, we learned that several "ancient" wrecks were believed to be lying in the Western Branch, one of which had actually been discovered by the owner and his father but had been torn up to make way for a landing. Another, further upstream and referred to as the Iron Pot Wreck, had never been seen, but when the creek and surrounding marshes froze, its outline could be discerned by the gas bubbles, trapped and frozen in the ice, which had emanated from its rotting timbers.[16]

The Iron Pot Wreck was believed to be, as were most wreck sites in the region, one of Barney's barges. A penetration into the marshy waters failed, unfortunately, to locate any vestige of the purported vessel. An underwater investigation off the narrow strip of land that joined the upland plateau, upon which Mount Calvert was ensconced, with the waters of the Western Branch, where the landing had been erected, also failed to produce even a fragment of a wreck. The site did, however, provide other benefits. The area, like most tributaries of the river, was quite shallow from centuries of runoff and siltation, which had filled the channel once navigable for seagoing ships of up to three hundred tons. The channel banks, composed largely of clay, were sharp and still quite well defined from the dredging that had kept the waterway to Marlborough open to traffic to the end of the eighteenth century. Visibility in the coffee-and-cream-colored water was measured in millimeters. Yet the relics of ages gone by—the detritus of the seventeenth, eighteenth, and nineteenth centuries—were encountered in profusion. Here were brickbats, broken bottles, iron scrap, potsherds, and miscellaneous materials of all sorts covering the full historic span of occupation at Mount Calvert. Our objective, however, was not to collect artifacts but merely to assess the environment in which the resources lay. Thus, only a single artifact in relatively good condition was recovered.[17]

The artifact was a trivet, a round, three-legged stand made of iron and used to support and keep a kettle simmering over coals in a hearth. It was a piece of ironwork typical of a type employed in homes from the seventeenth through the nineteenth centuries and one that was not an altogether surprising find. The hillside adjacent to the house had clearly been regularly employed as a refuse dump for many years, and the refuse of centuries had just as regularly found its way, through erosion, into the creek.

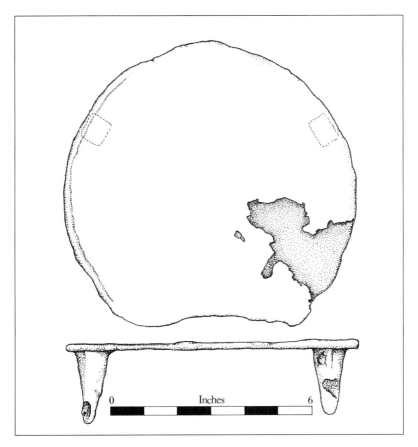

An iron trivet from the waters of the Western Branch off Mount Calvert, near the first county seat of Prince George's County.

The strategically defensive peninsular site had been as inviting to prehistoric peoples as it had been to the first white settlers. The plateau was rich with signs of prehistoric occupation, which was well attested to by the personal collections of lithics gleaned from the nearby plowed fields and displayed by the owner of Mount Calvert.[18] Yet, private artifact collections notwithstanding, it was again time to move on.

□   □   □

The finds encountered during the summer reconnaissance had, indeed, been exciting, but it was in the reach between Pig Point, now known as Bristol Landing, and old Queen Anne's Town, wherein lay the remains of the Chesapeake Flotilla, that the focus of our attention now turned. But the stretch of river was far more important than being merely the resting place for Barney's barges.

179

Native American settlements between Mount Calvert and Queen Anne's had, by the onset of the eighteenth century, been all but forgotten except in local place names. Of course, here as elsewhere along the river valley, colonial development had followed much the same pattern. In 1684 the town of "Pig Pointe," in Anne Arundel County, had been established by an act of the Maryland General Assembly, and fifty acres of land was allocated upon which the town was to be erected. Pig Point was connected to Prince George's County by a ferry, and to Herring Bay on the Chesapeake by overland road, and became a thriving crossroads but never a full-blown town. By 1706, when Marlborough and Queen Anne's Town were founded, urban port development on the river's shores had reached the saturation point. Still, many merchants, such as Stephen West, who owned stores in all three upriver locales, and agents for such important syndicates as Wallace, Johnson, and Muir continued to profit from a healthy maritime trade. In 1782, Bartholomew Bromley opened a ferry service, one of the last to be established on the upper Patuxent, at Mount Pleasant Landing, near Marlborough and above a small, marshy islet called Spyglass Island.[19] The great river highway upon which the service depended, however, had already begun its decline. And few seemed to notice or care, until it was too late.

The most dramatic event in the upriver reaches, the loss of the entire Chesapeake Flotilla—thirteen seventy-five-foot and fifty-foot armed barges, a row galley, a lookout boat, a hired supply schooner, the flagship *Scorpion,* and thirteen merchantmen—would soon dramatically illustrate the impact siltation was having. Had it not been for the heavy sedimentation which was already beginning to choke off riverine access to several of the northernmost towns and landings, the flotilla might have been saved.

Among the most important communiqués dispatched by Secretary of the Navy William Jones to Barney and rediscovered by Fred Hopkins was a letter instructing Barney to bring the fleet to Queen Anne's Town and from there to portage it overland to South River.[20] Barney immediately directed his son, Major William B. Barney, to take soundings of the Patuxent River from Nottingham to Queen Anne's and to examine the road from that place to South River. William quickly carried out his mission and reported back:

The depth of the water from this place [Nottingham] to Pig Point being already well known, I did not sound it. From Pig Point to Scotchmans Hole, about 4 miles higher up, is a sufficiency of water for the *Scorpion,* above that place she could not be carried without lightening and then only about one mile from this upwards there is not more than 4¼ to five feet at most—the river varies in width—above Pig Point and to within a mile of Queen Ann's it is narrow, not exceeding in some places 80 to 100 yards, its channel frequently crossing from side to side. For the last mile it is quite narrow and very winding but no where wider than to admit more than one barge to row up at a time, as far as the bridge at the town.[21]

Though the road to South River was passable, it was clear that many of the flotilla vessels might find it difficult, if not impossible, to reach Queen Anne's.

On August 21, 1814, Barney received orders from Jones to retreat with the flotilla to Queen Anne's, leaving only enough men behind to destroy it if necessary, and march to the defense of Washington. The commodore did his best, but with the shallowness of the river and the British nipping at his heels, there was little choice but to abandon the flotilla and its covey of merchantmen, well below Queen Anne's, to the charge of Captain Solomon Frazier and a hundred picked men with orders to scuttle it at the first sight of the enemy. The rest was history.[22]

When John Weems, whose property bordered on the river where the flotilla had been sunk, undertook the salvage of the fleet with the permission of the Navy, he was first obliged to halt the pillaging of the wrecks already under way by local inhabitants. Yet Weems was a resourceful man, and from a base of operations erected at Mount Pleasant Landing, just above the derelict fleet, he managed to salvage twenty-two of thirty-two cannons, along with large quantities of munitions, ship's anchors, and other items. The mission, however, proved far more difficult than he had anticipated, and larger support was needed. He requested the assistance of two Navy vessels on the Chesapeake to raise *Scorpion*, so that he might burn her down for her metal. But naval assistance was not forthcoming. Weems persisted and managed to raise or drag two barges onto the shore near Queen Anne's. Soon afterward, he raised a third but, in a fit of anger induced by the Navy's alleged refusal to pay him for his efforts, gave her over to a private citizen in Prince George's County. Barney's own battle-weary flotilla men were then inducted into a naval salvage effort and managed to recover the remainder of the guns, carriages, cambooses, shot, and most of the portable Navy property. But the boats themselves could not be moved and were abandoned to sink ever deeper into the Patuxent muds that had barred them passage.[23]

The remains of Barney's barges became a landmark of sorts on the upper Patuxent. In 1878, sixty-four years after their abandonment, many of the hulks were still visible in the shallow river waters.[24] In 1907, ninety-three years after their loss, Spenser Cosby, of the Army Corps of Engineers, after surveying the river for a proposed dredging project, reported: "A short distance above Hills landing there are visible at extreme low tide the hulks of some old vessels reported to have been sunk by the British during their attack upon Washington in the War of 1812."[25]

The oral traditions relating to the flotilla were, as elsewhere along the river, strong among the old-line families of the upper Patuxent. Here, too, were heard the well-told tales of cannonballs found along the shores, anchors recovered by watermen, and the pieces of wrecks occasionally snagged by fishermen. Indeed, a late eighteenth century anchor dragged up from the waters near Hills Landing by a local fisherman and donated to the museum was tantalizing. But without provenance, it was an artifact without a story. Yet, as elsewhere, every story, report, and clue was pursued with the thoroughness of an FBI investigation. And there were many red herrings.

Typical of the accounts told to us that, on the surface, seemed extremely promising was one provided by a waterman who had reported the loss of his fishing nets years earlier on a purported shipwreck above Hills Bridge. The nets had been weighted with hundreds of pounds of lead, which represented a substantial investment for the fisherman. When they became irretrievably entangled on the obstruction, they also represented a serious financial loss, and one that the fisherman would long remember. Guided by his directions, we attempted to relocate the site with a grapple hook. A target was soon snagged in the precise location we had been given. Diver investigation, however, revealed the obstruction to be not a wreck at all, as we had hoped, but a large tree which had toppled from the eroding shoreline and lay partially buried in the bottom, replete with fragments of fishing net and a few lead weights still entangled.[26]

Other targets reported to us simply could not be found, perhaps because they were buried deeply beneath the sediments, such as the one in Lyons Creek. Three sites said to lie in the vicinity of Back Channel Creek, which had been independently reported on by several informants, were cases in point. Repeated grappling and diving failed to yield the slightest hint of the three wrecks. Indeed, an examination of the wide marshes through which Back Channel Creek flowed, believed by some to have once been the open shallow reach above Pig Point mentioned by Admiral Sir George Cockburn, was examined by boat and on foot with equally negative results.[27]

Yet the geographic and historic parameters that also guided our search were quite clear. The first of these, of course, was that the fleet, according to Cockburn, had been blown up and sunk in the reach above Pig Point. We also knew, from Major William B. Barney's assessment of the river, that the *Scorpion* would have been unable to proceed much further than Scotchmans Hole without lightening (which was not done). Cockburn had reported that the flagship was "the headmost vessel," that is, the closest to the British fleet, and therefore the southernmost of the American squadron on the river, "with the remainder of the flotilla extending in a long line astern of her." The fleet, we concluded, must have all gone

The ruins of Hills Landing (modern Green Run Landing), the northernmost steamboat stop on the Patuxent, is still visible, but only during extremely low water. The landing closed to steamer service in 1885 owing to silting in of the river channel. Modern Hills Bridge lies several hundred yards to the north.

down or been captured above Scotchmans Hole. When Weems began his salvage work, his base of operations had been established at Mount Pleasant Landing, a ferry operations site that had continued in service until at least 1822. When Cosby produced his report on the Patuxent in 1907, he noted that many hulks could still be seen at low water above Hills Landing, now Green Run Landing.

The boundaries of the search area were thus clearly defined. The reach between Pig Point and the approximate area of Mount Pleasant Landing was three miles long. Between Hills Bridge and Mount Pleasant Landing the distance was less than a mile and a half. A total of twenty-nine American vessels had been lined up behind *Scorpion* when the British first

183

appeared. Calculating the average merchantman at seventy-five feet long, together with the known lengths of most of the flotilla vessels, the fleet would, if placed bow to stern, have formed a line over two thousand feet long. One barge had been captured by Cockburn, along with an unknown number of merchantmen, perhaps as many as half a dozen. Three more barges had been salvaged by Weems, leaving perhaps as many as twenty vessels littering the bottom of the river between Scotchmans Hole and Mount Pleasant Landing.

In October 1978, during an extremely low tide, we discovered the pilings, stretchers, and crib walls of the nineteenth century steamboat wharf at Hills Landing a short distance south and within sight of modern Hills Bridge. All we needed to do now was to ascertain the precise locations of Scotchmans Hole and Mount Pleasant Landing, and the rest, with the assistance of the proper remote-sensing equipment, would be duck soup. Or so we hoped.

Based upon the archival data, contemporary maps of the Patuxent, and British engineer's plan drawings of the march on Washington, which provided a general position for the flotilla, a bathymetric survey was laid out. We would be charting the river depth north of Hills Landing in an effort to locate the probable site of Scotchmans Hole and, hopefully, the Mount Pleasant Landing of 1814. Utilizing our little aluminum pram *Sneaky Seaweed* as a survey platform and equipment loaned to us by the Navy, we proceeded with the final phase of our reconnaissance of the Patuxent during the late fall.

Within hours of the start of the survey, barely half a mile above Hills Bridge, we discovered a gouge, over twenty-five feet in depth, in the otherwise shallow river channel. It was immediately conjectured to be Scotchmans Hole. Confirmation was not long in coming. Within a quarter mile further, the water shoaled up to barely eight feet in the channel, and within a few hundred yards more, to less than five feet.[28]

Our search for Mount Pleasant Landing was equally rewarding. A short distance above Spyglass Island and on the western shore of the river, spread at a distance of roughly one hundred feet apart, were the remains of three log structures exposed only at low tide and preserved by the river muds. All of the structures were similar in design and consisted of two parallel rows of logs, spaced one to two feet apart, and driven into the river bottom, with both lines extending perpendicular from shore. Between the two rows, lines of logs, now collapsed, had been laid horizontally across to form a deck. Now stained black by the river muds, the logs had been stripped of bark, cut, and trimmed with an axe or adze. Although all three sites were in a state of decay, a conjectural reconstruction of their simple design was readily completed. The structures, we concluded, were all that remained of three very small and primitive piers that would have been suitable only for hosting small watercraft.

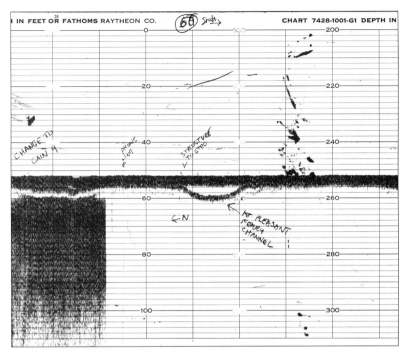

The vestige of the Mount Pleasant ferry channel across the Patuxent was located, as were the remnants of the ferry landing itself, during a bathymetric survey of the river above Spyglass Island.

The collapsed ruins of Mount Pleasant Ferry Landing. The primitive log site was encountered during extremely low water and is normally submerged.

185

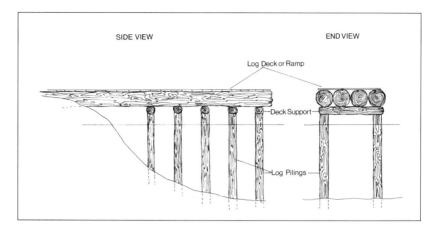

SIDE VIEW   END VIEW

Log Deck or Ramp

Deck Support

Log Pilings

Conjectural reconstruction of the Mount Pleasant Ferry Landing.

A bathymetric survey of the shallower waterway about the sites revealed that a trough, noticeably deeper than the surrounding riverbed itself (here only a few feet deep), ran diagonally across the river immediately below the piers. An intensive reconnaissance ashore failed to discover evidence of any habitation, roadbeds, trails, or access from the uplands beyond.

Were the three primitive piers all that remained of Mount Pleasant Landing? Based upon an atlas of Prince George's County published in 1878, which included the location of the landing as but a short distance above a small creek outlet on the western shore and immediately north of Spyglass Island, and comparative data provided by modern topographic maps, we were certain we had discovered our target. Here, we agreed, was the northernmost limit for the sepulcher of Joshua Barney's "much vaunted flotilla."[29]

Now, all we had to do was find it.

E L E V E N

Turtle Shell

In March 1979 Nautical Archaeological Associates and the Calvert Marine Museum jointly applied for and received a permit from the state of Maryland to conduct a formal underwater archaeological survey in the Patuxent River. It was to be the first permit ever issued by the state for such work, and as such established precedents that had not been hitherto addressed, not just for the Patuxent, but for Maryland and all of its submerged cultural resources.[1] It seemed obvious that what we did and how we did it was likely to affect the protocol and procedures for any similar endeavors that we or others might undertake in the future. It was somewhat sobering to speculate "that experience gained in this data-gathering operation may be employed in future projects in Maryland waters, . . . that the work undertaken in the Patuxent may form a model for investigations of other river systems."[2] Indeed, the impact of our simple but productive reconnaissance effort was already beginning to assert some influences on official state policy-making with regard to archaeology. By the spring of 1979, the Maryland Historical Trust, which had for several years been deeply involved in the evolution of an archaeological master plan for the state, began, for the first time, to seriously consider the incorporation of the submerged cultural resource base as an integral component in plan development.[3] If what we had confirmed in our first modest effort was any yardstick, the resources were there, and in great abundance. Just how great, we were certain, would be ably demonstrated by the next phase of the project. It was up to the state to utilize the data as it saw fit.

It was clear, from the limited information gained concerning the varying states of preservation of sites examined, the diversity of environments in which they were found, and the apparent relationship of certain types of resources to others, that our data base was far from adequate. Indeed, a synthesis of data assembled would not yet suffice if we were to attempt the formulation of a holistic model of the resource base of the Patuxent, nor would it permit the development of a suitable strategy for the evaluation of like riverine systems elsewhere in the Tidewater.

Only sites relatively well known or easily located had been examined, which limited the scope of the data base considerably. One thing, however, was sadly evident: there were serious stress factors impacting the survivability of the archaeological resources of the Patuxent Valley. Many of the sites had been visited by relic hunters or had been otherwise disturbed prior to our reconnaissance, and the archaeological integrity of some had already been critically injured. It was thus necessary, in the next phase of the project, that our principal objective be to locate and examine a representative portion of hitherto unknown or undiscovered sites which had not been impacted by stress.

In other words, the easy stuff was behind us. And, unlike the work undertaken in 1978, the next stage, incorporating remote-sensing technology, was going to cost money. Lots of it.

As early as the fall of 1978 Ralph Eshelman and I had begun to search for funding for the next phase of the project with "dog and pony" presentations to such institutions as the American Folklife Center, the National Trust for Historic Preservation, the National Endowment for the Humanities, and the Maryland Historical Trust. Our project design for the 1979 campaign was relatively simple and would consist of three subphases: 1) expansion of the ongoing literature search; (2) continuation of informant interviews and the examination of private artifact collections; and (3) the most important of all, the initiation of an intensive remote-sensing survey of four transects of the river, each representing a distinct environmental variable in which historic shipwrecks, structures, and insert sites might exist.[4]

The four transects selected for remote sensing would include the waters of St. Leonard's Creek, Nottingham, Lyons Creek, and a reach between Selby's Landing and the northern end of Spyglass Island, which represented, if not all environmental and historic variations, at least most of the extremes within the system (See Tables 2 and 3 on pages 128–29). A thorough examination of each transect, utilizing state-of-the-art remote-sensing instrumentation, would be executed, with field proofing on each new site located to be carried out by divers.[5]

Early in the reconnaissance phase it had become apparent that many archaeological sites in the Patuxent lay partially or entirely buried beneath the sediments that had been steadily filling the river since colonial times. Indeed, it seemed the further north we had gone, the deeper the burial. As suggested by the Lyons Creek site, some wrecks could lie as deep or deeper than ten feet below the bottom. The realities of the river's physical environment thus dictated the remote-sensing array that would be most suitable for search.

Three types of remote-sensing technologies were considered for the survey: side-scan sonar, sub-bottom profiling, and magnetometry. The physical location of the remains, as well as the specific environments in which they would be deployed, suggested that the first two might prove inappropriate. Side-scan (side-reading) sonar, quite effective for open seas and the bottom conditions that might be encountered on the Chesapeake or Atlantic, was deemed unsuitable for the often extremely narrow confines of the Patuxent. The value of side-scan lay in its ability to send out acoustical impulses and to record the profile of targets that those impulses encounter as they travel outwards and rebound off the obstructions. The rebound of the sound wave is picked up by a sonar receiver; the distance traveled is calculated and transmitted to a strip chart recorder, which provides a graphic picture of the acoustic data. The side-scan, however, was deemed impractical for two major reasons. First, considerable riprap, trees, and other debris were strewn about many sectors of the river bottom. Second, cultural materials, especially on the upriver reaches, very probably lay buried deep beneath the bottom sediments and thereby would offer few surface obstructions.

The sub-bottom profiler, an acoustical device designed to detect obstructions lying beneath marine sediments, was also considered but disallowed. In environments with great accumulations of vegetation, such as in tidal marshes or shallow river systems like the upper Patuxent, gases resulting from decaying matter percolate through the soft bottom and tend to distort or "fool" the profiler, often indicating anomalies where none exist.

The proton precession magnetometer, though possessing limitations of other kinds, was selected as the most suitable device for the job. For decades, the magnetometer, or "mag," has been recognized as one of the most versatile remote-sensing instruments in the archaeologist's electronic tool kit. Capable of detecting submerged and/or buried materials and features, it has successfully been used to locate a variety of materials and features, including anything made of ferrous metal as well as buried walls, kilns, ditches, pits, and even tombs. At shipwrecks, even those covered by sands or silts, the magnetometer can detect not only such iron artifacts as cannons, anchors, and fittings, but also some ballast stones, pottery, and kiln-fired clay items, which are also slightly ferromagnetic.

To appreciate the application of the proton magnetometer, it is first necessary to understand the types of magnetism that permit the creation of magnetic anomalies in ferromagnetic materials which can result in their detection. There are only two types of magnetism, induced and permanent. *Induced* magnetism is the combined effect of a magnetic property of the material (its permeability), the earth's magnetic field, and the shape and orientation of the object in that field. If magnetic permeability is high, such as for iron or steel, the material may be described as ferromagnetic. Such factors oblige the materials to act as a magnet in the presence of the earth's magnetic field. The shape and orientation of an object also serve to enhance induced magnetism, for the longer the object and the more nearly parallel to the earth's magnetic field it is, the stronger the magnet.

Permanent magnetism, or "perm," is a property related only to the object in question and not to its orientation or to the earth's magnetic field. Some objects, however, may attain a perm by remaining in the earth's magnetic field at a fixed orientation over a long period of time. Generally, the magnetic disturbance, or anomaly, recorded by the magnetometer will be the sum of both the induced magnetic effects and the perm. Still, the perm represents the most predominant property useful in searching for a buried or submerged object and will occasionally be as much as ten times the induced magnetism. Usually, materials such as water, air, sand, silt, or coral do not affect the magnetic anomaly of a given object, although igneous rock (absent in most of the Chesapeake) will.

It is possible to compute the size and shape of a target based upon the magnetic signature of an object in question and the distance from the sensor head, as the magnitude of a magnetic field is inversely proportional to the distance the target is from the sensor head of the magnetometer. The closer the sensor head to a target, the greater the recorded magnitude.

The proton precession magnetometer is an instrument designed to measure the total magnetic field of a given area. To accomplish this goal, it utilizes the precession torque of protons in a hydrocarbon fluid, generally kerosene encapsulated within wire coils in the sensor. This fluid is temporarily magnetized via direct current flow in the wire. When the current is removed the protons (hydrogen nuclei) then precess much like spinning tops all about the direction of the magnetic field of the earth at a frequency directly proportional to the magnetic intensity and independent of the direction of the sensor. The bottle containing the coil and kerosene of the sensor unit is sealed within a housing at the end of a durable, electronically suitable tow cable.

The frequency of the signal from the sensor is transmitted up the cable to a magnetometer console where it is measured by electronic circuits in the magnetometer unit with a resolution of generally one gamma, with measurements made at rates varying from one reading every six seconds to a high of three per second. The measurements are displayed on an analog chart recorder and can be digitally recorded as well. The data is presented on the chart at various sensitivity factors, which supply both resolution and dynamic range to portray local change caused by regional gradients or background.

The tow system, consisting of the sensor head and the cable unit, must be nonmagnetic and low in microphonic response. When deployed, its height or distance above the bottom, the length of tow, the environmental conditions during the search, and other considerations are all important factors in conducting a marine search. Instrument noise produced by the magnetometer itself, noticeable if there are violent motions of the sensor, may cause a Doppler effect, or "noise spikes," resulting in false anomaly observations by the magnetometer. Tidal or swell activity may produce an induced magnetic field anomaly because the activity represents a mass of conducting water moving through the earth's magnetic field, causing perturbations that will also be noted by the magnetometer. Atmospheric and regional interference, such as solar flares, electrical storms, the passing of a locomotive or an automobile, or interference caused by the instruments passing a bridge, radio tower, house, or another ferromagnetic structure, will also result in false observations. Fortunately, there were few such obstructions on the narrow Patuxent or in the myriad backwaters that we had selected to survey. All we needed was the financial support to secure the appropriate equipment and the experienced technicians to manage it.

In late March 1979, we were delighted to learn that a major matching grant application that we had submitted to the Maryland Historical Trust had been approved. The Trust, we learned, would serve as the administering agency for funds being provided by the Heritage, Conservation, and Recreation Service of the U.S. Department of the Interior. Within a week, negotiations had been entered into with a remote-sensing specialist, marine archaeologist Daniel Koski-Karell, of the Karell Institute of Alexandria, Virginia, and a contract was agreed upon.

The second season of the Patuxent Project was about to begin.

□   □   □

"You boys still huntin' fer shipwrecks?" the old waterman sitting by the dock at Zanheiser's Marina at Solomons asked me not long after the grant had been approved.

"Sure," I said, always looking for a lead. "Know of any?"

"Why don't you take a look at that old submarine out there off Point Patience? I heard she was sunk in the war with a treasure aboard," he replied matter-of-factly. "I hear she was one of them Nazi U-boats."

You could have knocked me over with a feather on that one, though I thought I had heard them all. This was one for the books, a preposterous tale of a sunken sub in the Patuxent, and a Nazi sub at that. It simply couldn't be true. Or could it?

The waterman in his canny way refused to elaborate, no matter how hard I pressed him, letting me stew in my own curiosity.

Several days later, while researching in the CMM library, I mentioned the incident to Leroy "Pepper" Langley. Born in 1915 at Solomons, Pepper was something of a local legend. A master wood carver, he had worked in and around boat building on the Patuxent since his childhood and was famed throughout the Tidewater for his beautiful carvings and ship models. He had, in fact, been one of the founding fathers of the Calvert Marine Museum. During World War II he had been employed in naval ship construction and testing at the M. M. Davis and Son yard and then at the Naval Mine Warfare Test Center at Solomons. If anyone would

191

know something about a submarine lost off Point Patience, it was Pepper Langley. "Indeed, we did have a submarine here," he said.

> She wasn't no Nazi, though. Navy boat she was. They had no use for it so they took it in this deep hole above Point Patience, and they sunk it in a hundred and twenty-six feet of water, mainly to give their divers something to train on and probably try to cut a hole in, rescue work, such as that. That's a very hazardous place where the water is squeezed down the most narrow of any place in the river, and creates an awful strong whirling tide.[6]

Although Pepper was unable to identify the ship, it now seemed probable that a sub did lie in the waters off the point.

Further research at the Naval Historical Center in Washington, D.C., soon verified that there was indeed a submarine sunk off Point Patience, one of a series of S-class boats designed in 1915 and produced in mass between 1918 and 1922. A total of fifty-one S-boats had been built before the London Naval Limitation Treaty of 1922, which restricted the number of capital ships and submarines that could be fielded by signatory nations, had brought the program to a close. According to U.S. Navy records, the boat lying in the deep trough of the Patuxent, indeed one of the deepest in the entire Chesapeake, was the *S-49*.

Laid down on October 22, 1920, by the Lake Torpedo Boat Company, of Bridgeport, Connecticut, the *S-49* was launched six months later, on April 23, 1921, commissioned on June 5 of the same year, and placed under the command of Lt. Ingram S. Sowell. She possessed a surface displacement of 933 tons and a submarine displacement of 1,230 tons. Measuring in at 240 feet in length, 21 feet 10 inches abeam, with a mean draft of 13 feet 6 inches, her top surface speed was put at 14.5 knots, and her submerged speed was 11 knots. Her first assignment had been as part of Submarine Division Zero, a submarine research and development unit at New London, Connecticut. She was later to be employed in secret experimental work. Yet her active career was to be short-lived. In 1926 she suffered two accidental hydrogen gas explosions in her battery room, which injured and gassed twelve men, four of whom died. After undergoing extensive repairs, she was relegated to training duties until being decommissioned on August 2, 1927. On March 21, 1931, the *S-49* was removed from the Navy list and soon after was sold to the Boston Iron and Metal Company for scrap. By 1936, though reduced to a bare hulk, she had yet to be broken up, possibly because of the depressed price of scrap metal. Several years later the Navy reacquired her for use "as equipment" in experimental work at the Naval Mine Warfare Proving Ground at Solomons. Soon after the onset of World War II she was accidentally sunk during testing off Point Patience and was finally abandoned.[7]

Precisely how *S-49* died remains a mystery. Some old-timers said the battered old sub was being used for training for divers sent down from the Navy's Diving and Salvage School at Washington, D.C. Others said that she had been rigged for sonar trials, mine testing, and submarine escape. Whatever had caused her demise, however, time and tide had served to erase her memory from all but a few senior residents of Solomons.

I was delighted to learn of the vessel's existence, and to be apprised of her approximate location from several watermen, not only because she was another addition to the growing inventory of historic shipwreck sites in the river, but because we now had a large verifiable ferromagnetic target of known dimensions, tonnage, disposition, and depth upon which we could test, calibrate, and fine-tune our remote-sensing gear before setting out on the survey of the four designated transects.

□　　□　　□

Koski-Karell and a Canadian marine archaeologist named Colin Drury Languedoc, with whom I had contracted to assist in the remote-sensing work, had been eager to get under way on the morning of June 1, 1979. A thirty-foot wooden-hulled Owens called *Sagittarius,* belonging to Nick Freda, was recruited into service as the principal survey vessel. A second boat, our own *Fincastle,* a thirty-two-footer, was employed to run interference with the heavy pleasure boat traffic of the region as we ran our survey patterns. With the sensor being towed as much as seventy-five feet astern of the survey boat, and with scores of powerboats and water-skiers tearing about all around us in the reckless abandon of summer, the danger of having the tow line severed and sensor head lost was considerable. The mission of *Fincastle* was doubly important.

Perhaps the most important consideration in conducting any remote-sensing search mode is the need for precise positioning controls, to enable appropriate mapping of site data gathered during the survey. In other words, you need to know where you are at all times so that once you find your target, you can relocate it. The then-most-recent innovations in the use of electronic positioning control and calculator-plotter systems for marine archaeological survey, most successfully deployed in the search for sixteenth century Spanish shipwrecks off Padre Island, Texas, and in the search for the wreck of the U.S.S. *Monitor,* off North Carolina, though highly accurate, were not within our modest budget.[8] Traditional Loran and magnetic compass bearings taken on prominent landmarks would have to suffice. Fortunately, the four transects that we would be surveying were all within the narrow confines of a riverine environment in which, at any given point, geographic landmarks could also be used for triangulation.

The *S-49* lay somewhere beneath a rectangular block of open water one-half mile wide and three-quarters of a mile long off the sandy pit of

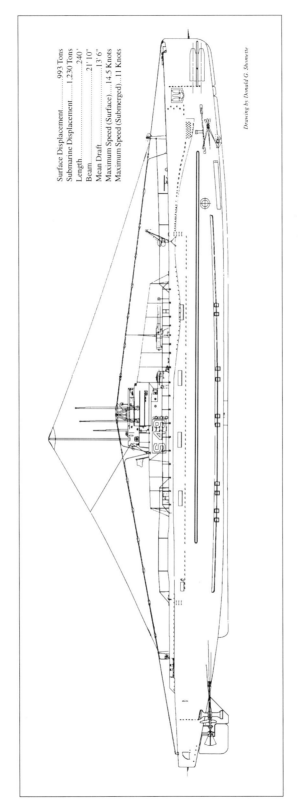

Surface Displacement..............993 Tons
Submarine Displacement......1,230 Tons
Length...............................240'
Beam..................................21' 10"
Mean Draft.........................13' 6"
Maximum Speed (Surface)....14.5 Knots
Maximum Speed (Submerged)...11 Knots

Drawing by Donald G. Shomette

Plan view of the United States Navy submarine *S-49*.

Point Patience. In April 1943 the area had been designated a restricted zone in which naval mine warfare tests were to be conducted. Our search sector was believed to contain not only the hulk of the submarine, but numerous dummy mines and other ordnance items used from 1943 to the end of the war as well.

Lane buoys, normally laid out as navigational guidelines, were not deployed during the field testing since the principal purpose of the operation was to check out instrumentation. However, radio coordinates and plots of magnetic and landmark bearings, utilizing the Point Patience light, the radio tower, radio poles, the Thomas Johnson Bridge struts, and several prominent headlands, provided ready positional reference. During the first trials, both sensor heads were tested and played out at various distances on the tow line. Fine-tuning of the magnetometer was conducted to establish the most appropriate repetition rate of signal transmission from the sensor head. And throughout the operation, *Fincastle* scuttled about like a nervous water bug, constantly keeping small boat traffic from entering the tow trail zone of the sensor, not only to prohibit the accidental severing of the tow line, but to prevent the magnetometer from registering false anomalies caused by metals associated with the "bandit" craft or their engines.

Despite some initial difficulties, an anomaly suitably large enough to be the sub was recorded just upstream from the point. The depth sounder verified that we probably had our sub, sitting proud above the bottom in 125 feet of water. A long scatter of debris, believed to be portions of the vessel blown off during mine testing, trailed off downriver from the wreck. It would later be determined by divers that the site was, indeed, the wreck of the *S-49*, sitting upright with a modest tilt to starboard, bow pointed downriver, as if ready to sail once more. Our instrumentation was working famously and was quickly transferred to a Boston Whaler to begin the survey of the shallow waters of St. Leonard's Creek.

The entirety of St. Leonard's Creek, over four nautical miles in length, of course, could not be completely surveyed. To insure that those areas most likely to possess submerged cultural resources were covered, the creek was divided into four discrete subtransects. Working in this beautiful, almost pristine little waterway, it was hard to imagine the thunderous events that once echoed across its surface. But imagination was all that was going to sustain us here, for aside from the remains of a derelict cabin cruiser and the brief reexamination of the sites that we had already investigated, the remote-sensing survey of St. Leonard's produced little in the way of new data—or sites. The survey of the next transect (Nottingham) we hoped, would prove far more interesting.

On June 6 *Sagittarius, Sneaky Seaweed,* and the Boston Whaler made the long trip up the Patuxent to the promising waters off the old port and began work the next morning. Here, we would be surveying a stretch of river beginning just below the town and extending a full nautical mile northward.

The magnetometer survey of the Nottingham transect took two and a half days to complete, but produced the first solid new discoveries of hitherto unknown sites. The first, a shipwreck site covered by coarse sand was promptly dubbed the Sand Wreck. The second, a target deeply buried beneath sediments but believed to be a second shipwreck site, was called the Mud Wreck. A reexamination of the Nottingham Cannon Wreck (1-NCW) also produced a superb magnetic record. Diver investigations of all three sites proved fruitful.

We reinvestigated 1-NCW with difficulty, as the shore-to-wreck line laid in the previous year had apparently snapped and could not be relocated. Nevertheless, making the first dive on the site, I was able to tie a marker buoy on a stable timber, which allowed ready access from the dive boats. A lengthy diver survey was then undertaken, even as Koski-Karell and Languedoc continued with the magnetometer work.

The Cannon Wreck was over 74 feet long, with two massive gaps, one eight feet wide and the second ten feet wide, torn in its hull. Many frames had totally collapsed, as a consequence of these tears. An effort to locate the seaward (eastern) side of the wreck, believed to have fallen away into the channel, was undertaken, but to no avail. The site, battered by the forces of nature and half a century of relic hunting, was in a terrible state of disfigurement. But a single frame was recovered for later diagnostic evaluation. The identity of 1-NCW had grown more intriguing than ever. Had she been one of the many merchantmen that had visited the town during its heyday, or perhaps a Revolutionary War era or federal-period ship, as suggested by the bottle fragments recovered from the site? Or had she been merely an old derelict abandoned after the town had declined? Perhaps we would never know, for the site was anything but easy to survey.[9]

In the near-zero visibility and high currents, which forced us to literally wrap our legs around sections of the wreck when taking measurements, accidents were an ever-present threat. Once a diver let go, he could be carried off downstream instantly, and with near zero-visibility no one would have known. On more than one occasion, divers became tangled in monofilament fishing line, totally invisible in the Stygian-hued waters, and were obliged to carefully cut themselves loose with their dive knives. Any obstruction or line was a potential hazard. Indeed, I even had the dubious honor of relocating the seaward end of the old shore-to-wreck line, which had remained tied to a frame on one end, while flapping wildly about in the currents with the other. Without my knowledge of its presence, the line had become wrapped around my tank valve. When I attempted to surface, my air having been all but expended, I found myself mysteriously anchored to the wreck. Fighting off panic I struggled to locate the means of my imprisonment and to cut it loose. The realization that in the mud-black water no one even knew precisely where I was on the site or of the difficulty I was in, even though my dive partner was within but a few feet of me was of little consolation. Within seconds, however, I had located the line, which was now wrapped about my waist as well, and cut myself free. Thereafter, buddy lines connecting every dive team became mandatory.

Survey of the Sand Wreck was far less dangerous. Lying barely fifty feet from shore, in less than seven feet of relatively placid water, the site was the first to be located during the survey by magnetometer, and then pinpointed by diver manipulation of the sensor head. Completely buried by sediments deposited from the outflow of a small creek, the parameters of the site remains were ascertained by piercing the bottom with iron rods to determine its overall dimensions. By hand-fanning the sand away, we could briefly expose portions of the wreck before the currents dusted it over again. Though some sections were under but a few inches of sand, others were deeply buried, and apparently disarticulated fragments lay scattered about the area in some profusion. The overall length of the largest single section of the wreck, a well-preserved fragment of hull, appeared to be forty-five feet, while the general span of the entire wreck area was more than seventy-five feet. No diagnostic artifacts associated with the site could be found. Was the site the remains of a second shipwreck or merely the other half of 1-NCW, which had broken away and come to rest here? Like those asked before, the question would have to be answered at some later date, for there was only so much time to devote to site analysis.[10]

The Mud Wreck, lying well upriver of 1-NCW, was the second site located by the magnetometer and lay inhumed beneath a thirty-foot-long mound of mud which was almost liquid in consistency. Using long iron rods, divers systematically probed the mound for signs of the origins of the magnetic anomaly. Penetrating to a depth of six feet below the ooze, Colin Languedoc discovered a soft, pulpy, wooden structure of undetermined size which, although impossible to verify as being a shipwreck or part of a wreck, was nevertheless chalked up as a strong candidate because of the strength of its mag signature.[11]

□   □   □

The finds at Nottingham, after the negative results of the remote-sensing survey of St. Leonard's, had served as a tonic to the occasionally flagging spirits of our survey team, several of whom had expected the bottoms to be littered with shipwrecks. There was, in fact, some justification for their hopes. Our archival research had indicated that more than 140 shipwrecks and derelicts once lay or still rested in the Patuxent proper and off its entrance.[12] Hence, the prospects of further discoveries in the next transect, Lyons Creek, were eagerly looked forward to, particularly

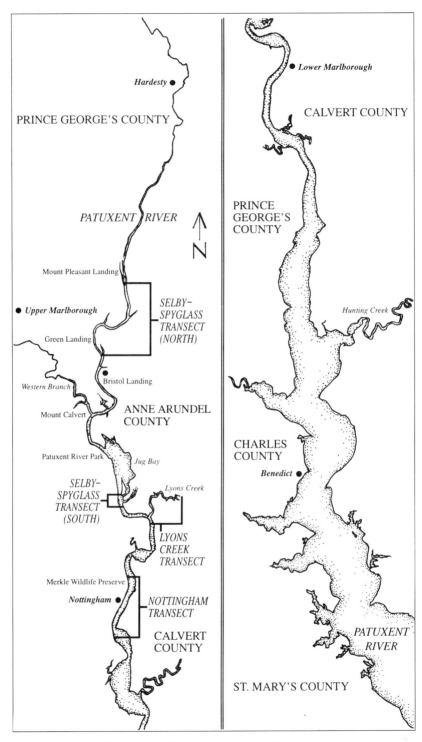

Map of the Nottingham, Lyons Creek, and Selby-Spyglass transects.

198

at the Schwenk site. To survey these extremely shallow waters, however, would require some experimentation in our survey methodology.

Hitherto, the sensor head had been towed a minimum of fifty feet behind the survey boat and at various depths. To traverse shoally, extremely narrow and twisting upriver waterways such as Lyons Creek, which were often clogged with debris, tree branches, and other obstructions, it would be necessary to keep the sensor head just above or on the surface of the water. A pole assembly, projecting the sensor head well ahead of the survey craft was tried but proved unsuccessful. A more successful approach that was used thereafter was to wrap a flotation jacket around the sensor head, thereby providing enough buoyancy to keep it barely submerged.

Survey patterns on St. Leonard's and at Nottingham had been laid out in lane intervals of twenty feet. This distance between lines, given the shallow water depths generally encountered (usually less than twenty-five feet), was chosen in order to permit the detection of all magnetic anomalies in each survey sector having a magnetic strength equal to that created by one hundred pounds or more of ferromagnetic material such as iron. It would, of course, also permit the location of much smaller items as well. We used sealed white plastic milk cartons as buoys to delineate each successive block being surveyed and to mark targets for positioning and for later diver investigation. Frequently, divers would be used to pinpoint smaller anomalies by hand-maneuvering the sensor head in inaccessible areas blocked by fallen trees or where they were deeply buried. When undertaking such maneuvers, however, the divers had to strip down to bathing suits only and free-dive, since metal items such as air tanks, knives, and even zippers or clips might affect the reading.

Two areas were surveyed in and about Lyons Creek. The first extended from the mouth of the creek upstream for nearly a mile, to the very headwaters of navigation. The second incorporated a survey at and below the ruins of the Lyons Creek steamboat landing. A total of three targets were registered, none of which produced anything but disappointment. The first target was the Schwenk site. Here, unfortunately, the mag signatures were totally obscured (and thus interpretively useless) at every pass over the "wreck" site by a series of iron mooring poles that had been driven into the creek bed by local property owners or that had fallen and now lay prone on the bottom. A second site proved to be nothing more than a recently collapsed boat dock. A third, buried beneath three feet of sediment nearly a mile up the creek, was a large rectangular metal anomaly believed to be either an engine block or a kitchen appliance such as a refrigerator.[13]

We tried to console ourselves with the old adage that even negative information is important and prayed that the last transect would be different. After all, there was a whole fleet of ships out there just waiting to be found!

On Monday, June 11, the day we were to begin the survey of the Selby-Spyglass transect, I entered into my log: "Go for the big one."

It was, indeed, the largest single transect to be examined during the survey, a range of nearly three miles of river from a point below Green Run Landing to Spyglass Island. A small sector of the transect further down around Selby's Landing had already been scrutinized but, with the exception of the *Peter Cooper* site, was without any noteworthy targets. Now it was time to find the flotilla.

The morning was warm but wet with a mild drizzle as we set off at eight o'clock from Patuxent Park in the Boston Whaler and the *Muskrat*. There were five of us aboard: Koski-Karell, Languedoc, Hollingshead, Hopkins, and myself. Survey of the sector, we knew, would be interpretively more difficult than any of the others. In several places large contemporary features were likely to obscure indications of those of earlier times. The twin iron spans of modern Hills Bridge, erected over the site of a nineteenth century bridge, would totally destroy any possibility of locating sunken vessels within several hundred yards north and south of the structure, in an area where local traditions suggested vessel remains still lay. Some distance above that, at the edge of a large trailer park near Wayson's Corner, the presence of a long wooden retaining wall fitted with iron bolts, sections of which had fallen into the river, might also mask signatures of features from earlier times. Owing to the sector's proximity to urban centers, there was also a considerable quantity of contemporary refuse, much of it likely to provide magnetic targets that would require hands-on identification and cost us substantial field time. The heaviest concentration of refuse, unfortunately, was to be found in the vicinity of the trailer park, directly in the reach in which we believed the flotilla remains to lie. Nevertheless, we set off with unbounded optimism.

We began the survey near a small creek well below Green Run Landing by following the now-familiar procedure of laying out buoys for lane lines, sighting in bearings, and then deploying the mag sensor. Within minutes of beginning our first run we began to register targets, even though we were more than a mile below Scotchman's Hole, the conjectured southern terminus of the flotilla. At each target a marker buoy would be cast and *Muskrat*, bearing our dive team for the day, would come up, establish site position, and dispatch a diver to investigate.[14]

Many sites proved to be of contemporary cultural affiliation, composed of little more than the flotsam and jetsam of modern society. Other targets, deeply buried beneath the sediments, were more problematic. One such, lying under an estimated ten feet of sediment off a small marsh outlet called Mill Creek, could not be identified. Another, lying off the ruins of the old steamboat wharf at Hills Landing in eight feet of water, proved to be large conglomerates of badly deteriorated iron of undetermined usage, but probably associated with the landing itself. Then, as we

Archaeologist Daniel Koski-Karell and assistant Colin Drury Languedoc conduct
a magnetometer survey in search of signs of the elusive Chesapeake Flotilla
in the lower sectors of the Selby-Spyglass Transect amidst the wetlands of Jug Bay.

approached Scotchmans Hole, the rain stopped and the sun, as if on cue, emerged. The targets became more numerous than ever.[15]

Dan Koski-Karell and I, after many days of drawing mostly blanks, rarely moved our eyes from the strip chart printout except when ordering a buoy dropped. The targets came so rapidly now that we dared not stop to investigate each lest the spell be broken, but continued pushing methodically northward toward Spyglass Island, back and forth, lane by lane. Finally, as we arrived at the reach above the island, the water shoaled so abruptly that we could no longer proceed without danger of snagging the sensor head on river debris or dragging it across the bottom. With more than forty buoys deployed, it was now time to begin hands-on investigations of our targets.

Less than half a mile above Scotchmans Hole, Colin Languedoc was dispatched to investigate our first and most impressive anomaly, which lay in six to eight feet of water in a narrows of the main channel. At first nothing could be seen. Fragments of wood sticking out of the bottom, believed to be buried remnants of yet another tree swept into the river from some eroded bank upstream, were located, but nothing more. Hollingshead jumped in to assist, and the sensor head was again deployed to manually pinpoint the anomalies. Despite the paucity of surface features, there was definitely a major target buried beneath the sedi-

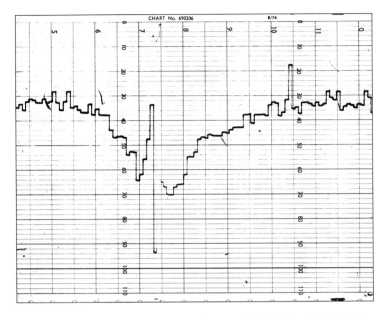

Magnetometer signature of unidentified anomaly in vicinity of Hill's Bridge.

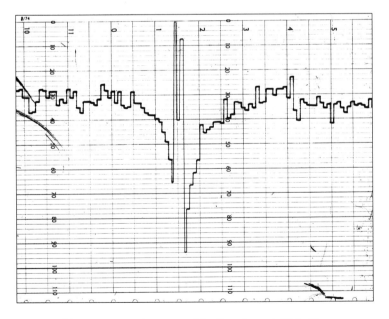

Magnetometer signature of the Scotchman's Hole Site.

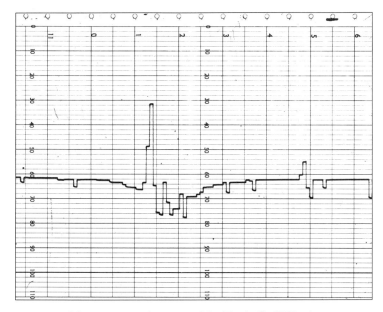

Magnetometer signature of the Turtle Shell Wreck.

ments. What it was, was anyone's guess, although it was located in the river well above the sites of most contemporary depositions and squarely in the stretch wherein the fleet was conjectured to lie. We decided to dig and find out.[16]

The following day, Eshelman arrived with a small water pump borrowed from the Chesapeake Biological Laboratory. The idea was to attempt to clear the sediments from a small sector of the target area, around two pieces of water-smoothed wood sticking eighteen inches out of the bottom where the signature was strongest.

I began the excavation with a prayer that we were not merely digging on another piece of floating junk buried by the river muds. My prayers were soon answered. Within minutes we had exposed another foot or so of the wood, which proved to be not a tree but squared timbers in which iron spikes had been driven. The typology of the spikes were typical of the period 1790-1820.

Excitedly, we began to use the pump hose and the water jet as a probe. Working to one side of the timbers, we discovered a solid wooden structure five feet beneath the mud but were prohibited from further excavation by the heavy current flow, which caused the hole to repeatedly collapse. Other areas adjacent to the timbers were probed, and at each, a solid wooden feature was encountered five feet down. We clearly had a substantial structure, well over forty feet long, made of wood, with por-

The first recovery from the Turtle Shell Wreck. Photograph by Nicholas Freda

tions of it fitted with iron spikes. But was it a shipwreck? And if so, did it, as we fervently hoped, belong to the flotilla?[17]

Although the iron fittings had given us a possible time frame, they had been badly corroded, and interpretive mistakes could easily be made. We needed something even more diagnostic. Yet further investigation with the limited resources in hand, in the turbid, swift environment, was likely to yield little. One last try was made. The only artifact to be retrieved from the site was brought up. It was a broken, heavily worn turtle shell, minus its original owner.

For lack of a better name, I dubbed the site the Turtle Shell Wreck.

□   □   □

At least seven other sites were tested by probing in the days following the discovery of the Turtle Shell Wreck (1-TSW). Though all were substantial targets, it had been impossible to acquire the same degree of even limited data we had uncovered at 1-TSW owing to severe environmental constraints and deep burial of the sites. Yet, it was abundantly clear that the sector was pregnant with potential.[18]

If the Turtle Shell Wreck was, indeed, a shipwreck as we all believed, that would have been important enough. But if it was part of the U.S. Chesapeake Flotilla, the sister ships could not be far away.

Though our conjecture was based upon the still circumstantial evidence only, I was convinced that we had found Joshua Barney's "much vaunted flotilla." There seemed to be little alternative now but to conduct a major underwater excavation and confirm it.

T W E L V E

Wedged Between Some Planking

The winter and spring of 1980 had been hectic, as we attempted to consolidate the two previous years' data and prepare a plan for the final campaign on the river. I knew that the Phase II operations had to be firmly based on the previous years of effort if we were to ascertain the survivability and condition of archaeological resources in a Tidewater riverine environment. Yet our final thrust would have to address all of the unknowns that had been avoided thus far. Ralph Eshelman and I were well aware that the results of survey work in the black and occasionally treacherous environment of the Patuxent River with then-current methodologies were considered in some professional archaeological circles to be of questionable value at best. We would be attempting, with largely volunteer and paraprofessional help, to survey and excavate sites in a zero-visibility underwater environment that would be difficult even in the clear waters of the Caribbean or Mediterranean. But we had come too far to stop in the final stretch. Again we submitted a grant proposal to the Heritage, Conservation, and Recreation Service through the Maryland Historical Trust. And again the grant was, to our great delight, approved.[1]

The project was to be divided into three discrete missions. The first was to develop specific techniques for the excavation, survey, and mapping of designated sites in each of the four transect areas laid out in 1979. In so doing we would be experimenting with a variety of site types, each of them ensconced in different marine environments spread out over a fifty-mile stretch of waterway. It was, as it turned out, more than a case of overoptimism. Few underwater archaeological projects in the United States had been able to carry out precision survey work, as we envisioned, in the variety of hostile blackwater environments such as those encountered on the Patuxent or had bothered to attempt to develop techniques to do so. To a certain extent, improvisation would be almost a mandatory adjunct to the scope of work. It followed, then, that our second mission would be to develop and refine modest but appropriate sampling procedures at each designated site. Our third objective was to develop a conservation facility suitable for handling low-level recovery of artifacts—an effort, we soon discovered, that would prove to be as labor intensive as the field work itself.[2]

We were also painfully aware that the Maryland Historical Trust, through which our modest eighteen thousand dollars in matching funds was being administered and which would approve or disapprove the final disbursement of moneys after the completion of the project, cared little about how we achieved survey results, but only that results be achieved. During the winter, I had become concerned, on the one hand, over the lack of official comprehension about what our work entailed, and was delighted, on the other, because there was so little interference. However, having personally borrowed a substantial sum of money to see the project through until I could be reimbursed at its completion, I was nagged by the thought of failure. What if we were digging dry holes after all? What if our pursuit of the flotilla was, indeed, a chimera? My confidence was severely tested during one pre-project meeting in Annapolis, when the Trust's chief archaeologist responsible for overseeing the program made it abundantly clear that if we failed in the effort, disbursement of the matching funds (against which we were employing equipment, money, and personnel as match) could possibly be delayed, reduced, or even withheld. But it was Ralph Eshelman, who had placed the good name of the Calvert Marine Museum on the line in supporting the project, who stood to lose the most. He had gone to bat with the museum's board of directors to secure permission to assemble a small conservation facility on museum property, and largely at museum expense, suitable to handle the artifacts recovered during our sampling efforts. And should we fail, his credibility in the eyes of his peers would certainly suffer. Yet his almost practiced nonchalance provided a constant source of humor and candor which continually reinforced our own self-confidence.

"Hell," he once quipped as I glumly mused over what would happen if the project was a bust. "We can always sell our homes!"

□   □   □

We had optimistically selected seven potential sites for testing during Phase II, each representing one of the three major site types: inundated, insert, and shipwreck. The sites specifically chosen included the Gunboat Wreck and the remains of St. Leonard's Wharf in St. Leonard's Creek, the Cannon Wreck and the Nottingham Beach site, the Lyons Creek Wreck, the *Peter Cooper* Wreck near Selby's Landing, and the Turtle Shell Wreck.[3]

To maximize the value of the resources in hand for the forty-five days of field activity, we had planned that the survey of the sites would be carried out by two field teams operating independently of each other, utilizing five vessels ranging in size from a thirty-foot cabin cruiser to a ten-foot-long pram. Nearly thirty paid and volunteer staff would be employed during the program, including archaeologists, paleontologists, historians, museologists, catalogers, draftspersons, engineers, a conservator, a diving safety officer, a paramedic, video technicians, divers, and miscellaneous handlers and roustabouts. The team had been assembled from as far afield as Colorado (diving safety officer Emily Graves) and Florida (archaeologist Galloway Selby), and as close as next door (an aspiring marine archaeologist named Sally Ruhl). It was a synergistic team whose whole was destined to prove greater than any of its parts. The team would be so successful, we would soon discover, that we quickly had to scale down our initial optimistic scope of work to focus on only three of the original seven sites: the Turtle Shell Wreck, the Lyons Creek Wreck, and St. Leonard's Wharf.

The equipment to be employed varied from spartan to the most sophisticated available. In the course of the survey, a specially designed hydrodredge and a standard airlift would be used, as would a common, commercially leased "trash" pump, to remove the many feet of overburden covering the sites in the river. An assemblage of pipes, fire hoses, and water pumps would be employed to produce high-energy water jet streams suitable for probing for structural features buried deep beneath the river silts at the upriver sites and for assisting in driving cofferdam pilings into the bottom. Divers would use both standard scuba and surface-supplied air systems. And for those utilizing the latter, a compressor unit, specially designed by our chief diver and engineer, Eldon Volkmer, would be deployed to provide air for as many as five divers at a time for an indefinite period at the maximum, albeit shallow, depths we expected to encounter.

One of the principal intentions of the project was to record the survey effort on film or video for public presentation in a museum environment, as well as for *in situ* documentation of the various site features themselves for later study. Owing to the high particulate content in the river's waters and consequent low light penetration, the chances for the successful use of standard underwater photography were deemed slim at best. However, state-of-the-art high-resolution, low-light underwater video, incorporating the use of an extremely powerful lighting system, surface monitoring capability, and direct diver-to-surface voice communications was considered suitable to compensate for such environmental pitfalls. And if it were successful, we would be producing the first underwater video documentation of a historic archaeological site in Tidewater history. After considerable deliberation, the firm of Oceans Data Systems, Inc., a leader in marine research, was contracted to carry out the task.

Surface video documentation of the project, day by day, from beginning to end, was considered of major importance, both to record the progress of the program and for scientific and educational purposes. Through the efforts of Nautical Archaeological Associates' Nick Freda, we had been fortunate, only a week before field work was to begin, to secure the support and services of a young television production company, Yellow Cat Productions, to record our work on the Turtle Shell Wreck. Nick's presentation had not only seduced the company's talented chief executive and producer, Michael Ford, to video-document the project, but to do so at the cost of videotape only. We bought the tape and Yellow Cat did the rest.

Many other pieces of equipment, such as generators, electrical saws, drills, survey tools, a survey grid system, underwater gear, and so forth, were soon being stockpiled and inventoried for the coming project at the project's upriver base of operations at Patuxent River Park's Jug Bay Landing, six miles downriver from the Turtle Shell Wreck.

In order to provide a stable platform for a semipermanent operations base at several of the sites, we needed a durable, watertight vessel of less than a foot draft. It had to be capable of bearing the weight of personnel, machinery, and construction supplies, spacious enough to provide working room, an enclosed shelter, and toilet facilities, and shallow enough to permit anchorage in the most shoally of waters. What was needed, in essence, was a barge.

After we had searched throughout February and March for such a vessel (without the least luck), a number of out-of-repair floating pontoon docks, recently acquired by Patuxent River Park from a defunct marina on the Anacostia River, were volunteered free-of-charge by the park's gregarious superintendent, Rich Dolesh. Dolesh's sole proviso was that it was up to NAA to make them seaworthy. Elated by Rich's call, I had accepted his offer of the pontoons sight unseen. To say that I was dismayed when I surveyed the hulks a week later would be an understatement. Most of the five-by-twenty-foot hulls had been drawn up in a corner of the park's utility yard several miles from the water, and all required major surgery. Every one of the units was bedraggled, rotten, and entirely unseaworthy. Gashes perforated most of their skins. Whatever paint had once covered them had long since blistered away, even as their plywood decks peeled and splintered in the sun. Still, there seemed little alternative but to either work the upriver sites from nearby shorelines (a major logistical nightmare) or roll up our sleeves, repair the pontoons, and assemble them into the working operations platform we needed.

With characteristic vigor, Ken Hollingshead and my brother Dale volunteered to restore the hulks to their former pristine seaworthy condition. Their word was as good as the miracle they performed. Over the next several weeks, gashes were plated and repaired. Wooden joints and seams were caulked. Gaping holes in the deck were covered. Permanent deck structures were erected. A floating sift box was manufactured. Fittings were installed. And everything was given several fresh coats of paint and made to look ship-shape. Finally, on April 26, four interchangeable dock units and the floating sift box were trucked down to the landing

Unloading one of the barges intended for the operations platform for the 1980 archaeological campaign. Photograph by Richard Dolesh

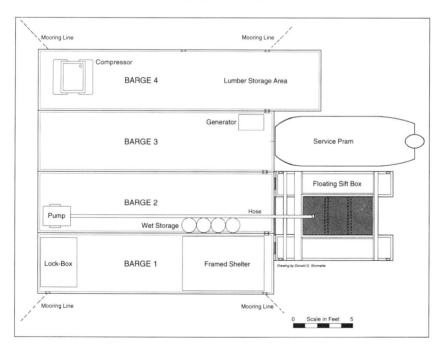

Plan of the operations platform.

at Jug Bay amid a driving rainstorm, launched into the Patuxent, and formally christened "Barney's Barge." For the next month, final outfitting of the platform and testing of gear would continue unabated. Finally, we were ready to begin.

By 8:00 A.M., June 1, the field team, fifteen strong, had gathered at Jug Bay Landing. From here the barge was to be towed by a park boat the half-dozen miles upriver to the Turtle Shell Wreck site for its first mission. I was to proceed with Fred Hopkins ahead of the barge to lay out marker buoys immediately south of the wreck site, while Eshelman attended to getting the operations platform off in good order. After conducting a final briefing on the project objectives, I set off aboard the park's big aluminum-hulled service boat *Muskrat* up a river that time had seemingly forgotten, barely twenty miles from the most important capital city in the world. As we passed several majestic blue herons picking about in the shoals of the adjacent marsh, I thought about the problems and promise that lay ahead.

The Turtle Shell Wreck lies squarely in the main river channel of the Patuxent, approximately a mile south of Spyglass Island. From the sounding survey carried out in 1978 and our hands-on evaluations the following year, we knew that the channel in this area was quite shallow, averaging eight feet of water or less, and shoaled considerably the further north one proceeded above the wreck site. It is a migratory streambed that frequently thwarts any uninitiated who take its course for granted, particu-

The operations platform and floating sift box.

larly in the reaches north of Jug Bay. From Hopkins's archival research, we had learned that during the 1814 campaign on the river, Commodore Joshua Barney's son, William B. Barney, commander of the *Scorpion*, during a reconnaissance of this section of the waterway, had also noted a similar serpentine aspect to its channel, running all the way from Nottingham to Queen Anne's Town.[4]

The shoreline to the west of the site was a flat, marshy wetland over half a mile wide, and drained by several small creeks. The most notable of these was Back Channel (which once may have connected to the main channel well north of the wreck site). In an earlier age, these flats were frequently festooned with thousands of wild geese, ducks, and other birds of all kinds, honking, quacking waterfowl that, at the slightest hint of danger, would rise in blankets that darkened out the sun. The opposite shore was equally marshy along the water's edge, but several hundred feet eastward the terrain sloped sharply upward to form a substantial terrace. The river itself was a dirty chocolate brown, attributable to siltation and runoff from upriver gravel pits and farm drainage, to tannins resulting from the decay of organic matter, and to raw sewage.

To call the upriver waters filthy, despite the beauty of the shores, would be an understatement. Indeed, through the little marsh to the east, a small rivulet struggled to flow past refuse and sewage-clogged bottlenecks to empty into the river. I winced a bit at the thought of diving here, for we had learned only days before the survey was to begin that a private sewage treatment plant, erected nearby to facilitate the needs of a local trailer park, was frequently on the blink and regularly discharged its untreated overflow into the river. On occasion, we had even seen raw human excrement floating by. Healthy marine and aquatic life beneath this stretch of river, despite the wishful thinking of hopeful fishermen who occasionally passed us in their little prams, seemed to have vanished. The once pristine Patuxent had become a sewer in which we would soon be working. The river which had offered its bounty to natives and colonists alike, and which had seen so much history, seemed, for all intents and purposes, dead.

□   □   □

Once the wreck had been relocated and *Barney's Barge* had been brought to a four-point anchor, the site's parameters were soon being ascertained by systematic water jet probing, even as a temporary datum point was being established on the eastern bank. The probing operation was a simple but drawn-out affair utilizing a calibrated ten-foot-long hollow iron pipe attached to a fifty-foot section of fire hose, which, in turn, was attached to a water pump mounted amidship on one of our prams. By forcing water through the narrow pipe at a high volume, it was possible to rapidly penetrate the layers of dead organic materials, mud, sand,

211

gravel, and clay. When solid objects were encountered (presumably structural features of the wreck, but often as not logs and stumps), probing would cease, the site would be marked and plotted, and the process would begin over again until each 100-foot square quadrant was examined. A total of thirty-two quadrants, or 70,000 square feet, was probed from shore to shore, 150 feet above to 150 feet below the site. In this manner, not only was the perimeter of the Turtle Shell Wreck site broadly defined, but several other anomalies, located but not identified during the 1979 mag survey, were also investigated. Within a day, we determined that the main and uppermost portion of the wreck lay between 2.5 and 5 feet below the bottom sediments in the very center of the river channel, which was itself now only 8 feet deep and less than 50 feet from the western shore.[5]

Our next objective was to conduct a small test excavation to establish the lie and condition of the site. To do so in the occasionally high-energy currents, which would quickly cause any trench or hole we could dig to fill in, we would first need to erect a small, temporary cofferdam (TCD) to provide an area in which divers could work protected from the current. The TCD, designed by my brother, Dale Shomette, was a simple but effective affair. Its framework could be assembled quickly aboard the operations platform from two-by-fours and half-inch-thick plywood sheets brought along for the purpose.[6]

Nearly a week was consumed in preparing to address the remainder of the survey programs at St. Leonard's Wharf and on Lyons Creek, however, before we were ready for the insertion of the TCD at the Turtle Shell Wreck site. With the aid of one of the boats, the buoyant framework of the TCD structure was inserted into the water with some difficulty, moored in position with heavy weights, and a plywood skin nailed to its sides. The unit was then secured by four-by-four pilings driven into the bottom at each corner angle and then nailed to it. The barge was reanchored downstream of the little coffer, and a small platform causeway erected between the two.[7]

Not until the afternoon of June 6 were we finally ready to begin excavation within the TCD. During the previous week, a continual debate had been raging among the team members as to what condition we would find the wreck in, or whether the site was, in fact, one of Barney's flotilla. Eshelman even laughingly suggested that it might not be a wreck at all, but the ruins of some upriver duck blind that had washed downstream in a forgotten storm many years earlier. For even offering such a notion he was nearly cast bodily from the platform. The team wanted one of Barney's boats, and that was that!

When excavation finally began, problems appeared almost immediately. Our dredging equipment refused to cooperate, and frequent

Archaeologist Galloway Selby wrestles an airlift hose down to divers working below in the test pit coffer.

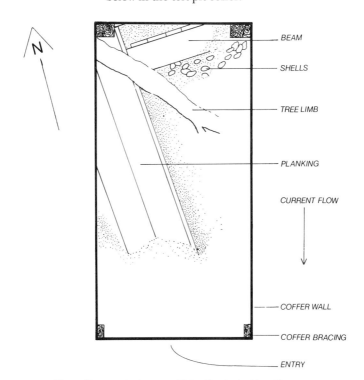

Plan of excavated area within the test pit coffer.

clogging of the hose lines added further delays. Visibility in the TCD enclosure, when sediments were not disturbed, was a good eighteen inches, but as soon as divers touched the bottom, the lights went out. Yet progress was made. As the test hole was gradually and carefully deepened by rotating teams of divers, and openings appeared below the coffer wall, additional sheets of plywood were driven down and secured to the frame. Finally, at about 5:00 P.M., while working upside down in the narrow confines of the coffer with diver John Burton, I encountered a single flat timber. Then a second. Both timbers ran almost due north. Excitedly, I directed that the dredging operation be temporarily halted. We would proceed with the excavation, but using only trowels and our fingertips.

Carefully, over the next two hours, several inches of sediment were cleared away, in total darkness. We found our progress blocked by a tree limb lying diagonally across the two planks and soon deduced it to be river debris swept into the site after the wreck's deposition. Then came a concentration of freshwater clamshells, identified by Eshelman as *Elliptio complanata* Lightfoot, a shellfish once common but extirpated in this century along this sector of the river. As we proceeded to clear the north end of the TCD, we discovered a beam that extended diagonally off from the planks. On the north side of the beam was the top of a line of vertical wooden slats running down into the mud. Several more planks, apparently unattached, were also discovered.[8] Our enthusiasm knew no bounds. We worked until darkness fell but even then, found it difficult to call it a day.

Here, it seemed, was a site with substantial local structural integrity. Was it merely a well-preserved component of a vessel, or could the whole site be intact? Few in the team slept soundly that night.

The following morning, examination of the test pit was renewed. Beneath the north beam, more clamshells, a spread of wood chips, and several peach pits were discovered. Excitement continued to build throughout the morning as more of the wreck was slowly cleared within the rigid confines of the TCD. Then, after lunch, I discovered a musket flint wedged between some planking, and a rose-headed spike, of a type commonly produced between 1790 and 1820, protruding from another timber.[9] The evidence was more than promising. Although outwardly calm, I could barely maintain my composure. Even though the indicators were still too sparse to permit any preliminary conclusions, I was convinced we had indeed found one of Barney's vessels. And having achieved what we had set out to do with the TCD, namely, to test the lie and condition of the site, I eagerly directed that the structure be disassembled. Within hours, the erection of a larger coffer was under way.

From the remains encountered within the TCD and the data acquired by systematic water jet probing, the wreck was determined to be oriented in a north-south direction running directly down the center of the river channel. Having determined the wreck's depth below the silts, probable size, and orientation we were now to begin the final phase of our three-year quest for the Chesapeake Flotilla.

The design, size, and construction of the main cofferdam (MCD) was based as much upon the limited building materials that our budget would permit and the time and manpower available to build it, as upon our findings. Again, my brother provided the construction plan. The mission of the structure would be much the same as that of the TCD: it would provide our divers with protection from the river currents while at the same time preventing excavated areas from filling in with sediments as we worked. It was also hoped that an additional benefit would be improved underwater visibility within the nonturbulent confines of the structure

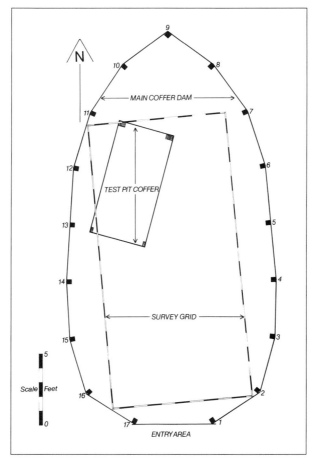

Plan of the test pit cofferdam, the main cofferdam, and the survey grid erected on the Turtle Shell Wreck site.

215

Project workers replace a wooden panel in the cofferdam which had been
undercut and loosened by the river.

itself. If the particulates in the water were allowed to settle over a period
of hours, it might even be possible to take underwater photographs on
site before work began each morning.[10]

The MCD was to be twenty-eight feet long, a maximum of fifteen feet
wide, and boat-shaped, with the pointed end facing upriver to deflect the
current flow and the downstream end flat and capable of being opened
or closed for diver entry. Never intended to be permanent, the structure
would be constructed of the same materials as the TCD, at a staggering
overall cost of $365. It was unquestionably the most inexpensive coffer-
dam ever erected for archaeological purposes in Tidewater history.

Soon, sixteen-foot-long four-by-four pilings were being driven into the
river bottom at four-foot intervals, at predetermined positions based upon
the findings from the water jet probing. Even as one team labored to drive
pilings in, a second struggled to attach the plywood skin to the frames,
both above and below the waterline, while a third constructed a bracing
rim-cum-walkway joining the caps of each piling together in a continuous
reinforcing band. The operations platform, which had been provided
with a stable four-point mooring at the downstream end of the structure,
was then connected to the coffer by a narrow walkway. Over the weeks to
come, as excavation within the MCD moved relentlessly downward, additional sheets of plywood would be added to prevent undercutting of the
structure, while constant and tedious patching of the sides would become
the first order of each day's schedule throughout the excavation.[11]

216

While work was progressing on the coffer, two more convenient and permanent survey stations were established on the nearby west shore, less than fifty feet from the wreck. A prefabricated metal grid system was assembled aboard the crowded work barge and then lowered into the coffer and fixed in position. The portable grid system, of my own design, featured a sliding graduated pair of parallel aluminum bars with a two-foot-square quadrant mounted between them. The grid frame was calibrated in feet and inches, as were the parallel bars. Once the positions and elevations of the grid's four corners were recorded, the locations of archaeological features falling within its confines could be readily determined by sliding the bars, and then the quadrant position over them, measuring the distances within the quadrant, and then taking elevations on the objects from the nearby shore.[12] In the end, however, accuracy was occasionally compromised, owing to what would prove to be a complex three-dimensional makeup of the site, and visibility of six inches or less. Countless resurveys of the same features were required to correct inaccuracies. But we would learn. And quickly.[13]

On the morning of June 7, 1980, when the excavation of l-TSW began in earnest, few in our team would have guessed that nearly a thousand man-hours would eventually be spent within the confines of our little coffer. And none of us could have predicted the remarkable condition of the site we were to uncover: nothing less than a largely intact military vessel from the War of 1812. One of Joshua Barney's own.

Cannonballs Galore

While work was under way on the Turtle Shell Wreck, a second team of investigators, led by Ralph Eshelman, was detached to conduct a limited but systematic survey of the Lyons Creek Wreck, several miles downstream. Eshelman's group was small, consisting of Fred Hopkins, Ken Hollingshead, Nicholas Freda, and Eldon Volkmer. Their task would prove, in many ways, to be far more trying—and rewarding—than the work being carried out at the same time on the Turtle Shell Wreck, well upriver.

The site, though quite near shore, lay beneath a virtual mudflat at low water, making access impracticable during much of the working day. Worse, the sediments were so soft that one could not walk upon them without sinking in chest deep. The bottom consistency, when covered by water, was similar to industrial sludge. Thus, the team was obliged to work only at flood tide when water depths approached several feet and personnel in the water could work in tandem with those aboard *Sneaky Seaweed*.

Utilizing the Schwenk wharf as a base for the heavy equipment, a water jet probe was first employed to determine the extent, distribution, and position of the site's hard subsediment features. A line of investigation was initially established to the east of the wharf, where the first of several hard targets was encountered. Two more lines, running north and south of this main trunk, were also systematically probed with the water jet but with negative results. A fourth line of investigation, running off the north end of the wharf, was then opened and penetrated, but with only one hit.

Most of the targets were found to be buried between eight and ten feet below the surface of the silts. Although it was immediately determined that excavation to these targets through the porous muds stood little chance of success without benefit of a cofferdam, Eshelman decided to try anyway. His decision was based on the premise that all spare resources were currently employed upriver and could not be used. Most would be returned to their owners or would be used up during the upriver survey, before the summer was over, without prospects for any future availability. It was, in essence, a now-or-never proposition. Thus, he wasted little time and quickly deployed a small dredge to conduct test excavations along each of the lines where hard targets had been encountered. As expected, however, digging in the nearly fluid silt beds proved all but impossible.

Hollingshead's wielding the cumbersome dredge hose in the shallow slop was reminiscent of one of those intrepid zoologists in the old "Wild Kingdom" television series wrestling an anaconda in an Amazonian backwater. As each test pit was opened and the spoil pumped ashore for sifting, the nearly liquid bottom would quickly slope into the hole, filling it within minutes. To produce a cone-shaped hole three feet deep (which would survive for less than half an hour untended), it was necessary to excavate a surface opening ten feet in diameter. The deeper the hole, the wider the opening had to be.

Working upside down in zero visibility while attempting to monitor the provenance of items encountered proved a hopeless task. The maintenance of stratigraphic integrity and the recording of artifactual provenance without the erection of a cofferdam was quickly determined to be impracticable. Penetrations of the bottom never exceeded five feet. By the beginning of each new day, the sites excavated the day before had completely filled in.

After days of labor with inconclusive results, and with no funds, resources, or manpower available to construct a cofferdam, we decided to close down the investigation until some later, more propitious time. After all, we reasoned, the site wasn't going anywhere and would be there when and if we might someday return, protected by the deep sediments that had frustrated us. Our mission had been simply to test, and not to conduct a full-scale excavation.[1]

Nevertheless, when I arrived on the creek to confer with Eshelman about closing down the investigation, he presented me with some tantalizing finds. There were several artifacts of interest that had been recovered with at least local provenance. These included sundry cannonballs, brick fragments, ceramics, kaolin pipe stems, pieces of worked wood, and possibly ballast stones.[2] But of the greatest interest were several wooden planks from the hull of the wreck itself. Was it possible that the vessel lay buried in only five feet of silt or less? Or had it been entirely disarticulated by the clam bucket which had first encountered the site and spread its various parts throughout the muds? Were our probe targets, encountered at eight to ten feet, portions of the wreck or merely river debris or protrusions from the ancient creek bed itself?

In the weeks and months that followed the 1980 field season on the Patuxent, the real work at evaluation of the site data and various artifact collections began in earnest. For most of those working on the project, the Turtle Shell Wreck, because of its condition, in historical terms, and the diversity of the artifacts recovered, was considered the most important site examined during the program's three-year history. In my opinion, however, the mysterious, fragmented vessel lying beneath the muck of Lyons Creek was of unparalleled importance, not only from a site-specific consideration, but possibly even on a national scale. If the artifacts were associated with the wreck, as suspected, it was possible that the site was one of the oldest small craft wrecks discovered to date in the United States. The thirty-three fragile structural components that had survived offered the exciting prospect that some information about the architecture of the vessel itself might be extracted as well. Perhaps a conjectural model of the actual boat might even be produced from the skeletal data in hand.

One of the most perplexing enigmas concerning the find was why more than six hundred pounds of cannonballs, which had been either dredged up or otherwise recovered during the excavation, had been associated with such an apparently small vessel site. To assist in rooting out an answer—if one could be found—we enlisted the expertise of Professor Charles R. Fisher of the University of Baltimore, a naval historian and expert in seventeenth- to nineteenth-century ordnance. Fisher's initial impression was that the pieces were probably intended for artillery of English manufacture. Though most Western European nations of the seventeenth and eighteenth centuries, he explained, produced standard artillery for the same approximate weight of ball, the actual bore size of the gun and the caliber of the ball varied slightly from one country to another. He pointed out as an example that during the period of the American Revolution, when casting had reached a high degree of sophistication, the diameter of a French nine-pound shot, in English measure, was 4.188 inches, while the diameter of an English ball of the same caliber weight was four inches. Fisher meticulously compared the relative diameters of American, English, French, and Spanish cannonballs with the average diameters of the best-preserved cannonballs from Lyons Creek, for all calibers, and determined that they had definitely been intended for use in English artillery.[3]

Of the forty-five cannonballs recovered, cleaned, measured, weighed, and analyzed, most had been excavated from the spoil pile prior to the June 1980 survey. Thirty-nine were entered into the collections of the Calvert Marine Museum, four remained in Peter Schwenk's hands, and two were sacrificed for metallurgical analysis. It had been impossible to examine, of course, the diameter of every shot with absolute accuracy until each had been cleaned and in some cases submitted to electrolytic reduction at the CMM conservation laboratory to remove the heavy concretions that had formed around the balls. Only after cleaning and conservation could we accurately measure and weigh each ball.[4]

With the help of the Metallurgical Division of the Bethlehem Steel Corporation at Sparrows Point, Maryland, a metallographic and chemical

A total of 45 cannonballs, of five different calibers and manufactured for use in English ordnance, were recovered at the Schwenk Site in Lyons Creek. Many of the artifacts had been hidden in dredge spoil until discovered by Peter Schwenk and reported to the Calvert Marine Museum. Additional cannonballs were recovered during archaeological excavations of the site. (Top) A pile of cannonballs lies on the shore soon after recovery by Peter Schwenk. (Bottom) Cannonballs after cleaning and stabilization by archaeological conservator Leslie Bright.

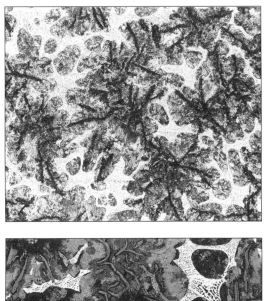

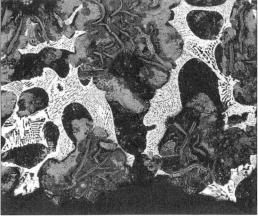

A microscopic metallurgical analysis of several of the cannonballs from the Schwenk Site was undertaken by the Bethlehem Steel Corporation. (Above, top) At 100 × magnification graphite flakes appear as very dark lines. The dark mottled areas consist of fine pearlite. The light areas are steadite. (Above, bottom) At 200 × magnification the light grey fingerlike areas are graphite flakes. Light and dark grey areas surrounding the graphite flakes are iron oxides. The areas that appear black are unaffected pearlite and the white areas are ferrite constituents of the steadite. (Opposite) The lamellar structure of the pearlite is resolved at 1000 × magnification.

analysis of the two sacrificial cannonballs was carried out. As a safety precaution, the two projectiles were first X-rayed to determine if they were bombs or solid shot. Both proved to be solid. One of the samples was then cut into sections while the second was cored by a diamond drill. The sections and fragments were then submitted to examination through

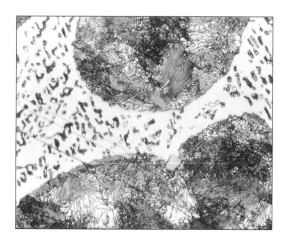

photomicrography. Sophisticated microhardness tests were then performed on a Tukon Hardness Tester, while macrohardness was measured on a Rockwell Hardness Tester.[5]

The sacrifice of the two cannonballs was well worth it. While the dates of origin could not, of course, be ascertained, some parameters had been set. The large percentage of phosphorous (1.3 percent of weight) indicated a high proportion of the mineral steadite in the ball and thus ruled out modern casting. According to Chief Metallurgist E.B. Shelly, who conducted the testing, both the projectiles were of unusual hardness, as evidenced by the high percentages of steadite and pearlite. Iron produced by later foundry processes contained an insignificant percentage of both elements. Therefore, modern production of the two artifacts was ruled out.[6]

The cannonball collection was found to be composed of five different calibers of ball. Though such projectiles were commonly listed by weight, actual caliber weight traditionally bore little and only relative relationship to actual weight. Hence, a 24-pounder might weigh 23.5 pounds or 24.7 pounds. We calculated that the collection was composed of three 24-pounders, eighteen 18-pounders, seven 10- or 12-pounders, fifteen 8-pounders, and two 6-pounders.[7] Despite the acquisition of a considerable body of data on the projectiles, it was still impossible to ascribe an independent time frame for their origins or the period in which they were lost based upon weight, dimensions, or the foundering process by which they were manufactured. Indeed, it was not even certain that their presence could be attributed to a military purpose, since both out-of-service artillery and munitions were known to have been used on occasion during the colonial period through the nineteenth century as ballast in sailing vessels. Or had the artifacts merely been dumped at the site from the nearby shore or, perhaps, from a visiting vessel?

We looked hopefully to the analysis of the kaolin smoking pipe fragments, ceramics, and broken bottle sherds for a more precise date on the site. As it turned out, the results from this next step would only add to the mystery. But we began with high hopes, for as the noted director of archaeology for Colonial Williamsburg, Ivor Noël Hume, once stated,

> The English kaoline tobacco pipe is possibly the most valuable clue yet available to the student of historical sites, for it is an item that was manufactured, imported, smoked, and thrown away, all within a matter of a year or two.[8]

Pipes are perhaps the most commonly encountered items on archaeological sites from the colonial period through the nineteenth century. Fortunately, techniques of dating them—from analysis of makers' marks, bowl and stem forms, armorial and other decorations, and the evaluation of stem fragments—had, over the recent three decades, become accepted tools of archaeological research. The evolution of bowl shapes and the documentation of makers' marks, first published on in 1951 by the English archaeologist Adrian Oswald, has long formed the heart of a major data base upon which historical archaeologists have come to rely. In 1954, the noted National Park Service archaeologist J. C. Harrington, after an intensive study of thousands of pipes in Great Britain and the United States, published a graph displaying the percentages of aperture diameter for pipes of five chronologically sequential periods between 1620 and 1800. The historical archaeologist's arsenal was again enlarged.

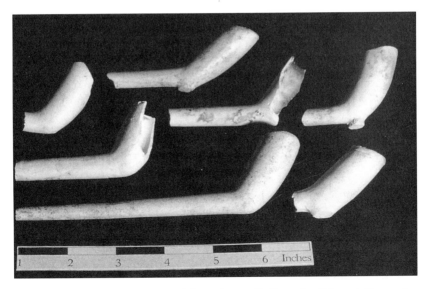

Kaolin smoking pipes recovered from the spoil pile at the Schwenk Site and during the excavation of the site in 1980 were among the many artifacts used by researchers in an effort to date the site.

Cannonballs Galore

The chart revealed that average diameters of pipe stem apertures tended to diminish measurably from the seventeenth century through the second half of the eighteenth century. Based upon Harrington's theory, Dr. Lewis Binford produced a mathematical formula that would permit dating of sites from which large numbers of pipe stems had been recovered, with an error factor of only ten to thirty years.[9]

Although the fifty-five kaolin pipe stem and bowl fragments recovered from the spoil pile at Lyons Creek were far from the two hundred or so considered necessary to provide an accurate date or an average date of the deposit from which they had come, the pieces would provide at least limited parameters that might reinforce data later gleaned from the ceramic and bottle sherd collection. Using the Harrington-Binford formula, I calculated a date of 1690. Typological comparison of bowl samples from existing collections as well as other characteristics gave us a broader dating frame of 1680-1720.[10]

The new data was more than exciting. There had been, we knew, a military revolution in Maryland in the summer of 1689, when Protestant fought Catholic for control of the colony, and the Patuxent River had served as a military highway (albeit briefly) for the combatants. Could the cannonball-strewn wrecksite in Lyons Creek have been related to that significant incident in Maryland history, a moment that ultimately led to the permanent removal of the colony capital from St. Mary's City to Providence Town, now modern Annapolis? Only further confirmation by the dating of the ceramics and bottle fragments could lend credence to our hypothesis.

Six substantial wine bottle fragments were recovered from the spoil pile, including three nearly complete basal sections and two intact necks, along with a wide assortment of miscellaneous body fragments. A considerable body of literature has been produced over the years concerning the evolution and typology of English wine bottles between 1650 and 1820, and we were hopeful that a study of the Lyons Creek collection would reinforce the time frame suggested by the pipe data. Our initial dating of the glass produced a period from 1685 to 1721.[11] Upon consultation with Ivor Noël Hume, who had graciously consented to examine the glass and ceramics, we were presented with a time span ranging from 1675 to 1680, with a single basal fragment dating between 1725 and 1730.[12]

We read Hume's analysis of the glass with interest, for, aside from the single late-dated bottle parts, which I secretly hoped was of random deposition, everything seemed to point to the possibility of the 1680-1720 period. The ceramic analysis, however, would ultimately widen the range by another ten years, and defuse my strong suspicions that the site dated from the revolution of 1689.

There were at least eleven and possibly as many as fourteen different ceramic types represented by the seventy-four sherds recovered, primarily from the spoil pile. One piece, a gravel-tempered sherd from North Devon, England, dated anywhere between 1610 and 1750. Twenty-five yellow lead-glazed earthenware fragments had belonged to a milk pan of European origins, possibly French or Flemish. Similar sherds were later recovered at another location on the Patuxent called the Kings Reach site, in Calvert County, and dated circa 1690-1715.[13]

Twenty polychrome tin-glazed earthenware sherds, portions of a plate probably manufactured in Bristol, England, and painted in lush floral designs of blue, red, and green, were dated by Hume at between 1715 and 1730. Three tin-glazed earthenware sherds, all decorated with a blue floral pattern, belonged to a bowl, a plate, and a punch bowl. Two lead-glazed earthenware sherds, slip-decorated in a scgraiffito design, possibly a crown, were the most difficult to assess. Hume deduced that both pieces were Germanic in character and if made in America would most likely have dated to the second half of the seventeenth century, but if of German or Rhenish origins, could have been much earlier.[14]

Clearly, placing the site in a time frame became more difficult with each new shred of data. There seemed to be no neat, well-trimmed answers after all. Yet, there were other artifacts to help us.

We had recovered a wide variety of miscellaneous artifacts from the spoil pile and the site itself. Most of them ultimately provided little in the way of datable evidence. Nevertheless, they too were possible clues to the life of the long-forgotten little boat, and most certainly they were important components of the overall site even if they did not relate to its maritime character. Some, such as a small, bent and battered copper pot, fragments of a large wrought-iron key, a piece of a knife blade, an imperfectly molded lead shot, a musket's trigger guard, scraps of a leather shoe with several small tacks still adhering, and a number of iron nails and spikes, provided ample evidence of human activity at the site, possibly even aboard the boat. It was even conceivable that four chunks of gray flint, two of which had been knapped, may also have been used by persons aboard the vessel, perhaps to kindle a fire for warmth or to cook their food. They may have eaten pork, deer, or even dog meat, as was indicated by several bones recovered from the site. There were also numerous fragments of brick, as well as several smooth cobbles larger than the normal gravels found in this particular geological environment. The presence of coal suggested the possibility that the brick might have been part of a deck camboose or maybe a waterfront structure, while the stone may have been used as ballast aboard the boat itself. The possibilities were endless. Because the site was first discovered by dredging, we were unable to determine the provenance of the artifacts dredged up. The true relevance of the myriad assortment in the collection could thus only be guessed at.

Cannonballs Galore

Timber fragments of the Lyons Creek Wreck, possibly one of the oldest
Euro-American small craft wrecks discovered to date in American waters.
Photograph by Tim Mihursky

The thirty-three frame, plank, and molding components of the wreck
were another matter. The majority of the wooden vessel parts had been
taken from the spoil pile, although several had been recovered during
the excavation. Close examination of these ancient pieces of wood revealed that they had been cut by a pit saw, an archaic manner of sawing
that was all but extinct by 1840. A number of wooden treenails (pro-
nounced "trunnels"), used to fasten overlapping sections together, were
shaped by hand to fit holes bored through framing members. It was
readily apparent that a spoke shave or similar tool, rather than a lathe,
had been employed to roughly round the treenails. The end product had
been irregularly sided treenails which, when driven into the bored holes
and wetted, would swell and prevent the fitting from coming loose.

Unlike the practice of most trained boatbuilders, the constructor of
the Lyons Creek boat had not driven a wedge into the treenail after its
insertion into the hole, a common procedure that further expanded the
surface of the treenail to insure a tight fit. Such casual workmanship
suggested the possibility that the vessel had not been constructed by a
regular shipwright or boatbuilder but by someone more attuned to dry
land carpentry. But there could, of course, have been an exception.
Eshelman later observed that there had been no wedges in the juniper
and hickory treenails employed in the construction of the Ronson Ship,

an unidentified eighteenth-century vessel discovered during an excavation project on Manhattan's lower east side in 1982.

Preliminary examination of the framing members of the Lyons Creek Wreck suggested that the vessel was of clinker or lapstrake construction; that is, the lower edge of the upper plank overlaps outside the upper edge of a lower plank. This boatbuilding design tradition existed in its earliest European form in Saxon and Viking shipbuilding, and became widespread throughout northern Europe and Great Britain, and eventually spread to North America.

From the shallow depth of the stepped incisions, it appeared that the boat had been lightly and crudely constructed. Both iron rose-headed nails and wooden treenails had held the planking to the frames while the overlapping planks of the hull were affixed by nails. A few planks possessed what appeared to have been crude, square iron washerlike pieces placed between the planks and fasteners.

In order to determine the type of wood employed in the construction, samples of planking and framing from the wreck were submitted to the Forest Products Laboratory at Madison, Wisconsin, for analysis. Both were identified as white oak of a variety common to the Tidewater. From the size and shape of the planking and framing pieces, we estimated that the overall length of the craft had not been more than sixteen to twenty-two feet—about the size of a small ship's boat for the late seventeenth to early eighteenth century.

☐ ☐ ☐

Although a return to the Lyons Creek site was not in the cards for the next seven years, historical research and expanded analysis of the vessel remains and artifact collection continued in fits and starts as time and funding would permit. And with each new shred of evidence, the wreck grew even more enigmatic. We continued to be perplexed, for it was impossible to state that the ceramics, bottles, shoe, key, copper pot, bones, and other items recovered from the spoil pile and adjacent waters were definitely contemporary to the wooden boat fragments recovered from the same place. It was indeed possible that the wreck site was located at a former boat landing or dump site where cultural detritus from two or more discrete sites or time units had become mixed by dredging, the fluidity of the matrix, and general environmental dynamics not yet understood.[15] Nevertheless, we were encouraged in that the artifacts as a totality suggested a period of deposition ranging from 1680 to 1730. And if they were in fact chronologically contiguous to the site of the vessel, the remains of the Lyons Creek Wreck could well represent the earliest small craft wreck of Euro-American manufacture located in the United States. Even if the vessel was not contiguous to the conjectured time frame, it certainly predated 1840, after which time the employment of pit saws by

boatwrights in English America ceased and the utilization of steam-powered sawmills prevailed.

If the artifacts and the boat were sunk at the same time in a single event,
it was probable that the craft had served as a military lighter, carrying
munitions on the Patuxent, perhaps to or from Mount Calvert or the
strategically situated heights above Lyons Creek for some nonpacific
purpose. The presence of over six hundred pounds of cannonballs, a
musketball, and fragments of a musket trigger guard strongly suggested
a possible military connection. The copper pot, ceramics, brick, and coal,
one faction of our team argued, might indicate the vessel was lived on,
even though it was quite small. Wine bottles would not have been out of
place. In fact, wine bottles had been among the few diagnostic artifacts
discovered on the Browns Ferry Wreck, a partially intact craft discovered
under similar conditions in South Carolina and dating circa 1733.[16]

We were already aware that the only major military event occurring
along the Patuxent watershed during the 1680-1730 period was the
revolution of 1689. At that time, a call for arms and munitions had gone
out from both Catholic and Protestant forces contending for control of
the Maryland colony during the tumultuous ascendancy of the Protestant
William III to the throne of England. Catholic troops, besieged at Mattapany, at the mouth of the Patuxent in St. Mary's County, eventually
succumbed to superior Protestant forces, and the revolution came to an
end. But during the brief struggle, the Patuxent had served as a conduit
for arms shipments. Yet no vessel of any kind had been documented as
having been lost on the river during the conflict. But then, who would
have bothered with a small boat only sixteen to twenty-two feet long?

While conducting archival research a year after the survey, I discovered
that only one vessel had, in fact, been documented as going down in
Patuxent waters between 1680 and 1730. This unfortunate craft, lost in
1707 and not during the struggles of 1689, had been called *Richard and
Mary* and was noted as being a pink belonging to one Captain George
Harris. A search for additional mention of the vessel proved fruitless.[17]
Tracking down the owner, however, was far more rewarding. Systematic
examination of colonial inventories, financial accounts, wills, and other
resources in the Maryland Hall of Records revealed that Harris had owned
and operated a store at Charles Town, not far from Lyons Creek on the
opposite side of the river, and owned property downriver at Nottingham
as well. Of equal interest was the discovery that he also owned a hundred-
acre tract of land called Illingsworth Fortune, which was documented only
as lying somewhere in Calvert County. I was very excited, however, to learn
that during Harris's day, the county's northernmost boundary was set at
the banks of Lyons Creek.[18] Harris's vessel, we later learned, had apparently been employed in some capacity by the Maryland provincial government, and the captain had been paid a compensation of thirty pounds

for her loss while in the colony's service. As the date of the demise of *Richard and Mary* fell within the conjectured time frame set for the Lyons Creek site, the possibility that the two vessels were one and the same was intriguing.[19] Could the vessel have, in fact, been serving the government as a military lighter? Was Illingsworth Fortune the same tract of land lying on the south shore of Lyons Creek, upon which the Schwenk estate now lay?

Unhappily, we were obliged to conclude that unless further intensive archaeological evaluation of the site were carried out, no definitive identification of the site's date of origin could safely be ventured.

Then we began to pursue another line of investigation. Could the materials deposited in the creek have been domestic and military refuse dumped in the river from the shore directly on a site where a small boat had come to rest either before, during, or after the 1680-1730 period? Access to the water's edge at the site was facilitated by a convenient and well worn hillside path terminating there. But as we walked the area over and over, it was hard to escape the suspicion that individuals occupying the upland of the south shore would have simply cast their refuse over the sides of the steep cliffs rather than carry it down to the water's edge, as random deposition at the site, beyond the range of the highland, would have required. Yet the accumulation of trash could well have taken place at the convenient little waterfront (with the probable exception of the heavy munitions which may have been dumped there for some unspecified purpose) over a period of years. I had noted many such sites throughout the Chesapeake, where deposition continues through to the present day, and where trash pits are inundated owing to natural sea-level rise.

The site could have provided an excellent landing for small boats during the colonial era or could have served as the terminus for ferry operations known to have run between Mount Calvert Landing, on the west shore of the Patuxent, and Lyons Creek, or as a sheltered small craft docking area or harbor of refuge during storms or inclement weather. Indeed, colonial records indicated that in 1673, a private ferry, one of the first on the upper river, was in operation across the Patuxent, with its terminus somewhere near the mouth of the creek. Upon close examination of the shoreline, however, it seemed more than likely to me that the ferry terminus itself would have been located on the more convenient riverfront, where a steamboat landing was erected in the early nineteenth century, than in the recesses of the creek itself.

As the years passed, we continued to fit bits and pieces into the complex mosaic that formed the Lyons Creek site. It was not until 1987, however, thirteen years after the inadvertent discovery of the site and seven years after the conclusion of the Patuxent Survey, that either Eshelman or I was ready to publish our findings.[20] Gradually, we had been drawn to the conclusion that most, if not all, of the artifacts recovered from the site were, in fact, not directly associated with the wreck itself. We had been greatly influenced by the weight of evidence that suggested that deposition of materials had occurred over a fifty-year period rather than during a single event, and by the diffuse range of artifact typologies.

We were strongly reinforced in our conclusion by the views of Hume after he examined the collections from the creek:

> I see [the collection] covering a 50-year span and being a curious mixture of English and European sherds. I should guess that the bottles are all English as are the pipes. If you were to tell me that the material came from a fifty-year-old ship that had traded with northern European ports before sinking in 1730, I should not be surprised. On the other hand, it does seem to be a rather improbable assemblage, and really is more likely to be the product of domestic discarding, albeit from a household with perhaps Huguenot connection.[21]

Yet we had neither a ship nor a household site. Ironically, we concluded, if the small-craft wreck was contemporaneous with the deposition of the recovered artifacts, the site could well represent one of those rare instances when a shipwreck had been dated by the aid of cultural materials not directly associated with the shipwreck itself. The site, even minus the wreck, however, was still an important assemblage of cultural materials from one of the earliest European occupation sites along the Patuxent River. But the Lyons Creek Wreck had still to reveal all her secrets.

FOURTEEN

Bucket Seats by Barney

Our operations platform for the Turtle Shell Wreck site, *Barney's Barge*, was anything but graceful looking. On one side we had erected a small tool shed; on the other a modest shelter covered by a garish Day-Glo waterproof tarp. The shed was definitely ugly, but extremely inexpensive to build. More importantly, equipped with a drafting table, chairs, a supply closet, and changing room manufactured from materials that had been procured by Eldon Volkmer at various sales and swap meets, it was extremely functional. Born with the keen eye and intuition of a military scavenger, bargains were Eldon's passion, and the art of the deal his first love. Indeed, it seemed at times that he had outfitted the entire operation with used gimcracks picked up at government surplus sales, estate auctions, or junkyards, at well below bargain-basement prices. Yet his real genius lay in an incredible ability to convert old pieces of metal and rubbish, which to anyone else seemed suitable only for the scrap heap, to functional machinery. Already holding several patents for various inventions, he could rebuild, adapt, or even invent any tool necessary to meet our peculiar and eclectic needs, be it a generator, an underwater dredge, or an entire electrical system. If anything broke, he could fix it; if we didn't have it, he could build it or invent a new one to replace it. To this day I am firmly convinced that every project needs an Eldon Volkmer on its team to succeed.

With the operations platform fully outfitted, we began excavation on June 7, 1980. We had planned that the barge, once anchored in its final position, would not be moved until the testing of the Turtle Shell Wreck site had been completed. Then it would be hauled downriver to the *Peter Cooper* Wreck where the entire process would begin anew in two weeks. But even the best-laid plans, of course, never seem to fall in line with the processes of discovery, especially those predicated on perpetually good weather or a shoestring budget. Late in the evening, after the field team had gone home, disaster nearly ended the project before it began when a sudden unexpected thunderstorm struck the Patuxent Valley. Hammering rains, high winds, runoff, and mud moved in a torrent down the river, suddenly and dramatically raising the water level and flooding the wet-

232

lands about the cofferdam. Full-sized trees were torn from eroding river-banks and carried swiftly along with the flash flood.

Sitting in the comfort of my home, listening to the rain pelting on my roof, and watching trees in my yard bend before the wind, I could only guess at what was happening to our dime-store cofferdam and jury-rigged operations platform. Why hadn't I assigned some personnel to watch over the site during the evening? But then, I reasoned defensively, perhaps it was better that no one was aboard the barge, for there was little anyone could do.

Early Sunday morning, with the storm over, I drove to the nearest point I could reach along the shore upriver from the cofferdam. Anxiously, I hiked along the bank for about a quarter-mile to a point on the eastern side of the river opposite the site. As I approached the site from a distance, I was relieved to discover that both the cofferdam and the operations platform were still there. When I came closer, however, it became distur-bingly clear that the upriver end of the platform had somehow been hove out of the water and had come to a precarious rest on the pilings at the southern end of the coffer. The platform's downriver end was completely submerged. The floating sift box was held in place only by a single line which had been employed as a backup precaution to an elaborate hinged arrangement (which had been destroyed) attaching it to the deck. The Day-Glo shelter was a shambles. Timbers and heavy equipment that had been firmly lashed down the night before rolled about freely on the now-sloped deck as it swayed back and forth on the waters. Worse, both the coffer and the barge, which partially rested upon it, quivered in the current as if they were about to break free and float away with the next strong surge.

For a moment I froze. Then, fearing that there was little time to run for help, I stripped to my shorts and swam over to the site. On boarding the platform, fortunately, I found that two of our four upstream anchor lines had held. Within minutes I was able to redeploy the remaining two by physically carrying them out, half swimming and half walking, and hand-planting them in the bottom. Upon inspecting the pontoons be-neath the platform I was relieved to find that there had been little damage, with the exception of a small puncture in one pontoon. The wound was temporarily patched with the single most important piece of equipage of any project—duct tape. (How the world ever got by without this simple but indispensible item, I will never know!) After securing the loose materials on the deck, my next goal was to pry the forward end of the barge off the coffer pilings, using both four-by-four timber and iron pipes. After more than a few imprecations, I was finally able to free the impris-oned platform and then hammer in and resecure the loosened pilings. By the end of the day, the barge and coffer were pretty much in the same condition they had been before the storm. When work was resumed the following morning, few of our team were even aware of the near disaster that had occurred—except Eldon, who quietly repaired some of the damaged equipment on the spot.

When excavation finally commenced in earnest within the main cofferdam, it rapidly became apparent that the sediments through which we were digging possessed a readily discernible stratigraphy. The uppermost stratum consisted of a coarse brown sand, which varied in thickness from five to eight feet, depending upon its location on the site. Beneath the sand was a thin layer of decomposed leaves, twigs, and other rotted vegetation varying from six inches to a foot in thickness, which was principally located beneath the timbered structure on the west side of the coffer. Below the decomposing vegetation was a third stratum consisting of sand, heavy concentrations of freshwater clam shells, and a scatter of pebbles. The last stratum to be encountered, and ultimately the most difficult to excavate, consisted of gray clay, from one to two feet thick.[1]

It was in this, the deepest layer of sediment, that the excavators were obliged to exercise the most care, for it was here, we learned, that the best and most fragile artifacts had been preserved. Later evaluation of the stratigraphy helped to reinforce the historic record and oral traditions pertaining to the site which we had earlier recorded. U.S. Army Engineers reports, as late as 1907, indicated the known presence of the flotilla wrecks in the river. They were then referred to as hulks, a term used by the corps to designate visible derelicts.[2] As late as the 1930s, according to oral tradition, at least two and possibly more of the flotilla hulks were still visible. Some had been used by local fishermen as platforms to fish off of. Thus, it seemed likely that the wrecks had slowly, rather than abruptly, settled into the bottom of the shallow riverbed. But how did the archaeological record affirm this hypothesis?

Analysis of sediment samples taken in the vicinity revealed that the clay found in the lowest stratum, in the hold, was created by particulates in the Patuxent, a by-product of the continual erosion of Paleocene clay deposits along various sectors of the river banks and upland areas. When allowed to settle within the lower confines of the hull, the suspended clay material blanketed everything lying beneath it with a solid mantle, a protective, anaerobic mass effectively sealing out most of the destructive biota that could consume organic materials. With the passage of time, the particulate matter, under pressure from additional sedimentary deposits settling on top of it, slowly congealed into an almost impervious aggregate. Later, the vessel settled ever deeper, and its upper wooden components gave way to the forces of the river or were worn down to heartwood by current flow. Heavier, coarser gravels and sands, pushed along by the river current, began to seep through hull fissures and into the hold of the wreck. The gravels began to provide purchase for small colonies of

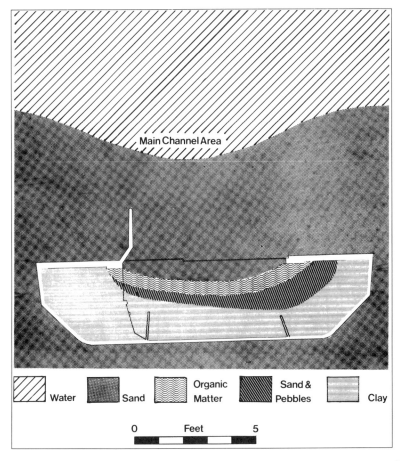

A stratigraphic profile of the Turtle Shell Wreck, viewed from the stern toward the bow, as it lay beneath the Patuxent sediments.

freshwater clams. Later, the slight depression, which had once been the hold of the ship, became a receptacle for leaves and other migrating river debris such as broken tree branches. As the river continued to scour around the hull, and the sediments increased within it, the wreck nestled ever deeper into its own pit. Finally, the putrid-smelling gray sands that now cover the river bottom erased all evidence of the vessel which, as late as the 1930s, had served as a visible reminder of the War of 1812.[3]

Over the next few weeks, as excavation progressed downward, stratum by stratum, the field crew grew increasingly competitive among themselves. Each dive team vied with the others for the most bottom time. Twelve- to fourteen-hour work days became the norm for the crew. And there was always the danger that weariness could lead to mistakes. The fine river silts continually fouled the divers' breathing regulators, and the

235

airlift was forever in need of unclogging. Equipment overhaul and repair became part of the daily regimen. The demands upon dive master Emily Graves and chief engineer Volkmer were unforgiving. Yet, thanks to their competence and ability, there would not be a single accident in nearly a thousand man-hours of diving on the site, nor a day lost owing to equipment breakdown.

Tedium was a constant companion. We removed each layer of sediment slowly and gingerly, in near total darkness, ounce by ounce, using the traditional archaeological trowel and even spoons. Each golfball-sized glob of clay was carefully examined on the spot to determine whether any artifacts were present before it was fed to the intake nozzle of the dredge hose. To prevent all but the smallest of artifacts from being admitted into the hose, Volkmer had designed a special expandable-contractable shield over the nozzle. Frequently, small metal rods were carefully inserted into an area about to be excavated to probe for the presence of larger items or disarticulated components of the ship itself, to prevent possible breakage during the actual excavation.

As the sediments were carried up the hose and spat out into the sieve box, they were carefully examined again by topside personnel who sifted endlessly through the debris. Many small artifacts, such as seeds, fruit pits, wood fragments, and the like, overlooked by the divers, were in this manner recovered.

Fred Hopkins, Iva Wesley, and Dale Shomette monitor the floating sift box for any small artifacts dredged from the Turtle Shell Wreck by the airlift.

Despite the deployment of the prefabricated grid system, its use was soon found to be impractical owing to its cumbersome management within the confines of the coffer, and the zero visibility. The grid was removed. Henceforth, the positions of all artifacts encountered on the bottom were triangulated from fixed points within the cofferdam with measuring tapes. We then shot elevations with an extended survey rod and a transit set up on the western shore, to insure proper recording of provenance. Owing to the frequent inaccuracies that occurred from working in black water, it was necessary to repeatedly recalculate or check many finds to insure exactness in our data.

Progress downward was painfully deliberate and was measured in inches rather than feet. We quickly fell behind schedule. Yet, as the cavity-like trench increased in breadth and depth, it was becoming increasingly apparent that something totally unexpected was being revealed to us. From the structural integrity of the site and the superb state of preservation of architectural features being exposed, we gradually came to the realization that we were not plotting the fragmentary ruins of a wrecked vessel as expected. We were, in fact, excavating down into the hold of a largely intact military craft from the War of 1812.

Structurally, the vessel remains appeared to be extremely well preserved owing to the oxygen-free environment in which they lay. The now-sterile sediments which had for so long masked its location had also acted as a shield against biotic-induced degeneration. The sediments also protected the site from the many natural and man-made stress factors that cause exposed wooden vessels to decline. And by a sheer stroke of good fortune, our excavation was progressing directly down into the open hold of the vessel's very heart. As we continued to peel back the layers of time, the complex mosaic of the wreck grew ever more understandable on our developing site plan. By a combination of systematic water jet probing outside of the coffer and excavation within, we were soon able to compute a conjectured overall length of the wreck at forty-eight feet seven inches, and a beam of sixteen feet.[4] She appeared to be a shallow-draft vessel, three feet deep in hold, with a relatively flat ceiling (floor) contour.[5]

At the downriver terminus of the wreck, immediately outside the confines of the cofferdam, a brief test excavation revealed cant framing timbers splayed outward as if crushed by the hands of some unseen giant. The timbers had suffered severe water erosion, and in some cases had been worn down to the very heart of the wood. Here we also discovered evidence of a fire, while the outward splay of the hull suggested a possible explosion. The shattered remains of a large brownstone water jug, apparently once stowed below deck, lay scattered about in the sediments. Like every other artifact encountered, each broken piece of pottery was carefully plotted, retrieved, and assigned a field number. As we proceeded to clear this section, it became evident that the area had indeed been

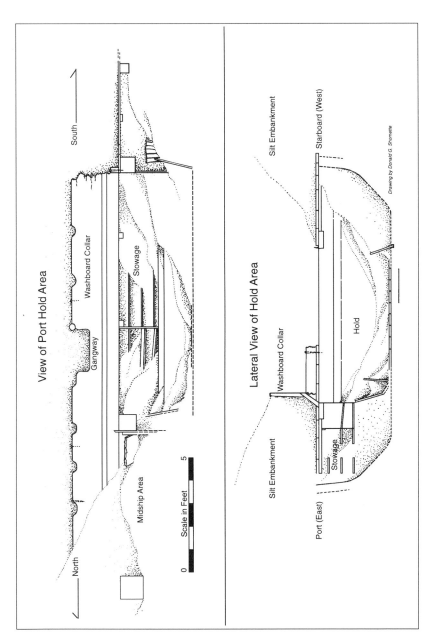

View of Port Hold Area

North

South

Midship Area

Gangway

Washboard Collar

Stowage

Scale in Feet

0   5

Lateral View of Hold Area

Silt Embankment

Washboard Collar

Silt Embankment

Port (East)

Stowage

Hold

Starboard (West)

Drawing by Donald G. Shomette

Plan views of the hold of the Turtle Shell Wreck.

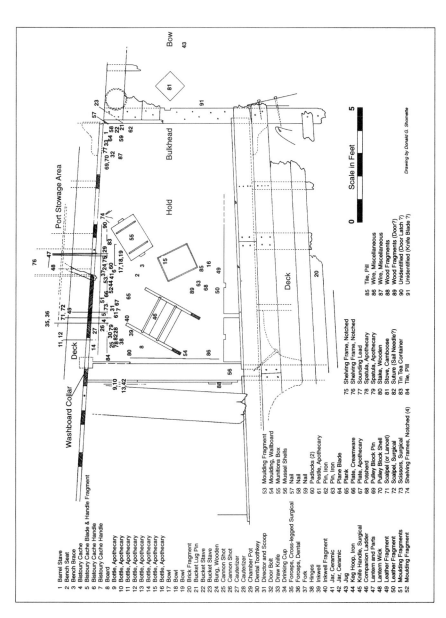

Top view of hold showing distribution of recovered artifacts in the Turtle Shell Wreck.

1	Barrel Stave	53	Moulding Fragment
2	Bench Seat	54	Moulding, Wallboard
3	Bench Brace	55	Munitions Box
4	Bistoury Cache	56	Mussel Shells
5	Bistoury Cache Blade & Handle Fragment	57	Nail
6	Bistoury Cache Handle	58	Nail
7	Bistoury Cache Handle	59	Nail
8	Board	60	Padlocks (2)
9	Bottle, Apothecary	61	Pestle, Apothecary
10	Bottle, Apothecary	62	Pin, Iron
11	Bottle, Apothecary	63	Pin, Iron
12	Bottle, Apothecary	64	Plane Blade
13	Bottle, Apothecary	65	Plank
14	Bottle, Apothecary	66	Plate, Creamware
15	Bottle, Apothecary	67	Plate, Apothecary
16	Bottle, Apothecary	68	Potsherd
17	Bowl	69	Pulley Block Pin
18	Bowl	70	Pulley Block Shell
19	Bowl	71	Scalpel (or Lancet)
20	Brick Fragment	72	Scalpel, Surgical
21	Bucket Lug Pin	73	Scissors, Surgical
22	Bucket Stave	74	Shelving Frames, Notched (4)
23	Bucket Stave	75	Shelving Frame, Notched
24	Bung, Wooden	76	Shelving Frame, Notched
25	Cannon Shot	77	Sounding Lead
26	Cannon Shot	78	Spatula, Apothecary
27	Cauterizer	79	Spatula, Apothecary
28	Cauterizer	80	Stake, Wooden
29	Chamber Pot	81	Stove, Camboose
30	Dental Toothkey	82	Suture (Sail Needle?)
31	Director and Scoop	83	Tin Tea Container
32	Door Bolt	84	Tile, Pill
33	Draw Knife	85	Tile, Pill
34	Drinking Cup	86	Wire, Miscellaneous
35	Forceps, Cross-legged Surgical	87	Wire, Miscellaneous
36	Forceps, Dental	88	Wood Fragments
37	Fork	89	Wood Fragments (Door?)
38	Hinges	90	Unidentified (Door Latch ?)
39	Inkwell	91	Unidentified (Knife Blade ?)
40	Inkwell Fragment		
41	Jar, Ceramic		
42	Jar, Ceramic		
43	Jug		
44	Keg Hoop, Iron		
45	Knife Handle, Surgical		
46	Companion Ladder		
47	Lantern and Parts		
48	Lantern Wick		
49	Leather Fragment		
50	Leather Fragment		
51	Moulding Fragments		
52	Moulding Fragment		

subjected to some violent force, probably resulting in a conflagration. I recalled Admiral Cockburn's vivid account of the last minutes of the flotilla:

> On nearing them we observed the sloop bearing the broad pendant [Barney's *Scorpion*] to be on fire, and she soon afterwards blew up. I now saw clearly that they were all abandoned and on fire with trains to their magazines, and out of the seventeen vessels which composed this formidable and so much vaunted flotilla sixteen were in quick succession blow up.[6]

Whatever vessel it was that we had been excavating, it seemed likely that a small charge had been set off in her downriver end, all but obliterating part of her deck and tearing asunder her frames and hull in that quarter. But had the charge been set in her bow or stern, or had the magazine blown up? And what, if any, further evidence could we find to support the explosion theory? Though many of Barney's vessels were double ended, apparently with removable rudders at their stern to facilitate the use of their long guns in action, we knew absolutely nothing about how such vessels were structurally reinforced in these areas. Did the forward carronade deck of a barge have greater reinforcement, special bulkheading or traverse pieces than the long-gun-bearing stern? What form of construction was adopted to host a removable rudder? There were, in fact, scores of questions we might answer if we could only determine which end of the vessel we were investigating in the dark. To find out, I directed that the excavation be intensified on the downriver end, both inside and outside of the coffer. Perhaps we might locate a rudder, gudgeon, strapping, sternpost, stempost, or some other recognizable indication to suggest just which end of the vessel it was that we were examining. Soon the excavation revealed the presence of certain carpentry and naval gear that would normally have been stowed in the forward section of the vessel. Though architectural details failed to aid in our quest for an answer, it was eventually assumed, but never absolutely confirmed, that the collapsed downriver end of the wreck may have been the bow.

Had Barney pointed his vessels downstream in the narrow river in the event he might have the opportunity to once again engage the enemy or perhaps make one last escape effort? Had the bow, upon which a carronade may have once rested, been blown up as initial evidence suggested, or was the collapse of the framing merely the result of extreme high energy currents in the river or the burdensome weight of tons of clay on the bottom? Several more days of careful excavation, we hoped, would give us our answer.

Abaft, or north of the collapsed cant frames, a small traverse brace was discovered, apparently laid in place to reinforce against the stress caused by the severe rake of the hull as it bent toward the juncture with the stempost. Exactly three feet eight inches abaft the forward brace excavation, the main forward bulkhead was revealed, replete with timber downslats which served to compartmentalize the bow from the rest of the vessel. Here we encountered further evidence of the terrible force that had undoubtedly sunk the ship. Remains of torn and fragmented deck timbers attached to the top of the traverse beam, as well as brutally bent and broken nails and spikes embedded therein, provided seemingly ample proof of the force of a sudden and violent shock in the "bow" section.

Despite the damage caused by the probable explosion beneath the forward deck, we were soon able to discern that the compartmentalization of the forward bulkhead had apparently absorbed much of the concussion. Aft of the bulkhead, the hold of the vessel, though littered with a profusion of items cast about by the shock, seemed to be in a relatively stable condition.

Excavation now progressed northward and widened to the borders of the coffer, commensurately increasing our understanding of the wreck. On the east side of the coffer, presumably the port side of the vessel, a singularly intriguing and complex set of features was revealed. The most interesting of these was believed to be a washboard collar running along the edge of the hold. The collar was without question among those features added as protection against the turbulent waters of the Chesapeake, at Barney's insistence, during the shakedown cruise of the flotilla in the spring of 1814. Careful inspection of the board revealed five half circles, presumed to be oar rests, equidistant from each other, and cut into the crown of the collar, as well as a gangway portal.

The collar was mounted on a deck which protected from beneath the coffer wall. Through water jet probing on the outside of the coffer and excavation from beneath the deck on the inside, we began to assemble data on the collar's construction. Excavation on the opposite side of the narrow hole, not unexpectedly, revealed another partially intact deck, but from which the collar had been separated, probably by the shock of the explosion.

Our next discovery, in what now seemed an unending series of delights, was the location of compartmentalized stowage sections beneath the port deck—replete with goods contained within. The compartments, which were clogged with stiff clay, were almost evenly divided into several subcompartments by wooden slats or partitions. Miraculously, a series of shelves were found still *in situ* attached to the partitions in the same position they had been when the vessel went down. Close examination of the compartment ceilings revealed what we believed to be tracks used to guide and hold partition slats in position, permitting the division or subdivision of the compartments into any sizes desired. The find was of great importance—if our interpretations were correct. If so, we had discovered the key to determining how shipboard goods and even private property were kept separated aboard a small warship where even modest personal stowage space would have been at a premium. The constructors had simply built into every usable area beneath the port deck, and probably throughout the entire vessel, stowage compartments that could be enlarged or reduced by merely adding or removing a partition slat.

Exploration beneath the starboard deck, however, revealed that any compartments in that quarter had either disintegrated or, more than likely, never been constructed. Instead, we found little more than a large empty space, quite suitable for bulk stowage, perhaps for line, sails, or use as an anchor locker. However, excavation in this section proceeded only far enough to confirm the apparent absence, for whatever causes, of stowage partitions and shelving. Beneath both port and starboard decks we also noted the expected support features such as lodging knees, bracings, traverse frames, and so forth. Gradually, the internal architecture of the ship began to fill in the great gaps on our site plan.

Excavation continued to progress toward the northern end of the coffer. Then, yet another bulkhead was discovered. Here, the main traverse beam, a large eight-by-ten-inch timber, with vertical slats extending from the beam downward to the ceiling, would provide the northernmost extent of the excavation area cleared within the coffer. Owing to diminishing time and financial resources, I decided now to concentrate all of our efforts in excavating this small forward hold area down to ceiling planking.

The focus of our efforts to clear the lower hold was undertaken with several objectives in mind. The first of these was to confirm or deny the presence of a conjectured mast step; the second was to determine the condition and realities about the hull and ceiling design. And finally, we hoped that artifactual components that could tell us something about everyday life aboard the vessel, as well as how she was sailed, manned, and fought, would be found lying at the base of the hold.

Our divers now began to experience increasing difficulties in maintaining provenance in the pitch-black water. Soon, the dive teams began to engage, head-on, the layer of thick clay that proved to be the most difficult sediments of all to remove. Again, the airlift was hand-fed a diet of presqueezed clay which had been delicately removed trowelful by trowelful from the bottom.

Excavation slowed to a crawl. Problems were now compounded by the discovery that some objects made of soft woods such as pine buried by the clay nearly 166 years earlier had become pulpy and fragile and were far inferior in terms of preservation to those that had been buried in sand and gravel. As a consequence, we dug through the clay with the ever-present danger of injuring wooden artifacts and delicate structural features of the vessel itself, such as trim fragments or even the ceiling planking.

Once again, we revised our strategy. We would not attempt a full excavation of the hold as earlier considered but instead would dig several trenches from port to starboard. In this way we would be able to explore and map the contour of the ceiling and other interior architectural features and sample artifacts encountered along the trench line, with only minimal hazard to the site itself.

The approach was something of an anachronism to the basic tenets of dry-land archaeological excavation, namely, the assumption that to dig a site one must in the process destroy it to extract the fullness of its data. But few dry-land sites are ever encountered almost entirely intact. We had, in essence, discovered the equivalent of a very fragile historic building, but underwater and buried beneath five feet of bottom sediment. And our initial objectives, after all, had been to merely test the site and develop the best methodology suitable to extract the most accurate data possible. Several trenches were thus begun, running from starboard to port, as were test excavations into several areas of the port stowage compartment. The contours of the hold area, and numerous architectural features within, rapidly began to take form.

One of the more interesting portable features of the ship was a small, removable two-stepped companion ladder with grooved runners that fit into a lip of the deck. Another was an oarsman's bench that had collapsed into the hold. The seven-foot-long bench, which once apparently ran

A wooden two-step companion ladder, pulpy and fragile after more than a century and a half of immersion, was slightly injured during recovery. It was later mended after more than two years of conservation treatment.

across half of the hold area, was unique in that it was contoured to fit the human posterior. "Bucket seats by Barney," quipped one of the divers.

The development of artifact sampling procedures and the recovery of a small number of diagnostically suitable artifacts were among the principal objectives of work on the site. The quantity, quality, condition, and variety of artifacts encountered within the small area of the coffer excavation, however, were totally unexpected. Most, owing to the oxygen-free environment in which they, like the ship itself, had been sealed, were in an excellent state of preservation. A wide variety of materials—animal, vegetable, and mineral—were excavated, among which were item types never before recovered from such sites.

One of the largest items rescued, and one that required extreme care in bringing up, was a large wooden munitions box. The soft, pulpy box was filled with clay and required singular attention. A special reinforced lifting cradle was contructed on deck and lowered into the hold by lines; the box was placed on top and lifted out. Once on deck, the clay within the box was carefully excavated in the event any artifacts were contained therein (even though the box had been discovered lying upside down). Throughout the excavation, the large artifact was kept wet and upon completion, was wrapped in plastic and immediately transferred to our conservation laboratory at Solomons.

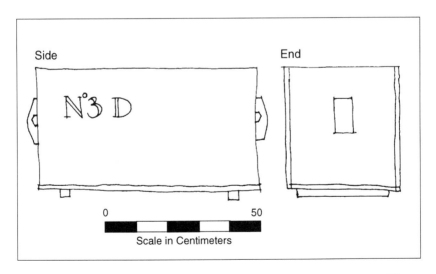

The wooden munitions box was wrapped in plastic to prevent drying. The insides were carefully excavated for any artifacts that might still be contained within. The inscription "No3 D" was found on one side. The D is believed to represent the firm of Christopher Deshon, the arms contractor responsible for supplying the flotilla with ordnance, side arms, and munitions.
Drawing by Carol Shomette

Bucket Seats by Barney

Upon recovery of each artifact, the item was tagged, numbered, measured, drawn to scale, bagged, and then transferred to the lab for stabilization and mending. Most small items were placed in Ziploc bags filled with water until they could be tended to by my wife, Carol, the project's draftsperson. More fragile items were photographed on the spot.

The artifacts recovered from l-TSW fell into six categories: (1) surgical/dental and related accoutrements, (2) military items, (3) carpentry tools, (4) domestic shipboard items, (5) maritime-related items, and (6) architectural features of the vessel itself.[7]

The surgical/dental items proved to be the most intriguing of the lot. These were originally stowed in a surgeon's field kit made of white pine. The kit, which had fallen to the deck, had become punky and was in the last stages of disintegration when excavated. Dental forceps, a vicious-looking dental tooth key, a bullet probe, surgical scissors, tortoise-shell-handled surgical knives, bistouries, probes, cauterizers, and other items were carefully recovered near the collapsed box, along with representative sections of the box itself, including its silver lock plate and brass hinges. These artifacts were of European manufacture. On the handles and blades of many instruments were engraved variations of the name "Nowill." After considerable research, it was learned that the instruments had been the product of the firm of Hague and Nowill, of Sheffield, England, makers of fine surgical tools since the time of the company's founding by Thomas Nowill in 1700.[8] Others bore the name "Evans" with

The imprint of the firm of Hague and Nowill, of Sheffield, England, makers of fine surgical equipment since the company's founding by Thomas Nowill in 1700, was in evidence on many surgical tools recovered from the wreck.
Photograph by Tim Mihursky

245

The imprint of John Evans and Company of London, a venerable firm founded in 1676, was discovered on several surgical items recovered from the Turtle Shell Wreck and was key to dating the site. The firm had been authorized in 1812 to bear the crown imprint above the company name after being designated as suppliers of surgical instruments to the Royal Navy. In 1813 the authorization was rescinded. Photograph by Tim Mihursky

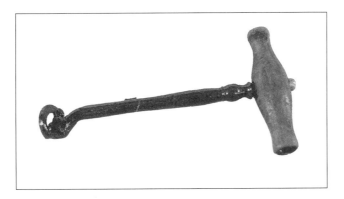

An instrument known as a toothkey, discovered aboard the Turtle Shell Wreck, was used in dental surgery. Photograph by Tim Mihursky

a small crown impression over it. These instruments had been produced by the firm of John Evans & Company, of 10 Old Change, London. The Evans firm had been founded about 1676, principally as a blacksmithing operation, but by 1783, when it was first known to operate at the Old Change address, the company was producing surgical instruments almost exclusively. Significantly, in 1812 the company became one of the principal suppliers of surgical instruments to the Royal Navy and was authorized to mount a crown over the name.[9] Had the instruments been part of the prize cargo taken from some Royal Navy vessel by an American privateersman, perhaps even HM Packet *Princess Amelia*, captured by Barney himself while commanding the *Rossie*? It was, indeed, a delightful idea, but one almost too savory to chew on for long.

These dental forceps were probably used by the flotilla's only surgeon, Thomas Hamilton, who served as both doctor and dentist, for tooth extraction.
Photograph by Tim Mihursky

These specialized cross-legged surgical forceps were used for bullet extraction. A bullet, flattened on one side, was found within a few inches of the forceps and may have been a "battle souvenir" intended for one of the surgeon's more fortunate patients. Photograph by Tim Mihursky

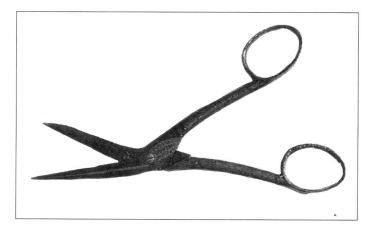

Surgical scissors bearing the Nowill imprint. Photograph by Tim Mihursky

Tidewater Time Capsule

A Nowill surgical scalpel with tortoise-shell handle. Photograph by Tim Mihursky

Pharmaceutical items recovered from the site included spatulas, cream-ware pill tiles, corked bottles (one with a creamy substance still captured within), a pestle head, and several Philadelphia-ware unguent jars, mixing bowls, and plates. The eight bottles recovered were of the same cylindrical shape common to seventeenth through early-nineteenth century pharmaceutical glassware, with solid bar empontiling suggestive of a terminal date of 1820–30.

The recovery of a single intact chamber pot was, perhaps, one of the most significant finds to be made. Since personal toilet facilities (for officers and men) on a vessel the size of l-TSW were not common in the early nineteenth century, it seemed probable that the vessel had been employed as a hospital ship, and that the pot was a component of the array of medical equipage aboard. Aside from an outbreak of flu and measles while the flotilla was stationed at the Patuxent port of Nottingham in July 1814 (during which time Barney himself was convalescent), health concerns aboard the squadron were not well documented. Indeed, muster lists of the flotilla discovered by Fred Hopkins indicated that the fleet was bereft of medical personnel. Only one surgeon, Dr. Thomas Hamilton, and a surgeon's mate, A. C. Thompson, had been enrolled. Hamilton's reported period of enrollment was from December 22, 1813, to April 6, 1814. Despite this information, which would seemingly dispel the probability of his presence aboard the flotilla at the time of its loss on August 22, 1814, expense lists of naval agent James Beatty indicated that Hamilton may have operated a field hospital at St. Leonard's Town during June 1814, when

One of many pharmaceutical bottles recovered, this phial contains a hardened vestige of medicine still sealed within. Photograph by Tim Mihursky

Several beautiful yellow and brown Philadelphia-ware apothecary bowls such as this were recovered from the wreck intact. Photograph by Tim Mihursky

This Philadelphia-ware jar with wooden stopper, one of several recovered, is believed to have served as an apothecary container in which salves and unguents were stored by Dr. Hamilton. Photograph by Tim Mihursky

An apothecary plate probably used by flotilla surgeon Dr. Thomas Hamilton or surgeon's mate A.C. Thompson. Photograph by Tim Mihursky

the squadron was blockaded within St. Leonard's Creek, suggesting that he may have served with the flotilla until its demise. Surgeon's Mate Thompson began service on July 17, 1814, at Nottingham and remained in service until September 7, 1814.[10]

Several vessels of the flotilla could have provided adequate facilities to accommodate a surgeon's needs. The first was either gunboat *No. 137* or *138*, one of which had been specifically converted at Baltimore to carry medical supplies and to serve as a hospital ship. Both vessels were scuttled in St. Leonard's Creek on June 26, 1814, which necessitated a shift of hospital duties to another craft. A second vessel which could conceivably have been employed thereafter was an unidentified merchant schooner belonging to William O'Neal of Washington, D.C., which had been hired to serve as an ordnance supply boat, and which had been destroyed with the flotilla.[11] The third candidate was Barney's own flagship, the U.S.S.

An apothecary's mixing spatula, one of several recovered bearing the Nowill imprint. Photograph by Tim Mihursky

Chamber pot recovered from the Turtle Shell Wreck. Photograph by Tim Mihursky

Swivel gun grip, used to direct a small anti-personnel weapon, usually mounted on a ship's rail, in close combat. Photograph by Tim Mihursky

251

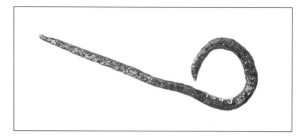

This gunner's pick was employed in clearing the touch hole of a small piece of ordnance such as a swivel gun. The recovery of both a swivel gun grip and the small gunner's pick were the first indications that the vessel was armed with more than large ordnance and the personal sidearms of the crew as indicated in the historic record. Photograph by Tim Mihursky

A small swivel gun shot which had struck the ship during battle is partially surrounded by the wood against which it impacted, probably during one of the engagements on St. Leonard's Creek. Photograph by Tim Mihursky

The musket ball pictured here appears to have been flattened on one side, possibly from impact. It was near the surgeon's kit box, approximately an inch away from the cross-legged surgical forceps used for bullet extraction. Was surgeon Thomas Hamilton saving a souvenir for someone? Photograph by Tim Mihursky

252

Scorpion, which had been withheld from combat in St. Leonard's Creek along with *Nos. 137* and *138.*

Among the military-related artifacts recovered were items such as small-caliber shot, a gunner's pick, a swivel gun grip, musket flints, and the munitions box. Owing to the salvage of practically all artillery, munitions, and weaponry by John Weems, the local citizenry, and Barney's own flotillamen immediately after the flotilla's loss, no cannon or other major military items associated with the fleet were encountered. Although there was a paucity of military artifacts, those recovered were nevertheless of importance. Both the swivel grip and the gunner's pick, suitable only for a small-bore weapon such as a rail gun, were recovered near one another on the forward port side, suggesting the vessel had been armed with small antipersonnel ordnance, a fact not indicated in the archival record. One small-bore shot, apparently an expended projectile that had struck the ship, was recovered with a section of the wood it had hit still tightly compressed around the shot—a distinct indication that the vessel saw combat. Another of the small shot retrieved was of such an imperfect mold that it would have been impossible to have been fired from a swivel gun and may have been employed as canister shot. If so, it was the first indication that canister may have been employed aboard the flotilla. A single musket shot, partially flattened, and which had obviously impacted against an object, was discovered within two inches of the bullet forceps. Was someone saving a grisly souvenir of battle? Elsewhere, three musket flints were retrieved. Interestingly, the list of purser's expenses for the flotilla indicated that musket flints had been procured in May 1814 in unit lots of 250 flints per lot at a cost of $2.50 per lot.[12]

An abundance of carpentry tools was encountered in the forward section of the hold, all probably part of the ship or flotilla carpenter's kit. Only three major items, however, were recovered: a plane blade impressed with a cryptic half impression of the letters "STONES" and the city of manufacture, Sheffield, England; a draw knife; and a punch. In addition to the tools, a large clump of white, claylike substance was recovered from the same section in conjunction with several small keg and bucket staves. The material was later determined to be white lead paint that had been allowed to harden within a container prior to its collapse. Naval agent Beatty's records indicated that numerous kegs of white lead paint had been purchased for the fleet at a cost of $7.50 per keg.[13]

The discovery of the carpentry tools was of paramount importance since there was but a single ship's carpenter enrolled aboard the fleet. His name was Charles Fleming, and he had signed aboard the *Scorpion* on September 5, 1812, while that vessel was still part of the Potomac Flotilla. He remained with the *Scorpion* until April 11, 1814, when he was transferred to Baltimore, presumably with his ship, to continue in service under

A carpenter's draw knife, possibly part of the tool kit of flotilla carpenter Charles Fleming, a member of the crew of the U.S.S. *Scorpion*. One handle of the tool was lost during recovery operations and remains on the site awaiting future archaeological investigation. Photograph by Tim Mihursky

A clump of white lead-based paint that had dried and hardened in its container prior to the loss of the flotilla. Kegs of white paint had been purchased for Barney's squadron for $7.50 a barrel. Photograph by Tim Mihursky

the command of Commodore Barney.[14] Unfortunately, *Scorpion*'s extant muster rolls do not include the period from February to August 1814, and it is impossible to determine whether Fleming continued in service aboard her.

The role of a ship's carpenter was an important one, for he had to be a complete craftsman capable of constructing everything from a ship's boat to a mast. Responsible for all repairs, he reported to the captain on the condition of the decks, masts, yards, hull, and pumps. He regularly checked for leakage, kept the pumps in good repair, and, in battle, plugged shot holes and mended the ship's wounds as necessary. Such was the work of Charles Fleming and, undoubtedly, a number of other artisans aboard the flotilla who served in a similar but undesignated capacity. It was, indeed, inviting to wistfully attribute sole ownership of the tools to Fleming, but a final determination would have to wait until all of the site data had been digested.

The recovery of a variety of domestic artifacts presented an array of everyday early nineteenth century life aboard ship seldom seen today. Many ordinary items were retrieved, such as a Liberty-head penny, leather shoe fragments, a wooden boot heel, ceramic bowls, water jugs, eating and drinking utensils, and even a small, portable galley stove, whose distribution patterns proved quite useful in the interpretation of shipboard activity.

Two major domestic items had been recovered from the bow area. The first of these was a small, handcut, sandstone galley stove known as a camboose. In appearance, the artifact is simply a square stone block,

A sandstone deck camboose. Photograph by Tim Mihursky

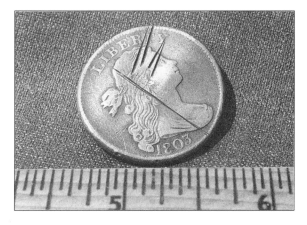

This 1803 large Liberty one-cent piece is believed to have served as a "chaw penny" upon which a seaman would cut a plug of tobacco. Photograph by Tim Mihursky

255

A tin-plated grog ration cup bearing the initials "CW" and numerous starbursts etched into its surface belonged to the ship's cook, Caesar Wentworth, the only enrolled member of the Chesapeake Flotilla with the initials CW.

This two-gallon stoneware jug, broken by the explosion that sank the ship, was found lodged behind several shattered cant frames. It required two days of underwater work to recover all but two pieces (which could not be found), and several more for conservator Leslie Bright to mend. Research by Dr. Fred Hopkins revealed that the jug had been purchased for the flotilla by naval agent James Beatty for $1.87½. Photograph by Tim Mihursky

hollowed out from one side to the other, and easily moved about at will. Owing to the danger of fire aboard wooden ships, deck stoves were usually set in a bed of sand or upon bricks laid out on the deck. Purser's records for the flotilla noted that "sand boxes" had been purchased at twenty-five

A creamware plate, one of many purchased for the flotilla at a cost of $5.00 per dozen. Photograph by Tim Mihursky

A small stamped brass button bearing the inscription "STAND & COLE LTD. LONDON" was probably a portion of a flotillaman's personal attire left behind during the hasty abandonment of the fleet. Photograph by Tim Mihursky

A pair of padlocks, still bearing traces of black paint, were recovered from the Turtle Shell Wreck. A total of thirty-six such locks were purchased by naval agent James Beatty for the Chesapeake Flotilla, two per vessel on the Patuxent, at a cost of $1.00 per lock. Photograph by Tim Mihursky

cents a box. Although no use for these boxes is indicated, they were probably to be employed as portable bases upon which the stoves were to be laid when in service. When cleaned, the camboose revealed extensive evidence of use, with carbon deposits heavily staining the inside of the block. Irregular chipping along the open top side suggested wear from some object laid across it, possibly a metal grate upon which items were placed to be heated or cooked. Indeed, the purser's records tell us that "grid irons" had also been purchased for the fleet. Although it has been suggested that the stove may have been employed to heat shot, several factors preclude such a probability. First, Barney noted in a report to Washington that he did not have shot furnaces. And second, the diminutive size of the artifact precluded heating of more than one cannonball at a time, a most unacceptable limitation in combat.

The location of the stove block indicated that it had been stowed beneath the bow deck. Its proximity to another large domestic artifact, a tall stoneware jug, which was probably employed to store water or some other consumable liquid, suggested that this section of the vessel had been used to stow domestic items. Access to this section beneath the deck would have been difficult, yet stowage aboard a small vessel of this size would have required that every unit of space be employed. The two-gallon stoneware jug had been found lodged, in a shattered condition, behind and beneath two collapsed cant frame timbers. Since the timbers were immovable, it took us more than two days to recover the jug's fragmentary remains. Happily, when restoration was later undertaken, only two sherds of the container were found to be missing. The purser's list for the flotilla had indicated that a number of two-gallon jugs had been purchased at a cost of $1.87½ per jug.[15]

The single Liberty-head large cent piece, dated 1803, which had been retrieved from the sift box topside, caused a flurry of excitement, for here was the first artifact to bear an actual date. The surface of the coin bore a number of incisions, as if cut by a knife, which had at first been interpreted as having been inflicted during the airlifting. However, the even, green patina on the surface and in the incisions indicated otherwise. Only months later would we learn that the incisions on the surface may have indeed resulted from a blade cut. Many Tidewater mariners of the early nineteenth century smoked and chewed tobacco cut from a rolled plug. To cut a plug on the deck surface of a vessel could cause splinters and posed a serious hazard to barefoot seamen. Custom thus forbade such actions, and it became common practice for seamen to carry a chew penny, a large cent piece, against which they could cut their plugs. We believed that we had found one such cent.

One of the most intriguing and personalized items to be found had been a small half-pint tin-plated grog ration cup. Although Beatty's list had revealed that several of these cups had been purchased at 12½ cents per mug, the most interesting detail about this particular artifact was that it was decorated with numerous stars of various sizes scratched upon its surface. Its owner was certainly patriotic. But the most interesting decoration of all was the owner's initials "CW." Examination of the flotilla's muster lists produced but a single flotillaman with the same initials. His name was Caesar Wentworth, one of twenty cooks enrolled with the fleet; he had served from September 10, 1813 until the end of the war.[16]

Several items also related to the ship's mess activity were recovered and included a creamware plate, a fork, and a tea tin. Beatty's records indicated that plates had been purchased in half-dozen lots at a cost of five dollars per dozen. Knives and forks, also procured in half dozen lots, also cost five dollars per dozen. (By mid-July 1814, however, well after the fleet had been blockaded within the Patuxent, the price for plates had dropped by 20 percent per dozen.)[17]

A single intact blue and gray stoneware inkwell, of the type commonly used with quilled pens, pierced with small holes around its crown, was recovered near the surgeon's chest. The common usage of quilled pens is generally accepted as having ended during the 1850s with the rise in popularity of steel-tipped writing pens. The common use of ceramic desktop inkwells such as the one recovered, however, is believed to have ceased about the beginning of the nineteenth century. Again, navy agent James Beatty's list of equipment purchased for the flotilla included inkwells, ink bottles, quills, and paper. Such items would likely have been used principally by the ship's officers, even Barney himself.[18]

Several items associated with personal apparel were retrieved, including a small stamped brass button marked with the inscription "STAND & COLE LTD. LONDON," which was of a type typical of the period 1800–30. A number of leather fragments, several of which showed stitch marks, are believed to have been portions of a shoe, as was a wooden heel fragment recovered near the munitions chest. The finds were of importance since the historic record had indicated that the flotilla had been abandoned in such haste that both officers and crews had been obliged to leave their personal belongings behind, primarily clothing, and later sued the federal government (unsuccessfully in the case of the officers) to be reimbursed for the loss. And here was some of the very evidence of their hasty retreat.

That on-board security was important was attested to by the discovery of a pair of padlocks, still clinched together and bearing the black paint or lacquer with which they were originally coated. Both were in working order and were among an assortment of items that had spilled out from the port stowage compartments. On May 22, 1814, shortly before the flotilla sailed on its fateful voyage from Baltimore, three double padlocks were purchased for Barney at a cost of one dollar per lock. On June 10 an additional thirty-three double padlocks were acquired for the rest of the fleet, bringing the total to thirty-six, or two per vessel on the Patuxent.[19]

Items of a naval or maritime character were few in number, undoubtedly owing to the efforts by John Weems and Barney's flotillamen, to recover as much navy property as possible during his salvage attempt in the fall of 1814. The three most important artifacts in this category consisted of a sounding lead, a pulley block, and a tin-plated lantern.

The sounding lead is quite similar in appearance to leads still in use today. Attached by a strap to a lead line, the sounding lead was managed by a leadsman. The lead occupied an important role in navigational decision making and was usually employed in the following manner: Tallow was placed in a recess in the base of the item. This was called "arming the lead." In shallow waters, a lead weighing from six to nine pounds, such as our artifact, was usually employed. In waters of twenty fathoms or more, a lead of up to twenty-five pounds was used. The leadsman, usually positioned at or near the bow of the vessel, would cast the lead to determine the depth of water. When the tallow-filled end of

The ship's sounding lead. Photograph by Tim Mihursky

260

A wooden block shell, possibly used in the standing or running rigging of the Turtle Shell Wreck, withered as a result of testing on several wooden "sacrificial" artifacts to determine the rate of shrinkage of waterlogged materials from the site when exposed to air and drying. Photograph by Tim Mihursky

the lead struck bottom, bits of the bottom mud, sand, gravel, shell, and so forth, would adhere to it. This information was of enormous assistance in helping a navigator determine his location, especially when nearing or working around a coast. Even today, navigational charts provide information on bottom makeup and depth to assist the modern mariner.[20]

In the same vicinity as the sounding lead, a small pulley and pin were excavated and recovered. Probably part of a single block assemblage, this artifact was bound with a strope, or rope ring, and would have been commonly employed suspended from masts, shrouds, and so forth, of a sailing vessel to increase the mechanical power of the lines used in handling the sails. It may also have been employed in a variety of other services as well, such as lifting cargo and deck gear, or as a component of the gun tackle. It is probable, however, that our artifact may have represented a spare part stowed until needed, as it had been found below the deck with other naval gear.[21]

The last major item with maritime connotations was a nearly intact "Paul Revere" lantern, replete with conical roof, hinged door, candle holder with elevator apparatus inside, and perforated sides. This wonderful artifact had been laboriously excavated and retrieved from the far recesses of the port stowage compartment, immediately below the shelving. The main lantern segments and what is believed to be a base and wick from a second lantern were recovered, encased in a large blob of clay, from inside the compartment by divers John Burton and Sally Ruhl. After being cleaned and stabilized, the entire lantern was eventually mended to a like-new condition.[22]

Owing to the dangers of fire aboard wooden ships and the frequency of accidental conflagrations, enclosed lanterns such as what we had recovered were commonly employed. The Revere lantern was, in fact, in com-

Tidewater Time Capsule

Stowed in a nearly inaccessible recess of the ship's port stowage compartments, this tin-plated "Paul Revere" lantern was probably little used. Photograph by Tim Mihursky

mon usage in the Tidewater during the early and middle nineteenth century. It was possible, though unlikely, that our model had been used as a shipboard beacon. However, from the position in which it was found, it seemed probable that the item had been deliberately stowed in the far recesses of the stowage compartment, so far back, indeed, that it would have been difficult to reach and was probably out of service.

During the course of excavation, six taxa of plants (nuts and seed pits), two of invertebrates (snail shells and clam shells), and four of vertebrates (bones and teeth) were recovered from the sift box without provenance or by divers. Though several of the items were certainly not associated with the ship and were undoubtedly part of the contaminants washed into the site, certain portions of the flora may well have been components of provisions consumed aboard. The flora included butternut, black walnut, hickory nut (water hickory or pignut hickory), pecan (not native to this area), and shagbark hickory. In addition to the nut family, several peach (*Prunus persica*) and plum (*Prunus* sp.) pits were also recovered. Of the invertebrate remnants retrieved, the most commonly encountered had been the flat filter clam (*Elliptio complanata* Lightfoot), one of the most widely distributed freshwater mussels on the Atlantic slope, and the Virginia River horn snail (*Goniobasis virginica*), a mollusk commonly found in slow-flowing waters typical of the Patuxent. A partial left jaw and incisor fragment of a muskrat (*Ondatra zibethicus*), and a patella of a white-

262

Bucket Seats by Barney

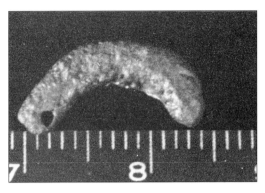

This reworked bone, possibly a personal adornment or jewelry of prehistoric origins
washed into the site from an eroding shoreline upriver, posed one of the greater
interpretive mysteries among the artifacts recovered from the Turtle Shell Wreck.
Photograph by Tim Mihursky

tailed deer (*Odocoileus virginianus*), both common to the Maryland Tidewater, were also retrieved.[23]

Two of the more curious items brought up were a stingray plate and
possibly a spine from the same species. Both plate and spine appeared to
have been reworked, but as the river in this region erodes through
Paleocene deposits of the Coastal Plain, which are rich in marine fossils,
the origins of these two ray parts seemed conjectural. The state of preservation, however, was more like that of a bony fish (not cartilaginous as are
rays) or a Holocene ray specimen. It seemed possible that the spine was
either a reworked fossil or in fact not a ray, or a reworked ray spine from
an aboriginal site (Native Americans were known to have used these spines
for spearing fish). Another possibility was that it was a curiosity brought
aboard the ship by a crew member. The presence of mineral formations on
the specimen further argued that it had been a reworked fossil.[24]

Architectural features of the vessel that were recovered included a
companion ladder, iron nails and spikes, miscellaneous wood trim fragments, the oarsman's bench, an iron doorlock, and a padlock bolt.[25]

The two-stepped, three-foot-tall companion ladder had been entirely
intact when found lying in the hold. It had obviously been intended to fit
into a lip at the deck level, as suggested by notches on its top end. The
absence of any nail, spike, or fitting holes suggested that it was portable
and could be employed anywhere where descent into the hold was
desired.

The oarsmen's bench, the first ever recovered from a vessel of this era,
was excavated and retrieved from the port hold area in two pieces but was
otherwise intact. Originally 7 feet long, 12½ inches wide, and tapered to
6¼ inches at one end, the piece was contoured longitudinally along its
full length, a feature that would have made the seat more comfortable for

Originally identified as a bayonet frog, this stitched boiled-leather artifact, recovered during the construction of the cofferdam, is now thought to be a component of the ship's pump. Photograph by Tim Mihursky

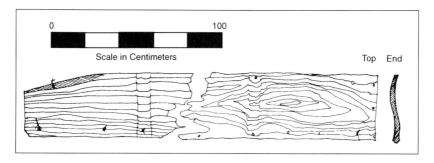

This oarsman's bench seat, recovered in two sections, was contoured to fit the human posterior to provide the maximum of comfort for a certainly less-than-comfortable task. Drawing by Carol Shomette

any individual sitting on it. Mounted on risers with bracings at either end, it had at one time spanned halfway across the hold. As many as nine complete benches would have been mounted on one of Barney's row galleys, thirteen on one of his 50-foot barges, and twenty on a 75-foot barge. From the prototype block sloop design of the 1812 period, from which *Scorpion* may have been adapted, Barney's flagship may have mounted as many as eleven complete oarsmen's benches.[26]

A number of wrought-iron rose-headed nails with beaten or hammered facets, dating circa 1790-1820, and three square-headed nails, of a type hitherto undocumented prior to 1820, were recovered from the sift box, along with a variety of trim and molding fragments. The trim and molding fragments were of six types, several of which still bore traces of red paint. Their presence as a decorative component of the architecture of the vessel suggested that the craft had not been constructed hastily,

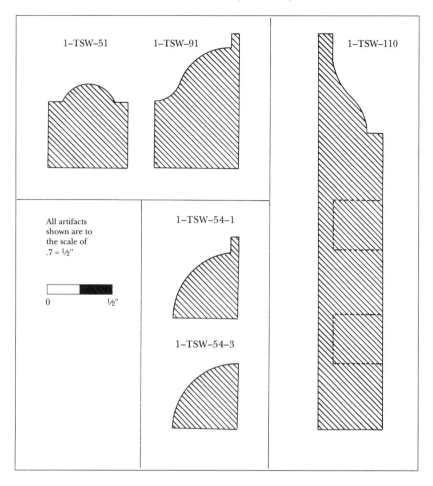

Five variants of decorative trim, some of which still bore traces of red paint and shown here in cutaway profile, were recovered from the Turtle Shell Wreck. The presence of such architectural amenities suggested that the vessel was probably not a hastily built craft such as the spartan barges constructed during the hurried building program initiated by Joshua Barney in late 1813.

as had the majority of Barney's barges, but with enough time and care that such marginal niceties could have been attended to.[27]

That the Turtle Shell Wreck, a largely intact vessel of the period of the War of 1812, had belonged to Barney's Chesapeake Flotilla, seemed a certainty. But exactly which vessel was she? That was a question that the assembled data and the marvelous, albeit small, collection of artifacts would soon answer.

Or so we hoped.

FIFTEEN

Working off the Brewhouse

There were few takers when I called upon the excavation teams working on the Turtle Shell Wreck for volunteers to accompany me to survey the St. Leonard's Wharf site on St. Leonard's Creek. Most of them had reasoned that a few piling stubs could not begin to compare in interest or glamour with an intact War of 1812 era warship or one of the oldest Euro-American small-vessel sites ever found in the United States. As usual, I fell upon the "A-Team," Volkmer, Hollingshead, Pugh, and Freda, for support.

The ruins of St. Leonard's Wharf, in brackish, turbid water just within the upper lip of the mouth of St. Leonard's Creek, were anything but glamorous. Yet the site, a possible typological representation of hundreds of others like it throughout the Tidewater that had passed into oblivion without record or note, was of significance. Moreover, unlike the other work carried out during the 1980 campaign, the St. Leonard's Wharf survey would be our only effort to evaluate an insert site, specifically one designed for the reception of watercraft. Although many other similar sites had been observed or visited in the previous two years, none had been thoroughly surveyed. Indeed, no intensive archaeological investigations of Tidewater Maryland wharf architecture had ever been carried out prior to the Patuxent Project.

Before the initiation of the St. Leonard's Wharf survey, we had discovered little pertinent archival or published data on the subject of Maryland wharf design. Extensive archaeological documentation had been carried out on a colonial wharf site at Yorktown, Virginia, and at several "cob" wharf sites in New England, which were instructive but proved to be of little direct value to our own endeavor.[1] Of greater relevance to our research was data provided by nineteenth and early twentieth century photographs of local wharves. The prints were housed in the collections of the Mariners' Museum, the Maryland Historical Society, and the Steamship Historical Society.[2] I had also encountered, in the manuscript and map collections of the Library of Congress, random inventories of building materials exported from Maryland for use in wharf construction at Alexandria, Virginia, as well as military engineering treatises and illustrative maps that revealed the formats for wharves in urban maritime centers such as Baltimore and Annapolis from the period of the Revolution to the end of the Civil War.[3] However, with the exception of several Army Corps of Engineers reports, data on the commonplace wharves and docks of the rural backwaters of the Tidewater was minimal. As for wharf architecture in general, there appeared to be a dearth of information on typology and even less on the logic governing design applications.

The St. Leonard's Wharf site, lying in five to twenty feet of water, had been selected as a survey target because it appeared to have existed in a variety of incarnations at a single, continuously occupied site, possibly from the seventeenth century on. Modern Mackall's Wharf, which stands only a few feet away from the earlier ruins of St. Leonard's Wharf, is situated on the north shore of St. Leonard's Creek, several hundred yards east of a small indentation in the shore known as Mackall's Cove, and a few hundred yards more from the entrance to St. Leonard's Creek. Its historic positioning was significant in that it was established astride a tract of land once known as the Brewhouse, or Johnsons Fresh, which had been settled in the mid-seventeenth century by Captain Peter Johnson, an enterprising Puritan colonist. Johnson had passed the property to his eldest son, Peter, Jr., who in turn bequeathed it to his own daughter Mary, who married Roger Baker, an English sea captain. Roger and Mary's daughter, Mary Baker, inherited the tract and married an English lawyer named Thomas Johnson, who had come to America in 1690 and is believed to have been a distant relation to her great-grandfather Captain Peter Johnson's side. The Thomas Johnsons took up residence at Brewhouse and in 1701 had a child, Thomas, Jr. In 1732, at about the time of the birth of his own son, Thomas III, Thomas, Jr., repatented Brewhouse, and from that time on, the estate was linked to one of Maryland's foremost historical figures.[4]

Thomas Johnson III was destined for greatness. As a youth, he studied law and was elected to the Provincial Congress. At the outbreak of the Revolution, he became a member of the Continental Congress and presented the nominating speech for his friend George Washington as commander-in-chief of the Continental Army. Johnson served as a member of the Maryland Convention, which ratified the Constitution of the United States. After serving three terms as the first elected governor of Maryland, he was appointed to the Supreme Court of the United States and later to the commission responsible for laying out the city of Washington.[5]

The Brewhouse remained in the Johnson family until it was sold to a family named Sollers, who, in turn, sold it to Dr. Richard Mackall about 1840. The Mackalls maintained ownership of the estate and its venerable works overlooking St. Leonard's Creek well into the twentieth century.[6]

Sometime in the mid-nineteenth century—no one knows for certain exactly when—a steamboat landing, named for the creek in which it had been erected, was built on the waterfront of the Mackall's Brewhouse tract to facilitate the operations of shipping, primarily by steamboats plying Patuxent waters. By the end of the steamboat era on the river, circa 1938, it had become a well-known, albeit irregular, stop for the various steamers serving the riverfront communities of southern Maryland. However, the old wharf, with its single dirt road connecting it to the outside world, was not destined to long survive the demise of the steamboats. Eventually, a newer, smaller dock, suitable for only the small craft that visited the creek from time to time, was erected immediately east of the original site.

An examination of title and probate records for the seventeenth century through the late nineteenth century had failed to reveal any data pertaining to the wharf or its possible antecedents. Indeed, archival research had produced scant indication that a wharf had ever existed here, aside from steamer route maps and occasional mention in the local newspapers. American military records in the National Archives in Washington and British naval records in the Public Record Office in London had also failed to note the presence of a wharf in the War of 1812 combat zone that St. Leonard's Creek had once been. It thus seemed likely that it was not until well after 1821-22, when steamer traffic began to regularly ply Patuxent waters, that major wharf development on the river and creek had begun. Our preliminary investigation during 1979 had suggested that the site would have once covered a substantial area, possibly in a T-shape formation of nineteenth- or early twentieth-century construction. But did an earlier site, possibly from the seventeenth or eighteenth centuries, exist? And what were the realities of the known site remains? What could they tell us about Tidewater wharf design and construction and the logic behind it?

To facilitate our investigation I had brought down to Mackall's one of our large survey vessels, the double-planked cabin cruiser *Sagittarius*, to house our dive team, and the *Sneaky Seaweed* for use as a light surface support boat. Both standard scuba and a small hookah (surface-supplied air) unit would be employed to support diving activities.

Preliminary examination of the supposed T-end of the wharf, although conducted in near-zero visibility, suggested that the facility had been of substantial size. Our initial survey objectives were equally large: to map the entirety of the exposed ruins; to ascertain joinery and building methodology employed in the construction of the site; and to conduct artifact sampling. We initially hoped that we could make test excavations in four discrete subtransects of the site to uncover buried features and improve our overall data assemblage in the week-long period allocated for the investigation. Yet, owing to the extremely thick blanket of oyster shells covering the site and the fragility of the exposed timber remains therein, even limited test excavation was deemed too difficult to tackle with the resources available. Our excavation gear simply could not be brought up to the task without major modification. Reluctantly, I decided to reduce our objectives and focus on mapping the visible remains, collecting wood samples for speciation study, and assembling whatever diagnostic data we could from the exposed ruins.[7]

The majority of piling stubs, usually projecting mere inches from the bottom, were situated at or on the descending edge of the twenty-foot channel drop-off, more than two hundred feet from the shore. A six-foot-long underwater datum pole with a swivel ring attachment was driven into the bottom on the seaward side of the two large iron flywheels discovered the year before; a hundred-foot measuring tape was then securely attached to the ring. Then forty 180-degree radial surveys were carried out by divers using the datum as a hub while swimming clockwise at increments of five feet. Whenever a piling stub, timber, artifact, or other noteworthy feature was encountered, its position relative to the datum was determined by compass. Distance between the feature and the datum was then measured with the tape. With the aid of specially lengthened survey rods, elevations and ranges were then shot by transit from a second datum point established on the surface at the end of the extant wharf. Each piling that was discovered was examined for unique features, nails, treenails, wear marks, signs of sheathing, and so forth, after which its condition and dimensions were recorded. Despite inordinate difficulties caused by the constant snagging of survey lines on obstructions (a problem overcome by having divers take their fins off and walk the bottom, and lifting the line over obstructions whenever they were encountered), mapping of all exposed features was completed in five days.[8]

The condition of the ruins was readily apparent. Most of the larger, exposed and collapsed pilings were in an advanced state of decay, owing to general rot and shipworm damage. Many of the stubs and lumber fragments found lying on or partially exposed on the surface were spongy and porous from the ravages of the worms and other biota. Interestingly, none of the pilings (later determined to be white pine) betrayed any evidence of sheathing, creosoting, tarring, resin application, or other treatments commonly employed in the Tidewater as protection against worm and rot in either this century or the last. Nor had we detected any presence of the original tree bark still attached to the pilings, a feature common to certain eighteenth-century wharf architecture, such as in the cobb-style wharves of New England.[9]

From the site plan that had been developed, however, the wharf apparently had been a T-shaped structure typical of Tidewater river port wharves of the nineteenth century and possibly earlier, but thus far documented in Maryland, at Annapolis, only as early as 1860. The wharf was a simple affair consisting of a series of vertical pilings driven into the bottom in a hollow T formation. Across the top of the structure, the builders had laid down a deck of 2-by-12-inch lumber. The overall length of the structure had been 205 feet from shore to the head of the tee. The walkway supports were evidenced by only three pilings, which gave us an estimated walkway width of over 16 feet, substantial enough for two average animal-drawn carts of the mid-nineteenth century to pass without difficulty. The tee itself measured 48 feet 6 inches by 25 feet. Along the seaward edge of the tee, where visiting vessels would have tied up to the wharf, we found clusters of larger pilings abutting each other and similar in configuration to those frequently pictured in nineteenth century photos and prints of Tidewater wharves. The sides of the tee were not as heavily reinforced. The landward end of the wharf appeared to have featured a small wooden quay supported only by a line of light pilings. Unfortunately, we had been unable to discover any physical evidence of how the structures had been held together, whether it was by nails, spikes, bolts, treenails, or reeved line. A number of lesser support poles, possibly edge pilings or headers from an earlier, smaller structure, were plotted within the rectangle area formed by the tee, as were several poorly preserved 12-inch planks and sawed fittings, believed to be the remnants of a collapsed deck.[10]

Although we had hoped that the St. Leonard's Wharf site would provide verifiable evidence of the evolutionary progression of Tidewater wharf development, perhaps even some insight into eighteenth century southern Maryland marine construction, it was not to be—at least not entirely from the archaeological record. Even though several bricks and random large cobblestones had been encountered, no datable or diagnostic artifacts were found, except two iron flywheels and the rusted remains of a small boiler, probably manufactured circa 1880-1910.[11] Equally frustrating was the impossibility of decoding the progression of designs, if, indeed, there had been one. Tree-ring analysis from two pilings on the tee periphery later gave us the imprecise date of 1878-1920.

To enhance our understanding of the limited information we had assembled, we needed to turn to European sources for detailed comparative data concerning the construction and architecture of early-nineteenth century marine facilities. The Maryland Tidewater environment, we assumed, did not possess many of the factors that determined the type of port facilities developed in European shipping centers. At the St. Leonard's Wharf, however, there were shared factors too important to ignore.

To begin with, the location and construction of even the most primitive marine facility in historic times required the presence of certain environmental conditions. Entrance to a harbor or the approach to a wharf always demanded that there be seaward access and sufficient sea (or basin) room for maneuvering so as to prohibit the act of a vessel's docking from becoming unmanageable at the moment of "taking the port." During the age of sail, the direction of the entrance or approach necessitated the coincidence of a vessel's forward motion with the heaviest wave or current activity, and with a favorable wind. Although the advent of the steam age

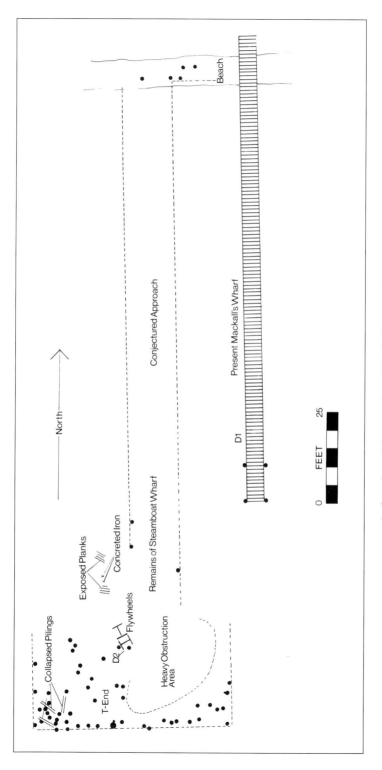

North

Collapsed Pilings

Exposed Planks

Concreted Iron

Flywheels

D2

T-End

Heavy Obstruction
Area

Remains of Steamboat Wharf

Conjectured Approach

Present Mackall's Wharf

D1

Beach

FEET

0   25

A plan view of the remains of the St. Leonard's Wharf Site.

provided mariners with the means to manage their watercraft in ways hitherto impossible under sail, the prevalence of small and large sailing craft on the Tidewater well into the twentieth century made it necessary for harbors, wharves, and docking facilities of all kinds to be laid out with reference to prevailing winds and currents. Yet it was not until 1875 that the precise angle of approach, with the prevalent winds, was scientifically ascertained to be twelve degrees. From this finding, subsequent orientation for small and large harbor and port facility construction proceeded throughout Europe, and to a lesser extent in America.[12]

With the introduction of the internal-combustion engine as an adjunct to sailing craft, harbor and port construction again experienced a subtle alteration, for now even sailing vessels were fitted with auxiliary engines and could approach a dock from any quarter with minimum coverage for windage. Yet approach to a facility in early times was a major determining factor in the placement of a suitable wharf site. There had to be a sufficient distance landward to the mouth of a harbor to permit a vessel with full weight on her to shorten sail or, if she were a steamer, to back engines. By 1885 the allowable recommended space in Britain was approximately a thousand feet. When entering an inner basin or coming about within a given basin to a dock or pier, no circle less than two hundred yards in smooth water was recommended for the ordinary class of coastal steamer, and considerably more was recommended for sailing vessels. Of equal importance was a good "loose," or open space that permitted a vessel on leaving a wharf or harbor to shape a course free of obstruction on the lee shore. Although rocks or reefs were of no concern on the Patuxent, sand bars, shallow water snags, and forest overhangs frequently were. Thus a deep-water "loose" was always desirable. The importance of this requirement is echoed in the wreck rate in the Maryland Tidewater. During the period 1886-95, for instance, 110 vessels were lost in Maryland waters owing to strandings, and many of them succumbed during entry into or departure from a port area or an estuary or within the offshore shallows of the Atlantic seaboard. By the beginning of the twentieth century on the Patuxent the upriver landings and wharves at Hills Bridge, Bristol, and Selby's were already closed because of the poor "loose" caused by siltation.[13]

Capacity, size, and design of a facility varied with the exposures, sizes, and types of vessels using it. Measurable absolutes in harbor vessel population (of particular importance in heavily visited basins such as Baltimore Harbor) were often important in determining the extremes of permissible sizes in wharf and dock construction. The tonnage of vessels utilizing the marine facilities, however, played the most important role in the determination of construction design during the age of steam and presumably during the earlier age of sail as well.[14]

The environment into which the foundations for a structure were inserted, often by mechanical means such as a pile driver, had to be considered not only in terms of safe and easy ingress and egress for vessels, but also in terms of the serviceable longevity of the structure itself. A dock would not normally be built in the Tidewater in a manner which would challenge the natural flow of water unless there were no alternatives. Landings and docks would often be erected at the edge of a slope or shallows for protection against collision from errant vessels approaching from deeper waters and to avoid obstructing the erosive flow of water. Thus only the exposed seaward end would protrude into the deeper waters. Since the seaward end offered the largest single target for an errant vessel missing stays or losing control, it was always the strongest and most heavily buttressed section of a facility.[15]

The commercial value of a given site along a navigable river was dependent on the depth of the channel connecting it to the sea (which governed the size—hence profitability—of vessels that might be admitted) and the access to the produce and commerce of a given area via the connecting links of the marine installations. Facilities like St. Leonard's Wharf insured such access. Yet they afforded additional advantages, for vessels could be accommodated in the smallest space and still remain afloat, whereas in tidal estuaries or coastal areas served only by landings, they were apt to be stranded and even damaged when "taking the ground" to unload.

One prominent authority on European design noted that as a general rule of thumb in the design of marine facilities, the availability of work that could be done per yard length of the quay varied directly in proportion to the different facilities afforded to land traffic flow to and from the quay. Conversely, the utilization of a given marine facility (as well as its size and design) depended upon the availability of the nearby shore transportation system and space on the grounds behind the quay. It was generally desirable, at least during the late nineteenth century, to provide a minimum hundred-foot breadth behind a quay to facilitate traffic flow. For each sixty to seventy feet of water frontage, adequate space for a single moderate-size steam-powered vessel could be provided. St. Leonard's, with less than fifty feet, was substantially smaller than deemed adequate in Europe (certainly a reflection of its rural setting and the limited regional commerce offered by southern Maryland in general). Still, the design and construction features of St. Leonard's Wharf, its relationship to the geography and environment of St. Leonard's Creek, and its physical stance within that geography and environment all suggested that many of the sophisticated European design considerations of nineteenth-century waterfront facilities held true as well for the simple needs of a rural Maryland waterway such as the Patuxent.[16]

Examination of pictographic portrayals of Patuxent landings and other Tidewater river ports in Maryland and Virginia provided additional evidence of our interpretation of the St. Leonard's site. Typical of riverfront steamboat wharf construction was the clustering of large pilings at the

The steamboat *St. Mary's* approaches St. Leonard's Wharf sometime between
1889 and 1907. Note the abbreviated L-shape of the wharf. Courtesy of
Calvert Marine Museum

waterfront end and the presence of a shed, house, or houses upon one
section of the structure, usually the seaward end, to shelter passengers,
store merchandise and produce awaiting shipment, and to house steamboat company gear and offices. The landward end usually terminated at
a juncture with a road or, as at St. Leonard's and the county wharf at
Bristol, a small quay as well. In some cases, such as at Lower Marlboro,
the wharf was built large enough to permit vehicular access to the wharf
deck. At Bristol, two wharves, side by side, one a T-shape and the other a
smaller Y-shape with a quay, were in operation when the Patuxent channel
approach was surveyed by the U.S. Army Office of Engineers in 1889.[17]
Both of these were undoubtedly typical of the structural types prevalent
on the Patuxent during this period, and both contained in their layout,
features similar to those of St. Leonard's.

The typical scheduled stop at St. Leonard's Wharf in 1921 by upriver-
bound steamers such as the Weems Line side-wheeler *Westmoreland* was
preceded by a stop at St. Cuthberts Wharf on the south shore of the
Patuxent and followed by another to St. Leonard's, and then a third at
Sollers, on the south shore of St. Leonard's Creek. Steamboats descending the Patuxent would call first at Sotterley, on the west bank of the river,
and then turn into the creek for a stop at St. Leonard's first and Sollers,
on the opposite side of the creek, second. In both cases inbound steamers

always called at St. Leonard's first and Sollers second.[18] This would indicate that steamboats approaching the former enjoyed sufficient sea room on both port and starboard sides to permit maneuvering room on each side until the last minute, when they would take the port. Current flow, although minimal, would tend to meet the inward-bound vessel obliquely until the last minute of taking the port. At that point the current would meet the bow of the vessel head-on until she was able to maneuver into a parallel position with the wharf. Moored flush to the seaward end of the wharf, the vessel would again face a slightly oblique current to help keep her in place. Upon departure, she would then enjoy a luxurious basin of approximately two thousand feet within which to maneuver for her approach to Sollers. This approach would bring her directly across the prevailing current flow of the creek but would allow her to come about in deep water without fear of grounding in the shallows beneath and adjacent to Sollers. At both St. Leonard's and Sollers, the pier facility extended directly out to the edge of the channel or deep-water drop-off. Maneuvering of a steamer to the shoreward of either facility would have certainly caused grounding.

Although of regional significance, the rural nature of St. Leonard's Wharf probably negated any concern on the part of its constructors for harbor population. Nevertheless, the builders most assuredly considered the sizes of prevalent vessel types that used the harbor in their deliberations. Owing to the increasingly shoally nature of the harbor's access after the eighteenth century, it is likely that the largest ships to visit St. Leonard's were the bay steamboats of the nineteenth and early twentieth centuries. These vessels, occasionally of up to six hundred tons' burden, were generally of shallow draft, averaging seven to nine feet, powered by steam, and propelled by side-wheel paddles or propellers. Such vessels normally tied up flush with the seaward end of the wharf. Loading into and unloading out of large side bay doors or from the deck itself was carried out by donkey engines, and human and/or animal labor.

Had the St. Leonard's Wharf been primarily intended for the reception of sailing vessels, as it undoubtedly was from time to time, its configuration probably would have possessed the typical long wharf format of the eighteenth century, which was evidenced in many contemporary plans of major American seaports rather than the prevalent T-shape design of the nineteenth century. Its overall length would undoubtedly have been increased to provide incoming vessels with the luxury of the deeper (thirty-foot) channel waters farther out. Shallow-draft vessels operating under steam power would not have needed this longer wharf, since their maneuverability was far greater than sailing vessels and the dangers of stranding were considerably less.

Although our survey findings had been less dramatic than either at the Turtle Shell Wreck site or in Lyons Creek, the conclusions drawn from it and the subsequent research on Tidewater wharf construction were no less important to an understanding of the river's history. The remains of St. Leonard's Wharf most likely represented a typical configuration of the type of wharf common to the period 1860–1920 in the Maryland Tidewater. Its service was primarily as a steamboat landing wharf, although it undoubtedly served other vessels as well. Its crude but organized construction was typical of that of many other riverfront facilities of the same period, yet its lie within the riverine environment where it was erected suggests that it was constructed along guidelines in common usage from at least the middle of the nineteenth century.

Not long after the conclusion of the survey, a remarkable photograph, believed to be of St. Leonard's Wharf, the only one of that site located to that time, was donated to the Calvert Marine Museum. The photo was enormously significant to our investigation, for it pictured not only the configuration of the wharf at some stage in its development—a reverse L type—as well as a tiny building on its seaward end, a small quay, and the road leading to it, but also the big side-wheeler *St. Mary's* making her approach to the wharf. Here was the only pictorial evidence of what the wharf had looked like at a particular stage in its existence. The presence of the *St. Mary's* in the picture indicated that the photo had been taken sometime between 1889, when the ship was rebuilt from the hulk of the steamboat *Theodore Weems,* and December 5, 1907, when she was burned to the water's edge on Holland Point Bar in the Patuxent. Thus, the T-shaped wharf revealed by our survey may have either evolved from or devolved to the reverse L wharf in the picture. Given the historical circumstances, the latter seemed to be the most likely choice. Between 1910 and 1930, the people of the Tidewater had rapidly begun to turn to alternative and cheaper modes of transportation, as the automobile, truck, and train began to lure commerce and passengers away from the water routes. The steamboat lines, of course, slipped into a decline from which they would never recover. Most companies, stricken by the dramatic decrease in revenues, struggled to hold on by reducing expenditures allocated for the maintenance of their vessels and for the wharves and landings along each of their routes. St. Leonard's, a relatively unimportant stop by the late 1920s, was permitted to degenerate in scale and service until the demise of steamboat activity above Solomons in 1928 sealed its fate. Thus, the photograph of St. Leonard's Wharf almost certainly represented a reduction of the earlier T wharf.

Here, for the first time, the physical evidence provided by underwater archaeology had dovetailed with, reinforced, and enhanced the sparse historical record regarding Tidewater wharf design and its evolution. The discovery was neither dramatic nor revolutionary, but it boldly confirmed what history had implied: as local commerce had withered and died with the demise of the steamboat, so had St. Leonard's Wharf.

SIXTEEN

Scorpion

When Wes Hall arrived at my doorstep one evening at the end of June after a ten-hour drive from Wilmington, North Carolina, he brought with him the accoutrements of the then-state-of-the-art underwater video technology for which I had contracted from the firm of Oceans Data Systems. It had been our plan, once the Turtle Shell Wreck had been excavated and the other two survey targets of the 1980 campaign had been addressed, to attempt to document l-TSW using high-resolution low-light underwater video. It was an ambitious scheme which was to be the first effort of its kind ever to systematically record an underwater archaeological site in Tidewater history, a first that none of us had even considered at the time and the last project objective of the campaign. We were all far more excited by the prospect of seeing more than six inches at a time of the ship we had been working so hard to uncover than by making history!

The most important gear Wes had brought with him was a Kinergetics Observer II underwater video camera, with an 8.5 millimeter lens. The ratio of subject to recorded imagery that could be provided by the camera's 61-degree wide-angle lens was one-to-one, which was all we could have hoped for. A Birns and Sawyer ll0-volt Snooper underwater lighting system, capable of up to one thousand candlepower, would provide illumination. Imagery would be recorded on a Sony half-inch reel-to-reel recording console and surface monitor. Of equal importance in Wes's bag of tricks was a Desco full-facemask diver-to-surface communications and recording system that would facilitate topside management and documentation of the underwater work. Although the video system was supposed to produce high-resolution color imagery in low-light environments, Wes had suggested that even better resolution of targeted areas might be had in the turbid waters within the main cofferdam (MCD) if we used black and white video instead.[1]

During the early days of the excavation several attempts had already been made to document the site, its architectural features, the artifacts *in situ*, and the progress of the underwater work using conventional underwater photography. We had expected such efforts to prove fruitless unless the silts that were constantly being stirred up within the MCD were allowed to settle. But as the high-energy currents coursed around the coffer, the

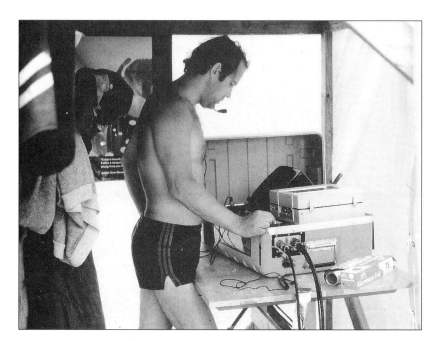

The author watches the video monitor aboard "Barney's Barge" as the first pictures of the Turtle Shell wreck appear. Photograph by Nicholas Freda

The underwater camera unit used to record features of the Turtle Shell Wreck in the first effort at video documentation of a submerged archaeological site in the Tidewater.

Scorpion

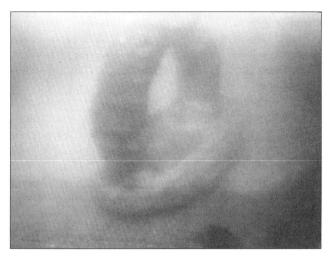

Video image of an iron fairlead, used to channel line, on the deck of the Turtle Shell Wreck.

protective plywood sheeting was continually being undercut or penetrated through even the smallest of openings. This in turn led to a percolating effect: the waters within the MCD remained in a constant state of mild agitation, prohibiting the settlement of particulates. Successful conventional photography was out of the question.

Still, there were moments when we had greater than normal visibility. These were first observed in the mornings, after a maximum period of settlement had occurred and before anyone had entered the water. It was also noted that when the airlift or hydrodredge was deployed but allowed to remain stationary on the bottom, the areas immediately around the intake nozzles became clearer, albeit only infrequently permitting visibility to extend beyond a foot. A several thousand-candlepower lighting system failed to do anything but exacerbate the problem as the dense particulate matter caused severe backscatter of the light. Thus the use of high-resolution low-light underwater video held intriguing possibilities. We were so positive about its potential that we scheduled the first and only press conference of the season to capitalize on the results.

That was a mistake.

Lacking a power source suitable for the video system, Wes had requested that a five-kilowatt generator be brought out to the barge. Although I suggested that five-kilowatts far surpassed the power needed for the camera unit, Wes decreed otherwise. He was, after all, the expert.

The initial deployment of the unit was to be conducted by Wes, who was first given a hands-on underwater familiarization tour of the site and was then provided with a set shooting sequence that would be monitored and voice-managed from the surface. Diver-monitor voice communication was imperative, both to facilitate and record descriptive commentary and to maintain video-target control. Since the diver could seldom see the target as well as his camera could, the surface manager would be acting, through the camera imagery presented on the surface video monitor, as his eyes.

To maximize the photographic potential of underwater video, the diver first needed to devote a considerable period of time to each target, slowly examining it from all possible angles to permit a three-dimensional evaluation of the architectural features of the vessel itself. Individual dead-on stills and slow pans of selected areas would also be undertaken in hopes that, by selectively rephotographing the video, a photo-assemblage of sequential shots would permit us to produce a montage of sections of the vessel. Talk about overreach!

We had been able to lease the unit for three days at a bargain-basement price. We soon found out why. On the very first dive, the console unit experienced a malfunction caused by a circuitry overload. A second unit had to be flown into Washington National Airport from New Orleans that evening. The following morning, the new unit was successfully deployed. As the entire survey team hovered around the video console, the first black-and-white pictures ever taken of one of Joshua Barney's warships appeared. For the first time, we could see the enhanced images and details in the murk that had previously gone unnoticed by divers. Saw marks made by the artisans who had constructed the vessel could be plainly seen on the screen, when their existence had gone unrecorded during the hands-on survey. The effects of current erosion and timber shrinkage along various sectors of the starboard deck and the port washboard collar, which would have otherwise gone undetected and would have led to an incorrect evaluation of measurements already taken, were duly noted. Nail and spike heads on eroded surface areas of the cant frames, we discovered, had been incorrectly noted as knots in the wood until identified by the camera. Details of various joints, scarfing, and the minutiae of the vessel's construction exposed by our excavation were all being seen and systematically recorded on videotape for the first time.[2]

Our delight was short-lived. Again, the diver-monitor communications system broke down. Without surface control, the diver's efforts were without order or sequence and the dive was concluded while repairs were once again attempted. Our efforts proved fruitless. Another unit was flown in. A third shooting program was launched the next day despite a forecast of poor weather. A thunderstorm had been predicted and, as we prepared for another try, now seemed close at hand. The voice link again failed. Wes and I hurried to create and memorize a shooting sequence that could be carried out without benefit of communications. This time, I would do the shooting, and he would tend the monitor. The effort proved successful, and another full 90 minutes of tape was completed just as the thunderstorm struck. Operations for the rest of the day were scrubbed, but that evening, as we reviewed the fruits of our labors, I was elated. The morrow, the last productive day of the project, was scheduled for a show-and-tell for the press and the state agencies managing the funding. The live video of the site would be the cornerstone of the presentation. Unfortunately, our joy was to be short-lived.

The following morning a small press conference was held at Patuxent River Park to formally announce our discoveries. Now was our chance to crow. After a brief slide show documenting the project's progress, the reporters and state officials were taken upriver aboard several park boats to view the operations and to see the wreck first-hand. When the boatloads of press arrived, everyone on the survey team was on his or her best behavior—except the underwater video unit. Murphy's Law had once again prevailed. The entire video unit, including the monitor, had blown its fuse and was useless. We couldn't even run the tapes we had shot the day before!

Thus ended the last day of active investigation of the Turtle Shell Wreck, both ignominiously and in triumph.

The following morning backfilling of the wreck began. It was an expedient that had been deemed necessary to prevent injury to the site by the currents after we removed the MCD, to restore the anaerobic environment, which would insure its continued preservation, and to remove all traces of excavation. The last measure was specifically intended to discourage the relic hunting that was likely to follow even as news of our work was being made public. The spoil that had been dredged from the site was now carefully pumped back, with care being taken to fill the most fragile areas, such as the port stowage compartments and under the starboard deck, first. Simultaneously, the MCD was dismantled.[3]

In the evening, I made the last dive on the site before it was completely covered, taking with me a plastic milk carton with the names of our survey team sealed within. The carton, bearing each of our signatures, would be buried with the ship, beneath five feet of sediment.

□　　　□　　　□

The excavations of the Turtle Shell and Lyons Creek wrecks were not undertaken without a deep sense of responsibility for the preservation of the sites and the artifacts therein that were to be recovered. Indeed, artifacts from any marine environment are likely to produce far more serious problems for the conservator, the individual who must stabilize, mend, and preserve them, than do those recovered from sites on dry land. Most materials that have survived the rigors of long term immersion—electrolytic reduction, cellular collapse, attack by marine biota, rot, and the myriad other harmful components of the undersea environment—face an even greater danger of destruction and rapid disintegration upon being brought into contact with air.

In view of this concern, it had been necessary to establish a conservation facility capable of handling the cleaning, stabilizing, mending, and possibly even restoration of any artifacts that might be recovered. Ralph Eshelman and I had decided as early as mid-1979 that a facility would be needed that could provide space, public road and waterfront access, security, water, humidity control, and ventilation. Moreover, a seasoned conservator, with a background in the specialized field of treating waterlogged materials and who possessed a thorough knowledge of the specimens likely to be encountered would have to be hired. The conservator's task would be monumental in that he or she would not only have to treat the artifacts, but actually have to put together the laboratory to do the work with a threadbare budget.

With less than two thousand dollars in funds available for even limited conservation (half of which was being generated through our "shoestring" grant), it was impossible to locate a commercial facility suitable for our needs. Calvert Marine Museum, then situated in the old Solomons Island schoolhouse built in 1925, had little space to spare even to house those collections that might be resurrected. The only conservation facility in

The J.C. Lore Oyster House, converted into a temporary preservation laboratory for service during the Patuxent Project, became the first conservation facility in the Maryland Tidewater capable of large scale stabilization, mending, and preserving of waterlogged materials from underwater archaeological sites.
Courtesy of Calvert Marine Museum

southern Maryland even remotely suitable was the archaeology lab at St. Mary's City—and that was already overextended. Fortunately, in late 1979 CMM had acquired the J.C. Lore Oyster House, an old oyster packing plant built in 1934, which was scheduled to become an out-facility and exhibition center for the museum. Ralph graciously offered it for use as a temporary conservation facility.[4]

Having failed to learn my lesson from such generous but untested donations in the past, my enthusiasm upon accepting the offer, sight unseen, was immediately tempered by the first visit to the old oyster house. Although scenically situated adjacent to the "Tidebox," a modest bridge spanning a narrow waterway that divided Solomons Island from the mainland, the oyster house was dingy, dirty, and in desperate need of paint. There was no electricity, water, heat, ventilation, or other important assets necessary for conservation work. Worse, at extreme high tides, the concrete floor in the back of the building facing a waterway on the east side of the island called The Narrows was under as much as a foot of seawater. There were, however, certain virtues to the site, which Ralph was quick to point out. In the empty east wing of the plant there was plenty of open working space, concrete tables, floor drainage, cold-storage rooms with heavy security doors, waterfront and public road access, large sliding bay doors, and an abundance of stainless steel containers left over from the building's oyster packing days. With a few volunteers, he suggested optimistically, the place could be made shipshape in no time at all.

And so, in April 1980, when Nautical Archaeological Associates contracted with Leslie Bright, a senior archaeological conservator with the North Carolina state government, it was with the proviso that he design and supervise the erection of the necessary facilities in the oyster house. Leslie was not a novice to such a task, for he had been instrumental in helping to establish the Fort Fisher underwater conservation facility at Kure Beach, North Carolina, for the North Carolina Division of Archives and History. The Lore Oyster House, however, would prove to be a *major* challenge even for him.[5] He attacked the problem with zeal and ingenuity.

By May, Leslie had produced the first working design for the modification of the east wing interior of the oyster house. CMM and NAA recruited volunteers, and within a short time, an electrical system was installed. For the first time in years, fresh water flowed unhindered through the ancient water pipes of the old building. The museum staff, ably assisted by Eldon Volkmer, pillaged southern Maryland for necessities. A stove, a freezer, small tools, and so forth, were scavenged, borrowed, or otherwise found their way into the operation. Giant stainless steel cooking vats were donated by NAA for the administration of alcohol and freshwater baths. Storage shelves were constructed in the main work area. A large electrolytic reduction chamber was built, while a ventilation system was installed by museum volunteers. A large set of shelved closets was provided by the museum for the security storage area. Fifty-gallon drums of expensive chemicals such as polyethylene glycol were trucked in and stored to await use. And so it went, right down to the beginning of the 1980 campaign.

Despite the considerable expense, manpower, and time involved in the erection of the conservation lab, the facilities were far from adequate or even comfortable, partly because they were never intended to be permanent, having been designed only to handle limited collections. Indeed, the lab's capacity was the determining factor in just how far excavation of the Turtle Shell Wreck would go, for there was a finite amount of money available, limited conservatorial talent, and even less time to devote to the collections. Nevertheless, by June 1, the J.C. Lore Oyster House, the first marine conservation facility ever established in Maryland, was operational.

The artifacts recovered from the Turtle Shell and Lyons Creek wrecks were of animal, vegetable, and mineral origin, and 95 percent of them were in good to excellent states of preservation owing to the anaerobic condition in which they had lain for well over a century and a half. Nevertheless, the process of conservation began immediately after recovery. No artifact was permitted to begin the drying process prematurely, but was placed in water-filled Ziploc bags or larger water-filled containers and kept immersed until transported to the lab. Specially constructed braces were sometimes built to reinforce large or fragile wooden objects. Individually designed cushions were employed to prevent vibrations from damaging frangible artifacts being transported from site to lab. Upon arrival at Solomons, all artifacts were immediately transferred to stainless steel containers filled with distilled water in which they would remain until they could be individually treated.

In July, under Bright's direction, CMM registrar David Bohaska and Ralph's wife, Evelyne Eshelman, a nuclear chemist at the Calvert Cliffs Nuclear Power Plant, began the onerous task of hand-cleaning each artifact, while volunteers from NAA and the Chesapeake Biological Laboratory began to photodocument the collections. To facilitate records management of these proceedings and the conservation process, Leslie had instituted a card system to document procedures employed in the treatment of each item and to keep track of their whereabouts and dispositions.[6]

The system (in this pre-personal-computer era) was simple but expedient. Every artifact submitted for treatment was assigned a laboratory number next to its field number. Each step of the examination, treatment, and mending process of every artifact was then recorded on the lab record card. Information on each card included the following: name of item, laboratory number, field number, site number, photograph number, museum accession number, recovery date, name of the person who recovered the artifact, artifact treatment code, treatment date, artifact description, and general remarks (disposition, condition, etc.). It was well that a system had been implemented, modest as it was, for the deluge of cultural materials requiring treatment was substantial and diverse.

The artifacts recovered from the Turtle Shell and Lyons Creek wrecks, once cataloged, were treated in a variety of ways, each dependent upon the materials with which it was made, its condition, size, and so forth. After each artifact was cleaned, stabilized, mended, and cataloged, it was moved to the cold-storage room and shelved. Every treatment, however, was slightly different.

Glassware was leached in fresh water, immersed in 10 percent solutions of citric acid to slough off concretions and marine growth, then air-dried. Ceramics were also leached for weeks in fresh water and then soaked in a solution of oxalic acid to remove iron oxide stains. Waterlogged wooden artifacts were leached in fresh water and then given repeated alcohol baths before being submitted to a long-term (six months to two years) cellular stabilization process using polyethylene glycol impregnation to prevent shrinkage and destruction. In several instances, large wooden objects, such as the munitions box and the oarsmen's bench, were first disassembled; each piece was numbered and then submitted to a leaching process with distilled water, alcohol, and finally polyethylene glycol impregnation in a specially constructed container. Iron objects were cleaned by electrolysis, with a low-voltage current being sent through a solution of sodium hydroxide covering the artifact. Many artifacts needed little treatment other than leaching and hand-cleaning. Certain substances, however, such as medical salves and liquids, which had been found in the pharmaceutical containers, were dispatched to Johns Hopkins University for analysis.[7]

Leslie Bright's task seemed endless, but somehow he managed. And the Turtle Shell Wreck collection was preserved for all to see. On June 26, 1981, on the 167th anniversary of the climactic battle of St. Leonard's Creek, and less than a year after the conclusion of the Patuxent Project, the Calvert Marine Museum and Nautical Archaeological Associates, Inc., jointly opened a full-scale exhibition, to a standing-room-only crowd, on the history of the U.S. Chesapeake Flotilla and the excavation of the Turtle Shell Wreck. The popular exhibit, entitled "War on the Patuxent," reinforced by a video documentary of the project, entitled "Turtle Shell and Toothkey," would eventually tour the state of Maryland for more than a year, from the World Trade Center in Baltimore to the Eastern Shore and back again to southern Maryland. At CMM it would stand for nearly eight years, bringing to life a long-ignored piece of American history as it had never been seen before.[8]

Many questions had been answered by the excavation, and many more had been posed. But the principal one, Was the Turtle Shell Wreck one of Barney's Flotilla, and if so, which one? had finally been laid to rest by the evidence produced by the survey. Although only a portion of the ship had been examined, the information we had gained—archival, artifactual, and architectural—presented a strong confirmation that the vessel belonged to the Chesapeake Flotilla, lost on that fateful day of August 22, 1814.

That the wreck had definitely been lost between the years 1812 and 1815 was proven by several key artifacts. The first of these, which provided the earlier date, was the surgical scalpel with the imprint of the British firm of John Evans & Co. accompanied by a small crown. The crown imprint provided perhaps the most significant interpretive piece of data to be extracted from the wreck, for it indicated that the instrument had been produced for the Royal Navy in 1812, the only year the Evans firm had been authorized to use the crown impression. Thus, the vessel could not have been lost prior to 1812. The second item, or items, which provided a terminal date of sorts, were the numerous nails and spikes employed in the construction of the vessel, none of which predated 1790 or postdated the period 1815-20. Indeed, the majority of datable artifacts fell within the period 1790-1830, with many, such as bottles, the 1803 penny, and others providing a relatively tight time frame. No vessels other than those belonging to the Chesapeake Flotilla and a number of merchantmen under its protection were ever documented as having been lost between 1790 and 1830 in the reach of river in which 1-TSW was found. Which vessel, then, was she?

From the examination of the architectural features of the ship and several structural components that had been recovered, it appeared that the vessel was well assembled, fitted with iron, and not constructed in a hurry. The molding strips and painted trim that were recovered would undoubtedly not have been employed in the building of the twenty-one-day wonders of the flotilla which had been constructed at Baltimore and St. Michaels. Such additions would have been nonutilitarian and too time-consuming for the artisans and shipwrights building the vessels to have added. From the structural integrity of the vessel, also, it would appear that 1-TSW could not have been easily dismembered, nor was it intended to be.

Yet on June 21, 1814, in St. Leonard's Creek, the flagship *Scorpion*, two gunboats, the lookout boat, and six of the thirteen barges were either partially or totally dismantled in a single day at the direction of Secretary of the Navy Jones, in preparation for transport overland for reassembly on the Chesapeake side of Calvert County. Fortunately for Barney, the order was rescinded. On another occasion, masts were unstepped so that the flotilla might close with the enemy naval forces without being discovered beforehand. Just before the flotilla escaped from the creek, at least thirteen masts belonging to the barges, the yards belonging to the row galley, and several gun slides were removed and carried ashore. The

Scorpion, however, apparently retained her mast, for it is recorded that on the afternoon of June 26, the fleet of barges, with the flagship in the lead (noted by an observer at that point as a "topsail sloop"), arrived at Benedict after breaking through the blockade of St. Leonard's Creek. Later, Jones suggested to Barney a second plan for the dismemberment of the flotilla, which would entail the breaking down of the fleet at Queen Anne's Town on the upper Patuxent, hauling it overland with horses and wagons, and reconstructing it on the banks of the South River. Each of these incidents suggests that most of the flotilla vessels were capable of being easily dismantled and reassembled. Since there was only one ship's carpenter assigned to the squadron, the nature of vessel construction would have had to be relatively simple in order to accomplish such a feat. To what extent the vessels could be, or were, dismantled is not known, but it would appear that disassembly merely consisted of unstepping masts and removing gun slides, artillery, anchors, and perhaps smaller features such as oarsmen's benches, stoves, and the like. The Turtle Shell Wreck, although quite well fitted, is a relatively simple piece of naval architecture. Her shoal, flat-bottomed design indicates that she was meant for service in shallow waters rather than on the open sea, a capability that Commodore Barney required in all of the vessels of his flotilla. "I am," he wrote on July 4, 1813,

> of [the] opinion the only defence we have in our power, is a kind of barge or row-galley, so constructed, as to draw a small draft of water, to carry oars, light sails, and one heavy gun. These vessels may be built in a short time, say 3 weeks.[9]

Barney's original design of a typical barge suggests a vessel probably closer to the famous prototype Jeffersonian-era gunboats designed by Commodore James Barron than to the barges ultimately drafted by Chief Naval Constructor William Doughty that were produced for the flotilla, which carried a single long gun and a carronade.

Of the eighteen flotilla vessels used by Barney, seven were 75-foot-long barges (referred to in Doughty's plans as row galleys) and six were 50-footers. Since both gunboats *No. 137* and *No. 138* were scuttled in St. Leonard's Creek, their dimensions are not important to this discussion. No dimensions are recorded for Barney's lookout boat, the row galley *Vigilant*, or for his flagship *Scorpion*. Nor are dimensions recorded for the Georgetown merchant schooner, owned by William O'Neal, which had been hired by Barney as a supply ship. Nothing is known of the merchant schooners lost along with the flotilla.[10]

Certain conjecture, however, might be made regarding the *Scorpion*. Barney's flagship has been variously described as a gunboat, a topsail sloop, and a block sloop. Constructed before the war, possibly as early as

1806, she was the oldest vessel of the squadron. Rebuilt in 1812 at the Washington Navy Yard, she served on the Potomac and in the Virginia theater in 1813, fighting in several actions, after which she was refitted, probably at Baltimore, during the winter and spring of 1813-14. Although naval historians such as George F. Emmons have long referred to her as simply a gunboat, the late Howard I. Chapelle of the Smithsonian Institution stated that she was one of two block sloops (a vessel serving more as a floating battery than a maneuverable sailing ship) in naval service at the outbreak of the war. The first of these served on the Delaware and was of a verifiable design. The second block sloop design, termed a prototype, was unnamed and radically different from the Delaware vessel. The prototype measured 48 feet 8 inches on deck, 17 feet 8 inches molded beam, 18 feet 2 inches extreme beam, and 4 feet 6 inches in the hold. Prior to 1809, the U.S. government had contracted for 172 gunboats. *Scorpion* was built as *No. 59*. Soon after submission of the initial designs for this series by Commodore Barron, the gunboat plans were severely altered. Now the boats were to measure 50 feet on deck, 15 feet abeam, and 5 feet in the hold. The *Scorpion*, built by naval constructor George Hope at Hampton, Virginia, may have been altered at this time to block sloop status before completion, since she carried four guns instead of the usual two mounted on most gunboats of the series.[11]

Like *Scorpion*, the row galley *Vigilant* was not specifically constructed for the flotilla but was, instead, purchased by the U.S. Navy for eighteen hundred dollars. Although her genealogy is uncertain, it is possible that she may have been the same vessel constructed in 1811 as a schooner-rigged revenue cutter by Benjamin Marble at Newport, Rhode Island, and subsequently cut down for service as a row galley.[12] Several plans of row galley types were produced before and during the War of 1812, most of which vary in size from 40 to 75 feet in length. No dimensions are known to exist for the *Vigilant*, although she may have been among the smaller of those in the flotilla, since she was capable of carrying only a single gunnade.

The overall measured dimensions of the wreck site, as determined by systematic water jet probing and excavation, were 48 feet 7 inches in length and 16-plus feet abeam. Depth in hold was exactly 3 feet, and depth to the foot of the keel is estimated at 4 feet. Although it would be impossible to declare with absolute certainty that the probed and excavated areas definitely constitute the entirety of the site, the likelihood, considering the state of preservation, is quite strong that they do. Moreover, systematic probing revealed not only the probable extremities of the site but produced a roughly V-shaped contour at the north end of the site, presumably the stern end of the vessel. This strongly suggests that the craft was indeed relatively intact, but more important, that the dimensions established may be reasonably accurate. If the above dimensions do represent the entirety of the vessel, her identity as one of the 75-foot class of barge can be ruled out. The hired store ship, a schooner of undetermined size, may also be eliminated, for she was noted as having been sunk in Scotchmans Hole in waters apparently deep enough to prohibit salvage. Two of the 50-foot class barges were able to swim as far north as Queen Anne's, where they were blown up to prevent capture. One was later salvaged. Of the thirteen merchant schooners under Barney's protection, eight were blown up and/or burned and five were captured. The fates of the lookout boat and the *Vigilant* are unknown, although they undoubtedly perished with the fleet. "The Wreck of the *Scorpion*," salvor John Weems noted nearly two months after the flotilla's loss, "is yet very valuable." *Scorpion*, however, either proved too difficult to salvage or raise, or by the time Weems was up to the task, he had abandoned the project in disgust when the Navy refused to pay him. Thus, there were fifteen possible candidates to choose from for l-TSW: *Scorpion*, *Vigilant*, the lookout boat, four of the 50-foot barges, and eight merchantmen.

A thorough review of the artifacts indicated that the wreck had been a military vessel, thus reducing the list by eliminating the merchantmen. Given the duties of the lookout boat, it would seem unlikely that the same vessel might have served in the capacity of hospital ship, as suggested by the presence of so many surgical instruments, pharmaceuticals, and apothecary items. The overall length of the wreck, 48 feet 7 inches, is only one inch less than that given by Chapelle for the unnamed prototype block sloop. However, the maximum beam of the wreck was not computed, since the widest portion, at its midships, was not excavated. The depth in hold varies only somewhat between the estimated 4-foot depth of l-TSW and the 4 feet 6 inches of the prototype block-sloop.

Despite such similarities, certain architectural features suggest that the wreck could have been a vessel other than *Scorpion*. The most notable of these is the washboard collar on the port side of the vessel. Upon completion of the shakedown cruise, Barney had discovered that the smaller 50-foot class of barge was unsafe. The eighteen-pounder cannons were replaced with twelve-pounders, and an 8-inch-high washboard collar was built around their decks to prevent them from being awash in rough seas. At the same time, the commodore noted that he could carry only limited supplies in the open barges and requested that a special vessel be provided for the surgeon, Dr. Charles Hamilton, and the sick. This request was never fulfilled, and Barney had to make do with either gunboat *No. 137* or *No. 138*.

The presence of the washboard collar seemed at first to suggest that the vessel was one of the 50-foot barges, yet its l-foot-7-inch height more than doubled the size requested for that class. Since 1-TSW likely served as a hospital ship, it seemed possible that the extra-high collars were added as further protection from the sea for the sick and wounded. The construction quality of the washboard, when compared to that of the rest of the vessel, appeared somewhat inferior, especially where cuts were made, most noticeably along the board's crest where the oar rests and gangway portal had been cut out. It was readily inferred that the cuts had been made after the vessel departed Baltimore and its skilled pool of artisans for the last time.

The washboard collar notwithstanding, one major factor tended to refute the possibility of 1-TSW being one of the 50-footers: size. Although the overall length of the small barge class, at 50 feet, and depth, at 3 feet 6 inches, were quite close to those of the Turtle Shell Wreck, the beam of the 50-footers was 12 feet, a full 4 feet less than the widest portion of the wreck. Again, the field of candidates had been reduced to either *Vigilant* or *Scorpion*. And it was the artifacts recovered from the site that would solve the riddle.

That the Turtle Shell Wreck had served in both a military and a medical capacity has already been illustrated. Only one surgeon, Thomas Hamilton, and one surgeon's mate, A. C. Thompson, were listed in military records as having served with the flotilla; the presence of surgical tools and pharmaceutical and apothecary items indicated that one or both most likely served aboard 1-TSW at the time of her loss. During the last few naval engagements on St. Leonard's Creek, the *Scorpion* was absent despite her firepower. During that period, Hamilton was recorded as managing a field hospital in St. Leonard's Town, at the head of the creek and behind American lines. It seems probable that the hospital, which was located in the only building spared by the British on their raid of July 2, 1814, was transferred to the flotilla after the retreat up the Patuxent, as the lower Calvert County peninsula was in danger of being cut off.

Although the identity of the ship Hamilton and his mate served upon is not documented in the written record, the vessel aboard which flotilla carpenter Charles Fleming served is certain. Fleming served aboard *Scorpion* prior to its transfer from the Potomac Flotilla to Baltimore and served upon her there as well, for he was transferred to that station along with the ship. The presence of a number of carpentry tools aboard 1-TSW, although not conclusively belonging to Fleming (such instruments might well have been carried aboard any or all of the flotilla vessels), lends further circumstantial evidence to the identity of the wreck.

By process of elimination, dimensional characteristics, artifactual evidence, and a moderate dose of surmise, the answer seemed clear: the Turtle Shell Wreck was none other than the flagship of the U.S. Chesapeake Flotilla, the USS *Scorpion*.

S E V E N T E E N

Wrap-up

On the morning of Saturday, June 28, 1980, the final reburial of the Turtle Shell Wreck commenced. Sediments from spoil originally dredged from the site were pumped back into the coffer at an astonishing rate, even as the containment itself was being dismantled. In less than three hours, the site was returned to the condition in which it had been found, minus only ninety-one artifacts removed for diagnostic and display purposes. Within days, to further frustrate possible relic hunting, all evidence of the coffer had been removed from the area by the local Youth Conservation Corps, under the direction of Patuxent River Park director Rich Dolesh—and none too soon.

In less than a week, the story of Joshua Barney's long-forgotten flotilla and its discovery had hit the pages of the local and then the national press.[1] The Turtle Shell Wreck soon achieved a glorious, albeit short-lived, fame, that was boosted by the news media, exhibitions, publications, and a seemingly unending round of lectures by many of the project members. Within the year, the 750-page final report of the survey was published by the Maryland Historical Trust in its manuscript series, while numerous scientific papers on the history and archaeology of the river and its now-famous fleet were presented in academic forums from Annapolis to San Antonio.[2] Scientific and historical publications such as the *Journal of Maryland Archaeology, NOAA Magazine,* and *The American Neptune* began to publish the findings of the survey, guaranteeing the Patuxent River a long-denied place in history.[3] Joshua Barney was resurrected as one of Maryland's and the nation's greatest patriots, and suggestions were even being fielded by prominent Annapolitans that a statue honoring his memory be erected in the state capital.[4]

Yet, even as the fanfare blossomed and then began to fade, the river grudgingly continued to yield her secrets. During the winter of 1981, for instance, a waterman named Joe Dodson, living on a little backwater of the Patuxent known as Schoolhouse Cove, on St. John's Creek, discovered the remains of an unknown wreck while driving piles to repair his storm-damaged boat shed. Cognizant of the potential importance of the find, he notified the Calvert Marine Museum and Nautical Archaeological

291

Associates. An immediate hands-on investigation was launched, albeit in subzero weather, to determine the type and condition of the site.

The wreck, we soon discerned, lay beneath three feet of gummy black silt and five feet of water, with its bow less than ten feet from shore, and sitting squarely under Dodson's ruined boat shed. Although awkward to excavate, the wreck was in a location that had undoubtedly saved it from the untender attentions of the local derelict removal program that had swept the little tributary clean of at least seventeen known wrecks during the late 1970s.

As we gradually excavated a test trench to expose the shattered remnants of her hull, it became apparent that we were excavating the ruins of a five-log canoe approximately fifty feet long. Not a single metal fitting had been found. Indeed, the hull appeared to have been entirely wood-fitted, and in a unique and most unexpected manner.

The antecedents of the Chesapeake Bay log canoe can be traced directly to the traditions of Native American dugout canoe manufacturing, embraced early on by the first white settlers in the Tidewater, wherein a log was simply hollowed out by means of fire and by chopping and scraping with shells or iron. The rapid adoption of the dugout canoe by the settlers of Virginia, Maryland, and the Carolinas, most of whom were poor artisans and had come ill prepared for their venture in the new world, is well known. Despite early efforts to import shipwrights to build "Ships, Boates, and other Vessels whereof the Colony had great need," by 1623 the dugout canoe, or "Hogg trough," as one prominent settler called it, was already being utilized by Virginia colonists for oystering.[5] Later, adaptations of the basic canoe design to a catamaran form, employing two canoes lashed together with cords to carry heavy hogsheads of tobacco, spread throughout the Tidewater. By 1686, the settlers' use of single logs for canoe manufacture had been largely abandoned in lieu of two and even three logs, squared off, joined along a centerline, and hollowed out as a single unit with an adze.[6] By the early to mid-nineteenth century, wing logs had been added to provide additional carrying capacity and stability, and four-, five-, and even seven-log canoes were soon proliferating throughout the Tidewater.

Those constructed along their own unique lines on the lower Eastern Shore of Maryland were generically referred to as Pocomoke canoes, which varied somewhat in design from those constructed on the upper Chesapeake, called Tilghman canoes. A third breed of vessel and the most famous of its kind, built principally in Virginia, was known as the Poquoson canoe.

Although each of these log canoe types differed somewhat in form and fit, their genealogy and shell-first construction techniques were basically the same. All logs were squared and temporarily fitted together first, roughly hewed down with an adze as a single unit and then disassembled, after which each unit was further formed and shaped. The logs were then joined once again with the seams between them hugged together in such a way as to assure a close fit. "Some builders have such a delicacy and sureness of cut with adze and axe," noted maritime historian Marion V. Brewington from personal observation, "that they can fit the logs together without recourse to even a joiner plane."[7] Once the logs were thus jammed into position as snugly as possible, the builder could proceed to further cut and trim them from one end of the seam to the other with a handsaw, sawing rough spots down until each log was perfectly matched with its mate. The logs were then fitted together again and held in place by matching holes, bored into the seams, into which iron bolts (and in earlier times or when iron was unavailable, locust wood treenails) were driven as fastenings. Thus permanently fitted together, the whole boat was turned right side up for further shaping and finishing. The ends were tied together with bolts, holes plugged with wooden dowels, and final touches added to the inside and exterior. Then the masting assemblage, centerboard case and seat, knees, combings, stem and sternposts, and oak rubbing strakes were put in place, and the whole painted and finished off and made ready to sail. Thus was built the typical five-log canoe, grand-daddy of the famous Chesapeake Bay bugeye. Or so it was recorded.[8]

The Schoolhouse Cove canoe, however, was significantly different. Close examination of the seams revealed that at regular intervals, mortise and tenon joinery, blocked in position by two wooden pegs each, had been employed to hold the logs together. These were reinforced at irregular intervals along the seams by wooden "butterfly" fittings, typical of Mary-land-built canoes, tightly fitted into both logs to further stabilize the hull and prevent movement and chafing of one against the other. The concept was simple and, in retrospect, a logical approach to the shell-first method of boatbuilding. Yet, nothing like it had been documented in the Tide-water from archaeological remains, although some were to be found in museum collections. The few artifacts retrieved from the site, primarily bottle glass and one inkwell, suggested the wreck was of relatively recent vintage, dating from circa 1865. Archival research failed to turn up any vessel losses of that period or later in this particular reach of water. The site was chalked up to abandonment—another boat that had simply outlived its usefulness.

We were to learn later, however, that this boat, with its mortise and tenon fittings, was perhaps more unique than we had guessed.

In January 1982, during an archaeological conference in Philadelphia, Eshelman and I met with Professor J. Richard Steffy, the brilliant, inter-nationally known archaeological ship constructor from Texas A&M Uni-versity, to secure some insight into the fittings of the Schoolhouse Cove Wreck. Steffy, himself a native of the Eastern Shore, was greatly impressed when presented with the sample fittings, drawings, and photographs of

Tidewater Time Capsule

Nearly identical mortise and tenon fittings employed in the hull-first construction of the 19th-century Schoolhouse Cove Wreck (pictured here) and the Kyrenia boat of 288 B.C. suggested commonalities in the social dynamics, economics, and technologies of mankind that have governed the evolution of boat design and construction for 2,300 years and half a world apart.

the site. The mortise and tenon joinery, he declared, was almost a duplicate of that used to build an ancient merchantman sunk over 2,300 years ago in the Mediterranean Sea near Kyrenia, on the north coast of Cyprus. The Kyrenia wreck had first been surveyed by Dr. George Bass and members of the Institute of Nautical Archaeology in 1967 and proved to be the finest preserved ship of the late classical period of Greek civilization ever found. It ultimately took archaeologists eight years to complete the survey and to raise, preserve, and finally, under Steffy's hand, assemble and display the hull in a crusader castle at Kyrenia. The Kyrenia ship had been, like the Schoolhouse Cove Wreck, of shell-first construction, using interlocking mortise and tenon fittings, and possessed a typological ancestry of considerable significance.

The earliest example of shell-first construction had been revealed by the discovery of a great river barge buried about 2,500 B.C. as a component of the Egyptian King Cheops's funeral assemblage in an airtight chamber south of the great pyramid of Giza. Discovered in 1952, the barge was the oldest known vessel of shell-first construction ever encountered in the Mediterranean and the earliest to feature a smooth-planked carved hull. It was a tradition that would survive in various forms until the end of the Roman Empire. There had, of course, been numerous archaeological finds of shell-first-built vessels of antiquity, such as the Yassi Ada and the Pantano Longarini boats, which had buttressed the genealogy of the

294

vessel type. Yet, until the discovery of the Schoolhouse Cove Wreck, little address had been given to the evolution of such types in the Western Hemisphere, and less to the social dynamics that had determined their evolution. What, indeed, had triggered the transition from shell-first to frame-first construction? Had the same forces influenced the evolution in Euro-American shipbuilding as they had in classical Mediterranean cultures of antiquity?

Peter Throckmorton, the noted pioneer of marine archaeology who had worked on many of the Mediterranean sites, cautiously suggested that the decline in shell-first boat construction might have been attributable to the change from a slave-based economy of classical times to something closely approximating a free-market economy in which labor and materials became substantially more expensive. The transition, he proposed, was undoubtedly facilitated by simple economics. Frame-first vessels could be produced more cheaply and easily, particularly in a social setting that enhanced the concept of mass production, rather than the more labor-intensive production required for shell-first boats, even though the end product of the former was not likely to be as durable.[9]

The similarities of two vessels types, which had evolved independently in widely separated locations on the globe, with several millennia between them, introduced questions familiar to anthropologists the world over regarding the very processes of invention. They were questions which, with only the slimmest archaeological evidence to go by, we were unprepared to answer. Was there some dynamic commonality inherent in both classical Mediterranean and rural Tidewater culture prior to the end of the Civil War, such as the institution of and reliance upon slavery? Or was it merely a logical process of invention? Perhaps, it was, as L. Sprague De Camp once noted in his famous study of the evolution of engineering technology in antiquity, *The Ancient Engineers,* simply that "every invention contains some borrowing and every borrowing some invention."[10]

□   □   □

One of the most important but ignored finds of the Patuxent Project had been the 1978 discovery of large concentrations of prehistoric shell middens and the hints of seventeenth- and eighteenth-century occupation along the north shore bluffs and fields overlooking the entrance to St. Leonard's Creek. Although the walkover of the tract by Ralph Eshelman and myself had failed to pinpoint the precise location of Joshua Barney's batteries which had been here (and which had been the principal objective of our visits), the finds that were made were more than compensation. And the indirect spin-off was destined to have a major impact on Maryland archaeology.

Not long after the final report of the project had been submitted to the Maryland Historical Trust, Eshelman and I were asked to provide a walkover tour of the site to the Trust's Southern Maryland Regional Archaeologist, a savvy, no-nonsense fellow named Mike Smolek. To say that Smolek was stunned at the extent of surface evidence of early occupation and the potentials of yet-to-be-discovered sites would be an understatement. The Trust, with Smolek's recommendations, moved quickly.

The lands upon which these promising historic and prehistoric sites lay, a tract totalling 512 acres of rolling pastures, woodlands, and agricultural fields fronted by nearly 2.5 miles of waterfront, belonged to Mrs. Jefferson Patterson. It had been a singular stroke of good fortune that the estate was in the hands of a keen lover of history, for Mrs. Patterson had long been a supporter of CMM's efforts to document and promote the heritage of the Patuxent Valley. The widow of a foreign service envoy in the Eisenhower administration and heir to the Goodrich Tire fortune, she had also provided us with unrestricted access to her estate during the Patuxent Project, access that had directly resulted in our discoveries. Mrs. Patterson, a vigorous septuagenarian who preferred the life of Washington society to that of a remote country heiress, was nevertheless delighted with the finds and Maryland's great interest in them. Yet the great depth of her own interest and support caught everyone by surprise, for she had resolved to donate the entire estate to Maryland for development as an archaeological park. The gift was to be made with the provision that the estate's overall agrarian character not be despoiled, that the lands be maintained in perpetuity for scholars and others to research, interpret, and preserve their archaeological resources for the public benefit. Though Mrs. Patterson stipulated that she continue to have domestic access to her eleven-thousand-square-foot mansion and outbuildings for the remainder of her life, her offer was indeed one the state of Maryland could not refuse.

On June 16, 1983, on the green, rolling bluff overlooking St. Leonard's Creek and the Patuxent River, in a ceremony presided over by Governor Harold Hughes and the Honorable Comptroller of Maryland Louis L. Goldstein, the great tract was formally turned over as the largest single private donation ever made to the state of Maryland. And the Jefferson Patterson Archaeological Park and Museum was born.

Under the capable leadership of its first executive director, former Maryland Historical Trust archaeologist Wayne Clark, the park immediately began to take shape. The facility soon included a visitors' center and exhibit area, a limited archaeological conservation laboratory and storage area, and picnic grounds. Extensive archaeological research was soon under way, replete with public participation projects for both children and adults. A major early seventeenth century settlement site, at first believed to have been that of the first (albeit short-lived) St. Leonard's Town, was discovered, and documentation of innumerable prehistoric sites followed in quick succession.

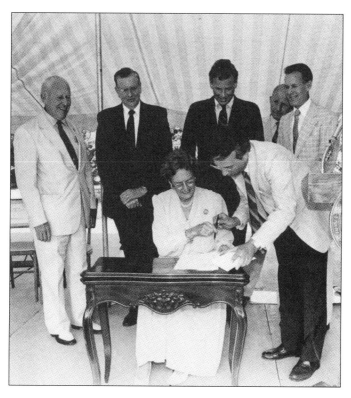

J. Rodney Little, Director of the Maryland Historical Trust, assists Mrs. Jefferson Patterson in signing the transfer of 512 acres of land overlooking St. Leonard's Creek and the Patuxent River to the State of Maryland, as Governor Harold Hughes (center standing) and other prominent Maryland officials look on. The land transfer, the largest private donation in state history, was undertaken to create the first archaeological park of its kind in Maryland. Courtesy of Jefferson Patterson Park and Museum

Not all of the discoveries, however, were made directly on park land. Indeed, one of the first was made quite by accident by my brother Dale Shomette and myself while on a family outing on a gloriously warm Sunday afternoon in early June 1984. While swimming from our boat in a shallow inset of Mackall's Cove directly adjacent to Park property, we encountered, quite by chance, the bones of a sunken derelict centerboard schooner, which had been overlooked during the 1979 remote-sensing survey, in waters less than eight feet deep. The remains of the bow of the boat were still moored by a few remaining threads of rotten line tied to a fallen stake once anchored in the bottom. Close evaluation of the few identifiable components of the wreck suggested that the vessel was approximately fifty feet long and fourteen to sixteen feet abeam and featured the fragmentary remains of a centerboard well and casing. It seemed a good bet that she had probably been constructed during either the latter half of the nineteenth or first quarter of the twentieth century and abandoned within recent memory.

Inquiry among the local residents of the creek by the CMM's curator of maritime collections, Paula Johnson, uncovered some tantalizing clues to the ship's identification. Two quite elderly sisters of a recently deceased waterman and fish huckster named Lawrence Gross had remembered the vessel as having sunk sometime during the second decade of this century. The sisters, Pauline Gross Willis and Annie Gross Parker, recalled that the boat once belonged to J. Cook Webster, a prominent Solomons Island mariner, and that the vessel's name may have been *Dash*.[11] Others suggested that her name had been *Dashway,* and that she had last belonged to a black waterman named Johnson who traded in used vessels. The boat, said some, had been involved in the Potomac River lumber trade. Yet nothing seemed certain until archival research by Fred Hopkins provided an additional clue.

A schooner named *Dashaway,* Fred discovered, with the same dimensional characteristics as the Mackall's Cove wreck, had indeed once sailed the waters of the Tidewater. Built in 1883 in Washington, D.C., she was

A deadeye from the wreck of the schooner *Dashaway.* As part of the standing riggings of the vessel, the piece was probably used as a purchase for the shrouds.

sixteen tons gross and fifteen tons net displacement. She measured in at 51.6 feet in length, 15.3 feet abeam, and had been 2 feet deep in hold. She had last been registered at Georgetown and then simply disappeared from the record as did most abandonments.[12]

Were *Dashaway* and the Mackall's Cove wreck indeed one and the same? Or was the wreck another vessel whose identity would remain an eternal mystery, another blank tile in the mosaic of Patuxent history. Perhaps we would never know.

□   □   □

For the next few years I had little contact with the Patuxent though I lived less than a few minutes from its fertile shores. Yet her allure could not be long ignored. Even as the Patuxent Project had been winding down, cleanup efforts to return the waterway to its once pristine condition had been initiated by an alliance of environmental groups, civic organizations, and county and state governments. Ever so slowly life began to creep into her roots, up her trunk, and into her myriad branches. But it was a hard-fought battle as the ever-encroaching developments of urbanization continued to press hard against her banks.

In February 1987 I had enjoyed the privilege of codirecting a remote-sensing survey of underwater sites in Lake Champlain, New York, for the National Geographic Society. It was, at the outset, an expedition that seemed to have little relevance to the Chesapeake. Unlike most shipwreck surveys, the Champlain expedition was not to be carried out by diving from boats or from the shores, but by radar, sonar, and remotely operated vehicles, through the thick winter ice covering the lake. Indeed, the project's objectives had been not only to locate historic shipwrecks, primarily from the period of the American Revolution, but to experiment with a variety of new technologies for underwater investigation and to explore new applications for already proven technologies, while employing the lake ice rather than a boat as our survey platform.

One of the experimental applications we hoped to test was the use of an already well known tool in the archaeologist's bag of tricks called subsurface radar, commonly known as ground-penetrating radar, or GPR. GPR had been employed for a number of years by geologists to detect and graphically display subsurface soil interfaces on dry land, and by archaeologists to locate artificially emplaced objects, structures, or features in soils to depths of as much as one hundred feet. We hoped that GPR could be used to penetrate the lake ice and the freshwater column beneath it to detect the presence of shipwrecks lying on or buried beneath the bottom sediments.

The GPR was to be managed by one of National Geographic's more formidable technical experts, Claude "Pete" Petrone, a grizzled ex-marine and veteran of more than three decades of service with the society as head of its Photographic Special Projects Office. Usually dressed in cowboy boots and hat and given more to riding Harleys than driving Fords, Pete Petrone is the owner of the original aw-shucks demeanor, a disarming attribute entirely out of character with his unique expertise. For years Petrone had been in the vanguard of field applications for such now-common technologies as fiber-optic and high-resolution photography. He had participated in innumerable history-making expeditions, such as the discovery of the *Titanic*. His most significant effort, however, had been in the contribution to and fielding of a specialized vacuum-lock and fiber-optic camera unit specifically designed to penetrate and remotely photograph an unopened, unexplored pharaonic solar boat tomb near the Great Pyramid of Cheops. The effort had been a magnificently successful technological tour-de-force that had contributed greatly to Egyptology and made headlines around the world.[13]

Now, by addressing GPR to the survey of marine environments, Pete Petrone was hoping to explore new uses for old technologies, and in nontraditional ways. The Champlain Project, however, undertaken in the dead of winter at forty degrees below zero Fahrenheit two miles out on an open, frozen lake, was destined to encounter setbacks—and big ones at that. Just as the GPR system was getting cranked up and the bugs were being eliminated one by one, Mother Nature stepped in and began to break up the lake ice beneath our feet. The project was forced to move further afield, into the protected confines of Burlington Bay. The GPR effort, however, had to be abandoned until some better opportunity came along.

It was then that I suggested we give it a try on the muddy waters of the Patuxent River. If we could test the system over a site of known disposition lying beneath the river's silts, a wreck that had already been mapped and documented, we might acquire not only an interpretable signature, but one suitable for comparison to and identification of other sites of like condition but unknown disposition. I proposed that our initial target be the Turtle Shell Wreck, sleeping quietly beneath five feet of sediment and eight feet of turbid water. If we were able to successfully obtain interpretable imagery from *Scorpion*, it might then be possible to locate additional flotilla wrecks that had escaped discovery during the 1979 survey. Both Pete and the Geographic enthusiastically agreed to the test.

On the morning of June 7, Pete, a U.S. Navy remote-sensing technician named Bob Reele who had worked with us on Lake Champlain, and I set off in a small boat managed by my father, Grady Shomette, from Hills Bridge and Landing on the Patuxent and headed upriver for the Turtle Shell Wreck site. We towed behind us a small Zodiac inflatable provided by the navy, in which the GPR antenna was mounted to avoid the interference that a metal boat hull might cause. A transducer control cable linked the antenna, via the tow line, to the SR-8 control unit and power system in the towboat. A line scan recorder would be employed to provide graphic imagery of any bottom and sub-bottom features we might encounter.

The actual operation of the GPR system we were to employ, a unit produced by a New Hampshire company called Geophysical Survey Systems, was simple. In a normal terrestrial operation, the transducer is towed by a vehicle or manually by an operator. The transducer is connected to the control unit by a control cable having a maximum length of two hundred feet. Mounted within the top center of the antenna is the transceiver electronics, which transmits a radar impulse into the ground at a rate of fifty kilohertz. The antenna receiver section receives reflected energy and sends a replica of the reflected pulse through the control cable to the control unit and recording instruments in the vehicle. The only difference this time was that there would be a water column between the antenna and the soil, and the vehicle was a boat.

As we approached the wrecksite from the bend above Hills Bridge, Pete activated the control unit while Reele managed the cable assemblage between the two boats. Just ahead lay the wreck nestled in its muddy blanket beneath the bottom. On the nearby marsh where our survey station once stood, a large beaver lodge had been erected by some of the river's residents who had returned to reclaim lost territory. A distinct

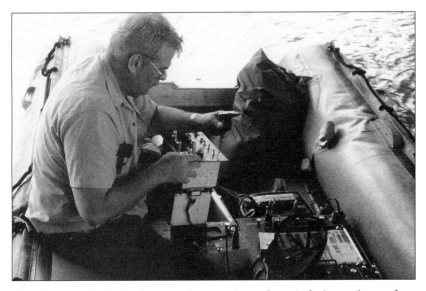

Pete Petrone "field strips" a ground penetrating radar unit during testing on the Turtle Shell Wreck site.

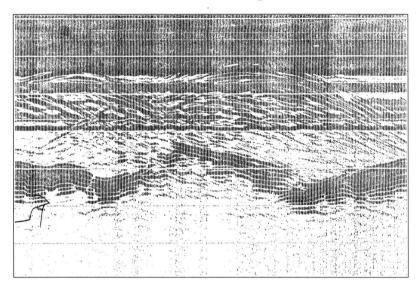

A ground penetrating radar signature of the *Scorpion* wreck made by Pete Petrone of the National Geographic Society and the author in June 1987. The signature reveals the wreck as lying on a hard bottom beneath six to seven feet of very loose sediments, tilted at a slight angle, and with evidence of a small sub-bottom scour downstream (left).

feeling of *déjà vu* crept over me. It was the first time I had been back on this section of the river since we buried the Turtle Shell Wreck almost eight years earlier. Little, it seemed, had changed. The river was just as beautiful as it had been when I last left it.

Quietly the control unit hummed its high-pitched tune. From time to time Pete would shout to Reele to let out or take in some cable, and the Zodiac would react accordingly. Then, the first pass over the site. A strange swirl pattern appeared on the recorder. A second pass, and the same. Deftly, Petrone modified the calibration of the pulse range. Again we passed over the site, and a newer, sharper pattern of swirls appeared on the recorder. More calibration changes. Ten nanoseconds per pulse. Another pass. Bingo. The imagery was stunning. Not only was the target, lying beneath five feet of sediment, identifiable as a large, solid object with a hard, flat surface, almost certainly the wreck, the actual angle of the tilt of the deck was clearly visible, matching that which we had computed during the actual hands-on survey in 1980.

Excitedly, we ran over the site at least a dozen times more, each time altering our angle of approach, calibrations, and so forth, testing and retesting for the best result. And each run told us something new about the use of the system.

302

"Let's take a look at some of the other sites picked up with the magne-tometer," I suggested. Immediately, we headed downriver, running back and forth across hot spots encountered during the remote-sensing survey in 1979. At Scotchmans Hole we had a definite target, and another less than two hundred yards away. Two more targets appeared near shore below that. Again and again we ran the tests, and each time targets appeared, although none of them had the same definitive form as that of the Turtle Shell Wreck. All of them, however, were buried beneath many feet of sediment. Yet, there were other targets as well, which we believed to be mostly river debris, trees, and sunken flotsam and jetsam. And there were many targets of unidentifiable nature. To say that we were euphoric would be an understatement, for we had field tested the use of GPR in an environment where it had never before been used successfully—and had succeeded.

And Pete Petrone had barely started. Four years later, in a remote waterway called Lake Phelps in North Carolina's Great Dismal Swamp, we would use GPR to conduct, in concert with the North Carolina Division of Archives and History, the first successful controlled GPR search for, and ground truthing of, submerged and buried prehistoric Indian log canoes, pottery, and other cultural features ever undertaken.[14]

But it had been at the site of the Turtle Shell Wreck, in the murky waters of the upper Patuxent River, that the revolutionary new applications of an old technology had been successfully tested for the first time in history.

□　　□　　□

The last word is something few archaeologists will risk claiming. The Patuxent had been deeply plumbed and her archaeological riches as-sessed. But there had been many more questions uncovered than an-swered. And some of the greatest question marks of all had been posed by the Lyons Creek Wreck. What type of vessel had she been? Had she been built in the Tidewater, or had she been imported from Europe? And what was her role in the river's history?

The thirty-three fragments of the wreck hull that had been dredged up in 1974 or excavated during the 1980 survey had lain undisturbed in a dark storage room of the Calvert Marine Museum with their secrets intact for the better part of seven years. Yet, amidst these battered, cracked, and splintered pieces of wood, most certainly lay the key to a better under-standing of the Lyons Creek Wreck itself, and at least a few answers to the questions about her. It would take the diligent efforts of a dedicated graduate student in marine archaeology named Bob Neyland to unlock the mysteries of the site even further.

Neyland, a student of Dick Steffy at Texas A&M, had first been apprised of the Lyons Creek Wreck after the presentation of a paper on the site by

Eshelman and myself at an archaeological conference in Nashville, Tennessee, in 1987. He was intrigued with the site's discovery, but more so with what remained to be learned, and quickly resolved to find out for himself. With Eshelman's assistance, he tore into the wreck's remains with considerable zeal.

Neyland's principal objective was to systematically analyze each of the boat's surviving structural components and then to attempt to reconstruct a portion of the hull from them to determine the realities of the boat's architecture and its possible national origin. It was more than a challenge, for many of the timbers, though stabilized with polyethylene glycol, were in very poor shape, often little more than damaged fragments. Absolutely no structural integrity of the original vessel remained owing to the ravages of the dredging project that had brought it up. But the young archaeologist was not deterred.[15]

Sorting through the collection he determined that the remains primarily consisted of planking and frames, with a few pieces of gunwale, a stringer, a clamp, and possibly a keel plank, all of white oak or similar species. Nine of the planks had been torn apart by force, broken at the point of contact with the frames. The remaining sections also showed various signs of demolition, leading Neyland to conclude that the vessel had been intact before the dredging.

Neyland's examination was both macroscopic and microscopic. Saw marks, as had already been determined, indicated that the planks had been sawn with a pit saw. Frames had been cut from naturally curved timbers. Distinctive tool marks gave evidence that the pieces had been shaped by an axe and adze. The hull, he deduced, as we had, was of clinker construction, with overlapping planks fastened together with iron rivets, and with the outboard face of each frame trimmed in step fashion to fit over the hull planking. Significantly, the outboard face of the frames also revealed gouge areas that had been cut to permit them to be easily fit over the rove-ends of the rivets. All of these features suggested that the boat was of shell-first construction. But could a hypothetical model of even a portion of the hull be constructed from the few remains in hand? Bob Neyland thought so and resolved to try.

There had been fifteen frames recovered from the Schwenk spoil pile that could readily be separated into three sections: floor timbers, futtocks, and top timbers. The majority of frames were determined to have come from an area forward of the midships line. After considerable calculation it was ascertained that the three frame types had been originally placed in sets with an alternating pattern rather than fastened together in a rigid frame.

Neyland closely examined all of the frames and noted even the most minute features of each, anything that would assist him in his reconstruction effort. Trimmed to fit snugly against the hull, each of the frames featured a stepped and beveled aspect on its outboard side, thereby duplicating the shape of the hull. Step lengths provided information on the width of planks. Bevels across the outboard faces of the steps permitted an assessment of orientation of the frames between midships and one end of the boat. Moreover, the overall shape of the frames reflected the contour, shape, and breadth of the hull, while the fastener angles (both iron and treenails) provided patterns that helped determine the position of the frames. Trim marks, wear patterns, and even barnacle marks helped in visually arranging the frames in relationship to each other. Utilizing the information derived from a thorough analysis of these extant features, it was possible to hypothetically reconstruct an additional three frame sections and a pair of half-frames. The end result revealed a part of the boat forward of midships with seven strakes on each side of the keel, mounted on frames estimated to have been almost equally spaced at sixty centimeters apart.

Neyland next examined the strakes. Distinctive features such as wear marks were analyzed to determine the degree of overlapping. In some cases, double wear marks and an excess of rivet fastenings offered ample evidence that repair work had been undertaken. Fragments of caulking, probably pine resin, containing animal hair and plant fibers were found to have been used to seal the hull against leakage. Several strakes had been fastened by a row of iron nails, while another had been beveled to fit the rabbet at either the stempost or sternpost. And yet another contained the remains of a dozen tacks, further indications that repair work had been carried out or, perhaps, that sheathing had at some point in time been applied. The planking had been fastened together with iron rivets and roves with regular spacing between the former, except where repairs had apparently been made.

A single fragment believed to have been a keel plank was studied with considerable interest. Although the piece was very badly damaged, evidence of a surviving bevel along one edge closely matched the reconstructed angle of the garboard and keel of the boat. A lone treenail hole indicated that either a floor timber, or possibly a skeg or false keel, had once been fastened to the piece.

The seventh strake was the sheerstrake, which was overlapped on its upper edge by two fragments of the gunwale, fastened on by rivets. There was evidence that a clamp piece had also been fitted to the gunwale, and of four reliefs for rovers that fastened the gunwales to the sheerstrake. A notch on the clamp was believed to have served as a row lock.

Neyland's analysis next turned to the fastenings. Both treenails and iron nails had been used to hold floor timbers and futtocks together. Some of the iron nails had obviously been for repair, such as where they had been clustered together or had actually been driven through wooden treenails. Had the vessel originally been fitted with treenails and then repaired with iron nails? Neyland thought so.

But what did the Lyons Creek boat look like? The young researcher's hypothetical reconstruction revealed a shell-first, clinker-built craft comprising fourteen strakes with an arch bottom and upright sides. The boat probably had a keel plank beneath which a false keel might have been

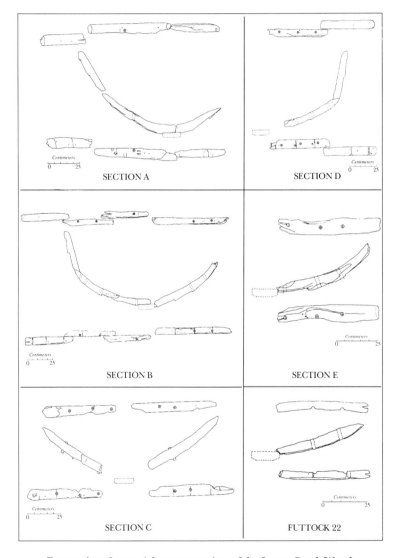

Frame plans for partial reconstruction of the Lyons Creek Wreck.
Courtesy of Robert S. Neyland

attached. Although the actual vessel length was conjectural, its broadest beam was calculated at 173 centimeters with a depth of 60 centimeters. Its thin oak planking provided a light, somewhat flexible hull, partially stiffened by frames shaped from grown crooks, with its sheerstrakes topped off by a gunwale-clamp arrangement, protecting it from damage and strengthening the boat's upperworks. The craft had been extensively repaired and possibly even refitted, and some evidence even suggested that efforts had been made to tighten the hull at the turn of the bilge.

Although it was difficult to reliably identify the watercraft's type and function, many facts had become obvious with Neyland's remarkable detective-like analysis and reconstruction. He concluded that the vessel was probably a workboat:

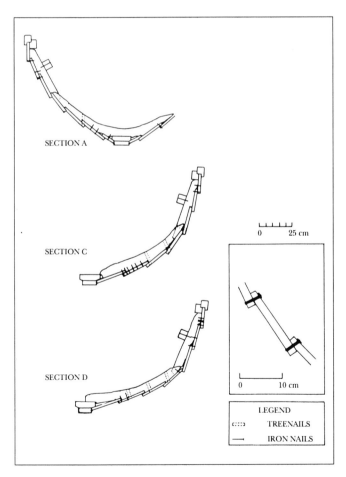

Plank, frame, and keel reconstruction of the Lyons Creek Wreck.
Courtesy of Robert S. Neyland

307

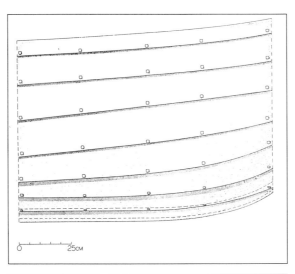

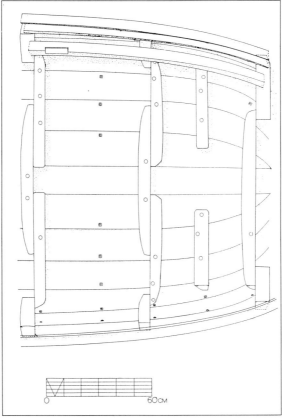

Lateral plan view of reconstructed segment of the Lyons Creek Wreck (top) and top view (bottom). Courtesy of Robert S. Neyland

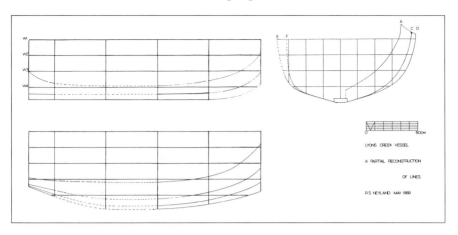

A partial reconstruction of the lines of the Lyons Creek Boat.
Courtesy of Robert S. Neyland

The boat was probably relatively small, and certainly not designed for long voyages over open water. Many of the construction features suggest an open working boat. A relatively lightweight hull is desirable in boats that are intended to be hauled in and out of the water a great deal. The stiffening along the sheerstrake, with [the] gunwale-clamp arrangement, is important in a work boat, particularly if the boat has to carry a heavy load or come alongside other craft a great deal.[16]

But what type of vessel had the Lyons Creek Wreck been? Sadly, the archival record was of little assistance. The most common vessel types alluded to in the seventeenth and eighteenth century records of the Patuxent were sloops, shallops, and on occasion, pinks, all of which were used as either boats or small freight haulers. All these names, unfortunately, were also generic terms that changed with the times and the writer and provided little precise data on rig, construction, or function.

Many small boats had, early on, been employed seasonally on the river, having been transported as ship's boats from Europe *en fagot,* that is, disassembled to facilitate storage on board and reassembled upon arrival in the colony. Others were simply of local construction. "It is interesting to speculate," Neyland noted in this regard, "that evidence of a refit and the puzzling fastening patterns of the Lyons Creek boat could be the result of transporting the boat in a knocked-down fashion, with the upper strakes removed."[17]

There were other historic scenarios that were equally inviting. Europeans had inhabited Lyons Creek as early as 1670, as evidenced by several plantation sites on the waterway that had been indicated on the Augustine Hermann map of Maryland in that year. As early as 1673 a ferryboat had been in operation between Lyons Creek and Mount Calvert, on the opposite side of the river. Could the Lyons Creek boat be the bones of the ferry? Had she been some forgotten vessel lost or scuttled while carrying munitions on the river during the revolution of 1689? Or was she indeed Captain George Harris's little pink, the *Richard and Mary*, lost while on government business in 1707? Neyland addressed these questions.

> The boat remains raise more questions than they answer. The style of construction and perhaps, if positively associated, the ceramics of Rhenish manufacture, suggest North European connections. Whether or not the vessel was built in the North America colonies or is of European manufacture remains a mystery. However, the technology which produced this vessel is certainly well-founded in the North European tradition.[18]

Neyland's efforts were to be among the last, to date, produced as a direct result of the Patuxent River Project. The modestly funded effort, though officially lasting only three years, had continued to bear fruit of unexpected historic and archaeological importance for nearly ten years after. We had reached beneath the turbid, polluted waters, through centuries of silt, debris, and detritus to extract and study the past. And we have learned from it.

Someday, perhaps, we will return.

Notes

The following is a list of short titles and abbreviations for the notes presented hereafter.

Admiralty   Admiralty Records, Public Record Office, London
Archives   *Archives of Maryland*
CL   Captains Letters to Secretary of the Navy, National Archives and Record Service, Washington, D.C.
CMM   Calvert Marine Museum, Solomons, Md.
CSM   *Chronicles of St. Mary's*
DGSC   Donald G. Shomette Collection, Dunkirk, Md.
LC   Library of Congress, Washington, D.C.
MHM   *Maryland Historical Magazine*
MHS   Maryland Historical Society, Baltimore, Md.
MLR   Miscellaneous Letters Received by Secretary of the Navy, National Archives and Record Service, Washington, D.C.
MVUS   *Merchant Vessels of the United States*
NARS   National Archives and Record Service, Washington, D.C.
NDAR   *Naval Documents of the American Revolution*
PAXS   *The Patuxent River Submerged Cultural Resources Survey*
PRO   Public Record Office, London
SHA   Society for Historical Archaeology
SNL   Secretary of the Navy Letters to Officers, Ships of War, National Archives and Record Service, Washington, D.C.

Chapter 1: Of a Lesse Proportion

1. For a thorough discussion on early Spanish territorial claims and explorations on the Chesapeake Bay in the sixteenth century see Clifford M. Lewis and Albert J. Loomie, *The Spanish Jesuit Mission in Virginia 1570–1572* (Chapel Hill: University of North Carolina Press, 1953).
2. Ibid., 191.
3. It has been conjectured that Father Oré's account was probably published at Madrid about 1617, nineteen years after Gonzáles's voyage and ten years after the establishment of the Jamestown settlement. An eyewitness account, known to have been written by Juan Menendez Marques, Gonzáles's second in command, has never been found.
4. John Smith, *The Generall Historie of Virginia, New England, and the Summer Isles* (London: Printed by I. D. and I. H. for Michael Sparkes, 1624), 24.
5. Charles Francis Stein, *A History of Calvert County, Maryland* (Baltimore: pri-

vately printed, 1960), 60; James C. Bradford, *Anne Arundel County. A Bicentennial History 1649–1677* (Annapolis, Md.: Anne Arundel County and Annapolis Bicentennial Committee, 1977), 74.

6. The native towns on the Patuxent indicated on Smith's map of 1612 and reprinted in his *Generall Historie* in 1624 were the following: (east shore) Opament, Quomocac, Pawtuxunt, Onnatuck, Wascocup, Tauskus, Wepanawomen, and Quactataugh and (west shore) Acquintanacsuck, Wasmascus, Acquaskack, Wasapokent, Macocanaco, Pocatamough, Quotough, Wosameus, Mattapament, and Nacotchtanek (John Smith, *Virginia*, 1608 [1612], John Work Garrett Library, The Johns Hopkins University).
7. Stein, 7.
8. Nathaniel C. Hale, *The Virginia Venturer: A Historical Biography of William Claiborne, 1600–1677* (Richmond, Va.: Dietz Press, 1953), 118.
9. By 1635 Fleet "had lived many yeeres among the Indians, and by that meanes spake the Countrey language very well, and was much esteemed of by the natives" (Clayton C. Hall, ed., *Narratives of Early Maryland, 1633–1634* [New York: Barnes & Noble, 1910], 72).
10. Thomas Harriot, *A Briefe and True Report of the New Found Land of Virginia* (1590; reprint, New York: Dover Publications, 1972), 55.
11. Regina Combs Hammett, *History of St. Mary's County, Maryland* (Ridge, Md.: privately printed, 1977), 55.
12. John Thomas Scharf, *History of Maryland* (1879; reprint, Hatboro, Pa.: Tradition Press, 1967), 1: 189–90.
13. Bradford, 206.
14. Stein, 9.
15. Ibid.
16. Ibid., 29, 30.
17. Thomas J. Wertenbaker, *Virginia under the Stuarts 1607–1688* (New York: Russell & Russell, 1959), 99–101.
18. Stein, 19–20.
19. Hall, 203–204.
20. Ibid., 242; Stein, 19–20.
21. Hammett, 36.
22. Stein, 21–22.
23. Hall, 242–44, 265–67; Stein, 22.
24. Stein, 23.
25. Lois Carr, "The Metropolis of Maryland: A Comment on Town Development along the Tobacco Coast," *MHM* 69, no. 2 (Summer 1974): 128.
26. Stein, 31.
27. Donald Shomette, *Londontown: A Brief History* (Londontown, Md.: London Town Publik House Commission, 1978), 38; Carville V. Earle, *The Evolution of a Tidewater Settlement System: All Hallows Parish, Maryland 1650–1783* (Chicago: University of Chicago Department of Geography, 1975), 152.
28. *Archives* 5: 31; John Ogilby, *America: Being the Latest, and Most Accurate Description of the New World* (London: 1671), 189.
29. *Archives*, 5: 47–48; ibid. 7: 278–80.
30. John W. Reps, *Tidewater Towns: City Planning in Colonial Virginia and Maryland* (Williamsburg, Va.: Colonial Williamsburg Foundation, 1972), 103.
31. *Archives* 7: 265, 266.

32. Ibid., 609–19. For a comprehensive overview of town planning and development in seventeenth- and early eighteenth-century Maryland see Reps, chapter 5.
33. The name Coxtown was changed in 1704 in honor of the Duke of Marlborough, the victor and hero of the recently fought battle of Blenheim (1703). In 1706, when the town of Upper Marlborough was founded, Marlborough (formerly Coxtown) became Lower Marlborough, a name later shortened to Lower Marlboro. See Stein, 56–57, for comments on new town legislation in Calvert County.
34. *Archives* 7: 609–19.
35. Ibid.
36. Ibid. 25: 602.
37. Stein, 53.
38. Andrew Burnaby, *Travels through the Middle Settlements in North-America in the years 1759 and 1760 with observations upon the state of the Colonies . . .* 2nd. ed. (reprint, Ithaca, N.Y.: Cornell University Press, 1976), 56.
39. "Itinerant Observations in America, 1745–1746," *Collections of the Georgia Historical Society* 4 (1878): 29.
40. Arthur Pierce Middleton, *Tobacco Coast: A Maritime History of Chesapeake Bay in the Colonial Era* (Newport News, Va.: The Mariners Museum, 1953), 244–45; Earle, 166.
41. Earle, 143.
42. Augustin Herrman, *Virginia and Maryland As it is Planted and Inhabited this present Year 1670 Surveyed and Exactly Drawne by the Only Labour & Endeavour of Augustin Herrman* (London: W. Faithorne, Sculpt., 1673), LC.
43. Charles M. Andrews, *The Colonial Period of American History,* (New Haven: Yale University Press, 1934), 1: 372; Hammett, 37.
44. Hammett, 79–80.
45. Andrews, 1: 101–7, 156.
46. Hammett, 38; Stein, 81.
47. *Archives* 13: 487; ibid. 26: 426.
48. Stein, 90.
49. Reps, 100.
50. *Archives* 26: 636–37.
51. Reps, 100.
52. *Archives* 26: 64; Reps, 100.
53. Bradford, 1.
54. *Archives* 32: 370.
55. Earle, 153.
56. Anne Arundel County Judgements, 1720–1721, f.54, Maryland Hall of Records, Annapolis.
57. Ibid., 1722–1723, f.50.
58. Ibid.
59. *Archives* 39: 121–22, 483–85.
60. Iron ballast pigs bearing the inscription "Patuxent" have been recovered from an eighteenth-century shipwreck in Canadian waters by archaeologists and are believed to have been a product of the iron industry of the upper Patuxent Valley. One of the pigs is on permanent display at the CMM. A nearly identical pig was recovered by a resident of Nottingham from the nearshore of the old town site and loaned to the Prince George's County Historical Society.

61. Earle, 153.
62. Anne Arundel County Judgements, IB-5, f.14.
63. Earle, 153; Anne Arundel County Judgements, IMB-2, f.14.
64. *Maryland Gazette*, 10 June 1729.
65. Ibid., 20 May 1729.
66. Scharf, 1: 66.
67. In 1698 Maryland's governor, Francis Nicholson, reported that more than 470 negroes had been imported to the colony during the year, of which 399 had arrived directly from Guinea, 50 more via Virginia from Guinea, 20 from Pennsylvania, and several more from Barbados and other places (Elizabeth Donnan, ed., *Documents Illustrative of the History of the Slave Trade in America* [New York: Octagon Press, 1965], 4: 17, 18, 19). Among the first known slave ships to enter the Patuxent was the *Fly* in 1697. Captained by George Lewis, the vessel utilized the sheltered anchorage in St. Leonard's Creek before offloading her human cargo (*Archives* 22: 306–7).
68. Donnan, 4: 24.
69. Ibid.
70. *Maryland Gazette*, 6 June 1771.
71. Ibid., 1 May 1751, 21 June 1753, 28 June 1753.
72. Hyde Papers, 1765–1813, MS 1324, MHS.
73. Edward C. Papenfuse, *In Pursuit of Profit: The Annapolis Merchants in the Era of the American Revolution, 1763–1805* (Baltimore: Johns Hopkins University Press, 1975), 170.
74. West's stores on the Patuxent were located at St. Leonard's Town, Queen Anne's Town, Pig Point, and Upper Marlborough (Louis Joyner Heinton, *Prince George's Heritage: Sidelights on the Early History of Prince George's County, Maryland, from 1696 to 1800* [Baltimore: Maryland Historical Society, 1972], 126–27).
75. Stein, 81.
76. Earle, 22; Anne Arundel County Judgements, TB-3, f. 140.
77. *Archives* 39: 121; ibid. 46: 470.
78. *Maryland Gazette*, 3 May 1770.
79. Ibid., 10 May, 7 and 21 June, 5 and 26 July 1759.
80. Stein, 96.
81. See Heinton, 121–32, for the early history of Upper Marlborough.
82. Earle, 229; Shomette, *Londontown: A Brief History,* 58.
83. *Archives*, 46: 453–55.
84. U.S. Department of Commerce, Bureau of the Census, *Historical Statistics of the United States, Colonial Times to 1957: A Statistical Abstract Supplement* (Washington, D.C.: Government Printing Office, 1971), 766; Earle, 99.
85. See Papenfuse, 5–34, and Earle, 96–100, for a synopsis of the effects of the Tobacco Inspection Act of 1747.
86. *Maryland Gazette,* 12 April 1770.
87. See Heinton, 169–96, for Prince George's County's contributions to the American Revolution.
88. Richard Walsh and William Lloyd Fox, *Maryland: A History 1632–1974* (Baltimore: Maryland Historical Society, 1974), 72.
89. *Maryland Gazette,* 16 February 1774.
90. See "The Burning of the *Peggy Stewart,*" *MHM* 5, no. 3 (September 1910), for a complete account of the burning of the *Peggy Stewart.*

Chapter 2: Up the Patuxent Plundering

1. *Calendar of Maryland State Papers* (1943; reprint, Baltimore: Genealogical Publications Company, 1967), no. 5: 40, item 301; *Archives* 2: 221, 228, 276.
2. *NDAR* 5: 1066, 1078–80, 1093, 1106, 1119, 1134–35, 1145–46, 1249, 1263, 1275, 1312–16, 1339–48.
3. *Archives* 16: 182–83.
4. *Calendar of Maryland State Papers,* no. 4: 204, item 1300.
5. *Archives* 45: 10; ibid. 43: 258.
6. Ibid. 43: 270; ibid. 45: 77, 113, 115.
7. Ibid. 45: 173; Stein, 133.
8. *Archives* 47: 37–38.
9. Ibid.
10. Ibid., 37–38, 40.
11. Ibid., 151.
12. Ibid., 177.
13. Ibid.
14. Ibid., 151.
15. Ibid., 203, 214.
16. Ibid., 214; John Thomas Scharf, *History of Maryland* (1879; reprint, Hatboro, Pa.: Tradition Press, 1967) 2: 203.
17. *MHM* 6: 306, 317.
18. *Archives* 47: 402; ibid. 45: 562; Edwin W. Beitzell, *St. Mary's County, Maryland, in the American Revolution Calendar of Events* (Leonardtown, Md.: St. Mary's County Bicentennial Commission, 1975), 144.
19. *Archives* 45: 142.
20. Ibid. 48: 106–7.
21. *Calendar of Maryland State Papers,* no. 4, part 1: 211, items 1226, 1227.
22. *Archives* 48: 360–61, 364–65.
23. Ibid., 365–66.
24. Ibid., 376.
25. See John C. Emmerson, Jr., *The Chesapeake Affair of 1807* (Portsmouth, Va.: privately printed, 1954), for comprehensive documentation of the *Chesapeake–Leopard* incident and its repercussions.
26. See Donald G. Shomette, *The Othello Affair: The Pursuit of French Pirates on Patuxent River, Maryland, August 1807* (Solomons, Md.: Calvert Marine Museum Press, 1985), for a complete account of the so-called *Othello* affair.
27. President Madison issued his message to Congress, calling for a declaration of war against Great Britain on 1 June 1812. On 4 June the U.S. House of Representatives passed the measure by a vote of 79 to 49. On 17 June, the Senate also passed the measure by a vote of 19 to 13. The following day, war was declared. The British government, already enmeshed in a great conflict against Napoleonic France, waited until 13 October before responding with its own declaration of war against the United States.

Chapter 3: I Am Anxious to Be at Them

1. William M. Marine, *The British Invasion of Maryland 1812–1815* (1913; reprint, Hatboro, Pa.: Tradition Press, 1965), 21.

2. *Niles' Weekly Register* 7: 190; George Coggeshall, *History of American Privateers* (New York: privately printed, 1856); Marine, 15; George F. Emmons, *The Navy of the United States from the Commencement, 1775 to 1853* (Washington, D.C.: Gideon and Company, 1853), 170–210; Mary Barney, ed., *A Biographical Memoir of the Late Joshua Barney from Autobiographical Notes and Journals in Possession of His Family, and Other Authentic Sources* (Boston: Gray and Bowen, 1832), 252; Fred W. Hopkins, Jr., *Tom Boyle, Master Privateer* (Cambridge, Md.: Tidewater Publishers, 1976), 13–55.

3. Lords Commissioners of the Admiralty to Admiral Sir John B. Warren, 26 December 1812, PRO Admiralty 2/1375.

4. Lt. John Polkinghorne to Warren, 3 April 1813, PRO, Admiralty 1/503; Admiral Sir George Cockburn to Warren, 19 April 1813, Cockburn Papers, Letters Sent, 3 February 1812 to 6 February 1814, vol. 9, LC; ibid., 3 May 1813; ibid., 6 May 1813; Captain John Cassin to Secretary of the Navy William Jones, 26 June 1813, MLR 1813, RG45, M125, R29, NARS; Colonel Sir Thomas Sidney Beckwith to Warren, 28 June 1813, PRO, Admiralty 1/503; Marine, 28, 29, 32, 52; G[ilbert] Auchinleck, *A History of the War between Great Britain and the United States of American during the Years 1812, 1813 and 1814* (Redwood City, Calif.: Arms and Armor Press and Pendragon House, 1972), 264–78.

5. Polkinghorne to Commodore Loraine Baker, 10 August 1813, PRO, Admiralty 1/503; Warren to First Secretary of the Admiralty John W. Crocker, 23 August 1813, PRO, Admiralty 1/504; Marine, 53; *Niles' Weekly Register* 4, no. 22 (31 July 1813) and no. 23 (7 August 1813); Edwin W. Beitzell, "A Short History of St. Clements Island," *CSM* 6, no. 11 (November 1958), 246; Regina Combs Hammett, *History of St. Mary's County, Maryland* (Ridge, Md.: privately printed, 1977), 95.

6. On paper, the southern Maryland region between the Patuxent and Potomac drainages was protected by nearly 9,000 infantry and 1,150 cavalry, all militia, and a single regular army unit, the 36th U.S. Infantry Regiment, although militia actually fielded rarely exceeded more than 30 percent of given strength at any time (Donald G. Shomette, *Flotilla: Battle for the Patuxent* [Solomons, Md.: Calvert Marine Museum Press, 1981], 12–13).

7. See Hulbert Footner, *Sailor of Fortune: The Life and Adventures of Commodore Barney, U.S.N.* (New York: Harper & Brothers, 1940), and Mary Barney for the most concise and authoritative biographies of Joshua Barney.

8. Barney's voyage in the *Rossie* resulted in the capture of eighteen British vessels, totalling 3,698 tons. The value of his prizes, captured, burned, sunk, or ransomed, was well over $1.5 million and included HM Packet *Princess Amelia* and the letter of marque *Jeannie*, both of which were taken after spirited engagements (Barney, 252–53; Footner, 252–57).

9. Joshua Barney to Jones, 4 July 1813, "Defense of the Chesapeake," James Madison Papers, series 1, vol. 52, no. 73, LC.

10. Ibid.

11. Ibid.

12. Secretary of the Navy William Jones to Barney, 20 August 1813, MLR 1813, RG45, N149, R11, NARS.

13. Defense of Baltimore Papers, MS 2304, R2, MHS; Jones to Barney, 27 August 1813, SNL 1813, RG45, M144, R11, NARS; Barney to Jones, 31 August 1813, MLR 1813, RG45, M124, R57-58, NARS; Jones to Barney, 2 September 1813, SNL 1813, RG45, M144, R11, NARS.

14. Defense of Baltimore Papers, MS 2304, R2, MHS; Thomas Kemp Papers, Wade Point Farm, McDavid, Md.; Howard I. Chapelle, *The History of the American Sailing Navy: The Ships and Their Development* (New York: W. W. Norton and Company, 1949), 246.

15. Chapelle, *American Sailing Navy*, 26.

16. Ibid., 222, 223, 225; Barney to Jones, undated, MLR 1813, RG45, M124, R63, NARS; Williams S. Dudley, ed., *The Naval War of 1812: A Documentary History* (Washington, D.C.: Naval Historical Center, Department of the Navy, 1992), 2: 331, 335, 349, 352, 387.

17. Chapelle, *American Sailing Navy*, 229; Emmons, 22–23; Dudley, 323, 330, 333, 335, 349, 366, 368, 378, 380, 387.

18. Barney to Jones, 15 December 1813, MLR 1813, RG45, M124, R59, NARS; Footner, 264; *American & Commercial Daily Advertiser*, 25 December 1813; *American State Papers. Documents, Legislative and Executive, of the Congress of the United States*, (Washington, D.C.: Gales & Seaton, 1832), vol. 1, *Naval Affairs*, 308; Barney to Jones, undated, MLR, RG45, M124, R11 and 63, NARS. Barney ultimately stripped the USS *Ontario, Adams* and *Shark* of at least sixty-one men to flesh out his manpower needs for the flotilla. See Shomette, *Flotilla*, 198–212, for those men originally enrolled aboard regular Navy warships that were transferred to the U.S. Chesapeake Flotilla.

19. Footner, 264.

20. Ibid., 264–65.

21. *American & Commercial Daily Advertiser*, 9 May and 9 June 1814.

22. Barney, 255; Footner, 265–66.

23. Captain Robert Barrie to Cockburn, 1 June 1814, Captains Letters, vol. 38 of Cockburn Papers, LC; *American & Commercial Daily Advertiser*, 8 June 1814.

24. Ibid.

25. Ibid.

26. Ibid.

27. Ibid.; Walter Lord, *The Dawn's Early Light* (New York: W. W. Norton and Company, 1972), 126; Footner, 270. Barney was able to secure one of the expended missiles and sent it to Washington for study. It was the first sample of the greatly feared "terror" weapon to reach the capital and set off considerable controversy regarding the "uncivilized" mode of war adopted by the enemy.

28. *American & Commercial Daily Advertiser*, 8 June 1814; Barrie to Cockburn, 1 June 1814, Captains Letters, vol. 38 of Cockburn Papers, LC. The British landed at Cedar Point and plundered the plantation of a Mr. Sewell, carrying off both slaves and livestock.

Chapter 4: Determined to Something Decisive

1. Barrie to Cockburn, 11 June 1814, Captains Letters, vol. 38 of Cockburn Papers, LC; log of HMS *Loire*, 6 June 1814, *CSM* 8, no. 10 (October 1960); log of HMS *Jaseur*, 6 June 1814, *CSM* 8, no. 12 (December 1960); log of HM Schooner *St. Lawrence*, 6 June 1814, *CSM* 11, no. 12 (December 1963); log of HMS *Dragon*, 6 June 1814, *CSM* 13, no. 8 (August 1965).

2. Hulbert Footner, *Sailor of Fortune: The Life and Adventures of Commodore Barney, U.S.N.* (New York: Harper & Brothers, 1940), 269; log of HMS *Loire*, 7 and 8 June 1814; log of HMS *Jaseur*, 7 June 1814; log of HM Schooner *St. Lawrence*, 7 June 1814; log of HMS *Dragon*, 7 June 1814.

3. Log of HMS *Loire,* 8 June 1814; log of HMS *Jaseur,* 8 June 1814; *American &
Commercial Daily Advertiser,* 9 June 1814.
4. Barrie to Cockburn, 11 June 1814.
5. Footner, 269, claimed that Barney was only two miles up St. Leonard's Creek
when the British first attacked. Barrie, however, claimed the fleet to be six miles
up the creek. Today, St. Leonard's is only five miles long, although in 1814 a
point of land and shoal extended perhaps a quarter- to a half-mile further
into the Patuxent from the northern lip of the entrance. Two miles east of the
present entrance, between modern Breedens Point and Johns Creek, the channel is only eleven feet deep and would have offered a fine defensive position
against Barrie's deep-draft warships (Barrie to Cockburn, 11 June 1814).
6. Mary Barney, ed., *A Biographical Memoir of the Late Joshua Barney from Autobiographical Notes and Journals in Possession of His Family, and Other Authentic Sources*
(Boston: Gray and Bowen, 1832), 256–58; Footner, 270; *American & Commercial Daily Advertiser,* 13 June 1814.
7. Log of HM Schooner *St. Lawrence,* 8 and 9 June 1814; log of HMS *Loire,* 8 June
1814; Barrie to Cockburn, 11 June 1814.
8. Barney to Jones, 9 June 1814, CL 1814, RG45, M124, R64, NARS.
9. Ibid., log of HM Schooner *St. Lawrence,* 9 June 1814; log of HMS *Loire,* 9 June
1814; Barney, 256.
10. Barney, 256.
11. Log of HMS *Loire,* 10 June 1814; *American & Commercial Daily Advertiser,* 18
June 1814; *Daily National Intelligencer,* 27 June 1814; Barney, 257.
12. Log of HMS *Loire,* 10 June 1814.
13. Barrie to Cockburn, 11 June 1814; Barney, 256.
14. *American & Commercial Daily Advertiser,* 17 June 1814; Barney, 256; *Daily
National Intelligencer,* 21 June 1814; log of HMS *Loire,* 10 June 1814.
15. Log of HMS *Jaseur,* 10 June 1814; *American & Commercial Daily Advertiser,* 17
June 1814; Barney, 256.
16. Log of HMS *Jaseur,* 10 June 1814; Barney, 256.
17. Log of HM Schooner *St. Lawrence,* 10 June 1814; log of HMS *Jaseur,* 10 June 1814;
log of HMS *Loire,* 10 June 1814; log of HMS *Dragon,* 10 June 1814; Barney, 256.
18. Log of HMS *Loire,* 10 June 1814; Barney, 256; Barrie to Cockburn, 11 June
1814; *American & Commercial Daily Advertiser,* 17 June 1814.
19. *American & Commercial Daily Advertiser,* 17 June 1814; log of HMS *Loire,* 10
June 1814; Barney, 256–57.
20. Barney, 256–57.
21. *American & Commercial Daily Advertiser,* 17 June 1814; log of HMS *Loire,* 10
June 1814; Barney, 256–57; Barrie to Cockburn, 11 June 1814; log of HMS
Jaseur, 10 June 1814.
22. Log of HMS *Jaseur,* 10 June 1814; log of HM Schooner *St. Lawrence,* 11 June
1814; log of HMS *Loire,* 10 June 1814; Barney, 257; *American & Commercial
Daily Advertiser,* 18 June 1814.
23. Barney, 257; Barrie to Cockburn, 19 June 1814.
24. Log of HMS *Jaseur,* 11 June 1814; Barrie to Cockburn, 19 June 1814; *Daily
National Intelligencer,* 18 June 1814.
25. Barney, 258.
26. Log of HMS *Loire,* 13, 14, and 15 June 1814; log of HMS *Jaseur,* 13 and 14
June 1814; log of HMS *Jaseur,* 15 June 1814, *CSM* 10, no. 2 (February 1962);
Barrie to Cockburn, 19 June 1814.

27. Barrie to Cockburn, 19 June 1814; log of HMS *Jaseur*, 16 and 17 June 1814; *American & Commercial Daily Advertiser*, 20 June 1814. The value of tobacco lost at Lower Marlborough is based upon Barney's estimate of fifty dollars per hogshead as of 1 August 1814 (Barney to Jones, 1 August 1814, CL 1814, RG45, M124, R64, NARS).

28. Barney, 258, 262; Barney to Jones, 18 June 1814, CL 1814, RG45, M124, R64, NARS.

29. *Daily National Intelligencer*, 20 June 1814.

30. Ibid.

31. Ibid.

32. Ibid., 24 June 1814.

33. Ibid.; Captain Thomas Brown to Cockburn, 23 June 1814, Captains Letters, vol. 38 of Cockburn Papers, LC; log of HM Schooner *St. Lawrence*, 21 June 1814, *CSM* 13, no. 4 (April 1965); log of HMS *Loire*, 22 June 1814; *American & Commercial Daily Advertiser*, 27 June 1814.

34. Footner, 272. Similar efforts at dismantling, portaging, and then reassembling naval vessels had been successfully carried out by the British during the American Revolution when portions of a flotilla were transported from the waters of the St. Lawrence River and into Lake Champlain. The British fleet then defeated the opposing American naval force at the battle of Valcour Island, 10 October 1776. See Harrison Bird, *Navies in the Mountains* (New York: Oxford University Press, 1962), 186–95, for a complete account.

35. Barney to Jones, 20 June 1814, CL 1814, RG45, M124, R64, NARS.

36. Footner, 273.

37. Barney to Louise Barney, 22 June 1814, Joshua Barney Papers, Dreer Collection, Pennsylvania Historical Society, Philadelphia.

38. The British were well aware of the dangers of permitting the Americans to hold the high ground. "Should the enemy possess a decent proportion of spirit and enterprise," wrote Captain Thomas Brown, "I imagine from the thick woods near the entrance of the creek, and on the opposite bank of the river, they might get guns that would oblige us to drop further out, and perhaps eventually out of the river" (Brown to Cockburn, 23 June 1814, Captains Letters, vol. 38 of Cockburn Papers, LC).

39. *Daily National Intelligencer*, 7 July 1814.

40. Ibid.; Barney, 259.

41. Barney, 259, 261; *Daily National Intelligencer*, 29 June, 7 and 9 July 1814; Official Report of the Transactions at the Battery on the 25th and 26th June 1814, CL 1814, RG45, M124, R64, NARS.

42. Official Report of the Transactions at the Battery on the 25th and 26th June 1814, CL 1814, RG45, M124, R64, NARS.

43. On 23 June 1814 Keyser's troops were carried from Baltimore to Annapolis aboard the transport ship *Stephen Decatur* and from there marched to the town of Friendship where they bivouacked. On 25 June they set off from Friendship on a forced march overland to St. Leonard's Town, arriving there late the same night *(Daily National Intelligencer*, 9 June 1814; *American & Commercial Daily Advertiser*, 23 June 1814).

44. *Daily National Intelligencer*, 28 June and 7 July 1814; log of HMS *Loire*, 26 June 1814.

45. Barney, 261.

46. Brown to Cockburn, 29 June 1814, Captains Letters, vol. 38 of Cockburn Papers, LC.
47. Donald G. Shomette, *Flotilla: Battle for the Patuxent* (Solomons, Md.: Calvert Marine Museum Press, 1981), 90.
48. *Daily National Intelligencer,* 28 June and 2, 7, and 9 July 1814; Barney, 259–60.
49. Barney, 259–60.
50. *Daily National Intelligencer,* 28 and 29 June and 2, 7, and 9 July 1814.
51. Ibid., 2 and 7 July 1814.
52. Ibid., 7 and 9 July 1814.
53. Ibid., 29 June 1814; Official Report of the Transaction at the Battery on the 25th and 26th June 1814, CL 1814, RG45, M124, R64, NARS.
54. Barney, 260; *Daily National Intelligencer,* 28 June 1814; *American & Commercial Daily Advertiser,* 29 June 1814.
55. *Daily National Intelligencer,* 9 July 1814.
56. Ibid.; Brown to Cockburn, 29 June 1814.
57. Log of HMS *Loire,* 26 June 1814; Brown to Cockburn, 29 June 1814.
58. *American & Commercial Daily Advertiser,* 29 June 1814.

Chapter 5: The Only Fighting We Have Had

1. *Daily National Intelligencer,* 29 June 1814.
2. Ibid., 28 and 29 June and 2, 7, 9, and 14 July 1814; *American & Commercial Daily Advertiser,* 28 and 29 June 1814; Mary Barney, ed., *A Biographical Memoir of the Late Joshua Barney from Autobiographical Notes and Journals in Possession of His Family, and Other Authentic Sources* (Boston: Gray and Bowen, 1832), 258–60.
3. *Daily National Intelligencer,* 7 July 1814; Official Report of the Transactions at the Battery on the 25th and 26th June 1814, CL 1814, RG45, M124, R64, NARS; Lt. Solomon Rutter to Barney, 3 July 1814, CL 1814, RG45, M124, R64, NARS.
4. Captain Joseph Nourse to Admiral Sir George Cockburn, 4 July 1814, Captains Letters, vol. 38 of Cockburn Papers, LC; Captain Thomas Brown to Cockburn, 29 June 1814, Captains Letters, vol. 38 of Cockburn Papers, LC.
5. Official Report; Lt. Solomon Rutter to Joshua Barney, 3 July 1814.
6. Rutter to Barney, 3 July 1814; Nourse to Cockburn, 4 July 1814; Barney to Jones, 8 July 1814, CL 1814, RG45, M124, R64, NARS; log of HMS *St. Lawrence,* 2 July 1814, *CSM* 11, no. 12 (December 1963).
7. Rutter to Barney, 3 July 1814; Barney to Jones, 8 July 1814.
8. Barney, 262; *Daily National Intelligencer,* 2 July 1814.
9. Log of HMS *Albion,* 7 July 1814, Cockburn Papers, LC.
10. Donald G. Shomette, *Flotilla: Battle for the Patuxent* (Solomons, Md.: Calvert Marine Museum Press, 1981), 113; log of HMS *Loire,* 14 July 1814, *CSM* 8, no. 12 (December 1960); log of HMS *St. Lawrence,* 14 July 1814.
11. Log of HMS *Albion,* 14 July 1814, Cockburn Papers, LC; log of HMS *Loire,* 15 July 1814; Log of HMS *St. Lawrence,* 15 July 1814.
12. Cockburn to Vice Admiral Sir Alexander Cochrane, 17 June 1814, Cockburn Papers, vol. 24, LC.
13. Ibid.
14. Cockburn to Nourse, 15 July 1814, Cockburn Papers, vol. 44, LC.
15. Ibid.

16. Nourse to Cockburn, 23 July 1814, Cockburn Papers, vol. 38, LC; Charles Francis Stein, *A History of Calvert County, Maryland* (Baltimore: privately printed, 1960), 153.

17. Stein, 153.

18. *Daily National Intelligencer*, 15 and 22 July 1814.

19. Nourse to Cockburn, 23 July 1814; Stein, 153; Hulbert Footner, *Sailor of Fortune: The Life and Adventures of Commodore Barney, U.S.N.* (New York: Harper & Brothers, 1940), 277.

20. Nourse to Cockburn, 23 July 1814; Stein, 153.

21. Stein, 153; Footner, 277.

22. "A Personal Narrative of Events by Sea and Land, from the Year 1800 to 1815, Concluding with a Narrative of Some of the Principal Events in the Chesapeake and South Carolina, in 1814 and 1815," *CSM* 8, no. 1 (January 1960): 3–4.

23. Ibid.

24. Barney to Jones, 1 August 1814, CL 1814, RG45, M24, R64, NARS.

25. Ibid.

26. Ibid.

27. Walter Lord, *The Dawn's Early Light* (New York: W. W. Norton and Company, 1972), 27–28.

28. Log of HMS *Tonnant*, 17 August 1814, *CSM* 14, no. 8 (August 1966).

29. Lord, 59; Footner, 278.

30. Barney, 262.

31. See [George Robert Gleig], *A Narrative of the Campaigns of the British Army, at Washington, Baltimore, and New Orleans, under the Generals Ross, Packingham, and Lambert, in the Years 1814 and 1815 With Some Account of the Countries Visited* (Philadelphia: M. Carey & Sons, 1821), for an unofficial eyewitness account of the invasion of Maryland from the British point of view.

32. Jones to Barney, 20 August 1814, Joshua Barney Papers, Dreer Collection, Pennsylvania Historical Society, Philadelphia.

33. Ibid.

34. Barney's abandonment of Nottingham and retreat upriver served as the impetus for the entire population of the town and region to take instant flight. When Ross's troops occupied the town soon afterward, they found bread still baking in the ovens of private homes ([Gleig], 107–108).

35. Ibid., 107; Lord, 66–67.

36. Barney, 263.

37. Ibid., 322–23.

38. Cockburn to Cochrane, 22 August 1814, Cockburn Papers, vol. 24, LC.

39. [Gleig], 99.

40. Barney, 266–67.

41. Ibid. In his own report, published in the *Daily National Intelligencer*, 3 September 1814, Barney stated: "These [British] officers behaved to me with the most attention, respect and politeness, had a surgeon brought and my wound addressed immediately." Congressional reaction to the event was one of unquestionablé dismay. See *Niles' Weekly Register*, 17 December 1814, 241–50, for a complete transcript of congressional commentary regarding the affair.

42. For two comprehensive modern overviews of the campaign against Washington and Baltimore see Lord, and James Pack, *The Man Who Burned the White House: Admiral Sir George Cockburn, 1772–1853* (Annapolis, Md.: Naval Institute Press, 1987).

43. Log of HMS *Albion,* 25 August 1814, Cockburn Papers, LC.
44. *Niles' Weekly Register,* 24 September 1814, 24; ibid., *Supplement* to vol. 7, 156.
45. *Niles' Weekly Register,* 5 November 1814, 142.
46. See John Weems to William Jones, MLR, September–October 1814, RG45, M124, NARS, for a full account of the Weems salvage effort.
47. Although "deeply" injured by his wound, Barney nevertheless returned to duty after a short convalescence at his home in Elk Ridge. On 7 October 1814, he proceeded to Washington, from where he was sent the same day with a flag of truce. He was to meet with Admiral Malcolm, who was situated in the lower Chesapeake, to arrange for a prisoner exchange. Three days later Barney returned to Baltimore to resume command of the flotilla which had by then been augmented by several new vessels. Barney immediately set out upon a new recruitment campaign with authority to offer increased pay and bounty. The commodore continued outfitting the flotilla and recruitment, preparing for any emergency that might arise, until 14 February 1815, when word of the signing of the Treaty of Ghent reached Maryland. Congress immediately ordered the flotillamen discharged with four months pay as a gratuity, and the flotilla itself laid up (M. I. Miller, *Commodore Joshua Barney: The Hero of the Battle of Bladensburg. Incidents of His Life Gleaned from Contemporary Sources* [reprint from the *Records of the Columbia Historical Society,* Washington, D.C., 1911], 14: 158, 161).
48. Ibid., 161–64.

Chapter 6: Not Worthy of Further Improvement

1. Richard V. Elliott, *Last of the Steamboats: The Saga of the Wilson Line* (Cambridge, Md.: Tidewater Publishers, 1970), 3, 4.
2. Ibid.; Alexander Crosby Brown, *Steam Packets on the Chesapeake: A History of the Old Bay Line Since 1840* (Cambridge, Md.: Tidewater Publishers, 1961), 9, 150.
3. *Norfolk & Portsmouth Herald,* 23 April 1824.
4. Brown, 10; Robert H. Burgess and H. Graham Wood, *Steamboats Out of Baltimore* (Cambridge, Md.: Tidewater Publishers, 1968), 23.
5. *Evening Star,* 24 and 26 October 1878; *The Sun,* 25, 26, and 28 October 1878; Burgess and Wood, 4–8.
6. *St. Mary's Beacon,* 21 February 1861.
7. Daniel Carroll Toomey, *The Civil War in Maryland* (Baltimore: Toomey Press, 1988), 28.
8. Although the precise location of Camp Union is not known, it may well have been on the commanding heights overlooking the Anacostia River now occupied by the Fort Lincoln Cemetery, near where the British launched their attack against the American defenders of Washington in August 1814.
9. *War of the Rebellion: Official Records of the Union and Confederate Armies* (Washington, D.C.: Government Printing Office, 1880–1901), series 1, vol. 5: 385–86.
10. The occupation of polling stations in southern Maryland and the demonstration of Union authority were a direct consequence of orders by Major General John A. Dix to the U.S. marshall of Maryland and the provost marshall of Baltimore, issued on 1 November 1861, "to take into custody all such persons

in any of the election districts of precincts in which they may appear at polls to effect their criminal attempt to convert the elective franchise into an engine for the subversion of the Government and for the encouragement and support of its enemies" (Edwin W. Beitzell, *Point Lookout Prison Camp for Confederates* [Abell, Md.: privately printed, 1972], 7–8).

11. Ibid., 10–11.
12. Charles Francis Stein, *A History of Calvert County, Maryland* (Baltimore: privately printed, 1960), 12.
13. Toomey, 95. The steamer *Balloon* had been purchased by the Eastern Shore Steamboat Company on 11 December 1860. In 1861, before being chartered for federal service, she served under the command of Captain John R. Griffith, plying the waters of the Choptank, Wye, and Sassafras Rivers. Following the war, she would run independently, serving Annapolis and the West River. In 1858 the steamer *Cecil* served under the flag of the Baltimore and Susquehanna Steamship Company, running from Baltimore to the Sassafras River under the command of Captain William T. Rice. She was employed in 1860 on the run from Crumpton to Bookers Wharf on Spaniards Neck, Queen Anne's County. (Frederic Emory, *Queen Anne's County, Maryland: Its Early History and Development,* published for the Queen Anne's County Historical Society [Queenstown, Md.: Queen Anne Press, 1981], 547; Burgess and Wood, 10, 11).
14. Charles E. Fenwick, "Part of De La Brooke Manor," *CSM* 1, no. 6 (July 1951); *War of the Rebellion,* series 1, vol. 37, 163.
15. Department of the Navy, Naval History Division, comp., *Civil War Naval Chronology 1861–1865* (Washington, D.C.: Government Printing Office, 1971), part 5, 73.
16. Ibid., 91.
17. James C. Bradford, *Anne Arundel County. A Bicentennial History 1649–1677* (Annapolis, Md.: Anne Arundel County and Annapolis Bicentennial Committee, 1977), 75.
18. See Paula J. Johnson, ed., *Working the Water: The Commercial Fisheries of Maryland's Patuxent River,* published for the Calvert Marine Museum (Charlottesville, Va.: University Press of Virginia, 1988), for an overview of the development of the early fisheries industry at Solomons.
19. Stein, 183.
20. Basil Greenhill, *Archaeology of the Boat* (Middleton, Conn.: Wesleyan University Press, 1976), 151–52.
21. M. V. Brewington, *Chesapeake Bay Log Canoes and Bugeyes* (Cambridge, Md.: Tidewater Publishers, 1963).
22. See Bugeye, H-b5, History Files, CMM, for evolution of the "bugeye" nomenclature.
23. Brewington, 74, 100–110.
24. Ibid., 74.
25. Ibid.
26. Ibid.
27. The *Sun,* 20 April 1903.
28. *Calvert Independent,* 5 October 1977; the *Sun,* 2 October 1971.
29. *Calvert Independent,* 6 May 1976.
30. Ibid.

31. Ibid.
32. Ibid., 28 September 1977.
33. Ibid.; *Prince Frederick Recorder,* 15 April 1976.
34. *Calvert Independent,* 23 September 1954.
35. Ralph Eshelman and Clara M. Dixon, *Historical Tours through Southern Maryland: Solomons by Foot, Bicycle or Boat* (La Plata: Southern Maryland Today, 1983), 7; Drum Point Lighthouse, H-L2, History Files, CMM.
36. C. C. Yates, *Survey of Oyster Bars: Calvert County, Maryland* (Washington, D.C.: Government Printing Office, 1910), 87.
37. Ibid., 69–85
38. Brewington, 78–79.
39. Burgess and Wood, 23.
40. Ibid.; *Civil War Naval Chronology,* part 5, 80.
41. Burgess and Wood, 23.
42. Ibid., 24; U.S. Army, *Annual Report of the Chief of Engineers for the Fiscal Year Ending June 30, 1888* (Washington, D.C.: Government Printing Office, 1889), part 2, 851.
43. U.S. Army, *Annual Report of the Chief of Engineers . . . 1888,* part 2, 847–51.
44. Ibid.
45. Ibid., 848–49.
46. Ibid., 846.
47. Ibid., 847.
48. Ibid., 851.
49. Ibid., part 1, 998.
50. U.S. Army, *Annual Report of the Chief of Engineers for the Fiscal Year Ending June 30, 1890* (Washington, D.C.: Government Printing Office, 1891), part 1, 111–12; ibid., part 2, 1060; U.S. Army, *Annual Report of the Chief of Engineers for the Fiscal Year Ending June 30, 1905* (Washington, D.C.: Government Printing Office, 1906), part 1, 209.
51. U.S. Army, *Annual Report of the Chief of Engineers for the Fiscal Year Ending June 30, 1900* (Washington, D.C.: Government Printing Office, 1901), part 2, 1739–41.
52. Ibid., 1740.
53. Ibid., 1741.
54. U.S. Army, *Annual Report of the Chief of Engineers for the Fiscal Year Ending June 30, 1902* (Washington, D.C.: Government Printing Office, 1903), 1049.
55. Ibid., 1048.
56. Ibid., 1049.
57. U.S. Army, *Annual Report of the Chief of Engineers . . . 1905,* part 1, 209.
58. Burgess and Wood, 24, 84.
59. U.S. Congress, House, 60th Congress, 1st session, Document no. 531 (1911), 5.
60. Ibid.
61. Ibid.
62. Ibid., 3.
63. Ibid., 5.
64. Ibid., 6.
65. *MVUS* (1907), 287; *Washington Post,* 7 December 1907; Burgess and Wood, 88.
66. Burgess and Wood, 89.
67. Ibid., 103.
68. Ibid., 98.

69. Ibid., 123.
70. Ibid., 127.
71. Ibid., 127–28.
72. Ibid., 137–139.
73. *Calvert Independent,* 23 September 1954; Dewey Drydock, H-d2, History Files, CMM.
74. Merle T. Cole, *The Patuxent "Ghost Fleet," 1927–1941* (Solomons, Md.: Calvert Marine Museum Press, 1986); Ghost Fleet, H-g1, History Files, CMM.
75. *Calvert Independent,* 23 September 1954; Eshelman and Dixon, 5–6.
76. *Calvert Independent,* 23 September 1954.
77. *Bugeye Times* 3, no. 1 (Spring 1978): 1–2.
78. Ibid.
79. Ibid.
80. Ibid. 4, no. 2 (Summer 1979): 1.
81. Ibid.
82. Ibid., 2.
83. The *Skipjack* 7, no. 4 (April 1978).
84. *Calvert Independent,* 23 September 1954; Norman Alan Hill, ed., *Chesapeake Cruise* (Baltimore: George W. King Co., 1944), 50.
85. *Washington Post,* 9 September 1941; Regulations Governing navigation in the Patuxent River at Point Patience and Sandy Point, Maryland (9 April 1943). U.S. Navy—Mine Test, H-n2, History File, CMM.
86. *Bugeye Times* 3, no. 1 (Spring 1978): 1.
87. *Shore Erosion in Tidewater Maryland,* Bulletin 6 (Baltimore: Maryland Board of Natural Resources, Department of Geology, Mines and Water Resources, 1949), 68–69.
88. Merilyn Reeve, "Patuxent: More Waste than Water," *Maryland Waltonian* 4, no. 12 (September 1979): 1–2; Governor's Patuxent River Watershed Advisory Committee, *The Patuxent River: Maryland's Asset, Maryland's Responsibility* (Baltimore: July 1968); Maryland National Capital Park and Planning Commission, *Preliminary Master Plan for the Patuxent Scenic River* (June 1976).
89. *Bugeye Times* 3, no. 1 (Spring 1978): 1.

Chapter 7: Survey

1. Ralph Eshelman, personal communication; Calvert Marine Museum Mission Statement; *Bugeye Times* 3, no. 1 (Spring 1978): 1.
2. A. J. Eardley, *Structural Geology of North America* (New York: Harper and Row, 1962); D. R. Whitehead, "Palynology and Pleistocene and Phytogeography of Unglaciated Eastern North America," in *Quarternary of the United States,* ed. H. E. Wright, Jr. and D. G. Frey (Princeton, N.J.: Princeton University Press, 1965), 417–32; D. R. Whitehead, "Late Wisconsin Vegetation Changes in Unglaciated Eastern North America," *Quarternary Research* 3 (1973): 621–31; Steve Wilkie and Gail Thompson, *Prehistoric Archaeological Resources in the Maryland Coastal Zone: A Management Overview* (Maryland Department of Natural Resources, 1977), 27.
3. For an extensive contemporary view of the Tidewater environment and its bounty in the early seventeenth century see "A Relation of Maryland, 1635," in *Narratives of Early Maryland, 1633–1634,* ed. Clayton C. Hall (New York: Barnes & Noble, 1910), 70–83.

4. Johns Hopkins University Water Management Seminar, "Report on the Patuxent River Basin, Maryland" (Baltimore: Johns Hopkins University, 1966).
5. See Merilyn Reeve, "Patuxent: More Waste than Water," *Maryland Waltonian* 4, no. 12 (September 1979): 1–2, and Governor's Patuxent River Watershed Advisory Committee for the impact of pollution and urban development upon the biota of the Patuxent watershed.
6. Donald G. Shomette and Ralph E. Eshelman, "A Developmental Model for Survey and Inventory of Submerged Archaeological Resources in a Riverine System," in *Underwater Archaeology: The Challenge Before Us. The Proceedings of the Twelfth Conference on Underwater Archaeology,* ed. Gordon Watts (Fathom Eight Special Publication No. 2, 1987), 159–71; PAXS, 1: 41.
7. PAXS, 1: 41.
8. See PAXS, 1: 48–49, 52–53, 56–57, 59–60, 66, 68, 71 and PAXS, 2: 358, 387 for specific annotations on the diversity of historical and archaeological resources documented in the Patuxent River Survey.
9. Nautical Archaeological Associates, Incorporated, charter, DGSC.

Chapter 8: Shipwrecks and Saturday Night Specials

1. James H. Buys, personal communication.
2. PAXS, 1: 81; James H. Buys, personal communication.
3. *MVUS* (1902), 82. The *Henrietta Bach* disappears from the *MVUS* after 1931 but was not officially reported as abandoned. Vessels were often not documented as abandoned, however, until many years after their actual abandonment and were sometimes merely removed from the record. (Robert H. Burgess, *Chesapeake Circle* [Cambridge, Md.: Tidewater Publishers, 1965], 190).
4. Allan A. Sollers to Ralph E. Eshelman, personal communication; Mrs. Homer O. Elseroad to Emory Kristof, 8 February 1987; Mrs. Homer O. Elseroad to Donald Shomette, 16 April 1987, DGSC.
5. PAXS, 1: 83.
6. When word of the underwater archaeological survey work on St. Leonard's Creek eventually made its way into the local press, the result was considerable curiosity and a mild "feeding frenzy" among relic collectors who feared that the archaeologists would make off with all of the waterway's treasures.
7. Mackall's Cliff and the adjacent littoral would eventually yield remarkable finds from the Early Archaic period (7200–6900 B.C.) to the colonial era. By 1984, within a year of the founding of the Jefferson Patterson Park and Museum on the terrace overlooking the confluence of the Patuxent River and St. Leonard's Creek, numerous sites from the Woodland period (1000 B.C. to 1608 A.D.), including shell middens from the Accokeek Phase (900–500 B.C.), and at least six middens dating to the Shelby Bay phase (100–900 A.D.) had been found. No fewer than twenty Late Woodland sites bearing artifacts had also been located. Twenty sites from the colonial era, a dozen of which dated from the seventeenth century, including evidence of the location of the first St. Leonard's Town, had been discovered as well. By 1991 archaeological investigation had uncovered many additional sites, including the home site of Maryland's first attorney general (1658–1659), Richard Smith, Sr., and the Smith family cemetery. (*Jefferson Patterson Park and Museum: Final Master Plan*

[Annapolis, Md.: Maryland Historical Trust, 1984], 11–12; *Patterson Points* 6, no. 3 [1991]: 3–4; *Patterson Points* 7, no. 3: 3–4 [1992]).

8. PAXS, 1: 84, 87.
9. Ibid., 227–34.
10. Ibid., 210–15.
11. Ibid., 224–27.
12. Ibid.
13. See chapter 4; PAXS, 1: 84.
14. PAXS, 1: 197–204.
15. Ibid., 201–204.
16. James H. Buys, personal communication.
17. Paula Johnson, *Historical Tours through Southern Maryland: Broome's Island* (Solomons, Md.: Calvert Marine Museum Press, 1983), 1–16; Charles Francis Stein, *A History of Calvert County, Maryland* (Baltimore: privately printed, 1960), 30, 36, 246; Shipwrecks, H-s11, History Files, CMM.
18. *James E. Trott* was an 1870 Baltimore-built schooner of 59 gross tons, 56 net tons, 73.8 feet in length, last owned by Thomas Hance of Mutual, Maryland (*MVUS* [1935], 658–59; ibid. [1936], 1035).
19. Richard E. Stearns, *Proceedings of the Natural History Society of Maryland, No. 9: Some Indian Village Sites of Tidewater Maryland* (Baltimore: Natural History Society of Maryland, July 1943), 24–28.
20. *MVUS* (1907), 287; ibid. (1908), 382; Burgess and Wood, 24, 83, 84, 88, 211; *Washington Post,* 7 December 1907; Shipwrecks, H-s11, History Files, CMM.
21. In his first survey report of the Patuxent in 1943, Stearns documented eight sites on the east shore of the Patuxent but overlooked the Battle Creek site, although two shell middens were discovered immediately north of it on the farm of Alexander Duke. Stearns, *Proceedings*, 25–26.
22. PAXS, 1: 87–88.
23. Stein, 59, 308; Carey A. Litz, personal communication.
24. PAXS, 1: 308–13.
25. Craddock A. Goins, Jr., to Carey A. Litz, 5 January 1977 (photocopy), DGSC; William T. Tearman to Ralph E. Eshelman, 29 October 1979 (photocopy) DGSC.
26. *Archives* 44: 595–638; ibid. 46: 157–63; ibid. 50: 303–66; ibid. 56: 129; ibid. 58: 433–97; ibid. 61: 222; ibid. 64: 151–92; *American & Commercial Daily Advertiser,* 20 June 1814; Burgess and Wood, 103.
27. PAXS, 1: 89–93; Joseph Richards, personal communication.
28. PAXS, 1: 90.
29. Stearns, *Proceedings*, 24–25.
30. Mrs. Sudler Cockey to Ralph E. Eshelman, 20 January 1979, Lower Marlboro, H-LS, History File, CMM; Genevieve Frazier Cockey to Ralph E. Eshelman, September 1979, Archaeology Research—Phase 1, H-p4.1, History Files, CMM; *The Swampdoodle Book: A Walk through History—Lower Marlboro, Then and Now* (Lower Marlboro, Md.: funded by the Maryland Humanities Council through a grant from the National Endowment for the Humanities, 1983), 47–48.

Chapter 9: Nottingham

1. Louis Joyner Heinton, *Prince George's Heritage: Sidelights on the Early History of Prince George's County, Maryland, from 1696 to 1800* (Baltimore: Maryland Historical Society, 1972), 7, 11, 39, 42, 48, 50.

2. Prince George's County Land Records, Liber TT, f.237.

3. Prince George's County Court Records, Liber HH, f.398.

4. Ibid., Liber CC, f.312

5. *Maryland Gazette,* 1 April and 3 June 1773.

6. Minutes of the Board of Patuxent Associators, *MHM* 6 (1911): 305–17.

7. See H. Chandlee Forman, *Old Buildings, Gardens and Furniture in Tidewater Maryland* (Cambridge, Md.: Tidewater Publishers, 1967), 233–37, for discussion of the Governor Robert Bowie estate called The Cedars, also known as the Berry House or Nottingham Farm, at Nottingham. The house was destroyed by fire before the Patuxent project began, leaving only a few remnants of the structure and its colonial/Federalist–era occupation lying about the property.

8. George Robert Gleig, *A Narrative of the Campaigns of the British Army, at Washington, Baltimore, and New Orleans, under the Generals Ross, Packingham, and Lambert, in the Years 1814 and 1815 With Some Account of the Countries Visited* (Philadelphia: M. Carey & Sons, 1821), 107–108.

9. Ibid., 107; Walter Lord, *The Dawn's Early Light* (New York: W. W. Norton and Company, 1972), 66–67.

10. See Mark P. Leon, "Land and Water, Urban Life, and Boats: Underwater Reconnaissance in the Patuxent River on Chesapeake Bay," in *Shipwreck Anthropology,* ed. Richard A. Gould (Albuquerque: University of New Mexico Press, 1983), 173–88, for discussion on the impact of the War of 1812 on the urban development and its subsequent decline on the banks of the Patuxent Valley and along its shores.

11. David C. Holly, *Tidewater by Steamboat: A Saga of the Chesapeake* (Baltimore: Johns Hopkins University Press, published in association with the Calvert Marine Museum, 1991), 266.

12. John C. Schmidt, "Skin Divers May Have Found the Remains of Joshua Barney's Ships," *Sunday Sun Magazine,* 19 October 1958, 20.

13. Ibid., 19–20.

14. Ibid.

15. Ibid.

16. Donald Stewart, personal communication; Joseph Windsor, personal communication.

17. Edgar Merkle, personal communication.

18. Richard E. Stearns, "An Indian Site Survey of the Patuxent River, Maryland," *Natural History Society of Maryland Proceedings* 21 (1957): 3–20.

19. Ibid.; Wayne E. Clark, National Register of Historic Places Inventory—Nomination Form for the Nottingham Archaeological Site (August 1974), photocopy, DGSC.

20. PAXS, 1: 252–65.

21. Ibid., 270–73.

22. Edgar Merkle, personal communication; Richard Dolesh, personal communication; PAXS, 1: 273–81.

23. PAXS, 1: 278.

24. Primary research of title and probate records regarding the Nottingham mound and ditch complex was undertaken by Shirley Baltz under the direction of Maryland National Capital Park and Planning Commission historian John Walton. The first note of the Twiver (Twyford) tract is in Prince George's County Rent Rolls, vol. 3, f.464-HR.

25. Prince George's County Rent Rolls, vol. 3, f.464-HR; Prince George's County Patents, Liber DD5, f.624.
26. Prince George's County Deeds, Liber Q, f.623.
27. Forman, 52, 56, 58. A photocopy of an excerpt from the *Dictionary of Early English*, forwarded to the author by Maryland State Archaeologist Tyler Bastian, notes that "apart from the sound of laughter, but perhaps arising as an exclamation of surprise, haha has been used since the seventeenth century (also aha, ah ah, ha! ha!, hahah, haw haw) for a sunken fence, trench, ditch, or other boundary to a garden that does not obstruct the view and is not visible until one is right onto it. . . . It became an eighteenth century fashion, as [Daniel] De Foe noted in his *Towns of Great Britain* (1769) to be 'throwing down the walls of the garden, and making, instead of berms, haw haw walls.'" Ross Kimmell, historian for the Maryland Park and Forest Service, points out that there are land tracts in Anne Arundel County called Haha or Ahha, and one in Montgomery County called Gittings Haha. Perhaps the most famous of all hahas, however, was at Mount Vernon (Tyler Bastian to Donald G. Shomette, 23 May 1983, DGSC).
28. Baltz's research revealed that no fewer than thirty-four property ownership transections would be consummated on the Reed Farm tract, or major portions thereof, between the date it was patented in the late seventeenth century and 1969.
29. Campbell acquired the Reed Farm tract in 1761, two years after opening a store in Nottingham as a factor for the firm of Shortbridge, Gordon and Company of Glasgow. Campbell's store exported tobacco and imported European and East Indian goods via Glasgow, rum from the West Indies, and salt from Liverpool as well as a variety of other items. His plantation adjacent to the town, consisting of three tracts from the original Reed Farm, totalled 245 acres. Campbell apparently made frequent use of his riverfront property, considering his need of slaves who "had been used to the water." On November 1, 1764, he offered up the plantation for sale when, apparently as a consequence of the passage of the Revenue Act by Parliament to levy duties on colonial trade, his firm decided to recall him and close down the Nottingham operation. (*Maryland Gazette*, 22 November 1759, 21 February, 7 May, and 27 November 1760, 1 October and 5 November 1761, 8 and 22 July 1762, and 8 November 1764).
30. Prince George's County Deeds, Liber BB2, f.10; *Maryland Gazette*, 30 September 1773.
31. Prince George's County Deeds, Liber 125, f.496.
32. Ibid., Liber 3754, f. 327.
33. Joseph Windsor, personal communication.

Chapter 10: Frames, Flatties, and Trivets

1. PAXS, 1: 103.
2. Ibid., 104.
3. Ibid., 299.
4. Ibid., 305.
5. Ibid., 305–9.

6. Howard I. Chapelle, *American Small Sailing Craft: Their Design, Development and Construction* (New York: W. W. Norton and Company, 1951), 310.

7. The term "handscraper" was a name applied to dredge boats that employed hand-operated winches to haul a dredge. Most handscrapers were well under forty feet long (ibid., 312).

8. Ibid., 310.

9. See Chapelle, *American Small Sailing Craft,* 309–18, for further discussion on the evolution of the flattie.

10. Eric Christenson, personal communication; Port of Philadelphia Maritime Record, vol. 3, 1882–1884, section 4, Record of Wrecks, Philadelphia District, Pennsylvania Historical Society, typed transcript, LC.

11. Ibid., vol. 4, 1887–1888.

12. Richard Dolesh, personal communication; *The Planter's Advocate,* 31 January and 7 February 1855.

13. PAXS, 1: 352–54. The site was reexamined by the author and Kenneth Hollingshead in 1982 during a University of Baltimore field school in underwater archaeology, and in 1990 by the author and Dr. Ervan Garrison, chief of archaeology for NOAA's Marine Sanctuary Program.

14. See Louis Joyner Heinton, *Prince George's Heritage: Sidelights on the Early History of Prince George's County, Maryland, from 1696 to 1800* (Baltimore: Maryland Historical Society, 1972), 11–25, for a complete history of Charles Town.

15. Ibid., 23–25.

16. Edward Brown, Jr., personal communication. Similar observations were made within the controlled environment of a cofferdam erected in the York River, Virginia, to facilitate the excavation of a Revolutionary War shipwreck sunk in 1781 during the siege of Yorktown (John Broadwater, personal communication).

17. Edward Brown, Jr., personal communication; PAXS, 1: 98–101.

18. PAXS, 1: 101.

19. See Edward C. Papenfuse, *In Pursuit of Profit: The Annapolis Merchants in the Era of the American Revolution, 1763–1805* (Baltimore: Johns Hopkins University Press, 1975), for a synthesis of the mercantile history of the Patuxent drainage during the period of the Revolution.

20. Barney to Jones, 1 August 1814, CL 1814, RG45, M124, R64, NARS.

21. Ibid.

22. Mary Barney, ed., *A Biographical Memoir of the Late Joshua Barney from Autobiographical Notes and Journals in Possession of His Family, and Other Authentic Sources* (Boston: Gray and Bowen, 1832), 321–23.

23. It is possible that the many hulks of the flotilla that littered the narrow main channel of the Patuxent may well have contributed to the alteration of the river environment and accelerated the siltation process by blocking the free flow of sediment itself.

24. Dawson Lawrence, "Historical Sketch of Prince George County, Md.," *Atlas of Fifteen Miles Around Washington Including the County of Prince George, Maryland* (Philadelphia: G. M. Hopkins, 1878), 8.

25. U.S. Congress, House, 60th Congress, 1st session, Document no. 531, 2.

26. James Gebauer, personal communication; PAXS, 1: 106–9.

27. PAXS, 1: 106, 360–61.

28. Ibid., 106–107.
29. Ibid., 100–18.

Chapter 11: Turtle Shell

1. Application for Permit under Maryland Antiquities Act, March 25, 1979, photocopy, DGSC. The permit was issued through the Division of Archaeology of the Maryland Geological Survey, which was created by an act of the Maryland General Assembly in 1968. The Division of Archaeology was authorized to administer to all archaeological remains on lands owned or controlled by the state of Maryland, "including the bottoms of rivers, lakes, the Bay, and the Atlantic Ocean within three miles of the Maryland shore" (Division of Archaeology Mission and Jurisdiction, undated photocopy, DGSC).
2. Application for Permit, March 25, 1979.
3. Wayne E. Clark, "Suggestions for a Research and Management Plan for the Submerged Terrestrial Sites of Maryland," 1979, photocopy, DGSC; Donald G. Shomette, "Suggestions for the Development of a Comprehensive Approach to the Underwater Archaeological Master Plan for Maryland: Preliminary Overview," 1979, Archaeological Research Survey, H-p4-p4.3, History File, Calvert Marine Museum.
4. PAXS, 1:126; Ralph E. Eshelman and Donald G. Shomette, "A Proposal for the Survey of the Submerged Archaeological Resource Base of the Patuxent River, Maryland, Phase I, 1 June 1979–30 September 1979," proposal submitted to Maryland Historical Trust, Crownsville, Maryland. A total of $18,974 was requested for Phase I, of which $2,400 was to be allocated for magnetometer work.
5. PAXS, 1: 128.
6. Leroy "Pepper" Langley, personal communication, transcribed by the author and published with modifications in Melvin A. Conant, *I Remember: Recollections of "Pepper" Langley Growing Up in Solomons* (Solomons, Md.: privately printed, 1990), 66–67.
7. U.S. Department of the Navy, *Dictionary of American Naval Fighting Ships,* 8 vols. (Washington, D.C.: Government Printing Office, 1959–81), 4: 211–12; Dr. Joseph Beard, personal communication.
8. Sheldon Breiner, "Marine Magnetic Search," *Geometrics Technical Report No. 7* (May 1975); J. Barto Arnold III, "An Airborne Magnetometer Survey for Shipwrecks and Associated Test Excavations" (paper presented at the Tenth Conference on Underwater Archaeology, Nashville, Tennessee, 2–5 January 1979); M. J. Aitken and M. S. Tite, "Proton Magnetometer Survey of Some British Hill Forts," *Archaeometry* 5: 126–34.
9. PAXS, 1: 252–65.
10. Ibid., 265–67.
11. Ibid., 267–70.
12. Ibid., 71–77.
13. Ibid., 291–305.
14. Ibid., 335–51.
15. Ibid., 355–56.
16. Ibid., 356–61.

17. Ibid.
18. Ibid., 360–61.

Chapter 12: Wedged Between Some Planking

1. Ralph E. Eshelman and Donald G. Shomette, "A Proposed Survey of the Submerged Maritime and Archaeological Resource Base of the Patuxent River, Maryland" (1979), 34. The original proposal for the 1980 campaign on the Patuxent submitted to the MHT was for a matching grant. NAA and CMM would provide $37,471 in-kind services and cash, and the MHT would provide $38,856 from the Heritage Conservation and Recreation Service of the Department of the Interior upon completion of the project. Less than $16,000 was forthcoming, seriously reducing the extent of the project and achievement of its objectives.
2. Eshelman and Shomette, "A Proposed Survey," 8–10.
3. Application for Permit under Maryland Antiquities Act, March 27, 1980, photocopy, DGSC. The antiquities permit was approved by Harold M. Cassell, Chief, Wetland Permit Division, Water Resources Administration, on 22 May 1980, and by state archaeologist Tyler Bastian on 27 May 1980, only a few days before the field season was to begin. Owing to the drastic last-minute reduction in funding, however, the project objectives were reduced from seven sites to three.
4. Joshua Barney to William Jones, 1 August 1814, MLR 1814, RG45, M124, R64, NARS.
5. PAXS, 2: 389–92.
6. Ibid., 392–93.
7. Ibid., 393.
8. Ibid.
9. Ibid., 395.
10. Ibid.; Nautical Archaeological Associates, "Plan for the Construction of a Temporary Archaeological Coffer, Deplacement and Replacement of Bottom Sediments in Patuxent River, Anne Arundel County, Maryland," in Proposal to Dredge, Fill, Remove or Otherwise Alter Wetlands Notification and/or Application to the Water Resources Administration (27 March 1980), photocopy, DGSC.
11. PAXS, 2: 396–98.
12. Ibid., 401.
13. Ibid., 404.

Chapter 13: Cannonballs Galore

1. PAXS, 2: 512–16.
2. Ibid., 517–37.
3. Ibid., 518, 521.
4. The total collection of cannonballs included three 24-pounders, eighteen 8-pounders, seven 10-pounders, twelve 8-pounders, two 6-pounders, and three of uncertain size.
5. F. G. Fick to E. B. Shelly, 21 December 1979. "Investigation of Cannonballs Recovered from a Sunken Hull in a Tributary of the Chesapeake Bay." Report

reprinted in PAXS, II, Appendix C, Communications and Reports Concerning Artifacts Recovered from 1-LCS.

6. Ibid.

7. John Muller, *A Treatise of Artillery* (London: printed for John Millan, 1780), 11; PAXS, 2: 521.

8. Ivor Noël Hume, *Artifacts of Colonial America* (New York: Alfred A. Knopf, 1972), 296.

9. Ibid., 296–310.

10. PAXS, 2: 521–22.

11. Ibid., 527.

12. Ivor Noël Hume to Ralph E. Eshelman, 15 November 1985, Patuxent River— Lyons Creek, H-p3.1, History File, CMM; Ralph Eshelman and Donald Shomette, "On a Possible Seventeenth Century Small Craft Wreck, Lyons Creek, Calvert County, Maryland," in *Underwater Archaeology: Proceedings from the Society for Historical Archaeology Conference, Savannah, Georgia,* ed. Alan B. Albright (1987), 74.

13. Eshelman and Shomette, "Seventeenth Century Small Craft Wreck," 74–75; PAXS, 2: 522–27.

14. Hume to Eshelman, 15 November 1985.

15. PAXS, 2: 538–41; Eshelman and Shomette, "Seventeenth Century Small Craft Wreck," 74–75.

16. See George F. Bass, ed., *Ships and Shipwrecks of the Americas: A History Based on Underwater Archaeology* (London: Thames and Hudson, 1988), 119–25, for a complete overview regarding the Brown's Ferry Wreck.

17. *Calendar of Maryland State Papers,* no. 1 ("The Black Book"), 10, item 67.

18. Annie Walker Burns Bell, comp., *Maryland Inventories and Accounts,* 5 vols., (Annapolis, Md.: 1938); *Archives* 38: 281–83; Will Book, 8: 1, Maryland Hall of Records, Annapolis.

19. Harris is noted as also owning a store at Charles Town in the town's formative years, as well as property, including dwellings and a store, which were incorporated into the town of Nottingham in 1707 (Louis Joyner Heinton, *Prince George's Heritage: Sidelights on the Early History of Prince George's County, Maryland, from 1696 to 1800* [Baltimore: Maryland Historical Society, 1972], 12, 13).

20. Eshelman and Shomette, "Seventeenth Century Small Craft Wreck," 75–76.

21. Hume to Eshelman, 15 November 1985.

Chapter 14: Bucket Seats by Barney

1. PAXS, 2: 407–10.

2. U.S. Congress, House of Representatives, 60th Congress, 1st Session, *Document No. 531,* 2.

3. PAXS, 2: 407–10.

4. Ibid., 411.

5. Ibid.

6. Cockburn to Cochrane, 22 June 1814, Cockburn Papers, vol. 24, LC.

7. PAXS, 2: 447.

8. Ibid., 449–56; Elizabeth Bennion, *Antique Medical Instruments* (Berkeley, Calif.: Southeby Parke Bernet, University of California Press, 1979), 327.

9. PAXS, 2: 450–53; Bennion, 315. A year after the completion of the Patuxent River Survey, a document discovered in the National Archives by historian Scott Sheads of the National Park Service totally rebutted the *Princess Amelia* theory. Sheads discovered a letter of 14 April 1814 from Secretary Jones to Barney stating: "Mr. [James] Beatty will deliver to you the Medicine chest of one of the sloops [*Ontario*], together with the instruments the whole of which you will preserve in perfect order to be returned to the ship unbroken prepared for service." Furthermore, all petty officers, seamen, and ordinary seamen belonging to *Ontario* were to be transferred to the flotilla as all of her commissioned officers and warrant officers were being ordered to Sacketts Harbor. Moreover, Beatty was to deliver to Barney's purser "such slops from the *Erie* (which ship has a vast superabundance) as you may require and whatever stores of a perishable nature may be onboard either ship he will deliver on your requisition for the consumption of the Flotilla" (Juin A. Crosse to Ralph Eshelman, 26 June 1981, photocopy, DGSC; Jones to Barney, 14 April 1814, SNL, RG45, M149, R11, NARS).

10. PAXS, 2: 453–57; John Munsey, *Collecting Bottles* (New York: Hawthorn Books, 1970), 47; Henry Miller, personal communication; Clement Hollyday to Urban Hollyday, 12 July 1814, LC; *Daily National Intelligencer,* 24 July 1814; Payroll Records of the Chesapeake Flotilla, Navy and Old Army Branch, NARS.

11. PAXS, 2: 457.

12. Ibid., 457–59.

13. Ibid., 459; James Beatty Papers, Records of the Fourth Auditor of the United States, Judicial and Fiscal, NARS.

14. Payroll Records of the Chesapeake Flotilla, NARS.

15. PAXS, 2: 461–63; James Beatty Papers, NARS.

16. PAXS, 2: 463–65; Payroll Records of the Chesapeake Flotilla, NARS.

17. PAXS, 2: 465; Payroll Records of the Chesapeake Flotilla, NARS; James Beatty Papers, NARS.

18. PAXS, 2: 467; Munsey, 120; James Beatty Papers, NARS.

19. PAXS, 2: 467–69; James Beatty Papers, NARS.

20. PAXS, 2: 469.

21. Ibid., 469–70.

22. Ibid., 470–71.

23. Ibid., 476–79.

24. Ibid., 479.

25. Ibid., 471–75.

26. Ibid., 434–36.

27. Ibid., 472–74.

Chapter 15: Working Off the Brewhouse

1. Charles W. Snell, "Central Wharf," in *Historic Structures Report: Historical Data* (Denver: Denver Service Center, U.S. Department of the Interior, July 1974); Charles W. Snell, "Derby Wharf and Warehouses," in *Historic Structures Report Historical Data* (Denver: Denver Service Center, U.S. Department of the Interior, July 1974). For discussions on late nineteenth- to early twentieth-century wharf design and construction see Carlton Greene, *Wharves and Piers: Their Design, Construction, and Equipment* (New York: McGraw Hill, 1917) and

Cunningham Brysson, *A Treatise on the Principles and Practice of Harbour Engineering* (London: Charles Griffin & Company, 1918). For recent archaeological evaluations of wharf design and construction see Janice Artemel, Andrea Heintzelman, and Margaret Orelup, Back Street Waterfront, New London, Connecticut, Report from Deleuw Cather/Parson to U.S. Department of Transportation (May, 1984); John W. Durel, "From Strawberry Banke to Puddle Dock: The Evolution of a Neighborhood, 1630–1850" (Ph.D. dissertation, University of New Hampshire, 1984); Andrea J. Heintzelman, "Southern New England Colonial Wharf Construction" (Paper presented at the Third Annual Symposium for Southern New England Maritime History, Mystic, Connecticut, 5 November 1983); Andrea J. Heintzelman, "Late Seventeenth and Eighteenth Century Wharf Technology: Historical and Archaeological Investigations of Three Eastern U.S. Examples" (Master's thesis: American University, Washington, D.C., 1985).

2. Few photographs or illustrations of Tidewater wharves were produced with the structures themselves as the main topic. Rather, wharves were usually incidental to pictures illustrating the comings and goings of vessels. Of some value, however, were U.S. Army Corps of Engineers site plans, which often accompanied reports on dredging or other operations of the Corps near waterfront structures. These usually provided general typological features as well as bathymetric data.

3. For specific construction materials necessary to build a typical colonial Tidewater wharf and warehouse on the Potomac River at Point Lumley, Alexandria, Virginia, see Richard Harrison & Company Ledger, 1774, f. 284–85, LC.

4. Charles Francis Stein, *A History of Calvert County, Maryland* (Baltimore: privately printed, 1960), 66–67, 279–81.

5. Ibid., 281.

6. Ibid.

7. PAXS, 1, 220–21; ibid., 2: 544–46.

8. Ibid.

9. Ibid., 2: 546–49.

10. Ibid.

11. Ibid., 547.

12. Thomas Stevenson, *The Design and Construction of Harbours: A Treatise on Maritime Engineering* (Edinburgh, Scotland: Adam and Charles Black, 1876), 141, 143–44.

13. Ibid., 143–44; *Annual Report of the Operations of the United States Life-Saving Service for the Fiscal Year Ending June 30, 1895* (Washington, D.C.: Government Printing Office, 1896), 434–35.

14. Stevenson, 144.

15. Ibid.

16. Ibid., 162–63.

17. Bristol Bar, Patuxent, Maryland (chart), in U.S. Army, *Annual Report of the Chief of Engineers for the Fiscal Year Ending June 30, 1890* (Washington, D.C.: Government Printing Office); photoprint of the steamboat wharf at Lower Marlboro, Mariners Museum, Newport News, Virginia.

18. Robert H. Burgess and H. Graham Wood, *Steamboats Out of Baltimore* (Cambridge, Md.: Tidewater Publishers, 1968), 103.

Chapter 16: Scorpion

1. PAXS, 2: 382.
2. Ibid., 491–94.
3. Ibid., 496–97.
4. Ibid., 480.
5. Ibid., 481.
6. Ibid., 483–84.
7. Ibid., 483.
8. *Bugeye Times* 6, no. 2 (Summer 1981): 1–3; ibid. 7, no. 2 (Summer 1982): 3.
9. Joshua Barney to Jones, 4 July 1813, "Defense of the Chesapeake," James Madison Papers, series 1, vol. 52, no. 73, LC.
10. The O'Neal schooner is believed to have served as an ordnance supply vessel and may have become trapped along with the flotilla after running the blockade into the Patuxent.
11. Howard I. Chapelle, *The History of the American Sailing Navy: The Ships and Their Development* (New York: W. W. Norton and Company, 1949), 222–26.
12. Defense of Baltimore Papers, MS 2304, R2, MHS; Chapelle, *The History of the American Sailing Navy,* 246.

Chapter 17: Wrap-up

1. *Calvert Independent,* 2 July 1980; *Courier,* 3 July 1980; *Sunday Sun,* 13 July 1980.
2. For further accounts of the project published in scholarly proceedings, see Donald G. Shomette, "The Patuxent River Shipwreck Inventory," in *In the Realms of Gold: The Proceedings of the Eleventh Annual Conference on Underwater Archaeology,* ed. Wilburn A. Cockrell, Fathom Eight Special Publication no. 1, 1981; Symposium: Patuxent River Submerged Cultural Resource Survey, *Underwater Archaeology: The Challenge Before Us. The Proceedings of the Twelfth Conference on Underwater Archaeology,* ed. Gordon P. Watts, Jr., Fathom Eight Special Publication no. 2; Donald G. Shomette, "The Turtle Shell Wreck: A Narrative of the Discovery and Excavation of an Early 19th Century Warship in the Patuxent River," *Calvert Country* 9, no. 3 (July 1980).
3. Donald G. Shomette, "The Much Vaunted Flotilla," *Journal of Maryland Archaeology* 17, no. 2 (September 1981); Kenneth R. Hollingshead, "Archaeology Beneath the Chesapeake," *NOAA Magazine,* Summer 1981: 25–27; Donald G. Shomette and Fred W. Hopkins, Jr., "The Search for the Chesapeake Flotilla," *The American Neptune: A Quarterly Journal of Maritime History* 43, no. 1 (January 1983): 5–19.
4. Philip M. Evans, "We Need Local Heroes," *Annapolitan,* March 1988: 6.
5. Thomas Harriot, *A briefe and true report of the new found land of Virginia* (1588; reprint, New York: Dover Publications, 1972), 55; Smith, 31; Robert Beverly, *The history and present state of Virginia,* ed. Louis B. Wright (1705; reprint, Chapel Hill, N.C.: Institute of Early American History and Culture, 1947), 3: 61; Edward Beers Quinn, ed., *The Roanoke Voyages 1584–1590. Documents to Illustrate the English Voyage to North America under the Patent Granted to Walter Raleigh in 1584* (New York: Dover Publications, 1991), 1: 104–105, 432–33; Rusty Fleetwood, *Tidecraft. An Introductory Look at the Boats of Lower South Carolina, Georgia, and Northeastern Florida: 1650–1950* (Savannah, Ga.: Coastal

Heritage Society, 1982), 3–4; M. V. Brewington, *Chesapeake Bay Log Canoes and Bugeyes* (Cambridge, Md.: Tidewater Publishers, 1963), 2, 4.

6. Brewington, 3; William Tatham, *Essay on the Culture of Tobacco* (London: 1800).
7. Brewington, 8–10.
8. Ibid., 8–14.
9. Peter Throckmorton, ed., *The Sea Remembers: Shipwrecks and Archaeology* (New York: Weidenfeld & Nicholson, 1987), 94.
10. L. Sprague de Camp, *The Ancient Engineers* (New York: Ballantine Books, 1987), 9.
11. Paula Johnson to Wayne E. Clark, 28 June 1984, Archaeology Research Survey, H-p4, History Files, CMM.
12. Donald G. Shomette, Field Notes on the Mackall's Cove Wreck, 16 June 1984, DGSC; *MVUS* (1900), 42.
13. Farouk El-Biz, "Finding a Pharaoh's Funeral Bark," *National Geographic Magazine,* 153, no. 4 (April 1988): 513–34.
14. Donald G. Shomette, "A Sub-surface Radar Exploration of Lake Phelps, North Carolina," Report prepared for the North Carolina Division of Archives and History, Raleigh, North Carolina, 1993.
15. Robert Neyland, "The Lyons Creek Boat Remains" (unpublished study), 1989, Lyons Creek, H-p3.1, History Files, CMM; Robert S. Neyland to Ralph E. Eshelman, 10 June 1989, Lyons Creek, H-p3.1, History Files, CMM.
16. Neyland, "Lyons Creek Boat Remains," 9–10.
17. Ibid., 11.
18. Ibid.

Bibliography

Manuscripts and Documents

Admiralty In Letters. Admiralty Record 1/503. Public Record Office, London.

Admiralty Out Letters. Admiralty Record 2/1375. Public Record Office, London.

Application for Permit under Maryland Antiquities Act, 25 March 1979. Donald G. Shomette Collection, Dunkirk, Maryland. Photocopy.

Application for Permit under Maryland Antiquities Act, 27 March 1980. Donald G. Shomette Collection, Dunkirk, Maryland. Photocopy.

Anne Arundel County Judgements, 1720–1721. Maryland Hall of Records, Annapolis, Maryland.

Archaeological Research Survey, H-p4.3, History Files. Calvert Marine Museum, Solomons, Maryland.

Archaeology Research—Phase I, H-p4.1, History Files. Calvert Marine Museum, Solomons, Maryland.

Bugeye, H-b5, History Files. Calvert Marine Museum, Solomons, Maryland.

Calvert Marine Museum Mission Statement. Calvert Marine Museum, Solomons, Maryland.

Captains Letters to Secretary of the Navy, 1814, RG45, M124, R64. National Archives and Record Service, Washington, D.C.

Clark, Wayne E. National Register of Historical Places Inventory—Nomination Form. The Nottingham Archaeological Site, August 1974. Donald G. Shomette Collection, Dunkirk, Maryland. Photocopy.

Clark, Wayne E. Suggestions for a Research and Management Plan for the Submerged Terrestrial Sites of Maryland, 1979. Donald G. Shomette Collection, Dunkirk, Maryland. Photocopy.

Defense of Baltimore Papers. Maryland Historical Society, Baltimore, Maryland.

Dewey Drydock, H-d2, History Files. Calvert Marine Museum, Solomons, Maryland.

Drum Point Lighthouse, H-L2, History Files. Calvert Marine Museum, Solomons, Maryland.

Eshelmen, Ralph E., and Donald G. Shomette. A Proposal for the Survey of the Submerged Archaeological Resource Base of the Patuxent River, Maryland, Phase I, 1 June 1979–30 September 1979. Maryland Historical Trust, Crownsville, Maryland.

Eshelman, Ralph E., and Donald G. Shomette. A Proposed Survey of the Submerged Archaeological Resource Base of the Patuxent River, Maryland, 1979. Donald G. Shomette Collection, Dunkirk, Maryland.

Field Notes, 16 June 1984. The Mackall's Cove Wreck. Donald G. Shomette Collection, Dunkirk, Maryland.

Bibliography

Ghost Fleet, H-g1, History Files. Calvert Marine Museum, Solomons, Maryland.

Henry G. Granofsky Customs Collection, MS 2231, Box 6, Wreck Report Log. Maryland Historical Society, Baltimore.

Hyde Papers, 1765–1813, MS 1324. Maryland Historical Society, Baltimore.

James Beatty Papers. Records of the Fourth Auditor of the United States, Judicial and Fiscal. National Archives and Record Service, Washington, D.C.

James Madison Papers. Series I, vol. 52, no. 73. Library of Congress, Washington, D.C.

Joshua Barney Papers, Dreer Collection. Pennsylvania Historical Society, Philadelphia.

Lower Marlboro, H-LS, History Files. Calvert Marine Museum, Solomons, Maryland.

Maryland Geological Survey, Division of Archaeology. Mission and Jurisdiction. Donald G. Shomette Collection, Dunkirk, Maryland. Photocopy.

Miscellaneous Letters Received by Secretary of the Navy, 1813, RG45, M124, R11. National Archives and Record Service, Washington, D.C.

Miscellaneous Letters Received by Secretary of the Navy, 1813, RG45, M124, R29. National Archives and Record Service, Washington, D.C.

Miscellaneous Letters Received by Secretary of the Navy, 1813, RG45, M124, R59. National Archives and Record Service, Washington, D.C.

Miscellaneous Letters Received by Secretary of the Navy, 1813, RG45, M124, R63. National Archives and Record Service, Washington, D.C.

Miscellaneous Letters Received by Secretary of the Navy, 1813, RG45, M124, R64. National Archives and Record Service, Washington, D.C.

Nautical Archaeological Associates. Charter. Donald G. Shomette Collection, Dunkirk, Maryland.

Nautical Archaeological Associates. "Plan for the Construction of a Temporary Archaeological Coffer, Deplacement and Replacement of Bottom Sediments in Patuxent River, Anne Arundel County, Md." In Proposal to Dredge, Fill, Remove or Otherwise Alter Wetlands Notifications and/or Application. Submitted to Water Resources Administration 27 March 1980. Donald G. Shomette Collection, Dunkirk, Maryland. Photocopy.

Payroll Records of the Chesapeake Flotilla. Navy and Old Army Branch, National Archives and Record Service, Washington, D.C.

Port of Philadelphia Maritime Record. Vol. 3, 1882–84, section 6, Records of Wrecks, Philadelphia District, Pennsylvania Historical Society. Library of Congress, Washington, D.C. Typed transcript.

Prince George's County Court Records. Prince George's County Courthouse, Upper Marlboro, Maryland.

Prince George's County Deeds. Prince George's County Courthouse, Upper Marlboro, Maryland.

Prince George's County Land Records. Prince George's County Courthouse, Upper Marlboro, Maryland.

Prince George's County Patents. Prince George's County Courthouse, Upper Marlboro, Maryland.

Prince George's County Rent Rolls. Prince George's County Courthouse, Upper Marlboro, Maryland.

Regulations Governing Navigation in the Patuxent River at Point Patience and Sandy Point, Maryland, 9 April 1943. U.S. Navy—Mine Test, H-n2, History Files. Calvert Marine Museum, Solomons, Maryland.

Richard Harrison & Company Ledger, 1774. Library of Congress, Washington, D.C.

Secretary of the Navy Letters to Officers, Ships of War, RG45, M149, R11. National Archives and Record Service, Washington, D.C.

Bibliography

Shipwrecks, H-s11, History Files. Calvert Marine Museum, Solomons, Maryland.

Shomette, Donald G. Suggestions for the Development of a Comprehensive Approach to the Underwater Archaeological Master Plan for Maryland: Preliminary Overview, 1979. Archaeology Research Survey, H-p4-p4.3, History Files. Calvert Marine Museum, Solomons, Maryland.

Published Documents

American State Papers. Documents, Legislative and Executive, of the Congress of the United States. 38 vols. Washington: Gales & Seaton, 1832–61.

Annual Report of the Operations of the United States Life-Saving Service for the Fiscal Year Ending June 30, 1895. Washington, D.C.: Government Printing Office, 1896.

Archives of Maryland. Baltimore: Maryland Historical Society, 1883–present.

Auchinleck, G[ilbert]. *A History of the War between Great Britain and the United States of America during the Years 1812, 1813 and 1814.* Toronto, London, and Redwood City, Calif.: Arms and Armor Press and Pendragon House, 1972.

Beitzell, Edwin W. *St. Mary's County, Maryland, in the American Revolution Calendar of Events.* Leonardtown, Md.: St. Mary's County Bicentennial Commission, 1975.

Bell, Annie Walker Burns, comp. *Maryland Inventories and Accounts.* Annapolis, Md., 1938.

Beverly, Robert. *The history and present state of Virginia.* 3 vols. Edited by Louis B. Wright. 1705. Reprint. Chapel Hill, N.C.: Institution of Early American History and Culture, 1947.

Burnaby, Andrew. *Travels through the Middle Settlements in North-America in the years 1759 and 1760 with observations upon the state of the Colonies.* 2nd. ed. Reprint. Ithaca, N.Y.: Cornell University Press, 1976.

Calendar of Maryland State Papers. 1943. Reprint. Baltimore: Genealogical Publications Company, 1967.

Clark, William Bell, and W. J. Morgan, eds. *Naval Documents of the American Revolution.* 9 vols. Washington, D.C., 1964–present.

Donnan, Elizabeth, ed. *Documents Illustrative of the History of the Slave Trade in America.* 4 vols. New York: Octagon Press, 1965.

Dudley, William S., ed. *The Naval War of 1812: A Documentary History.* 2 vols. Washington, D.C.: Naval Historical Center, Department of the Navy, 1985–92.

Eddis, William. *Letters from America.* Edited by Aubrey C. Land. Cambridge: Belknap Press and Harvard University Press, 1967.

Emmerson, John C., Jr. *The Chesapeake Affair of 1807.* Portsmouth, Va.: privately printed, 1954.

[Gleig, George Robert]. *A Narrative of the Campaigns of the British Army, at Washington, Baltimore, and New Orleans, under the Generals Ross, Packingham, & Lambert, in the Years 1814 and 1815 With Some Account of the Countries Visited.* Philadelphia: M. Carey & Sons, 1821.

Hall, Clayton C., ed. *Narratives of Early Maryland, 1633–1684.* New York: Barnes & Noble, 1910.

Harriot, Thomas. *A briefe and true report of the new found land of Virginia.* 1588. Reprint. New York: Dover Publications, 1972.

"Itinerant Observations in America, 1745–1746." *Collections of the Georgia Historical Society.* Vol. 4 (1878).

Jefferson Patterson Park and Museum: Final Master Plan. Annapolis, Md.: Maryland Historical Trust, 1984.

340

Bibliography

Log of HMS *Albion*. Cockburn Papers. Library of Congress, Washington, D.C.

Log of HMS *Dragon*. *Chronicles of St. Mary's*. Vol. 13, no. 8 (August 1965).

Log of HMS *Jaseur*. *Chronicles of St. Mary's*. Vol. 8, no. 12 (December 1960), and vol. 10, no. 2 (February 1962).

Log of HMS *Loire*. *Chronicles of St. Mary's*. Vol. 8, no. 10 (October 1960), and vol. 8, no. 12 (December 1960).

Log of HM Schooner *St. Lawrence*. *Chronicles of St. Mary's*. Vol. 11, no. 12 (December 1963), and vol. 13, no. 4 (April 1965).

Log of HMS *Tonnant*. *Chronicles of St. Mary's*. Vol. 14, no. 8 (August 1966).

Maryland Rent Rolls: Baltimore and Anne Arundel Counties, 1700–1707, 1705–1724. Baltimore: Genealogical Publications Co., 1976.

Merchant Vessels of the United States. Washington, D.C.: Government Printing Office, 1866–present.

"Minutes of the Board of Patuxent Associators." *Maryland Historical Magazine*. Vol. 6 (1911).

Ogilby, John. *America: Being the Latest, and Most Accurate Description of the New World*. London, 1671.

Patterson Points. Vol. 6, no. 3 (1991), and vol. 7, no. 3 (1992).

Percy, George. *Observations Gathered out of "A Discourse on the Plantations of the Southern Colony in Virginia by the English, 1606."* Edited by David B. Quinn. Jamestown Documents. Charlottesville: University of Virginia Press, 1967.

"A Personal Narrative of Events by Sea and Land from the Year 1800 to 1815 Concluding with a Narrative of Some of the Principal Events in the Chesapeake and South Carolina, in 1814 and 1815." *Chronicles of St. Mary's* 8, no. 1 (January 1960).

Quinn, Edward Beers, ed. *The Roanoke Voyages 1584–1590. Documents to Illustrate the English Voyages to North America under the Patent Granted to Walter Raleigh in 1584*. 2 vols. New York: Dover Publications, 1991.

Shore Erosion in Tidewater Maryland. Bulletin no. 6. Baltimore: Maryland Department of Geology, Mines and Water Resources, 1949.

Smith, John. *The Generall Historie of Virginia, New England, and the Summer Isles*. London: Printed by I. D. and I. H. for Michael Sparkes, 1624.

U.S. Army. *Annual Report of the Chief of Engineers for the Fiscal Year Ending June 30, 1888*. Washington, D.C.: Government Printing Office, 1889.

———. *Annual Report of the Chief of Engineers for the Fiscal Year Ending June 30, 1890*. Washington, D.C.: Government Printing Office, 1891.

———. *Annual Report of the Chief of Engineers for the Fiscal Year Ending June 30, 1900*. Washington, D.C.: Government Printing Office, 1901.

———. *Annual Report of the Chief of Engineers for the Fiscal Year Ending June 30, 1902*. Washington, D.C.: Government Printing Office, 1903.

———. *Annual Report of the Chief of Engineers for the Fiscal Year Ending June 30, 1905*. Washington, D.C.: Government Printing Office, 1906.

U.S. Congress. House. 60th Congress, 1st session (1911). *House Document 531*.

U.S. Department of Commerce, Bureau of the Census. *Historical Statistics of the United States, Colonial Times to 1857: A Statistical Abstract Supplement*. Washington, D.C.: Government Printing Office, 1971.

War of the Rebellion: Official Records of the Union and Confederate Armies. 128 vols. Washington, D.C.: Government Printing Office, 1880–1901.

Yates, C. C. *Survey of Oyster Bars: Calvert County, Maryland*. Washington, D.C.: Government Printing Office, 1910.

Bibliography

Papers, Theses, Dissertations, Reports, and Studies

Arnold, J. Barto. "An Airborne Magnetometer Survey for Shipwrecks and Associated Test Excavations." Paper presented at the Tenth Conference on Underwater Archaeology, Nashville, Tennessee, 2–5 January 1979.

Artemel, Janice, Andrea Heintzelman, and Margaret Orelup. "Back Street Waterfront, New London, Connecticut." Report from Deleuw Cather/Parsons to U.S. Department of Transportation, May 1984.

Breiner, Sheldon. "Marine Magnetic Search." *Geometric Technical Report no. 7,* May 1975.

Durel, John W. "From Strawberry Banke to Puddle Dock: The Evolution of a Neighborhood, 1630–1850." Ph.D. dissertation, University of New Hampshire, 1984.

Governor's Patuxent River Watershed Advisory Committee. "The Patuxent: Maryland's Asset, Maryland's Responsibility." Baltimore, July 1968.

Heintzelman, Andrea J. "Southern New England Colonial Wharf Construction." Paper presented at the Third Annual Symposium for Southern New England Maritime History, Mystic, Connecticut, 5 November 1983.

————."Late Seventeenth and Eighteenth Century Wharf Technology: Historical and Archaeological Investigation of Three Eastern U.S. Examples." Master's thesis, American University, 1985.

Maryland National Capital Park and Planning Commission. *Preliminary Master Plan for the Patuxent Scenic River.* June 1986.

Neyland, Robert. "The Lyons Creek Boat Remains." Unpublished study, 1989. Lyons Creek, H-p3.1, History Files, Calvert Marine Museum, Solomons, Maryland.

"Report on the Patuxent River Basin, Maryland." Johns Hopkins University Water Management Seminar. Johns Hopkins University, Baltimore, 1966.

Shomette, Donald G. "A Sub-surface Radar Exploration of Lake Phelps, North Carolina." Report prepared for the North Carolina Division of Archives and History, Raleigh, North Carolina, 1993.

Shomette, Donald G., and Ralph E. Eshelman. *The Patuxent River Submerged Cultural Resources Survey, Drum Point to Queen Anne's Bridge, Maryland: Reconnaissance, Phase I, and Phase II.* 2 vols. The Maryland Historical Trust Manuscript Series no. 13. Annapolis, Md.: Maryland Historical Trust, 1981.

Snell, Charles W. "Central Wharf." In *Historic Structures Report: Historical Data.* Denver: U.S. Department of the Interior, Denver Service Center, July 1947.

————. "Derby Wharf and Warehouses." In *Historic Structures Report: Historical Data.* Denver: U.S. Department of the Interior, Denver Service Center, July 1947.

"Symposium: Patuxent River Submerged Cultural Resources Survey." In *Underwater Archaeology: The Challenge Before Us.* Gordon P. Watts, Jr., ed. Fathom Eight Special Publication no. 2.

Wilkie, Steve, and Gail Thompson. *Prehistoric Archaeological Resources in the Maryland Coastal Zone: A Management Overview.* Maryland Department of Natural Resources, 1977.

Letters

Tyler Bastian to Donald Shomette (23 May 1983). Donald G. Shomette Collection, Dunkirk, Maryland.

Genevieve Frazier Cockey to Ralph E. Eshelman (September 1979). Archaeology Research, Phase 1, H-p4.1, History Files. Calvert Marine Museum, Solomons, Maryland.

Bibliography

Mrs. Sudler Cockey to Ralph Eshelman (20 January 1979). Lower Marlboro, H-LS, History Files. Calvert Marine Museum, Solomons, Maryland.

Juin A. Crosse to Ralph Eshelman (26 June 1981). Donald G. Shomette Collection, Dunkirk, Maryland. Photocopy.

Mrs. Homer O. Elseroad to Emory Kristof (8 February 1987). National Geographic Society, Washington, D.C.

Mrs. Homer O. Elseroad to Donald G. Shomette (16 April 1987). Donald G. Shomette Collection, Dunkirk, Maryland.

Ivor Noël Hume to Ralph E. Eshelman (15 November 1985). Patuxent River—Lyons Creek, H-p3.1, History Files. Calvert Marine Museum, Solomons, Maryland.

Craddock A. Goins, Jr., to Carey A. Litz (5 January 1977). Donald G. Shomette Collection, Dunkirk, Maryland. Photocopy.

Clement Hollyday to Urban Hollyday (12 July 1814). Library of Congress, Washington, D.C.

Paula Johnson to Wayne E. Clark (28 June 1984). Archaeology Research Survey, H-p4, History Files. Calvert Marine Museum, Solomons, Maryland.

Robert S. Neyland to Ralph E. Eshelman (10 June 1989). Lyons Creek, H-p3.1, History Files. Calvert Marine Museum, Solomons, Maryland.

William T. Tearman to Ralph E. Eshelman (29 October 1979). Donald G. Shomette Collection, Dunkirk, Maryland. Photocopy.

Periodicals

American & Commercial Daily Advertiser (Baltimore, Maryland)
Annapolitan (Annapolis, Maryland)
Bugeye Times (Solomons, Maryland)
Calvert Independent (Prince Frederick, Maryland)
Daily National Intelligencer (Washington, D.C.)
Maryland Gazette (Annapolis, Maryland)
Maryland Historical Magazine (Baltimore, Maryland)
Maryland Waltonian
Niles' Weekly Register (Baltimore, Maryland)
Norfolk & Portsmouth Herald (Norfolk, Virginia)
The Planter's Advocate (Upper Marlboro, Maryland)
Prince Frederick Recorder (Prince Frederick, Maryland)
The St. Mary's Beacon (Leonardtown, Maryland)
The Skipjack
The Sun (Baltimore, Maryland)
The Sunday Sun Magazine (Baltimore, Maryland)
The Evening Star (Washington, D.C.)
The Washington Post (Washington, D.C.)

Books and Articles

Aitken, M. J. and M. S. Tite. "Proton Magnetometer Survey of Some British Hill Forts." *Archaeology* 5.

Andrews, Charles M. *The Colonial Period of American History*. 2 vols. New Haven: Yale University Press, 1934.

Barney, Mary, ed. *A Biographical Memoir of the Late Joshua Barney from Autobiographical Notes and Journals in Possession of His Family, and Other Authentic Sources*. Boston: Gray and Bowen, 1832.

Bibliography

Bass, George F., ed. *Ships and Shipwrecks of the Americas: A History Based on Underwater Archaeology.* London: Thames and Hudson, 1988.

Beitzell, Edwin W. "A Short History of St. Clements Island." *Chronicles of St. Mary's* 6, no. 11 (November 1958).

———. *Point Lookout Prison Camp for Confederates.* Abell, Md.: privately printed, 1972.

Bennion, Elizabeth. *Antique Medical Instruments.* Berkeley, Calif.: Southeby Parke Bernet, University of California Press, 1979.

Bird, Harrison. *Navies in the Mountains.* New York: Oxford University Press, 1962.

Bradford, James C. *Anne Arundel County. A Bicentennial History 1649–1977.* Annapolis, Md.: Anne Arundel County and Annapolis Bicentennial Committee, 1977.

Brewington, M. V. *Chesapeake Bay Log Canoes and Bugeyes.* Cambridge, Md.: Tidewater Publishers, 1963.

Brown, Alexander Crosby. *Steam Packets on the Chesapeake: A History of the Old Bay Line Since 1840.* Cambridge, Md.: Tidewater Publishers, 1961.

Brysson, Cunningham. *A Treatise on the Principles and Practice of Harbour Engineering.* London: Charles Griffin & Company, 1918.

Burgess, Robert H. *Chesapeake Circle.* Cambridge, Md.: Tidewater Publishers, 1967.

Burgess, Robert H., and H. Graham Wood. *Steamboats out of Baltimore.* Cambridge, Md.: Tidewater Publishers, 1968.

"The Burning of the *Peggy Stewart.*" *Maryland Historical Magazine* 5, no. 3 (September 1910).

Carr, Lois. "The Metropolis of Maryland: A Comment on Town Development along the Tobacco Coast." *Maryland Historical Magazine* 69, no. 2 (Summer 1974).

Chapelle, Howard I. *The History of the American Sailing Navy: The Ships and Their Development.* New York: W. W. Norton and Company, 1949.

———. *American Small Sailing Craft: Their Design, Development and Construction.* New York: W. W. Norton and Company, 1951.

Coggeshall, George. *History of American Privateers.* New York: privately printed, 1856.

Cole, Merle T. *The Patuxent "Ghost Fleet," 1927–1941.* Solomons, Md.: Calvert Marine Museum Press, 1986.

Conant, Melvin A. *I Remember: Recollections of "Pepper" Langley Growing Up in Solomons.* Solomons, Md.: privately printed, 1990.

de Camp, L. Sprague. *The Ancient Engineers.* New York: Ballantine Books, 1987.

Eardley, A. J. *Structural Geology of North America.* New York: Harper and Row, 1962.

Earle, Carville. *The Evolution of a Tidewater Settlement System: All Hallows Parish, Maryland 1650–1783.* Chicago: University of Chicago Department of Geography, 1975.

El-Biz, Farouk. "Finding a Pharaoh's Funeral Bark." *National Geographic Magazine* 153, no. 4 (April 1988).

Elliott, Richard V. *Last of the Steamboats: The Saga of the Wilson Line.* Cambridge, Md.: Tidewater Publishers, 1970.

Emmons, George F. *The Navy of the United States from the Commencement, 1775 to 1853.* Washington, D.C.: Gideon and Company, 1853.

Emory, Frederic. *Queen Anne's County, Maryland: Its Early History and Development.* Published for the Queen Anne's County Historical Society. Queenstown, Md.: Queen Anne Press, 1981.

Eshelman, Ralph, and Clara M. Dixon. *Historical Tours through Southern Maryland: Solomons by Foot, Bicycle or Boat.* La Plata, Md.: Southern Maryland Today, 1983.

Bibliography

Eshelman, Ralph, and Donald G. Shomette. "On a Possible Seventeenth Century Small Craft Wreck, Lyons Creek, Calvert County, Maryland." In *Underwater Archaeology: Proceedings from the Society for Historical Archaeology Conference, Savannah, Georgia.* Edited by Alan B. Albright. 1987.

Evans, Philip M. "We Need Local Heroes." *Annapolitan.* March 1988.

Fenwick, Charles E. "Part of De La Brooke Manor." *Chronicles of St. Mary's* 1, no. 6 (July 1951).

Fleetwood, Rusty. *Tidecraft: An Introductory Look at the Boats of Lower South Carolina, Georgia, and Northeastern Florida: 1650–1950.* Savannah: Coastal Heritage Society, 1982.

Footner, Hulbert. *Sailor of Fortune: The Life and Adventures of Commodore Barney, U.S.N.* New York and London: Harper & Brothers, 1940.

Forman, H. Chandlee. *Old Buildings, Gardens and Furniture in Tidewater Maryland.* Cambridge, Md.: Tidewater Publishers, 1967.

Greene, Carlton. *Wharves and Piers: Their Design, Construction, and Equipment.* New York: McGraw Hill, 1917.

Greenhill, Basil. *Archaeology of the Boat.* Middleton, Conn.: Wesleyan University Press, 1976.

Hale, Nathaniel C. *The Virginia Venturer: A Historical Biography of William Claiborne, 1600–1677.* Richmond, Va.: Dietz Press, 1953.

Hammett, Regina Combs. *History of St. Mary's County, Maryland.* Ridge, Md.: privately printed, 1977.

Heinton, Louise Joiner. *Prince George's Heritage: Sidelights on the Early History of Prince George's County, Maryland, from 1696 to 1800.* Baltimore: Maryland Historical Society, 1972.

Hill, Norman Alan, ed. *Chesapeake Cruise.* Baltimore: George W. King Co., 1944.

Hollingshead, Kenneth R. "Archaeology Beneath the Chesapeake." *NOAA Magazine,* Summer 1981.

Holly, David C. *Tidewater by Steamboat: A Saga of the Chesapeake.* Baltimore: Johns Hopkins University Press, published in association with the Calvert Marine Museum, 1991.

Hopkins, Fred W., Jr. *Tom Boyle: Master Privateer.* Cambridge, Md.: Tidewater Publishers, 1976.

Hume, Ivor Noël. *Artifacts of Colonial America.* New York: Alfred A. Knopf, 1972.

Johnson, Paula. *Historical Tours through Southern Maryland: Broome's Island.* Solomons, Md.: Calvert Marine Museum Press, 1983.

————, ed. *Working the Water: The Commercial Fisheries of Maryland's Patuxent River.* Charlottesville: Published for the Calvert Marine Museum by the University Press of Virginia, 1988.

Lawrence, Dawson. "Historical Sketch of Prince George County, Md." *Atlas of Fifteen Miles Around Washington Including the County of Prince George, Maryland.* Philadelphia: compiled, drawn and published by G. M. Hopkins, 1878.

Leone, Mark P. "Land and Water, Urban Life, and Boats: Underwater Reconnaissance in the Patuxent River on Chesapeake Bay." In *Shipwreck Anthropology.* Edited by Richard A. Gould. Albuquerque: University of New Mexico Press, 1983.

Lewis, Clifford M., and Albert J. Loomie. *The Spanish Jesuit Mission in Virginia, 1570–1572.* Chapel Hill: University of North Carolina Press, 1953.

Lord, Walter. *The Dawn's Early Light.* New York: W. W. Norton and Company, 1972.

Marine, William M. *The British Invasion of Maryland, 1812–1815.* 1913. Reprint. Hatboro, Pa.: Tradition Press, 1965.

Bibliography

Middleton, Arthur Pierce. *Tobacco Coast: A Maritime History of Chesapeake Bay in the Colonial Era.* Newport News, Va.: Mariners Museum, 1953.

Miller, M.I. *Commodore Joshua Barney: The Hero of the Battle of Bladensburg. Incidents of His Life Gleaned from Contemporary Sources.* Reprint from the *Records of the Columbia Historical Society,* Washington, D.C., 1911.

Muller, John. *A Treatise of Artillery.* London: printed for John Millan, 1780.

Munsey, John. *Collecting Bottles.* New York: Hawthorn Books, 1970.

Navy, U.S. Department of. Naval History Division. *Civil War Naval Chronology 1861–1865.* Washington, D.C.: Government Printing Office, 1971.

Pack, James. *The man who burned the White House: Admiral Sir George Cockburn, 1772–1853.* Annapolis, Md.: Naval Institute Press, 1987.

Papenfuse, Edward C. *In Pursuit of Profit: The Annapolis Merchants in the Era of the American Revolution, 1763–1805.* Baltimore: Johns Hopkins University Press, 1975.

Reeve, Merilyn. "Patuxent: More Waste Than Water." *Maryland Waltonian* 4, no. 12 (September 1979).

Reps, John W. *Tidewater Towns: City Planning in Colonial Virginia and Maryland.* Williamsburg, Va.: Colonial Williamsburg Foundation, 1972.

Scharf, John Thomas. *History of Maryland.* 3 vols. 1879. Reprint. Hatboro, Pa.: Tradition Press, 1967.

Schmidt, John C. "Skin Divers May Have Found the Remains of Joshua Barney's Ships." *The Sunday Sun Magazine,* 19 October 1958.

Shomette, Donald G. *Londontown: A Brief History.* Londontown, Md.: London Town Publick House Commission, 1978.

———. "The Turtle Shell Wreck: A Narrative of the Discovery and Excavation of an Early 19th Century Warship in the Patuxent River." *Calvert Country* 9, no. 3 (July 1980).

———. *Flotilla: Battle for the Patuxent.* Solomons, Md.: Calvert Marine Museum Press, 1981.

———. "The Much Vaunted Flotilla." *Journal of Maryland Archaeology* 17, no. 2 (September 1981).

———. "The Patuxent River Shipwreck Inventory." In *In the Realms of Gold: The Proceedings of the Eleventh Annual Conference on Underwater Archaeology.* Edited by Wilburn A. Cockrell. Fathom Eight Special Publication no. 1, 1981.

———. *The Othello Affair: The Pursuit of French Pirates on Patuxent River, Maryland, August 1807.* Solomons, Md.: Calvert Marine Museum Press, 1985.

———. *Pirates on the Chesapeake.* Centreville, Md.: Tidewater Publishers, 1985.

Shomette, Donald G., and Ralph E. Eshelman. "A Developmental Model for Survey and Inventory of Submerged Archaeological Resources in a Riverine System." In *Underwater Archaeology: The Challenge Before Us. The Proceedings of the Twelfth Conference on Underwater Archaeology.* Edited by Gordon Watts. Fathom Eight Special Publication no. 2, 1987.

Shomette, Donald G., and Fred W. Hopkins, Jr. "The Search for the Chesapeake Flotilla." *The American Neptune: A Quarterly Journal of Maritime History* 43, no. 1 (January 1983).

Stearns, Richard E. *Proceedings of the Natural History Society of Maryland No. 9: Some Indian Village Sites of Tidewater Maryland.* (July 1943).

———. "An Indian Site Survey of the Patuxent River, Maryland." *Natural History Society of Maryland Proceedings.* Vol. 21 (1957).

Stein, Charles Francis. *A History of Calvert County Maryland.* Baltimore: privately printed, 1960.

Bibliography

Stevenson, Thomas. *The Design and Construction of Harbours: A Treatise on Maritime Engineering.* Edinburgh, Scotland: Adam and Charles Black, 1876.

The Swampoodle Book: A Walk through History—Lower Marlboro, Then and Now. Lower Marlboro, Md.: funded by the Maryland Humanities Council through a grant from the National Endowment for the Humanities, 1983.

Tatham, William. *Essay on the Culture of Tobacco.* London, 1800.

Throckmorton, Peter, ed. *The Sea Remembers: Shipwrecks and Archaeology.* New York: Weidenfeld & Nicholson, 1987.

Toomey, Daniel Carroll. *The Civil War in Maryland.* Baltimore: Toomey Press, 1988.

U.S. Department of the Navy. *Dictionary of American Naval Fighting Ships.* 8 vols. Washington, D.C.: Government Printing Office, 1959–81.

Walsh, Richard, and William Lloyd Fox. *Maryland: A History 1632–1974.* Baltimore: Maryland Historical Society, 1974.

Weller, M. I. *Commodore Joshua Barney: The Hero of the Battle of Bladensburg. Incidents of His Life Gleaned from Contemporary Sources.* Reprint from the *Records of the Columbia Historical Society.* Vol. 14. Washington, D.C.: 1911.

Whitehead, D. R. "Palynology and Pleistocene and Phytogeography of Unglaciated Eastern North America." In *Quarternary of the United States.* Edited by H. E. Wright, Jr., and D. G. Frey. Princeton, N.J.: Princeton University Press, 1965.

———. "Late Wisconsin Vegetation Changes in Unglaciated Eastern North America." *Quarternary Research* 3 (1973).

Maps and Atlases

Herrman, Augustin. *Virginia and Maryland As it is Planted and Inhabited this present Year 1670 Surveyed and Exactly Drawne by the Only Labour & Endeavour of Augustin Herrman.* London: W. Faithorne, Sculpt. 1673. Library of Congress, Washington, D.C.

Smith, John. *Virginia.* 1608 [1612]. John Work Garrett Library, Johns Hopkins University.

Personal Communications

John Broadwater, Yorktown, Virginia.

Edward Brown, Jr., Mount Calvert, Maryland.

James H. Buys, St. Leonard's, Maryland.

Eric Christensen, Calvert County, Maryland.

Richard Dolesh, Baden, Maryland.

Dr. Ralph E. Eshelman, Lusby, Maryland.

James Gebauer, Calvert County, Maryland.

David Holly, Heritage Harbour, Annapolis, Maryland.

Leroy "Pepper" Langley, Solomons, Maryland.

Carey A. Litz, Calvert County, Maryland.

Edgar Merkle, Washington, D.C.

Dr. Henry Miller, St. Mary's City, Maryland.

Joseph Richards, Baden, Maryland.

Allan A. Sollers, Norfolk, Virginia.

Donald Stewart, Baltimore, Maryland.

Joseph Windsor, Nottingham, Maryland.

Index

Index

George Weems at, 104; as commercial partner with Patuxent region, 105; steamboat departures from, 111; merchants back Western Shore Steamboat Company, 112; Patuxent fish sold at, 115; southern Maryland in urban orbit of, 118; wharves studied, 267; Chesapeake Flotilla exhibit visits, 285; *Scorpion* refitted at, 288; mentioned, 45, 75, 102, 108, 113, 148, 158, 160, 253, 286, 290

Baltimore, Chesapeake and Atlantic Railway Company, 112

Baltimore and Virginia Steamboat Company, 112

Baltimore Harbor, 272

Barbados, 33, 34

Barnes, Col. Richard, 45, 49

Barney, Com. Joshua, fame as privateersman, 52; career, 56; denied Navy commission, 56; plan for defense of Chesapeake Bay, 56, 58, 287; appointed commander of Chesapeake Flotilla, 60; begins development of flotilla force, 60, 62–63; begins recruitment campaign, 63; learns of enemy barge construction program at Tangier Island, 63; arrives at Drum Point, Md., 64; engages British in Battle of Cedar Point, 64–66; retreats into Patuxent River, 66; retires into St. Leonard's Creek, 67; in First Battle of St. Leonard's Creek, 68–71; comments on Congreve rockets, 68; Barrie's strategy against, 72–73; holds low opinion of local militia and U.S. Army, 74; dispute with Carberry, 74; blamed for bringing war to southern Maryland, 74; skeptical of hauling flotilla overland, 75; ordered to destroy flotilla, 76; reinforcements sent to, 76; holds council of war, 76; critical of battery positions, 77; engages in Second Battle of St. Leonard's Creek, 77–81; escapes from St. Leonard's Creek, 80; abandons gunboats, 82, 143; retreats to Benedict, 82; attends conference in Washington, 83; orders flotilla to defense of Benedict, 83; fails at interdiction effort, 87; orders Major William Barney to sound the Patuxent, 88, 180; comments on Jones plan for retreat to South River, 88; learns of arrival of invasion fleet, 89; ordered to destroy flotilla and join defense of Washington, 90; retires from Nottingham, 90; heroic stand at Battle of Bladensburg, 92; paroled by British, 92; convalescence at Elk Ridge, 92; congressional criticism of, 94; secures compensation for his men, 94; salvages materials from flotilla wrecks, 94, 253; death of, 94; considered builder of the Lookout Creek mounds, 166; installs washboard collars on flotilla, 241, 289; convalescence while at Nottingham,

248; comments on lack of shot furnaces, 258; purchases padlocks for use of fleet, 260; discussion on gunboat designs by, 287; requests hospital ship for service, 289; resurrected as a hero, 291; mentioned, 10, 95, 133, 136, 143, 146, 150, 157, 186, 204, 217, 240, 247, 264, 265, 295

Barney, Maj. William B., saves burning barge in St. Leonard's Creek, 68; carries messages during First Battle of St. Leonard's Creek, 70; sounds the Patuxent River, 88, 180; mentioned, 182

Barney's Barges, records of destruction located, 131; oral traditions regarding, 155; early search for remains at Nottingham, 158; Iron Pot Wreck believed to belong to, 178; location of conjectured, 179–80; location reported by U.S. Army Engineers, 181

Barrie, Capt. Robert, blockades Potomac River, 64; conducts reconnaissance of St. Jerome's Creek, 64–65; directs British at Battle of Cedar Point, 65; plunders plantations along Patuxent, 66; reinforcements sent to, 67; transfers flag to HMS *Loire*, 67, leads attack into St. Leonard's Creek, 67; reliance on Congreve rockets, 68; establishes blockade of St. Leonard's Creek, 69; interdicts reinforcements bound for Barney, 69; retreat from St. Leonard's Creek, 70–71; lands Royal Marines, 71; adopts new strategy against Barney, 72–73; begins raiding on Patuxent River, 73; reinforced by HMS *Narcissus*, 73; conducts raids on Benedict and Lower Marlboro, 73; leaves Patuxent blockade to confer with Cockburn, 76; leaves command of Patuxent to Captain Brown, 77

Barron, Com. James, designs gunboats, 62, 287; mentioned, 146

Bass, Dr. George, on importance of water craft, 8; survey of Kyrenia Wreck, 294

Battle, Sussex, Eng., 23

Battle Creek, Md., Indian village at, 19; origins of name, 23; Calverton erected at, 25, 148; British destruction of town at, 87, 148; Union arsenal erected at, 97; Confederate spy activities at, 98; housing development planned for, 118; archaeological reconnaissance of, 148; wreck of *James E. Trott* near, 148

Battle of Bladensburg, 91–92

Battle of Cedar Point, 64–66

Battle of Craney Island, 54

Battle of Hastings, 23

Battle of St. Leonard's Creek, First, 67–73, 141; Second, 77–81; exhibit on anniversary of, 285; mentioned, 136

Battle of the Barges, see Battle of St. Leonard's Creek

Battle of the Severn, 24

Index

Beall, Maj. Ninian, forms Association of Protestant Gentlemen, 29

Beatty, James, records regarding supplies purchased for Flotilla, 245–46, 248, 253–55, 258–60

Belize, 130

Bellwood, 45–46

Benedict, Md., founded, 31; plundered by Joseph Whaland, 49, 148; Barrie's raids on, 73; rumored destruction of, 74; skirmish at, 75; arrival of flotilla at, 82; Wadsworth's troops march from, 84; reports of additional British attacks upon, 84; recommended as best place to launch invasion of America, 90, 148; Nourse lands near, 87; British invasion launched from, 58, 104; burning of Washington noted at, 92; Camp Stanton established at, 97, 148; Union raid on Virginia launched from, 97, 148; Army Engineers study silting at, 105; steamer landing at, 111; impact of end of steamboat era upon, 113; ferry service at, 114; archaeological reconnaissance near, 147; as possible site of Wasmacus, 148; destruction of steamboat *St. Mary's* near, 149–50; barges employed in bridge construction found, 150; mentioned, 106

Benedict-Leonard Town, Md., see Benedict, Md.

Bennett, G. Gordon, 141

Bennett, Richard, leads Puritan emigration to Maryland, 22; effects upon Patuxent settlements, 23

Berkeley, Gov. William, 23

Bermuda, 53

Berry, William, 25

Besche, Joseph E., 159, 160

Binford, Dr. Lewis, 255

Bishop, Henry, 19

Bishops Head, Md., 175

Black Colonial Corps, formation of, 64; employed in raid on Benedict, 73

Black Swamp Creek, Md., 118

Blackistone Island, Md., 54, 64

Bladensburg, Md., siphons commerce from Patuxent region, 36; Camp Union established at, 96; see also Battle of Bladensburg

Board of Patuxent Associators, 48, 150, 157, 168

Bohaska, David, 284

Booth, John Wilkes, 98

Bordeaux, Fr., 89

Boston, Mass., 41, 50

Boston Iron and Metal Company, 192

Bourne's Island, Md., 99

Bowie, Md., 118

Bowie, Gov. Robert, 157

Bowles, James, 34

Bowlington, Md., created by 1683 legislation, 26; failure of, 30

Boyle, Capt. Thomas, 52

Braine, Mast. John C., 98

Brand, John, 33

Breeden, George L., 134

Breeden, Laura, 134

Breeden, Capt. William E., 133, 134

Brewhouse, 267

Brewington, Marion V., 100, 293

Bridgeport, Conn., 192

Bright, Leslie, contracted for conservation work on Patuxent Project, 283; institutes artifact recording system, 284–85

Briscoe, Betty, 171

Bristol, Eng., 226

Bristol Bar, Patuxent River, Md., 105, 106

Bristol, Md., trade, 105; as terminus for Weems Line, 105; dredging at deemed imperative, 106; Army Engineers comments on importance of, 106, 108; difficulty for steamboat navigation at, 108–9; commerce discussed, 108; decline of, 109–11; impact of siltation upon, 110; end of port activity, 110–11, 272; Chesapeake flattie service, 175; wharf design at, 274; mentioned, 179

British Army, defeated at Yorktown, 48; landing at Benedict, Md., 89; departure from Benedict, 90; occupation of Nottingham, Md., 90, 158; at Battle of Bladensburg, 92

Brome, John, 147

Brome's Manor, 148

Bromley, Bartholomew, 180

Brooke Place Manor, 25

Brooke, Mary Baker, 23

Brooke, Robert, appointed Commander of Charles County, 22; leads council to rule Maryland, 23; builds Calverton, 25

Brooke, Thomas, 157

Brooklyn Navy Yard, N.Y., 100

Broome's Island, Md., reduction of river depth at, 124; archaeological reconnaissance of, 147; history of, 147–48; wrecks reported at, 148; failure to locate wrecks at, 149

Brown, Capt. Thomas, arrives on Patuxent, 67, commands squadron at St. Leonard's Creek, 77; at Second Battle of St. Leonard's Creek, 77; surprised by Barney's naval assault, 78; justifies British retreat from St. Leonard's, 79; observes the escape of the Chesapeake Flotilla, 80; reports on vessels remaining in St. Leonard's Creek, 83

Brown's Ferry Wreck, 229

Bryantown, Md., 98

Bull, Capt., 45

Burnaby, Andrew, 27

Butler, 134

Burton, John, 214, 261

Caldwell's Washington Riflemen, 75

Califf, Lt., 197

350

Index

California, 139

Calvert, Benedict, comments on Maryland's reliance on tobacco, 27

Calvert, Charles, moves to Mattapany, 24; orders seaports established, 24–25; comments on slow development of towns in Maryland, 26

Calvert, Leonard, permits Jesuits to settle among Indians, 19; takes control of Mattapany, 20

Calvert, Philip, 177

Calvert Cliffs Nuclear Power Plant, 284

Calvert County, Md., joined to St. Mary's County by Thomas Johnson Memorial Bridge, 15; established, 22; name changed to Patuxent County, 23; first towns described by Ogilby, 25; Coxtown established in, 26; partitioned into Prince George's and Calvert Counties, 30; county seat moved from Calverton to Prince Frederick, 37; British attacks on in 1780, 45; militia considered useless by Barney, 74; Nourse conducts raids against, 84–87; sympathetic towards Confederacy, 96; occupied by Union Army, 96–97; turns to oystering and fishing after Civil War, 99; patent tongs employed in, 101; statistics on oystering in, 102; *James Aubry* becomes county school boat, 114; Adams Ferry to St. Mary's County opened, 114; berry pickers from work Eastern Shore strawberry fields, 115; sport fishing in, 116; provides labor force for Patuxent Naval Air Test Center, 118; Maryland Derelict Boat Removal Program in, 147; Lower Marlboro becomes most prominent colonial port in, 155; Illingsworth Fortune in, 229; mentioned 29, 33, 40, 43, 47, 49, 68, 69, 75, 121, 152, 226, 286, 290

Calvert Manor, 177

Calvert Marine Museum, acquires Drum point Lighthouse, 203, 120; Eshelman takes charge of, 120; supports Patuxent River archaeological survey, 130; acquires *Henrietta Bach* collection, 134; houses *St. Mary's* artifacts, 149; artifacts from Magruder's Landing donated to, 153; Indian artifacts from Coxtown Creek donated to, 155; joint application with NAA for first underwater archaeology survey permit, 187; importance of Patuxent River survey to, 206; Lyons Creek cannonballs acquired by, 220; photo of St. Leonard's Wharf donated to, 276; donates Lore Oyster House for use as conservation facility, 283; recruits volunteers to assist in conservation program, 283; jointly sponsors War of 1812 exhibit with NAA, 285; learns of Schoolhouse Cove Wreck, 291; mentioned, 171, 191, 298

Calverton, Md., founded, 25; noted by Ogilby, 25; recognized in 1683 and 1688 bills, 26;

county seat moved from, 37; destroyed by British, 87

Cambridge, Md., 133

Camp Stanton, Md., 97

Camp Union, Md., 96

Campbell, Thomas, 169

Cannon Wreck, 162, 206

Carberry, Col. Henry, disputes with Barney, 74; at St. Leonard's Creek, 76, 77; troops flee battlefield, 79

Carberry, Fr. Joseph, 82

Carberry, Capt. Thomas, 82

Carcaud, David, 169

Caribbean Sea, 205

Carolinas, 175, 291; see also North Carolina and South Carolina

Cashner's Wharf, Md., 111

Catholics, first settlement of in Maryland, 19; seize Preston Plantation and Great Seal of Maryland, 24; seek peace along Patuxent River, 24; as religious minority in Maryland, 29; defense of Mattapany, 29; mentioned, 225, 229

Cecil County Historical Society, 155

Cedar Point, Md., merchant ship driven ashore at, 45; British landing at, 46; schooner captured at, 47, battle of, 64–66; mentioned, 15

Central America, 130

Cesarea, 2

Chalk Point, Md., 118

Chapelle, Howard I., documents Chesapeake flattie sloop, 174–75; states *Scorpion* was a block sloop, 288; mentioned, 289

Charles Branch, Md., 177

Charles County, Md., Calvert County established as, 22; sympathetic to Confederacy, 96; occupied by Union Army, 96; turns to oystering and fishing after Civil War, 99; mentioned, 32, 49, 121

Charles Reeder and Sons, 104

Charles Town, Md., founded, 31; county government moved from, 37; as county seat of Prince George's County, 177; development and decline of, 177

Charlotte Hall, Md., 97

Cheney, Lt., 97

Chesapeake Bay, archaeological resources of, 1–11; growth of during Holocene Epoch, 4; EPA study of, 4; impact of sea level rise and siltation upon, 4; importance of the boat in exploration of, 8–9; first European settlement on, 18; oysters from described, 18; meaning of name, 19; obstacles to navigation in, 27; British attentions focus on in 1780, 44–45; merchant fleet attempts to run blockade of, 45; raids continue on after Battle of Yorktown, 48; French aid sought for defense of, 49; French squadron blockaded

351

Index

Chesapeake Bay *(continued)*
in, 50; *Chesapeake-Leopard* Affair, 50; British blockade of in 1813, 52; devoid of defenses, 55; British strength in, 56, 58; first use of Congreve rocket on, 65; exposure to attack, 75; British invasion fleet arrives on, 84; first steamer activities on, 95; birth of oyster industry on, 99; impact of patent tongs on oystering in, 101; landings on siphon trade from Patuxent, 110; Baltimore and Virginia Steamboat Company operations on, 112; Chesapeake flattie service on, 175; first effort to video-document underwater archaeological site in, 207; similarities of St. Leonard's Wharf site to others in, 267; overland transport dooms steamboat operations on, 276; adoption of log canoe by settlers, 292; mentioned, 8, 15, 16, 17, 18, 20, 25, 30, 36, 48, 65, 67, 75, 89, 102, 103, 135, 143, 175, 181, 189, 190, 230, 241, 286, 299

Chesapeake Bay bugeye, earliest, 100; development at Solomons Island, Md., 100–101; yearly production at Solomons Island, 104; mentioned, 22, 116

Chesapeake Bay log canoe, natives' manner of construction, 22; wreck of found in Sawpit Cove, 142–43; discovery of a wreck in School House Cove, 292; adoption of use in Maryland and Virginia colonies, 292; development and regional variations of, 292; design and construction of, 292–93

Chesapeake Beach Railroad, 108

Chesapeake Biological Laboratory, 15, 113, 284

Chesapeake Flattie Wreck, discovery of, 173; description, 173–75; service and short life of, 175; interpretation of type, 175

Chesapeake-Leopard Affair, 50

Chester, Pa., 249

Chester River, Md., steamboat route sold, 112

Civil War, survey of prisoner of war camp at Point Lookout, 10; impact upon Patuxent River steamboat traffic, 96; in southern Maryland, 96–98; effects upon Patuxent River Valley, 98; wharves of period studied, 267; mentioned, 99, 104, 148, 153, 174, 295

Clagetts Landing, Md., 110

Claiborne, William, 19

Claiborne Project, 10

Clark, Wayne E., research on Nottingham sites, 161; as director of Jefferson Patterson Archaeological Park and Museum, 296

Cliffs of Calvert, Herrington Town to be erected upon, 25; tobacco from shipped, 36; British forces lay off during War of 1812, 47

Cochrane, Adm. Sir Alexander, seeks advice on best place to invade America, 84; approves of Benedict as invasion site, 89

Cockburn, Adm. Sir George, institutes blockade of Chesapeake, 53; attributes outrages at Hampton to Chasseurs Brittaniques, 54; Cochrane seeks advice on invasion, 84; recommends Benedict as invasion point, 84, 89; suggests plan of attack, 84; raids on Potomac, 84; vows to dine in Washington, 89; reports destruction of Chesapeake Flotilla, 91, 182; at Bladensburg, 92; report of flotilla loss missing from PRO, 131, discovery of personal papers at Library of Congress, 131; importance of reports to excavation of shipwreck site, 240; mentioned, 183

Cockley, Genevieve Frazer, 155

Cole's Farm, 97

Cole's Landing, Md., raided by British, 73

Collins, George, 168

Colonial Beach, Va., 114

Colonial Williamsburg, Va., 224

Colorado, 207

Confederate Army, guerrilla attacks of on Chesapeake Bay and Patuxent River, 98; mentioned, 96

Confederacy, 96, 97

Congreve, Sir William, 66

Congreve Rocket, 65, 68

Connecticut, 50

Constitution, 50

Contee, Alexander, 168

Continental Army, 267

Continental Congress, 44, 267

Continental Navy, 56

Coode, Capt. John, forms Association of Protestant Gentlemen, 29; captures Mattapany, 29

Coolidge, Capt. Judson, 35

Copley, Sir Lionel, 30

Cosby, Maj. Spenser, recommends dredging at Bristol, Md., 110–11; reports on presence of Chesapeake Flotilla hulks in Patuxent, 181, 182

Coster, Md., 115

Cousteau, Jacques, 9

Cove Point, Md., 111

Coxtown, Md.; founded, 26; survival of, 30, 31; redesignated in Act of 1706, 31; see also Lower Marlboro

Coxtown Creek, Md., 155

Crisfield, Md., 115

Cromwell, Oliver, 23, 28

Cuckhold's Creek, Md., 115

Cyprus, 294

Dare's Beach, Md., 111

Darnall, Henry, 29

David, Cmdr. John, 47

Davidson, Thomas, 33

de Camp, L. Sprague, 295

Index

Index

Index

Head of Elk, Md., 48

Hellen Creek, Md., 124, 141

Henderson, Capt. Perry G., 114–15

Heritage, Conservation, and Recreation Service, 191, 205

Hermann, Augustine, 28, 309

Herring Bay, Md., 96, 179

Herrington, Md., noted by Ogilby, 25

Hiersemann, Karl, 131

Higgenson, Gilbert, 36

Hills Bridge, Md., 182, 184, 200, 272, 300, 301

Hills Landing, Md., closed to steamers by siltation, 105; Army Engineers study of, 105; flattie service to, 175; reports of Chesapeake Flotilla wrecks lying near, 181, 182 18th-century anchor discovered at, 181; oral traditions of flotilla wrecks at, 182; discovery of steamboat wharf remains, 184; river above chartered, 184; magnetometer testing off of, 201; ground penetrating radar survey begins at, 300; mentioned, 110

Hills Marsh, Md., 155

Hollan, Joseph, 159

Holland Bar, Patuxent River, 111

Holland Point, Md., 111

Holland Point Bar, Patuxent River, 276

Hollands Cliffs, Md., 111, 150

Hollingshead, Kenneth, background of, 130; conducts underwater archaeology field school, 147; participates in archaeological reconnaissance at Nottingham, 162; excavation of Lyons Creek Wreck spoil pile, 171; in Selby-Spyglass remote sensing survey, 200; dives on Turtle Shell Wreck, 202–3; restores pontoons for operations platform, 208; conducts excavation of Lyons Creek Wreck, 218–19; at St. Leonard's Wharf Survey, 266

Hollowing Point, Md., see Hallowing Point, Md.

Holocene Epoch, 3, 4, 123

Holton, Thomas, 115

Hooper's Straits, Md., 64

Hope, George, designs gunboats, 63; builds Scorpion, 288

Hopewell, Md., 115

Hopkins, Dr. Fred W., Jr., as principal researcher for NAA, 130–31; findings on Nottingham wreck, 160; repudiates claims by Stewart, 160; discovers critical Jones letter, 180; begins Selby-Spyglass remote sensing survey, 200; in van to relocate Turtle Shell Wreck, 210; work on Lyons Creek Wreck, 218; discovers Chesapeake Flotilla muster list, 248; identifies Dashaway, 298

Horse Landing, Md., 115

Howard, Gen. O. O., 96

Howard County, Md., 121

Hume, Ivor Nöel, comments on archaeological value of kaolin pipe finds, 224; analy-sis of Lyons Creek bottle fragments, 225; conclusions regarding Lyons Creek site, 231

Hunting Creek, Md., archaeological reconnaissance in, 147, 150; shipwrecks in, 149, 150

Hunting Creek Bay, Md., 149

Huntingtown, Md., founded, 31; destroyed by British, 87, 149

Hyde, Isaac, 36

Illingsworth Fortune, 229–30

Indian Creek, Md., 148

Indians, arrival in Tidewater, 4; hostages of Spaniards, 17; Patuxent tribes, 18; provide name for Chesapeake Bay, 19; Jesuit settlement among, 19; Susquehannock attack on southern Maryland, 20; manner of boat building described, 20–21; missionary voyages to, 22; maintains ferry at Hallowing Point, Md., 24; rumors concerning slaughter of settlers by, 29; archaeological evidence of on St. Leonard's Creek, 137, 139–41, 295; relics at Windmill Point, Md., 141; prehistoric shell middens at Hallowing Point, 148; prehistoric occupation site at Prison Point, Md., 149; at Magruders Landing, Md., 153; shell midden at Coxtown Creek, Md., 155; sites at Nottingham discovered, 160,61, 165, 166; Mattapament site nominated to National Register of Historic Places, 161; lithics found at Mount Calvert, 178; on upper Patuxent River, 179; log canoe adopted by white settlers, 292; log canoes in Lake Phelps, N.C., surveyed, 303; mentioned, 16

Institute of Nautical Archaeology, 294

Iron Pot Wreck, 178

Isaac Solomon Oyster Canning Company, 16, 101, 102

Island Creek, Md., 147

Israel, 2

J.C. Lore Oysterhouse, utilized as a conservation laboratory, 283; mentioned, 16

J.S. Farrar & Co., 102

J.T. Marsh Shipyard, 16

Jack's Bay, Md., 148, 149

Jackson, Richard, 41

Jamaica, 2

Jamestown, Va., 18

Japan, 2

Jefferson Patterson Archaeological Park and Museum, foundation and development of, 296

Jesuits, settle at Mattapany, 19; mission attacked by Susquehannocks, 20; missionary voyage of described, 22

John Evans & Company, 246, 286

Johns Creek, Md., 70

Johns Hopkins University, study on sedimentation in Patuxent River, 123

Index

Johnson, Lady Bird, 147
Johnson, Mary Baker, 267
Johnson, Paula, 298
Johnson, Capt. Peter, 267
Johnson, Peter, Jr., 267
Johnson, Thomas, I, 267
Johnson, Thomas, Jr., II, 267
Johnson, Gov. Thomas, III, informed of weakness of southern Maryland to British attack, 44; birth of, 267; first elected governor of Maryland, 267
Johnson's Fresh, 267
Jones, Sec. of Navy William, aware of military dangers to Chesapeake, 56; reviews Barney's "Defense of Chesapeake" plans, 60; orders Chesapeake Flotilla dismantled on St. Leonard's Creek, 75; orders flotilla destroyed, 76, 286; orders marines to St. Leonard's Creek, 76; suggests flotilla be hauled overland to escape, 88, 180; informed of enemy landing at Benedict, 89; orders destruction of flotilla to prevent capture, 90, 180
Jordan, Col., 47
Journal of Maryland Archaeology, 291
Jowles, Col. Henry, 29
Jug Bay, Md., 133, 208, 210

Karell Institute, 191
Kennedy, President John F., 116
Kentucky, 94
Kemp, Richard, 33
Kemp, Thomas, builds barges for Chesapeake Flotilla, 60
Kent County, Md., 101
Kent Island, Md., 11, 54, 112
Kents Landing, Md., 73
Keyser, Maj. George, 77, 79
Kierstad, Capt. James, 45
Kilkenny Town, Md., ferry established at, 32; overland route to sought, 36
King Charles I, 22
King Charles II, 28
King Cheops, 294, 300
King George I, 37
King Henry VIII, 2
King Herod, 2
King James II, 28
King's Creek, Md., 160
Kings Reach Site, 226
Knowles, James, 151
Koski-Karell, Daniel, contracted to conduct magnetometer survey on Patuxent River, 191; begins remote sensing equipment tests on *S-49* site, 193; survey work at Nottingham, 196; begins Selby-Spyglass remote sensing survey, 200; mentioned, 201
Krohn, Commodore Hiacinthe, 50
Kure Beach, N.C., 283

Kyrenia Wreck, 294

Lake Champlain, N.Y., 299, 300
Lake Phelps, N.C., 303
Lake Torpedo Boat Company, 192
Lambert, Capt., 34
Langley, Capt. Leon, 118
Langley, Leroy "Pepper", recollections of a submarine in Patuxent River, 191–92;
Langley, Capt. Rodie, 114
Languedoc, Colin Drury, contracted to assist remote sensing effort on Patuxent, 193; survey work at Nottingham, 196; examines the Mud Wreck, 197; begins remote sensing in Selby-Spyglass Transect, 200; discovers possible wreck site, 201
Laurel, Md., 118
Lazaretto, Baltimore, Md., 92
Lee, Gov. Thomas Sims, 45, 47
Leipzig, Ger., 131
Leitch Wharf, Md., 111
Leonardtown, Md., 44, 49
Lexington Green, Mass., 42
Library of Congress, 131, 168, 266
Light Street Wharf, Baltimore, Md., 148
Lincoln, President Abraham, 97, 98
Liverpool, Eng., 50
Loame, Capt. Giles, 34
Loame, William, 34
London, Eng., 24, 28, 34, 131, 246, 268
London Naval Limitation Treaty of 1922, 192
Londontown, Md., 34, 88
Long Island, N.Y., 100
Lookout Creek, Md., 160, 165, 168, 170
Lord Baltimore, Puritans swear allegiance to, 22; erects Calvert County, 22; Cromwell commission divests authority over colony from, 23; orders Governor Stone to recover authority of proprietary government, 23; dispute with Puritans resolved, 24; orders the erection of seaports in Maryland, 24; issues the Ordnance of 1669 to control exports, 25; frustrated by slow development of towns in colony, 26; establishes 31 towns in 1683, 26; issues Proclamation of 1684, 27; ordered to inform of new colonial government under William and Mary, 29; supporters surrender to Protestant forces, 29; first slaves during proprietorship of Maryland, 33; mentioned, 30, 177; see also Cecil Calvert and Charles Calvert
Lord Cornwallis, 10, 48
Lord Dunmore, 43
Louisiana, 119
Love Point Ferry, 112
Lower Marlborough (Marlboro), established as Coxtown, 26, 154; raided by loyalists during Revolution, 47, 155; Captain

Index

Barrie's raid on in 1814, 73, 155; warehouse burned at, 73; Union Army units march on, 97; post-Civil War trade of, 105; importance of to river commerce, 110; steamboat landing at, 111; impact of end of steamer service to, 113; oral traditions of War of 1812 at, 155; archaeological reconnaissance at, 155–56; comments on wharf at, 274; mentioned, 150
Lumly, Capt. John Richard, 73
Lyons Creek, Md., ferry at, 24, 309; becomes head of steam navigation on Patuxent, 111, 112; end of river navigation at, 123; guns discovered in river near, 152; discovery of wreck site in, 171; discovery of the Chesapeake Flattie Wreck near, 173; *Peter Cooper* bound for, 176; selected as a transect for underwater archaeological survey, 188; remote sensing survey in, 199–200; wreck site in becomes target for archaeological excavation, 206; artifacts and wreck parts recovered from analyzed, 220, 225, 227, 228; as possible site of colonial store, 229; European habitations on, 309; mentioned, 182, 212, 225, 229, 275
Lyons Creek Hundred, 26
Lyons Creek Wreck, discovery and location of, 171; first investigations of, 171; artifacts from, 172; cannonballs from transported to museum, 173; Phase II survey begins on, 218; description of site, 218; importance of site, 220, analysis of artifacts from, 220, 222–25; theory on origins of, 225; conjecture regarding hull design, 227; as earliest Euro-American small craft wreck in U.S., 228; paper published on, 230; artifact conservation, 284; questions posed by, 303; Neyland begins study of, 304; findings of the Neyland study, 304–7, 309, 310; shell-first construction of, 304; appearance described, 305–10; conclusions regarding, 309–10

M.M. Davis Shipyard, establishment of at Solomons, Md., 99; builds the *Manitou*, 116; mentioned, 16, 191
MacCord, Howard, 161
Mackall, Benjamin, 49
Mackall, Dr. Richard, 267
Mackall family, 87, 267
Mackall's Cliffs, archaeological reconnaissance of, 136–40
Mackall's Cove, Md., discovery of wreck in, 297–99; mentioned, 267
Mackall's Wharf, steamboat wharf remains discovered at, 141; proximity to ruins of St. Leonard's Wharf, 267; survey vessels arrive at, 268
Mackinac, Mich., 116
Macquacomen, 19
Madison, Pres. James, declares war on England, 51, 52; aware of dangers to Chesapeake

Tidewater, 56; British vow to defeat, 89
Madison, Wis., 228
Magruders Landing, Md., merchants join non-importation association, 41; Capt. Barrie conducts raids on, 73, 153; steamboat landing at, 111; shoreline accretion at, 118; archaeological reconnaissance of, 153–54; cannon recovered from, 153; mentioned, 155; see also Hannah Brown's Landing
Manhattan, N.Y., 228
Marble, Benjamin, 288
Marianas Trench, 1
Mariners' Museum, 160, 266
Marion, Md., 115
Marques, Sgt. Maj. Juan Menendez, 17
Marsh, Charles L., 101
Marsh, Dr. Henry, 113
Marsh, James T., 100, 101
Maryland, shoreline erosion in, 4; wetland loss in, 4–5, enclosed aqueous systems in, 5; importance of maritime culture to, 8; first underwater archaeological surveys in, 9–10; treasure hunts in, 11; first Catholic settlement in, 19; Mattapany becomes military center of, 19; Providence Town erected, 22; capitulates to agents of the Commonwealth government in England, 23; Great Seal seized, 24; end of Puritan rule in, 24; seaports erected in, 25; new town acts opposed by planters of, 25–26; economic reliance on tobacco, 28; Hermann's map of, 28; Catholics become minority in, 29; protests against William and Mary, 29; Copley becomes first royal governor, 30; new towns created by legislation, 31; General Assembly passes additional new town acts, 31; primitive industry takes root in, 31; importance of slavery in, 33–35; tobacco inspection law, 39–40; impact of Seven Years War upon, 40; protests tea tax, 41; Council of Safety, 43, 44, 45, 46, 48; State Navy, 47; privateers in War of 1812, 52; British invasion of begins, 89; steamboat *Eagle* arrives in, 95; negroes from join Union Army, 97; raids on Virginia launched from, 97; rise of oyster fishery in, 99; impact upon by end of steamboat service, 112–13; horse racing in, 157; Charles Town founded by government of, 177; government establishes Pig Point, 179; approves first permit to conduct underwater archaeology, 187; evolution of wharf design in, 266–72; first marine conservation facility established in, 283; adoption of log canoe in, 292; Patterson donates land to, 296; mentioned, 8, 9, 10, 15, 35, 40, 42, 43, 44, 58, 64, 98, 99, 102, 103, 116, 120, 133, 140, 148, 157, 159, 170, 200, 262, 266, 267, 268, 285, 292, 295, 309
Maryland Convention, 267

Index

Maryland, Delaware and Virginia Railroad Company, acquires Weems Line, 109; maintains Patuxent River run, 109; criticism of, 109; impossibility of maintaining service to Bristol, Md., 110; loss of *St. Mary's*, 111, 148–49; acquisition of *Three Rivers*, 111; dismantled by Pennsylvania Railroad, 112; mentioned, 16

Maryland Department of Natural Resources, 147

Maryland Derelict Removal Program, removes shipwrecks in St. Leonard's Creek, 133; destruction of possible historic shipwrecks by, 147; removes wrecks in St. John's Creek, 291; mentioned, 149

Maryland Dredging and Construction Company, 109

Maryland Gazette, covers maritime events, 33; on slavery, 35; documents slave ship arrivals, 41; on nonimportation support in Prince George's County, 41; Reed Farm tract advertised in, 169

Maryland Hall of Record, 168, 229

Maryland Historical Society, 266

Maryland Historical Trust, considers submerged cultural resources in archaeological master plan, 187; funding for Patuxent Project sought from, 188; administers HCRS grant for Patuxent Project, 191; publishes final report on Patuxent Project, 291; moves to secure Patterson estate for Maryland, 296; mentioned, 146, 178, 295, 296

Maryland State Navy, 47

Maryland Steel Company, 111, 113

Mattapament (Mattapanient), Md., 18, 161

Mattapanian Hundred, Md., 19, 157

Mattapany, Md., given to Jesuits by Macquacomen, 19; attacked by Susquehannocks, 19; as a military center for Maryland, 19; Charles Calvert establishes residence at, 24; defended against Protestant forces, 29, 229; mentioned, 25, 49

Mattapany Landing, Md., 157

Mattox Creek, Va., 54

Mayr, Thomas, 161

Mears Creek, Md., 141

Mediterranean Sea, 2, 10, 205, 294

Merkle, Edgar, 160, 165

Merkle Wildlife Refuge, 160

Metallurgical Division, Bethlehem Steel Corporation, 220

Mexico, 130

Mill Creek, Calvert County, Md., 115

Mill Creek, Anne Arundel County, Md., 201

Mills, Charles, Jr., 159

Miller, Capt. Samuel, erects artillery battery at St. Leonard's Creek, 76–77; opens fire on British blockaders, 78; movements of, 78–79;

court inquiry on, 82; forces join Washington defense force, 90; at Battle of Bladensburg, 92; mentioned, 136

Millstone Landing, Md., Confederate spy activities at, 98; steamboats at, 111; ferry service to Solomons Island from, 114

Millstone Point, Md., 20, 111

Milltown Landing, Md., 118

Mississippi River, 114

Moll, Etinien, 19

Mollenson, William, 36

Molly's Leg Island, Md., 15

Monocacy Valley, 36

Monroe, Sec. of State James, engages British at Nottingham, 90, 158

Montgomery County, Md., 121

Moore, Capt. Thomas, 102

Morgan, Thomas P., 106

Moundbuilders, 166

Monument Circle, Baltimore, 160

Mount Calvert, Md., upper limits of oysters in prehistoric times, 123; discovery of shipwreck near, 177–78; search for shipwreck undertaken, 178; review of prehistoric collections from, 178; native settlements near poorly documented, 179; as possible destination of Lyons Creek boat, 229; landing at, 230; ferry at, 309

Mount Pleasant Landing, Md., ferry at, 32, 180; as base for salvage of Chesapeake Flotilla, 181, 182; search for location of site undertaken, 184; discovery of site, 184; mentioned, 183

Mount Vernon, Va., 56

Muckleroy, Keith, 6

Mud Wreck, 196–97

Mudd, Dr. Samuel, 98

Murray, Henry M., 61

Murray, James, see Lord Dunmore

Nanticoke River, 175

Napoleon Bonaparte, 50, 89

Nashville, Tenn., 303

Nassau, Bahamas., 98

National Archives and Record Service, 131, 168, 169, 268

National Endowment for the Humanities, 188

National Oceanic and Atmospheric Administration, 130

National Park Service, 9, 224

National Register of Historic Places, 161

National Trust for Historic Preservation, 188

Nautical Archaeological Associates, Incorporated, plans first holistic underwater archaeological survey of an entire river system, 16; joins forces with Calvert Marine Museum,

Index

130; charter and organization of, 130; initial investigations of Lyons Creek Wreck, 171; applies for first underwater survey permit in Maryland, 187; builds operations platform for work on Patuxent River, 208; contracts with Bright for conservation work, 283; recruits volunteers, 283; donates equipment to conservation laboratory, 283; sponsors exhibit on War of 1812, 285; notified about Schoolhouse Cove Wreck, 291; mentioned, 147, 160, 207, 208

Naval Historical Center, 192
Naval Mine Warfare Proving Ground, 192
Naval Surface Weapons Test Center, 16, 133
Negroes, runaways, 33; consigned by Royal African Company, 34; carried off by Joseph Whaland, 49; U.S. Colored Troops establish Camp Stanton at Benedict, Md., 97; settlement for erected at Cole's Farm on Patuxent River, 97; support needs spur Union raids into Virginia, 97; join U.S. Army, 97
New England, 266
New Haven, Conn., 102
New Jersey, 95, 130
New London, Conn., 192
New Orleans, La., 280
New York, 47, 105, 116, 299
Newcastle Terminal Company, 112
Newport, R.I., 288
Newport News, Va., 9
Neyland, Robert, develops interest in Lyons Creek Wreck, 303; study objectives of, 304; resolves to reconstruct Lyons Creek Wreck, 304; conducts architectural study of wreck fragments, 304–10; speculates on rig of vessel, 307, 309; conclusions regarding Lyons Creek Wreck, 309–10
Nicholson, Governor Francis, 30
NOAA Magazine, 291
Norfolk, Va., siphons off Patuxent River commerce, 58; *Cybelle* dispatched to in 1807, 50; expedition against pirates outfitted at, 51; British fail to capture, 54; as a primary British military target in Chesapeake, 58; Chesapeake Flotilla to help lift the blockade of, 64; mentioned, 75, 95
North America, 228
North Carolina, 193, 277, 283, 292, 303; Division of Archives and History, 283, 303
North Devon, Eng., 226
Northam, Capt. W.E., 102
Northern Europe, 228
Nottingham, Md., founded, 31, 157; slave market at, 35; attracts merchants to, 35; Wallace, Davidson and Johnson open store at, 40; merchants join nonimportation association, 41; as naval base for Board of Patuxent Associators, 48, 157; rumored destruction

of, 74; British raiders penetrate to, 74–75; Chesapeake Flotilla moves up to, 83; word on attack on Benedict arrives at, 84; Chesapeake Flotilla abandons, 90; Monroe encounters British Army at, 90, 158; post-Civil War trade at, 105; as end of navigation for seagoing vessels, 123; steamboat landing at, 111–12; impact of end of steamboat age on, 113; history of, 157–58; horse racing at, 157; fails to compete with Baltimore and Norfolk, 158; decline of, 158; Harris searches for Chesapeake Flotilla remains at, 158; Besche-DiJulio team discovers shipwreck at, 159–60; wreck fragments recovered by salvors, 160; Hopkins's research debunks salvor's accounts, 160; tales of cannon recovery at refuted, 160; wreck site used as a rescue squad practice area, 160; military fortifications reported at, 160; Stearns discovers major prehistoric site at, 161; Clark declares site is Mattapament, 161; prehistoric site nominated to National Register of Historic Places, 161; underwater archaeological reconnaissance begins at, 162; NAA surveys Nottingham wreck, 162–63; NAA discovers prehistoric remains at, 165–66; discovery of earthen mounds and ditches at, 165–66; theories about origins of mounds, 166, 168; title and probate research begins, 168; origins of mounds determined, 168–70; diatomaceous earth processed at, 176; selected for remote sensing survey, 188; magnetometer survey at, 196–97; discovery of unknown wrecks at, 196; survey of Nottingham Cannon Wreck at, 196–97; survey of Sand Wreck, 197; survey of Mud Wreck, 197; Harris property at, 229; outbreak of flu while Chesapeake Flotilla stationed at, 248; mentioned, 26, 89, 106, 150, 169, 170, 175, 180, 206, 211, 251
Nottingham Cannon Wreck, history of, 158–60; NAA begins preliminary survey of, 162; description of, 163; remote sensing survey over, 196; hands-on survey of, 196–97; selected as subject for Phase II survey, 206
Nourse, Capt. Joseph, orders reconnaissance of St. Leonard's Creek, 82–83; continues Royal Navy depredations on Patuxent River, 84–85, 87; encourages slave emigration, 85; invades and destroys towns along the Patuxent River, 87; mistakes floating storm debris for Chesapeake Flotilla, 88; mentioned, 88
Nowill, Thomas, 245

Oceans Data Systems, Inc., 207, 277
Ogilby, John, 25
Onantuck, 148
O'Neal, William, 251, 287

359

Index

Opament, 137
de Ore, Fra Luis Geronimo, 17
Oswald, Adrian, 224
Our Lady Star of the Sea Catholic Church, 16
Oyster Wars, 102

Paca, Gov. William, 49
Padre Island, Tex., 193
Pantano Longarini Wreck, 294
Paris, Fr., 94
Parker, Annie Gross, 298
Parker's Creek, Md., 37
Parker's Wharf, Md., 111
Parliament, 23, 41
Parran, John, 45
Patapsco River, Md., 48, 92
Patent tongs, 101
Patterson, Mrs. Jefferson, 296
Patuxent County, Md., see Calvert County
Patuxent Creek, Md., 168; see also Lookout Creek
Patuxent Indians, give lands to Jesuits, 19; Claiborne trades with, 19
Patuxent Naval Air Station, see Patuxent Naval Air Test Center
Patuxent Naval Air Test Center, 19, 116, 117
Patuxent Naval District, 27, 34
Patuxent River, historic sites on, 14–15; European discovery of, 17, Indian villages on, 18; exploration of, 18; European settlement on, 19; early travel on, 20; watercraft used on, 21–22; Puritans settle on, 23–24; ferry establishments on, 24, 177; development of towns and ports on, 24–27, 31; limits of navigation on, 27; annual arrival of tobacco fleet, 28; plantations, 28; first notice of siltation in, 30; survival of towns on, 30; discovery of iron deposits along, 31; called "Snowden's River", 31; first bridge on, 31–32; dredging above Queen Anne Town, 32, 36; slave trade, 33–35; attracts merchants after War of Spanish Succession, 35; continuing sedimentation of, 36–37; diminishing importance of, 37; tobacco inspection stations on, 40; impact of European wars of empire on, 41; merchants boycott importation of English goods, 41; American Revolution on, 43–50; Othello Affair on, 50–51; War of 1812 battles on, 65–94; arrival of Chesapeake Flotilla on, 64; British begin blockade of, 66; Barrie's raids upon, 73; British spies on, 74; recommended as best route for British invasion of America, 84; Nourse's depredations upon, 84–85, 87; William Barney takes soundings of, 88; arrival of British invasion force on, 89; retreat of Chesapeake Flotilla on, 90; destruction of Chesapeake Flotilla on, 91; flotilla salvage efforts in, 94; effects

of War of 1812, 95; first steamboats on, 95; Civil War on, 96–98, Union control established on, 96–97; oyster fleet raided by Union troops, 97; contraband settlement on banks of, 99; Confederate spies on, 98; efforts to capture Booth on, 98; first fishery established on, 99; construction of bugeyes on, 100–101; development of patent tongs on, 101; the Isaac Solomon Oyster Canning Company, 101; during oyster wars, 102; lighthouse built at Drum Point, 103; U.S. Torepdo Squadron on, 103; oyster beds surveyed, 103–4; Weems Steamboat monopoly on, 104; steamboat commerce after Civil War, 104; Army Engineers study of, 105; dredging on, 105–6; impact of increased siltation upon commerce on, 109–12; last steamboat operations on, 112–13; Dewey Drydock tested on, 113; commercial and sport fishing on, 115–16; World War II naval establishment on, 116; damage to fisheries by weapons testing on, 116; revival of ferry service, 116, 118; impact of erosion upon, 118; urban development sweeps in 118–19; Governor Thomas Johnson Bridge opened, 118; becomes an open sewer, 118; end of ferry service, 119; Calvert Marine Museum studies river, 120; geological description of, 120–24; deforestation along, 123; navigation of, 123; sedimentation rates documented, 123–24; Hopkins begins study of history of Chesapeake Flotilla on, 131; research on river history begins, 131; submerged cultural resource survey of begins, 133; Mackall's Cliff inspection, 138–39; evidence of prehistoric occupation on, 141; archaeological explorations of by Stearns, 148; search for wreck of St. Mary's in fails, 149–50; historic handguns recovered near Archer Hays plantation, 152; survey of Magruder's Landing site in, 153–54; oral traditions of War of 1812 along, 155, 181–82; first shipwreck salvage at Nottingham in 1932, 158–59; adoption of Chesapeake Flattie for freight hauling in, 175; loss of Peter Cooper on, 175–77; Pig Point founded, 179; last ferry establishment at Mount Pleasant Landing, 180; Chesapeake Flotilla barges as landmarks on upper river, 181; search for Scotchman's Hole and Mount Pleasant Landing in, 184; bathymetric survey at Mount Pleasant Landing, 184; first underwater archaeology permit in Maryland issued for survey of, 187; data base on considered weak, 188; buried archaeological sites in, 188; S-49 sunk in, 191–95; magnetometer survey at Nottingham begins in, 196; hostile environment of, 205; location of Turtle Shell Wreck in, 210; as a military highway, 225, 229; loss of Richard

Index

and *Mary* in, 229; earliest shipwreck site in, 230; environmental hazards to navigation on, 270; influence of geography and environment on wharf design in, 273; Schoolhouse Cove Wreck in, 291; land on donated to State of Maryland, 296; use of ground penetrating radar suggested for testing in, 300; ground penetrating radar survey in, 300–303; mentioned, 15, 30, 48, 75, 78, 88, 92, 127. 134, 140, 159, 165, 166, 181, 184, 189, 191, 229, 230, 234, 248, 262, 268, 274, 276, 287, 290, 299, 303, 309

Patuxent River Bridge, 115

Patuxent River Flattie, see Chesapeake Flattie

Patuxent River Park, provides vessel support for Patuxent River Survey, 133; as base of operations for Patuxent Project, 200, 208; volunteers use of pontoons for operations platform, 208; press conference held at, 218; mentioned, 165, 176, 291

Patuxent River Submerged Cultural Resources Survey, project design set, 124–27, 130; 1978 survey team, 130; reconnaissance of St. Leonard's Creek, 133–47; reconnaissance at Fort Hill, 133; first investigation of *Henrietta Bach*, 133–35; reconnaissance at Mackall's Cliffs, 136–39; oral traditions of War of 1812 relics in St. Leonard's Creek, 137–38; reconnaissance at Sollers Wharf, 140–41; first investigation at Mackall's Wharf, 141; discovery of the Sawpit Cove Wreck, 142; search for gunboats *Nos. 137* and *138*, 143–46; discovery of gun battery site, 143; discovery of Gunboat Wreck, 144–45; visit to White Sands Marina, 147; reconnaissance from Broome's Island to Benedict, 147–50; shell middens noted at Prison Point, 149; search for *St. Mary's*, 149–50; failure at Potts Point, 150; the handgun discoveries near Archer Hays, 152–53; reconnaissance at Magruder's Landing, 153–54; reconnaissance at Lower Marlboro, 154–56; investigation of Nottingham Cannon Wreck, 162–63; discovery of prehistoric sites at Nottingham, 165; discovery of the Lookout Creek mounds, 165–66; reconnaissance into Lyons Creek, 171–73; survey of the Flattie Wreck, 173–75; survey of the *Peter Cooper*, 175–77; reconnaissance at Mount Calvert and the Western Branch, 177–78; reconnaissance from Hills Landing to Mount Pleasant Landing, 181–84; Phase I permit approved by Maryland, 187; weakness of data base, 187; funding sources sought for, 188; 1979 project design, 188; remote sensing technologies considered, 188–91; Interior Department HCRS grant for approved, 191; remote sensing testing on *S-49*, 193, 195;

magnetometer survey of St. Leonard's Creek, 195; survey of Nottingham Cannon Wreck, 196–97; discovery of the Sand Wreck, 197; discovery of the Mud Wreck, 197; magnetometer survey of Lyons Creek, 199–200; magnetometer survey of Selby-Spyglass Transect, 200–204; Phase II project design, 205; funding for 1980 season approved, 205; problems over site selection, 206–7; methodology of excavation, 207; objectives of video documentation, 207–8; operations platform acquired, 208; Phase II survey begins, 210; extent of Turtle Shell Wreck site determined, 210–11; temporary cofferdam constructed, 212; main cofferdam constructed, 215; excavation of Turtle Shell Wreck begins, 217; Lyons Creek Wreck surveyed, 218–19; artifacts recovered from Lyons Creek site, 220; analysis of Lyons Creek site, 220, 222–31; storm damage to operations platform, 233–34; findings at the Turtle Shell Wreck site, 235–36, 238, 240–48, 251, 253–55, 258–65; St. Leonard's Wharf survey, 266–70; preliminary findings at wharf site, 266–68; wharf site description, 269; video documentation of Turtle Shell Wreck, 277, 279–81; termination of Turtle Shell Wreck excavation, 281; problems of conservation, 281–83; conservation project proceeds at Lore Oyster House, 283–85; final report on published, 291; importance of findings at St. Leonard's Creek, 295; mentioned, 10, 182, 230, 285, 296, 299, 310

Patuxent River Valley, out-migrations from, 36; commerce siphoned off by Baltimore and Bladensburg, 36; prosperity after American Revolution and subsequent decline, 50; as seat of combat in War of 1812, 51; Barrie's campaigns on influence future of, 73; effects of Civil War upon, 98; Stearns' archaeological surveys in, 155; mentioned, 158, 173

Patuxent Steam Express Company, 96

Pawtuxunt, 18, 148

Peabody Museum, 160

Peninsula Campaign, 89

Pennsylvania, 94

Pennsylvania Railroad, 109, 112

Perry, Capt. Oliver Hazard, 94

Persimmon Creek, Md., 115

Peter, Maj. George, 75

Peter's Georgetown Artillery, 75

Petrone, Claude "Pete", background, 299–300; pioneers ground penetrating radar in Lake Champlain Project, 300; conducts GPR survey of Turtle Shell Wreck, 300–303; conducts GPR survey at Lake Phelps, NC, 303

Philadelphia, Pa., 95, 99, 105, 175, 176, 293

Philippines, 113

Piankatank River, Va., 112

Index

Pig Point, Md., founded, 179; connected to Prince George's County by ferry, 179–80; importance to Chesapeake Flotilla navigation, 180; proximity to site of flotilla destruction, 90, 182; mentioned, 88, 91, 150
Pindell, Md., 110
Piney Point, Md., 116
Piscataway Indians, 18
Plater, Col. George, 49
Plum Point, Md., 111
Plummer's Plantation, 155
Point Lookout, Md., British landings at during Revolution, 44; raided during War of 1812, 54; British invasion fleet sighted from, 89; Civil War prisoner of war camp at, 97
Point Lookout Survey, 10
Point Patience, Md., ferry established at, 20; British attack upon, 45; Chesapeake Flotilla retreats to, 54; Somerville home destroyed at, 81; Navy Mine Test Station erected at, 116; Governor Thomas Johnson Memorial Bridge at, 118; depth of water at, 123; submarine sunk at 191–93; location of S-49 at, 195; mentioned, 15, 25, 99
Pooles Island, Md., 53
Popes Creek, Va., 97
Pope's Shoal, Patuxent River, 107
Poplar Island, Md., impact of sea level rise upon, 4; plundered by British, 53
Port Covington, Baltimore, 92
Port Royal, Jam., 2
Porter, Capt. David, 51, 92–93
Portsmouth, Eng., 2
Pory, John, 19
Potomac County, Md., see St. Mary's County
Potomac Flotilla, in War of 1812, 62, 253, 290; in Civil War, 98
Potomac River, Md., called Rio San Pedro by Spanish, 18; towns along established by legislation, 31; Lord Dunmore's raids on, 43; loyalist raids on, 49; Cockburn's raids upon in 1813, 54; Barney recommends obstructions sunk in, 58; Potomac Flotilla action on, 62–63; H.M.S. Dragon blockades, 64; Cockburn suggests diversionary attack upon, 84; invasion fleet arrives at, 89; Gordon's retreat upon harassed, 92–93; Confederate supplies sent across in Civil War, 96; Union naval patrols on, 97; watched to prevent Booth's escape, 98; steamboats employed on, 111, 112; mentioned, 44, 50, 65, 88, 89, 288
Potomac River Valley, out-migrations from, 36
Potts Point, Md., 149
Potts Point Wreck, 150
Poulten, Fr. Ferdinand, 19
Preston, Richard, 23, 24
Preston Plantation, 23, 24

Price, William, 62
Prince Frederick, Md., Calvert County seat moved to, 37; sacked by British, 87; Union Army sent to, 96
Prince George's County, Md., formed from Calvert County, 31; bridge construction on Patuxent, 32; empowered to make Patuxent navigable above Queen Anne's Town, 32; shares building cost of Queen Anne's Bridge, 32; county seat moved to Upper Marlboro, 37; merchants support nonimportation agreement, 41; occupied by Union Army, 96; connected to Pig Point by ferry, 179; mentioned, 121, 177, 181, 184
Prison Point, Md., 148, 149
Privateering, 52
Protestants, seek peace along Patuxent River, 24; become majority in Maryland, 29; forms association to support William and Mary, 29; captures St. Mary's City, 29; in Revolution of 1689, 29–30, 225, 229
Providence, Md., founded, 22; Governor Stone attempts capture of, 24; removal of Maryland capital to, 225
Public Record Office, 131, 268
Pugh, Larry, background of, 130; works on St. Leonard's Wharf survey, 266
Puritans, uprising of, 23; emigrations to Maryland, 23; removes links to Calvert administration, 23; victory at Battle of the Severn, 24; dispute with Baltimore resolved, 24; end of rule in Maryland, 24

Queen Anne's Town, Md., at head of Patuxent navigation, 27, 123; established, 31, 145; ferry established at 24, 32; bridge built at, 31; river made navigable above town, 32; attracts attention of merchants, 35; Hyde settles at, 36; the Great Road passes through, 36; river cleared for 25 miles above, 37; main street breached by flood, 37; Wallace, Davidson, and Johnson store at, 40; merchants support nonimportation association, 41; Chesapeake Flotilla to be hauled from, 88, 180, 287; flotilla ordered to, 90; flotilla fails to reach, 90, 181; Johns Hopkins University study of sedimentation at, 123; as terminal point of Patuxent River Submerged Cultural Resources Survey, 127; prehistoric sites near, 178; description of river channel at, 180; flotilla barges salvaged at, 289; mentioned, 150, 155, 179, 211
Queen Mary, 29
Queenstown, Md., 54–55
Quomacoc, 137

Rappahannock River, Va., 96, 111
Reed (Read), Richard, 168, 170

362

Index

Reed's Farm, 168, 169
Remote sensing, types considered for Patuxent River Survey, 188; side scan sonar, 188–89; sub-bottom profiler, 189; proton precession magnetometer, 189–90; magnetometer tow system, 190–91; survey of *S-49*, 193, 195; positioning controls for, 193; use of at Nottingham, 196–97, 199; alterations of methodology at Lyons Creek, 199; problems of in Selby-Spyglass survey, 200–201; ground penetrating radar survey of Turtle Shell Wreck, 299–303
Resurrection Hundred, Md., 22
Revolution of 1689, 29, 225, 229
Rhode Island, 288
Richards, Joe, 153
Robinson, Capt. Jonathan, 47
Rock Creek, Md., 118
Rodney Point, Md., 141
Rogers, Moses, 95
Ronson Ship, 227
Ross, Maj. Gen. Robert, commands British invasion army, 89; actions on the Patuxent at Benedict and Nottingham, 90; troops enter Upper Marlboro, 91; marches on Washington, 91; paroles Barney at Bladensburg, 92; considered as possible builder of Lookout Creek mounds, 166
Rousby Hall, 45
Royal African Company, 34
Royal Marines, conduct landings at First Battle of St. Leonard's Creek, 71; raids on Benedict, 73; at Second Battle of St. Leonard's Creek, 78; reconnaissance into St. Leonard's Creek, 83; aboard invasion fleet, 89
Royal Navy, strength at outset of War of 1812, 52; humiliated by Maryland privateers, 52; directed to blockade Chesapeake Bay, 52; raids on the Chesapeake, 53–54; strength in Chesapeake reported, 56, 58; gunners repel American attack at Benedict, 75; John Evans & Co. becomes surgical suppliers to, 246–47; mentioned, 136
Ruhl, Sarah "Sally", 207, 261
Russell, James, 168
Rutter, Lt. Solomon, commands *Vigilant*, 60; at First Battle of St. Leonard's Creek, 70; orders gunboats scuttled, 82; recovers naval gear and halts looting, 83; commands Chesapeake Flotilla at Baltimore, 83

St. Augustine, Fla., 17
St. Catherine's Island, Md., 54
St. Cuthbert's Wharf, 111, 274
St. George's Island, Md., Lord Dunmore's landings on, 43; loyalists attack on in 1783, 49; Cockburn's raids on, 54

St. Inigoes Manor, 82
St. Jerome's Creek, Md., merchant fleet driven ashore at, 45; Barrie conducts reconnaissance of, 64, 65
St. John's, Md., 30
St. John's Creek, Md., 291
St. Joseph's, Md., 30
St. Leonard's Creek, Md., first European settlement on, 19; St. Leonard's Town established on, 25–26; as slave ship anchorage, 34; tobacco grown along shipped to England, 36; Chesapeake Flotilla retreats into, 67; description of, 67; Barrie leads attack in First Battle of St. Leonard's Creek, 68; flotilla to be hauled overland from, 75; Wadsworth's plans to break blockade of, 76; 38th Infantry sent to defend, 76; Second Battle of St. Leonard's Creek begins, 77; Barney escapes from, 79, 286–87; gunboats scuttled in, 82, 143, 251, 287; Thomas Carberry retrieves artillery and wounded from, 82; Nourse orders reconnaissance of, 82–83; gunboats plundered in, 83, 143; steamboat landing on, 111; housing developments on, 118; archaeological reconnaissance begins in, 133; investigations at Fort Hill, 133; reported vessel sites investigated, 134; first examination of *Henrietta Bach* Wreck, 133–35; Breeden family on, 134; reconnaissance on Mackall's Cliff on, 136; Sollers Wharf surveyed, 140–41; discovery of Barney's battery site, 143; discovery of Gunboat Wreck in, 144–45; impact of Maryland Derelict Boat Removal Program on archaeological resources in, 147; Phase I transect selection of, 188; magnetometer survey begins in, 195; location of St. Leonard's Wharf, 166; geographic and environmental influences on wharf design in, 273; shell midden on, 295; archaeological sites in, 295; Patterson donates adjacent lands to Maryland, 296; mentioned, 141, 149, 155, 197, 206, 266
St. Leonard's Town, Md., founded, 25; officially recognized, 26; survival of, 30; redesignated by Act of 1706, 31; attracts attentions of merchants, 35; William Mollenson dominates regional trade from, 36; town moved by 1735 Act of Assembly, 36; Chesapeake Flotilla retreats to after First Battle of St. Leonard's Creek, 71; American base at stripped, 82; burned by British, 83, 143; archaeological reconnaissance to locate site of, 141; flotilla field hospital located at, 248, 290; site of first town discovered, 296; mentioned, 68, 70
St. Leonard's Wharf (Mackall's Wharf), steamboat service to, 111; remains of steamboat wharf discovered, 141; selected as target for

363

Index

Index

Smith, Col. Samuel, 46
Smith Point, Md., 44, 65
Smithsonian Institution, 151, 160, 174, 288
Smoleck, Michael, discovers War of 1812 battery site, 143; visits Mackall's Cliff sites, 296
Snowden, Richard, 35
Snowden's River, 31
Solent, Eng., 2
Sollers family, 267
Sollers Wharf, archaeological reconnaissance at, 140–41; employed by Weems Line, 274, 275; mentioned, 111, 142
Sollers and Dowell Oyster House, 141
Solomons, Isaac, establishes first major fishery on Patuxent River, 99; erects shipyard, 99; name adopted to island, 101; as owner of most of Solomons Island, 102
Solomons Island, Md., description of, 15–16, 101–102; German Lloyd Line "Ghost Fleet" at, 16, 113; shipyards at, 100, 104; bugeyes built at, 100–101, 104; named after Isaac Solomon, 101; cannery at, 101, 102; Farrar-Moore shipyard and fishery at, 102; U.S. Torpedo Flotilla at, 103; trade of, 105; steamboats service to, 111–12; U.S. Weather Bureau station at, 113; Dewey Drydock tested at, 113; Chesapeake Biological Laboratory at, 113; schoolboat service to, 113–14; ferry service, 114; as sport fishing center, 116; fisheries damaged by naval weapons testing in World War II, 116; modern town described, 119; Johns Hopkins University study of erosion rates at, 124; S-49 sinks near, 191–92, 193; end of steamboat service to, 276; mentioned, 102, 114, 116, 120, 133, 135, 282, 283
Somerset County, Md., 100
Somervell family, 99
Somervell's Island, Md., 99, see also Solomons Island
Somerville, Dr., 81
Sotterley Plantation, 69, 111, 115, 274
South Carolina, 229
South River, Md., Chesapeake Flotilla to be moved to, 88, 180, 287; mentioned, 28, 36
Southern Maryland, natives attacked by Susquehannocks, 20; threatened by Lord Dunmore, 43; fear of slave insurrection in, 64; opposition to War of 1812, 74; Union control of in Civil War, 97, 153; John Wilkes Booth escapes into, 98; enters urban orbit of Washington, Baltimore and Annapolis, 118; Drum point Lighthouse becomes unofficial symbol of, 120; described by first colonists, 123; Lower Marlboro as a commercial center of, 154; steamboats serving, 264; lack of archaeological conservation facilities in, 282; War of 1812 exhibit visits, 285; mentioned, 15, 48, 141, 270, 273

Sowell, Lt. Ingram S., 192
Spain, 89
Sparkman and Stephens Inc., 116
Sparrows Point, Md., 111, 113, 220
Spencer's Shipyard, 60
Spencers Wharf, Md., 111
Spesuite Island, Md., 53
Spout Farm, 141
Spyglass Island, Md., as terminus for Phase I survey tract in Patuxent Project, 188, 200; remote sensing work off, 201; mentioned, 180, 184, 186, 210
Stamp Act, 41
Stand & Cole Ltd., 259–60
Steamship Historical Society, 266
Stearns, Richard E., reports on prehistoric sites on Patuxent, 148, 155, 161; mentioned, 165
Steffy, Prof. Richard, 293, 303
Stein, Charles Francis, 20
Steward, Lt. John, 43
Stewart, Anthony, involvement in slave trade, 34–35; ship *Good Intent* turned back at Annapolis, 41; ship *Peggy Stewart* burned, 41–42
Stewart, Donald S., 160
Stockholm, Swed., 94
Stone, Gov. William, 23, 24
Straits of Tsushima, 2
Stringer, Thomas, 34
Stuart, Gen. George, 75
Stull's Georgetown Riflemen, 75
Submarine Division Zero, 192
Sun [Baltimore], comments on patent tongs, 101; provides account of first wreck salvage effort at Nottingham, 160;
Susquehanna River, 18, 53
Susquehannock Indians, 20
Sussex, Eng., 23
Swann, Thomas, 89
Swann's Point Bar, Patuxent River, 106
Swift, Capt. Ed, 114
Swift's Ferry Terminal, 16
Syckes, Gen. George, 96

Tangier Archipelago, 4
Tangier Island, Md.-Va., 63
Tangier Sound, Chesapeake Bay, 97
Taylor, Maj. Ignatius, 46
Taylor's Landing, Md., 40
Tearman, James, 151
Tennessee, 303
Texas, 193
Thames Street, Baltimore, 62
Thomas, James, 48
Thomas, Capt. John Allen, 43
Thomas, Col., 47
Thompson, A.C., 248, 290
Thompson, Thomas A., 149
Thompson, Lt., 97

365

Index

Index

sonal property of seamen found aboard, 259–60; proof that Turtle Shell Wreck belonged to, 263–65, 285–90; first underwater video of, 277–81; exhibit on, 285; vessel typology, 287–89; Turtle Shell Wreck as probable flagship of, 290; media reports discovery of, 291; mentioned, 95, 136, 150, 182, 183, 260
United States Coast and Geodetic Survey, 103
United States Coast Guard, 135
United States Congress, 94
United States Department of Agriculture, 168, 169
United States Department of the Interior, 191
United States District Court of Maryland, 112
United States Environmental Protection Agency, 4
United States Flotilla Service, 63
United States Government, selects Solomons for Dewey Drydock test, 113; contracts for gunboat construction, 288; mentioned, 153
United States Navy; strength at beginning of War of 1812, 52, 58; Barney denied commission in, 56; Barney recommends flotilla force separate from, 58; Department of, 60; Barney appointed commandant in, 60; employs Patuxent for U.S. Torepdo Flotilla speed tests, 103; establishes base on Patuxent in World War II, 116; Weems offers to salvage Chesapeake Flotilla for, 181; loans equipment for Patuxent Project, 184; records identify *S-49*, 192; purchases *Vigilant*, 288; mentioned, 162, 300; Diving and Salvage School, 193; Mine Test Station, 116, 191
United States Marines, to secure flanks of Chesapeake Flotilla at St. Leonard's Creek, 69; Miller's unit ordered to St. Leonard's, 76; ordered to defense of Washington, 90; makes stand at Battle of Bladensburg, 92; mentioned, 74
United States Supreme Court, 267
United States Weather Bureau, 113
University of Baltimore, 130, 147, 220
Upper Marlborough (Marlboro), Md., founded, 31, 177, 180; attracts attention of merchants, 35; county seat moved to, 37; merchants support nonimportation association, 41; disturbed by enemy raids on Patuxent in 1781, 47; menaced by British in 1814, 74; captured by British Army, 91; Union Army at, 96; post-Civil War trade, 105; turns to overland shipping, 110; weaned from dependence on steamboats, 113; urbanization swamps area, 118; competition with Charles Town, 177; mentioned, 15, 35, 150, 155, 180

Vail, Capt. Philip, 115
Van Ness, Maj. Gen. John P., 74
Versailles, Fra., 113

Vessels
USF *Adams* (frigate), 58
HMS *Aetna* (bomb ship), 87
HMS *Albion* (3rd rate man-of-war), joins Nourse squadron on Patuxent, 83; ship's log comment on destruction of Washington, 92
Alexander (slave galley), 34
Alexine (bugeye), 101
Anne Arundel (steamboat), 111
Antelope (privateer), 48
Aquarius (research vessel), 135
Ark (ship), arrival at St. Mary's, 19; first slaves at St. Mary's carried aboard, 33
HMS *Asia* (3rd rate man-of-war), brings news to Chesapeake of invasion army, 84
US Schooner *Asp* (schooner), joins Chesapeake Flotilla, 60; engagement on the Potomac, 60
B.S. Ford (steamboat), 112
Balloon (steamboat), 97
Barney's Barge (diving operations platform), constructed at Patuxent River Park, 210; anchored over the Turtle Shell Wreck, 211; description of, 232
Black Snake (row galley), 60
HMS *Brune* (5th rate man-of-war), 85
Calvert (steamboat), 112
Carrie (bugeye), 101
Catch-up (tender), 65
Cato (brig), 45, 46
Cecil (steamboat), 97
Chasseur (privateer schooner), 52, 60
USF *Chesapeake* (frigate), 50
Clytie (bugeye), 100
USS *Colorado* (battleship), 113
Commerce (steamboat), 104
USF *Constellation* (frigate), 55, 58
HMS *Contest* (gun brig), 63
Coral (bugeye), 100
Corsica (steamboat), 112
Cybelle (man-of-war), 50
Dashaway (schooner); discovery of wreck, 297; identity traced, 298–99
HMS *De Braak* (brig-sloop), 11
Dove (pinnace), landing at St. Mary's, 19; mentioned, 33
Dewey (floating drydock), 113
HMS *Dragon* (3rd rate man-of-war), establishes blockade of Potomac River, 64; at the Battle of Cedar Point, 64; cutter and barge from capture a schooner, 65; reinforced in blockade of Patuxent River, 67
Eagle (steamboat), 95, 96
Express (steamboat), 96
Federalist (miniature warship), 56
Felicity (privateer), 48
Fincastle (research boat), 193, 195
General Massena (pilot boat schooner), 50, 51
General Monk (ship), 56

Index

Index

news of reinforcements, 84; mentioned, 136
St. Mary's (schooner), 98
St. Mary's (steamboat), rebuilt from *Theodore Weems*, 109; history of, 148–49; search for remains fails, 149–50; important photo of donated to Calvert Marine Museum, 276; mentioned, 109, 111
San Lorenzo de Escoral (ship), 11
Santa Clara (ship), 11
Santa Rosalea (ship), 11
USS *Scorpion* (block sloop/gunboat), service on Potomac River, 63; assigned to Chesapeake Flotilla, 63; sails on flotilla shakedown cruise, 63; at Battle of Cedar Point, 65; sent to rear in Battle of St. Leonard's Creek, 69; to remain on station in the Patuxent, 83; retreats to Scotchman's Hole, 90; Cockburn's description of, 91; destruction of, 91; salvage attempts on, 94, 181, 289; wreck at Nottingham mistaken for, 160; inability to sail above Scotchman's Hole, 180, 182; importance of Cockburn's description of to excavation of Turtle Shell Wreck, 240; use as a hospital ship considered, 253; Fleming signs aboard, 253; dismantled at St. Leonard's Creek, 286; dimensions unknown, 287–88; as a candidate for Turtle Shell Wreck, 290; ground penetrating radar tested on wreck of, 300; mentioned, 89, 180, 183, 211, 264
Sea Horse, 33
HMS *Severn* (4th rate man-of-war), arrives on Patuxent River, 82; to prevent flotilla breakout from river, 83; tender capsizes on Patuxent, 99
USS *Severn* (ship), 103
Sneaky Seaweed (pram), supports magnetometer survey at Nottingham, 196; supports magnetometer survey in Lyons Creek, 218; employed in St. Leonard's Wharf survey, 268; mentioned, 133, 184
Surprise (steamboat), 95
Theodore Weems (steamboat), 104, 109, 148, 276
Three Rivers (steamboat), 111, 112
Titanic (ocean liner), 2, 300
HMS *Tonnant* (3rd rate man-of-war), 89, 92
Vaterland (steamship), 113
Vigilant (row galley), purchased by Navy, 60, 288; at Battle of Cedar Point, 65; sent to rear in Battle of St. Leonard's Creek, 69; dimensions unknown, 287, 288; conjectured history of, 280; considered as a candidate for the Turtle Shell Wreck, 289
Virginia (steamboat), 112
Volunteer (schooner), 51
Wenonah (steamboat), 104
Westmoreland (steamboat), 106, 112, 274
Virginia, Environmental Protection Agency studies erosion in, 4; native boat building

techniques in, 20; Puritans forbidden practice of beliefs in, 22; capitulates to Cromwell, 23; sends commissioners to Maryland, 23; tobacco inspection law serves as model for Maryland, 40; British defeat at Yorktown, 48; governor to act in concert with Chesapeake Flotilla, 58; Confederate invasion of Maryland from feared, 97; Union raid on, 97; Booth's death in, 98; wharf structure at Yorktown, 266; adoption of log canoe in, 292; mentioned, 5, 8, 9, 18, 19, 43, 44, 48, 54, 60, 95, 114, 174, 191, 262, 288
Virginia Capes, 44
Volkmer, Eldon, background of, 130; designs compressor, 207; work on the Lyons Creek Wreck, 218; outfits Phase II of Patuxent Project, 232; invents hose adapter, 236; work on St. Leonard's Wharf Site, 266; secures necessities for conservation facility, 283

Wadsworth, Col. Decius, plans flotilla breakout from St. Leonard's Creek, 76; attends council of war with Barney, 76; disapproves of battery positions, 77; learns of British flanking movement, 79; conduct criticized, 82; sent to Annapolis, 84; mentioned, 78
Wainwright, Capt. John, 92
Wallace, Davidson and Johnson, 40, 41
Wallace, Johnson and Muir, 180
Walton, John, 168
War of 1812; oral traditions regarding, 155; forts reported at Nottingham, 160; Turtle Shell Wreck attributed to period of, 265; mentioned, 10, 56, 95, 98, 131, 148, 153, 155, 159, 163, 181, 217, 235, 266, 268
War of Spanish Succession, 35
"War on the Patuxent", 285
Warman, F.C., 106
Warren, Adm. Sir John Borlase, 53
Washington, D.C., warships building at, 55; as a principal British target in Chesapeake, 58; concern over Barrie's motions on the Patuxent, 74; Thomas Carberry as mayor of, 82; rapid communications with Nottingham, 83; recommended as best target in America for British invasion, 84; Barney's certainty of British intentions towards, 89; General Ross presses towards, 91; destruction of, 92, 148; offers thanks to Barney for bravery, 94; Union Army marches into Maryland from, 96; learns of Booth's death, 98; southern Maryland enters urban orbit of, 118; departure of *Peter Cooper* from, 176; mentioned, 50, 68, 76, 89, 131, 166, 181, 184, 192, 193, 251, 258, 267, 268
Washington, George, 49, 56, 267
Washington National Airport, 280
Washington Navy Yard, *Blacksnake* outfitted at, 60; *Scorpion* rebuilt at, 63, 288

369

Index

War of Independence, see American Revolution

Warren's Reach Bar, Patuxent River, 106

Wascoup, 148

Wasmacus, 148

Watts, Capt. George Edward, arrives on the Patuxent, 67; orders *St. Lawrence* out of St. Leonard's Creek, 70; runs *St. Lawrence* aground, 71; retires from skirmish at Benedict, 75

Watts, Robert, 44

Wayson's Corner, Md., 200

Webster, Godfrey, 34

Webster, J. Cook, 298

Webster, Sir Thomas, 34

Weems, Capt. George, 95, 96

Weems, John, salvage effort on Chesapeake Flotilla, 94, 181, 183; establishes salvage base at Mount Pleasant Landing, 181; unable to recover *Scorpion*, 181, 289; mentioned, 182, 253, 260

Weems Steamboat Company, operations on Patuxent River, 95, 96, 104; returns to service after Civil War hiatus, 104; reports on Patuxent commerce, 105; Bristol Landing becomes Patuxent terminus, 105; encourages efforts to keep Patuxent open to traffic, 108; monopoly on business at Bristol Landing, 108; struggles to survive, 109; loss of *Theodore Weems*, 109; sells out to Maryland, Delaware and Virginia Company, 109; uses scows in upriver service, 110; use of St. Leonard's Wharf, 274

Wellington's Invincibles, 89

Welles, Sec. of Navy Gideon, 98

Wentworth, Caesar, 259

West, Stephen, Jr., establishes chain of stores on Patuxent River, 36; voices concern over British raids on river, 47; operates store at Pig Point, 180

West Indies, 33, 34, 48

Western Branch, Md., dredging financed by lottery, 37; Charles Town erected upon banks of, 177; Upper Marlborough founded at head of, 177; shipwreck reported in, 143; mentioned, 31

Western Europe, 220

Western Shore Steamboat Company, 112

Whaland, Joseph, 49

Whig Party, 28

White, Fr. Andrew, settles among Indians, 19; description of southern Maryland, 123

White, Lt. Even, 97

White Sands Marina, 147

Whites Landing, Md., 111

Wickes, Capt. Benjamin, 45, 46

Wilkinson, Joseph, 47

Wilkinson's Store, Md., 87

William and Mary, 28, 29, 229

William H. Skinner and Sons, 104, 148

Williams, Henry, 105, 108

Willis, Pauline Willis, 298

Wilmington, N.C., 277

Wilson, Pres. Woodrow, 113

Winder, Gen. William Henry, 87, 91

Windmill Point, Md., 141

Wisconsin, 228

World Trade Center, 285

World War I, 113

World War II, 16, 116, 124, 191

Wosameus, 157

Wye House, 169

Yassi Ada Wreck, 294

Yellow Cat Productions, 208

Yorktown, Va., 48, 266

Younge, William, 34

Youth Conservation Corps, 291

Yucatan, Mex., 130

Zanheiser's Marina, 191